NOT SO LONG AGO

By Lloyd Morris

BIOGRAPHY
The Rebellious Puritan: *Portrait of Mr. Hawthorne*
A Threshold in the Sun

DRAMA
The Damask Cheek (with John van Druten)

FICTION
Procession of Lovers
This Circle of Flesh

CRITICISM
The Celtic Dawn
The Young Idea
The Poetry of Edwin Arlington Robinson

TRANSLATION
The New Carthage (from the French of Georges Eekhoud)

SOCIAL HISTORY
Postscript to Yesterday: *America: The Last Fifty Years*

NOT SO LONG AGO

LLOYD MORRIS

Not so

long ago

RANDOM HOUSE · NEW YORK

Thanks are due to the following firms for permission to reproduce pictures from their collections: American Broadcasting Co., 2 pictures; Brown Brothers, 54 pictures; Culver Service, 38 pictures; Ford News Bureau, 7 pictures; General Motors, 1 picture; International News, 2 pictures; Museum of Modern Art, 16 pictures; National Broadcasting Co., 6 pictures; New York City Park Dept., 1 picture; Paramount Pictures, 1 picture; Press Association, 1 picture; Wide World Photos, 2 pictures

Manufactured in the United States of America by The Haddon Craftsmen, Inc., Scranton, Pa.

Designer: Ernst Reichl

To Nannine Joseph and Kendall Smith in grateful friendship

PREFACE

Like its predecessor, *Postscript to Yesterday*, this book is not a formal history.

In *Postscript*, I attempted to trace the effect, on the minds and hearts of Americans, of certain social changes that have taken place in our national life since 1896. The book was largely devoted to those writers and thinkers who, during that period, spoke for us most authoritatively and most deeply influenced our thought and feeling.

This book deals with the same spectacular era, but its subject is different. Since 1896, three agencies have profoundly and directly affected the lives of all Americans. For none of us has been left untouched by the influence of the motion picture, the automobile and the radio. Probably never before in human history have three instruments of such incalculable social power been developed in so short a time. All three were perfected in the United States, within the memory of a generation still active today. Yet, together, they have completely transformed our society, civilization and culture. The subject of this book is the changes they have brought about, and the effects they have produced in our lives.

My concern here is with social forces and social effects. And so, in dealing with motion pictures, the radio and television, I have ventured only incidentally into the field of criticism, for discussion of their achievements, as forms of art, does not lie within the province of this book.

In my research, I have used the resources of the New York Public Library (principally, the Division of Science and Technology, the Manuscript Division, and the Theater Collection); the Museum of Modern Art, with its notable Film Library and archives; and the New York Society Library. For courteous, helpful assistance I am grateful to their staffs. I am likewise grateful to the Automobile Manufacturers Association of Detroit, the Columbia Broadcasting System, Inc., the National Broadcasting Company and the Radio Corporation of America for information which they furnished. Miss Lillian Gish gave freely of her time to tell me about David Wark Griffith and her own work with him; I record my warm appreciation of her generous kindness. To Miss Phyllis Moir, John van Druten and other friends I offer thanks for discussing with me certain subjects relating to the motion pictures and to Hollywood. I am deeply grateful to Robert N. Linscott, of Random House, and to Miss Mary Barber, for their unflagging interest in the progress of my work, and their patient assistance during its course.

My debt is especially great to two friends: my agent, Miss Nannine Joseph; and Kendall Smith, who aided me in the long and extensive research which this book required. In dedicating it to them, I pay only inadequate tribute to their constant and solicitous collaboration.

L. M.

CONTENTS

ILLUSTRATIONS

PART THREE

Credits for Illustrations: CULVER SERVICE: Anna Held Enjoys a Peep Show, And
This Might Be the Picture that Anna Held Saw, An Early Newsreel, Between Films These Notices
Would Appear on the Screen, A Typical Nickelodeon, A Heartrending Scene from an Early
Biograph Film, Love and Laughter from a Biograph Film, Universal's First Outdoor Studio in New
York, D. W. Griffith as an Actor, *The Birth of a Nation,* D. W. Griffith Interviews Lillian Gish,
Richard Barthelmess and Lillian Gish in *Broken Blossoms,* Mary Pickford in Her Pre-Movie Days,
Mary Pickford in *Pollyanna,* The Keystone Cops, Sennett and His Celebrated Bathing Beauties,
Custard Pies Were Made for Throwing, Pearl White in *The Perils of Pauline,* Theda Bara Plays
the Vampire in *A Fool There Was,* Theda Bara—Fatally Alluring, To a Fate Worse Than Death,
A Million Hearts Beat Faster, Hollywood After, Cecil B. De Mille Takes *The Squaw Man* Com-
pany out on Location, The Inspired Architecture of Hollywood, Marlene Dietrich Starts the Day,
Charles Laughton and Hedda Hopper, Cleopatra—Played by Claudette Colbert, It Was Pictures Like
This That Led to Censorship, Gloria Swanson and Elinor Glyn, Gloria Swanson and Her Husband,
the Marquis, A Modern Studio, Automobile Advertisement, "Why Won't It Go"?, Mr. and Mrs.
W. K. Vanderbilt, Jr., The Well-Dressed Lady Motorist, A Spin in the Country. BROWN
BROTHERS: The Fetching New Styles of 1896, Ben Turpin and Bronco Billy Anderson,
America's Sweetheart, Charlie Chaplin in an Early One-Reeler, Charlie Chaplin in *Sunnyside,*
Hollywood Before, Marion Davies' Ninety-Room Home on the Beach, Duryea's First Horseless

NOT SO LONG AGO

INTRODUCTION

Rites of Spring

Spring had come at last, and the streets of American cities rang
with a shrill whirring of bells. For this was 1896, when modern-
minded young people were eagerly pursuing happiness on wheels.
The bicycle craze—newest ritual of triumphant national progress
—had swept the country. Old-fashioned folk deplored it. Genteel
conservatives were gratified when an eminent clergyman, Reverend Asa D. Blackburn, spoke in their behalf. The press com-
mended his sermon: "You cannot serve God and skylark on a
bicycle."

But even the highest circles of fashion had succumbed to this
vogue. And the approval of "society" promised to offset a merely

hypothetical divine displeasure. "My head is full of wheeling," a
young New Yorker noted in his diary, "and two great problems:
a saddle that is really comfortable, and a tire that will not slip in
mud. How far, today, we are from either!" The diarist was a
leader of cotillons, a perennial ornament of Mrs. Astor's balls. He
and his friends never wearied of wheeling. They flashed past
the glittering equipages and lumbering horse-drawn busses that
crowded Fifth Avenue. They pedaled through Central Park, and
out along Riverside Drive to Grant's Tomb. One day, chaperoned
by a married couple riding their tandem wheel, a party went far
afield, exploring rural Westchester. After enjoying a fine luncheon
at a country club, they returned to the city by train. The skirts of
his feminine companions often caught in the chains of their
'cycles, and the diarist had a hard time extricating them. But as
yet, American girls had not dared adopt the "bloomer cycling
costume" recently introduced in Paris; too many people professed
to be shocked at the exposure of ankles by shorter skirts. In spite
of delays, however, the diarist "got quite set up by passing pretty
much everything, and without effort" on the roads. The cult of
speed, already prevalent, was awaiting its appropriate vehicle.

The new freedom of circulation bestowed by the bicycle was
only one of many symptoms of social change. Although he found
life as a bachelor pleasant, the diarist was considering the prospects of marriage. His income from the practice of law was about
four thousand dollars, but this sum could no longer be considered
adequate. "I must say that the idea of my making enough to get
married on within a year by ordinary grubbing seems absolutely
impossible," he acknowledged ruefully. "I must strike in some
tremendous new line if I hope to do it, and the joke is I have not
even discovered the new line." To maintain one's position in
"society," wealth was becoming increasingly essential. Even within
the sacred citadel, old lineage was yielding to new gold. At one
of Mrs. Astor's receptions, he met "all the plain good people whom
she keeps on her list" but remarked that "the smart ones stayed
away, mostly." For the social dictatorship of old Mrs. Astor was
waning. The twilight of an era had arrived.

Tradition, decorum and gentility seemed to be vanishing from the world, and an old guard was making its last stand in their defense. The diarist's parents sternly refused to invite for dinner a lady whom he admired, because she had been divorced—and "on her own faultless application, too!" The parents of a young lady in his circle had provided her with a studio to paint in, but had obliged her to promise "to have no tête-à-têtes" there. Among the elect, chaperonage was inflexibly required. Bachelors found this exaction costly, and considered it foolish, yet had to comply with it. In order to entertain a young lady at dinner and theater, the diarist was compelled to play host to a party of four. They dined at the new Waldorf Hotel, went on to see *The Lady Slavey*, returned to the Waldorf for after-theater supper, and drove down Fifth Avenue to deliver the ladies to their homes near Washington Square. This evening's hospitality, as the diarist noted aggrievedly, represented an outlay of thirty-six dollars. (At the splendid new Waldorf, one might have for dinner a *filet mignon* for a dollar and a quarter; roast beef, for sixty cents; terrapin, for two dollars and a half; canvas-back duck, for four dollars. The supper menu offered such delicacies as lobster Newburg, at one dollar; Philadelphia reed-birds, also at a dollar; English snipe, or plover, or quail, at seventy-five cents; broiled squab, at eighty. For a mere twenty cents, the penurious could order a ham sandwich.)

The diarist thought New York social life agreeable, in 1896. Frequently, after the opera, he went on to supper and a ball, and danced until four in the morning. Dinner parties were brighter, too, for hostesses had finally conceded that conversation was a lost art, and were relying on professional entertainers to stave off boredom after coffee and liqueurs. In various homes, he enjoyed Professor Russell, "the king of cards" who performed feats of legerdemain; a clairvoyant; a singer of Virginia songs who likewise told stories in dialect. Even the staid Harvard Club surrendered to this new social necessity, and one evening provided "paid talent" to amuse the members with "funny stories till a late hour." Not to be outdone, the equally sedate University Club held a "story teller's night" which detained the diarist until after three in the morning. Nevertheless, he was convinced that gentlemen's clubs were "going to pot"—and this, too, was a symptom of social change.

One evening, he went to hear Lieutenant Robert E. Peary lecture on Arctic exploration. "I always hold to the idea that the North Pole is well worth visiting, and that it is a reproach that we have not been there and taken observations and so forth," he noted. "We cannot tell what we might learn in a scientific way, and we should assume that a visit there would be of great importance." Peary used good lantern slides to illustrate his lecture, so that it was "for all the world like going there, most graphic and real and interesting." But the diarist did not foresee that, within a very few months, another and more deceptive magic would make lantern slides, like stereopticons, forever obsolete. With the cult of speed, this desire for illusion still lacked an efficient instrument.

Elsewhere, the battle between progress and tradition was no less evident. The cult of speed received a setback in Morristown, New Jersey. There, two intrepid citizens, William Cook and Henry Armstrong, were tried for the misdemeanor of fast driving; they were charged with having urged on their horses to a pace "faster than a moderate trot." In Omaha, Nebraska, the city fathers were made anxious by novel, indecorous forms of freedom. Over the mayor's veto, they passed a curfew ordinance, thus opposing a dangerous tendency to gad about at unseemly hours. By promulgating a new rule, the American District Telegraph Company astonished many gentlemen, and provoked a brief mutiny by their own employes. To its messenger boys—aged fifteen to seventy-five —the company issued a decree forbidding the wearing of whiskers, goatees, mustaches and sideburns, all of which had been favored by convention ever since the War between the States. Irate at being deprived of their civil rights to hirsute adornment, the messengers protested that the company should either pay for shaves, or provide free shaving equipment. But the heartless corporation insisted that its staff keep up with the times at their own expense. There could be little doubt that masculine facial foliage was on its way out.

In Kentucky, an old code of gentlemanly violence appeared to be discredited, but democratic government was at a standstill. The whole country felt relief when the legislature of that state was forced to adjourn because the constitutional limit of its session had been reached. The lawmakers had spent the entire session in a fruitless effort to elect a member of the United States Senate. During the closing weeks, everyone in and around the state capitol had been carrying weapons, and bloodshed seemed likely to occur at any moment. When adjournment came, the lawmakers had failed to pass ordinary revenue and appropriation bills. Reformers, pointing to this fiasco, loudly approved the recent report of a committee of the Senate; it proposed a constitutional amendment providing that senators be elected by popular vote.

Though narrowly averted in Kentucky, violence broke out in Arizona. A murderous band of Apache Indians killed one Alfred Hands, a settler, then robbed and destroyed his home. The sparsely inhabited region was stricken by terror, for the event was believed to presage another Indian uprising. So a detachment of United States cavalry was sent to join the posse of cowboys that had set out in pursuit of the marauding band. Before this minor sensation died down, Americans were astounded by a spectacular case of banditry. Three masked men halted the east-bound 'Frisco Fast Express near Richland, Missouri, late one night. After intimidating its passengers and crew with gunfire, they dynamited the safe in the baggage car, withdrew from it an estimated one hundred thousand dollars, and successfully made their escape.

Tales of violence were likewise coming out of Cuba, where a revolution against Spanish rule was in progress. American sympathy for the Cuban insurgents mounted every day, nourished by provocative stories in the newspapers of Joseph Pulitzer and William Randolph Hearst. Congress had already recognized a state of belligerency in Cuba, but President Grover Cleveland, at odds with the Democratic party, took no further action hostile to Spain. But in Spain anti-American sentiment was running high; mobs trampled and burned the American flag. In several American colleges, students retaliated by burning the Spanish flag, and were rebuked for this "very objectionable sort of folly" by the judicious *Review of Reviews*, which reminded them that it might lead to

European misconception of American feeling. Nevertheless, a group of clergymen, in order to express their outrage at the mistreatment of Cuban rebels, organized a boycott of Spanish onions. Theodore Roosevelt and his friend Henry Cabot Lodge were even more bellicose. They were publicly advocating American military intervention in Cuba and a war with Spain. For such "jingoism" they were sternly denounced by President Charles W. Eliot of Harvard University.

Meanwhile political leaders were appealing to partisan spirit and class interests, for a presidential election was to take place in the autumn of 1896. It was already obvious that party strife would reach unprecedented intensity. For the major issue before the country was whether the United States should remain on the gold standard, as demanded by the Republicans, or resort to the free coinage of silver, an economic heresy originally proposed by the Populists and certain to be adopted by the Democrats. Over this issue, the nation was rapidly dividing into bitterly hostile camps.

Yet the extreme savagery of the presidential contest might have been avoided had Americans understood the implications of an event reported in the press. For the gold standard was a vital issue mainly because of the high price of that metal, of which the world supply was insufficient. Early in April, the steamer *City of Topeka* arrived at Port Townsend, Washington, from Juneau, Alaska. It brought news of the discovery of a new Eldorado. Just before the vessel sailed from Juneau, James McQuaid had returned there from the Yukon country, where he had been prospecting for eighteen months. He brought with him eighty-two pounds of gold dust, all that he had been able to carry from his rich strike. Hundreds of miners and adventurers were said to be stranded in Juneau without visible means of support. But shortly after the story of McQuaid's strike in the Yukon was published, fifteen vessels set out for Juneau from ports in the Northwest, carrying one thousand excited prospectors. A new gold rush had begun, and in Alaska the gold-fever became so acute that residents of Sitka, stirred to action, proposed to drain a near-by lake in the belief that its bed might be paved, to a great depth, with gold brought down by glaciers.

Unconcerned by these mundane affairs, American astronomers were making elaborate preparations to observe a total eclipse of the sun that would occur on the ninth of August. Sportsmen were looking forward to the American tour of an Australian cricket team, and to the victories of American athletes at the first modern Olympic games, to be held in Athens. To everyone's relief, the Continental Match Company had finally put an odorless match on the market. The latest marvel of science—Professor Roentgen's X-ray machine—was being displayed by Hilton, Hughes and Company, a New York department store. This progressive concern invited the public to come in and see it's own bones. More hospitable than scientifically accurate, it advertised that "the mystery of cathode rays is still a mystery, but you can see all there is to be seen about them and their production, the fluorescence in a Crookes tube, and actual pictures taken—one each hour." The enterprising makers of Vin Mariani, a popular tonic wine, were carrying progress in advertising even further. They had persuaded Miss Marie Tempest, the enchanting English comedienne, and E. H. Sothern, the celebrated romantic actor, to furnish signed endorsements of the product. And, however incredibly, they were making commercial use of these documents!

While gentlemen pondered foreign affairs, domestic politics and the complexities of monetary theory, ladies, as usual, were preoccupied by matters no less grave. In the onrushing tide of change, they turned to Edward Bok's *Ladies' Home Journal* as a citadel of permanence, a beacon of the eternal verities. The April issue of that magazine brought its customary reassurance. There were plans of a twenty-room Dutch Colonial residence; it could be built, anywhere in the United States, for five thousand dollars. There were suggestions for a garden pool, to be planted with water lilies, water hyacinth and lotus. Young girls were sensibly reminded that the best cosmetic was exercise in the open air; that they should watch their diet, and cultivate good, kind, hopeful thoughts that would bring pleasing expressions to their faces. Readers who required instruction in etiquette were assured that when calling on a married lady they should leave one of their own, and two of their husbands' cards, but when calling on an

unmarried lady they should leave only one of each. All this implied
that the familiar scene had not substantially altered. But, when
they came to the advertising pages of the magazine, many readers
received a nasty shock. For there, conferring obloquy upon a
dentifrice, was the picture of a female, announced as "the new
woman." Carrying a riding crop, and presumably about to mount
a horse, this brazen creature flaunted breeches like a man's—and
this could only mean that she sat her horse astride, as no true lady
had ever thought to, and would inevitably gallop to perdition
down a primrose path of dalliance. If this was progress, what could
the world be coming to?

In other publications, the fetching new styles received their
absorbed attention. Princesse skirts with corselet waistbands, so the
prophets of fashion asserted, were to be in vogue for summer
wear. Among many lovely costumes, who could fail to be attracted
by one "extremely simple, and yet stylish, little gown?" The
material of this creation was a brocaded mohair, silver gray in hue.
It had a full and flowing skirt, lined with *bleu de ciel* taffeta,
with a two-inch hem, above which were three tucks of equal
length; these, like the hem, were bordered with silver soutache
braid. The bodice had a pleat in front, edged with the same braid,
and a *patte* of violet velvet on each side of the pleat, also bordered
with braid and embellished with two antique silver coin buttons.
The collar was of violet velvet, covered with silver filigree work.
The upper part of the sleeves formed large, drooping puffs, with
three tucks in the center, edged with silver soutache; the forearms
were tight-fitting, and of violet velvet covered with silver filigree,
like the collar. Irresistible surely, if not, in sober reality, "extremely simple"!

Ladies of mature years—"painfully aware that nowhere do the
telltale signs of time show themselves so obviously as just behind
the ears and around the throat"—welcomed a new style in bonnets,
featuring lace strings that could be knotted under the chin. One
of these, "designed for a matron of forty or thereabouts," was
greatly admired. It was made of coarse black straw laid on in scales,
edged with jet, each scallop in front being decorated with a high
pointed cabochon of jet. On each side, there were little fans of

accordion-pleated black tulle edged with white, and from them trailed loops of old rose velvet. The center bore a white aigrette, rising from black accordion-pleated tulle edged with white Valenciennes lace, and a high loop of rose velvet. A wide black tulle scarf, edged with white, was fastened to the back of the bonnet by a jeweled pin; the ends of this scarf were brought forward and tied under the wearer's chin. This confection was described as "a dignified headdress and drapery which looks particularly well with hair *en pompadour*."

It was, no doubt, the vogue for such headgear that precipitated, among ordinarily docile American males, a brief but drastic revolution. For ladies avoided removing their hats in theaters, which made them an obstruction; but, if they did so, their hatpins made them a menace. Confronted by what appeared to be an unsolvable dilemma, yet deeply resentful, members of the Ohio legislature were goaded into unchivalrous action. They passed a law forbidding ladies to wear hats in theaters. In other states, ladies became apprehensive, for lawmakers elsewhere were looking to the results in Ohio for a plausible precedent.

The ladies could have struck back by refusing to attend the theater hatless, but who, in the spring of 1896, would have chosen, for whatever high principle or hat, to miss the excellent performances being offered throughout the country? The famous Italian tragedienne, Madame Eleonora Duse, after making a tour and playing a season of repertory in New York City, had lately sailed home, notably enriched by having dissolved thousands of Americans in tears. But early in April, Madame Sarah Bernhardt was offering a repertory of plays at the Lyceum Theater in Detroit. At the Auditorium in Kansas City, the sultry Miss Olga Nethersole, from England, could be seen in *Carmen, Frou-Frou* and *Denise*. At the Star Theater in Buffalo, Sir Henry Irving and Miss Ellen Terry were playing *The Merchant of Venice* and *The Bells*; their repertory comprised no less than fourteen plays. Buffalo would presently have lighter fare, for the shapely musical comedy star, Miss Della Fox, was touring in *Fleur de Lys*, and would play there after the departure of Sir Henry and Miss Terry. At the

Metropolitan Theater, in Saint Paul, Sol Smith Russell was alternating *The Rivals* with two other plays. In Boston, at the Tremont Theater, the comedian De Wolfe Hopper was appearing in John Philip Sousa's *El Capitan*, a favorite everywhere. In Baltimore, the beautiful Miss Julia Marlowe was playing in *Romeo and Juliet* at Ford's Opera House. And elsewhere, E. H. Sothern was touring in *The Prisoner of Zenda*; Nat Goodwin was playing *The Rivals*; and Miss Loie Fuller, inventor of a new form of dancing, was astonishing audiences by standing quite immobile except for her lovely arms, which sinuously shook out long chiffon banners while revolving colored lights played on her.

Who would have believed that, within another generation, the splendor of the touring companies was to be extinguished by a new form of entertainment, about to be born?

As usual, in the spring of 1896, Americans were relishing the disesteem of European visitors imported for profitable fault-finding expeditions. This year, the critical office was being filled by Madame Blanc, a not-too-celebrated French writer, who reported in the April issue of *The Forum* her misgivings about the state of the nation. Especially, she commiserated with the American husband, who so obviously was a martyr to the social aspirations of his wife and daughters. "I have visited houses," Madame Blanc recorded, "where he seemed only to have dropped in by accident, as one might say, evidently at a loss to recognize most of the invited guests, and yet showing himself most hospitable with the good-will of his handshake, his smile, and repeating almost as though he did not know to whom he was speaking that everlasting trivial phrase, 'glad to see you.' " She disapproved, too, of the systematic scorn of marriage expressed by young American girls who were ambitious "to be somebody, or do something"—to distinguish themselves in a career, and escape from the common ways of life. On the other hand, the lot of the independent "new woman" in America was happier than that of her spinster sister in France; "her intercourse with men, freed from the childishness of flirtation, bears a stamp of quietness and freedom which allows real and serious intimacies that no criticism could assail." On the whole, however, Madame Blanc felt that, "It would be to the advantage of rich and blasé Americans to refresh themselves from time to time by the good provincial customs; to return to those living springs, not only of their democracy, but of their true moral greatness"—and she recommended that, instead of traveling in Europe, they seek regeneration in isolated New England villages, remote districts of the Far West, or the South. There, at least, they might find "fathers of families who have preserved old-world ideas of authority, and housewives as we understand them." For to Madame Blanc one thing was clear: the most deplorable feature of American life was the disintegration of the family. In the high tide of its progress, the United States had seemingly lost all piety to the *foyer*.

Few Americans doubted, in the pleasant spring of 1896, that progress, already so great, would continue to even greater heights. Yet few suspected that, within a few short decades, their society, culture and civilization would be completely transformed. Three agencies, three forms of magic, were to contribute to this transformation, and all of them had lately been announced.

For in the spring of 1896 a horseless carriage made its appearance on the streets of Detroit. Moving pictures were shown in a theater in New York City. And, in London, a youthful Italian scientist transmitted a message, in Morse code, by wireless across the River Thames.

PART ONE

Life's but

a walking shadow

O, Pioneers

1 Miracle on Thirty-Fourth Street

On a late April evening in 1896, a crowd lingered in front of Koster and Bial's Music Hall, just west of Herald Square and the Great White Way. The street rang with a clatter of hooves as a long line of vehicles filed up to the entrance: public hansoms, livery-stable landaus, private opera coaches, broughams and coupés. Silk-hatted gentlemen, with feathered, frilly ladies clinging to their arms, pushed toward the brightly lit lobby. Fashionable New York was turning out in state, as if to attend the opera, half a dozen blocks farther up Broadway. Nobody had seen the like before. Koster and Bial's was the city's leading variety theater, and it catered to the middle classes. Gentlemen frequented it, of course; but only in their supposedly solitary hours. Decorum suggested that the fair companions whom they brought, or more likely found there, remain anonymous. But on this pleasant spring evening, everything was different. And the plain people, unable to secure admission to the theater, loitered to gape at the privileged.

Inside the large auditorium, all gilt and blue velvet brocade, you heard the rustle of well-bred excitement. The nominal headliner on the program was Albert Chevalier, a famous English music-hall star making his American debut. He would appear after the intermission, singing the quaint costermonger's songs that London adored: "My Old Dutch," "The Nipper's Lullaby," "Our Court Ball" and others. But it was not Chevalier who had aroused the audience to its high pitch of expectancy. Ladies were training their opera glasses on one of the stage boxes. There, grumpy and gray and apparently somewhat nervous, sat the electrical wizard, Thomas Alva Edison. Many also turned to stare at a strange object in the center of the balcony. From below, in the orchestra, it looked like the double turret of a big naval monitor, and the front of each half was pierced by two oblong holes. Would it work? Was it really going to project—as rumor had long been predicting—a series of extraordinary living pictures?

For this was Edison's latest reputed marvel, the vitascope, and the public was presently to see it in action for the first time. Impatience mounted during the turns of William Olschovsky, the Russian clown, and Cora Caselli, the eccentric dancer. There was little applause for The Three Delevines, in an original act billed as *Satanic Gambols*. The audience was equally cool to Paulinetti and Pico, and to Monsieur and Madame Ducreux-Geralduc, the French duettists. But you could hear a sigh of relief when The Brothers Horn, assisted by Miss Charlotte Hallett, finished a sketch called *London Life* and took a quick bow before the curtain. Now, at last, the vitascope . . .

A great white screen, twenty feet square and elaborately framed in gold like a painting, descended from the top of the proscenium. Suddenly, the auditorium was darkened. The vitascope began to

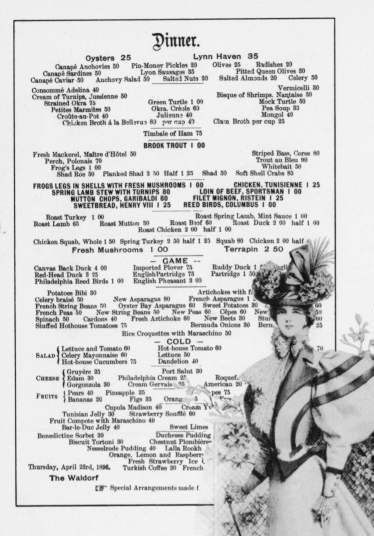

Dinner.

Oysters 25   **Lynn Haven 35**

Canapé Anchovies 50	Pin-Money Pickles 20	Olives 25 Radishes 20
Canapé Sardines 50	Lyon Sausages 35	Pitted Queen Olives 30
Canapé Caviar 50 Anchovy Salad 50 Salted Nuts 20		Salted Almonds 20 Celery 50

Consommé Adelina 40   Vermicelli 30
Cream of Turnips, Jussienne 50   Bisque of Shrimps. Nantaise 50
Strained Okra 75   Green Turtle 1 00   Mock Turtle 50
Petites Marmites 50   Okra, Créole 60   Pea Soup 35
Croûte-au-Pot 40   Julienne 40   Mongol 40
Chicken Broth à la Bellevue 80   per cup 40   Clam Broth per cup 25

Timbale of Ham 75

BROOK TROUT I 00

Fresh Mackerel, Maître d'Hôtel 50		Striped Bass, Corse 80
Perch, Polonais 70		Trout au Bleu 90
Frog's Legs 1 00		Whitebait 50
Shad Roe 50 Planked Shad 2 50 Half 1 25	Shad 50	Soft Shell Crabs 85

FROGS LEGS IN SHELLS WITH FRESH MUSHROOMS I 00   **CHICKEN, TUNISIENNE I 25**
SPRING LAMB STEW WITH TURNIPS 80   **LOIN OF BEEF, SPORTSMAN I 00**
MUTTON CHOPS, GARIBALDI 80   **FILET MIGNON, RISTEIN I 25**
SWEETBREAD, HENRY VIII I 25   **REED BIRDS, COLUMBUS I 00**

Roast Turkey 1 00   Roast Spring Lamb, Mint Sauce 1 00
Roast Lamb 65   Roast Mutton 50   Roast Beef 60   Roast Duck 2 00   half 1 00
Roast Chicken 2 00   half 1 00

Chicken Squab, Whole 1 50   Spring Turkey 2 50 half 1 25   Squab 80   Chicken 2 00 half

Fresh Mushrooms I 00   **Terrapin 2 50**

— GAME —

Canvas Back Duck 4 00	Imported Plover 75	Ruddy Duck 1 glish
Red-Head Duck 3 25	English Partridge 75	Partridge 1 50
Philadelphia Reed Birds 1 00	English Pheasant 3 00	

Potatoes Bibi 30   Artichokes with f.
Celery braisé 50   New Asparagus 80   French Asparagus 1
French String Beans 50   Oyster Bay Asparagus 60   Sweet Potatoes 30   60
French Peas 50   New String Beans 50   New Peas 60   Cèpes 60   New   50
Spinach 50   Cardons 40   Fresh Artichoke 60   New Beets 30   Stu   60
Stuffed Hothouse Tomatoes 75   Bermuda Onions 30   Bern   25
Rice Croquettes with Maraschino 50

— COLD —

SALAD	Lettuce and Tomato 60	Hot-house Tomato 60
	Celery Mayonnaise 60	Lettuce 50
	Hot-house Cucumbers 75	Dandelion 40
CHEESE	Gruyère 25	Port Salut 30
	Edam 30 Philadelphia Cream 25	Roquef.
	Gorgonzola 30 Cream Gervais 25	American 20
FRUITS	Pears 40 Pineapple 35	pes 75
	Bananas 20 Figs 35 Orang 5	Figs

Cupola Madison 40   Cream Y
Tunisian Jelly 30   Strawberry Soufflé 60
Fruit Compote with Maraschino 40
Bar-le-Duc Jelly 40   Sweet Limes
Benedictine Sorbet 30   Duchesse Pudding
Biscuit Tortoni 30   Chestnut Plombière
Nesselrode Pudding 40   Lalla Rookh
Orange, Lemon and Raspberry
Fresh Strawberry Ice (
Thursday, April 23rd, 1896.   Turkish Coffee 20   French

The Waldorf

☞ Special Arrangements made f

ABOVE:
Dinner at the Waldorf

RIGHT: The Fetching
New Styles of 1896

RIGHT: Anna Held Enjoys a Peep Show

ABOVE: This Might Be the Picture
That Anna Held Saw

BELOW: A Typical Arcade

ABOVE: A Typical Nickelodeon

LEFT: The Motion Picture
       Comes to Broadway

BELOW: Mr. Edison
       and His Kinetoscope

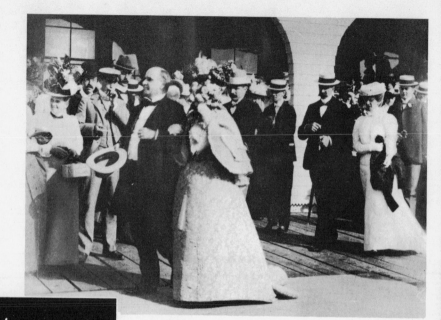

All that have seen the
entire Performance
are requested to pass
out and give others
a chance.

ABOVE: An Early Newsreel:
                President McKinley and His Wife

BELOW: The First American Motion Picture Studio.
The Edison Company's "Black Maria" at
                West Orange, N. J., 1893

buzz and roar, and a glaring white light flooded the screen.
Presently, a tinted background was thrown on it, and there appeared two blonde young women, wearing pink and blue dresses,
roguishly flirting their parasols as they danced. They vanished. An
angry surf rolled in toward the audience, crested into a mighty
wave, and crashed in jets of spume. There was a flurry of panic
among occupants of the front rows. Two comedians engaged in
a burlesque boxing match. They were followed by a comic allegory titled, *The Monroe Doctrine*. A ripple of laughter greeted
a brief, familiar scene from Charles Hoyt's popular farce, *The
Milk White Flag*. Then a blonde show-girl named Annabelle displayed her coquetry in *The Butterfly Dance*. As Annabelle faded
from view, the noise of the vitascope subsided and the houselights
were turned on. Awed, exhilarated by this miracle of science, the
audience cheered, applauded, and shouted for Edison. But the
wizard had left his box, and he did not reappear to acknowledge
the ovation. The great blue curtain was lowered. Gentlemen left
their seats for the intermission.

In the Grand Promenade, a babble of amazement drowned
out the music of Dr. Leo Sommer's Blue Hungarian Band.
Edison's incredible machine—so marvelously, so deceptively reproducing "true-life action"—had startled blasé New Yorkers into
genuine enthusiasm. An enterprising reporter, seeing a short,
tubby, dapper, middle-aged man momentarily alone, hurried over
to seek a verdict from Charles Frohman, maker of stars and tycoon
of the American theater. "That settles scenery," Frohman told
him. "Painted trees that do not move, waves that get up a few
feet and stay there, everything in scenery that we simulate on
our stages will have to go. Now that art can make us believe that
we see actual, living nature, the dead things of the stage must go."
Another spectator might have disputed this verdict. He was a
young man, known only as a scholar in medieval literature, who
had a passionate love for the theater. Later, he would publish a
dictionary of colloquialisms, write entertainingly about the stage
in many magazines, and become a leading theatrical press agent.
Thirty years after the eventful birth of moving pictures at Koster
and Bial's, Frank J. Wilstach read an account of it and noted,

in the margin: "I was there and was *not* impressed." But his low appraisal of the value of Edison's ingenious new diversion was scarcely more misguided that than of Edison himself.

For the great inventor was skeptical about this venture and reluctant to proceed with it. Indeed, he had been badgered into action by some of his younger associates, still grumbling, "Let's not kill the goose that lays the golden egg." The particular goose whose longevity he wished to insure was a prosperous gosling, the kinetoscope. This was a cabinet with a peep-hole and a slot for coins. It held a band of film on which photographs had been printed. When a spectator dropped his coin in the slot, an electric light illuminated the interior; a tiny motor revolved spools concealed at the sides; this caused the film to move past the peep-hole; for approximately one minute the spectator was regaled with pictures of people and animals apparently in lifelike motion.

The first of these machines had been installed in 1894, one in a store on the Gay White Way in New York, another in the Masonic Temple in Chicago, and had become sensationally popular. Several years earlier, Edison had put his gramophone into a similar coin machine equipped with listening-tubes. Enterprising men had rented stores, set rows of cabinets along the walls, and reaped a harvest of coins from customers who patronized each in turn to enjoy the novelty of listening to songs, speeches and instrumental music. "Phonograph parlors," as they came to be called, sprang up in all the larger American cities. The kineto-scope, which proved to be an even more alluring novelty than the gramophone, was quickly installed in most of them. On downtown streets in the cities, the "penny arcade" soon became a familiar attraction: an open-fronted store, garishly lit, with a stentorian barker at the entrance and, within, serried lines of Edison's new coin-machines, gramophones and kinetoscopes, providing amuse-ment for the masses. The Edison Company's plant at West Orange had difficulty in meeting a nation-wide demand for the kine-toscope. Edison himself, who had intended combining the kineto-scope and the gramophone in a single cabinet, thus synchronizing sound and animated pictures, lost interest, became engaged in other problems, and left exploitation of the increasingly profitable kinetoscope to his business partners.

In the opinion of Henry Ford, who met him in 1896 and had worshipped him from boyhood, Edison was the world's greatest genius and worst business man. To less reverent observers, he seemed an embittered man whose ambition to become an industrial tycoon, by means of his inventions, had been frustrated by the operations of men shrewder than himself. But, with respect to the kinetoscope, he was both indifferent and singularly obdurate. The thing was a toy; Edison, whose sole amusement was work, had no interest in toys. Yet it was a highly remunerative toy, and he cherished no prejudice against large profits. The thriftless masses seemed delighted to squander their pennies, in the slots of his machines, on the illusion of seeing a horse run, a man sneeze, a baby enduring a bath, a pretty girl dance. Edison lived in the narrow world of his laboratory, insulated from the general public. When his associates began urging that even larger profits could be made by lifting animated pictures out of the cabinet and projecting them on a curtain or screen, he refused to consider the idea. It would ruin the sale of kinetoscopes, and its success in replacing them was purely problematical. Why destroy the prodigal gosling?

Both the kinetoscope and a primitive movie camera had been developed under the supervision of one of Edison's laboratory assistants, W. K. L. Dickson. Edison had taken out patents on them in the United States, but stubbornly refused to spend any money for European patents. European experimenters succeeded in producing cameras very like his, and these were later to become instrumental in breaking a powerful American patent pool which sought to monopolize the new industry. The Edison camera operated on a principle of intermittent motion. It rolled the film up to the lens, held it there just long enough for a single photograph to be registered, and then repeated the process. The use of perforated film, moved by a sprocket wheel, insured regularity of motion and exposure. The camera took a series of pictures, separated by minutely brief intervals, which appeared to record continuous action.

Dickson likewise tried to develop a machine capable of projecting the animated pictures on a screen or curtain, just as the popular "magic lantern" projected its slides. This involved tech-

nical and scientific problems which he did not entirely solve. The
machine he devised was patterned on the kinetoscope and moved
the film continuously, but the effect produced was not satisfactory.
Meanwhile, other experimenters were likewise at work. Another
peep-show cabinet had been put on the market to compete with
the kinetoscope. Known as the "mutoscope," it met with success
and its promoters, presently joined by Dickson, perfected a
camera and projection machine for screen pictures, and set up in
business as the Biograph Company. Even earlier, in April, 1895,
a short-lived company organized by Major Woodville Latham, a
Virginia college professor, exhibited to the New York press a
projector described as a "pantopticon" and, one month later, in
a rented store on lower Broadway, threw on a screen the first
flickering, commercial motion picture: a four-minute film showing
Young Griffo and Battling Barnett in a boxing match.

More decisively, as it turned out, experimental work had been
done in Washington by Thomas Armat and C. Francis Jenkins.
Armat was in his thirtieth year, a part-time inventor engaged in
the real-estate business. He had been invited to invest in a kinetoscope parlor in Atlanta, Georgia, and although he had refused
this opportunity, it aroused his desire to invent a practicable
projector. Collaborating with Jenkins, he perfected one by the
summer of 1895, and patented it under the name of "vitascope."
Unlike Dickson, Armat rejected the principle of moving film
continuously past a lens. He conceived the theory that each individual picture must be held stationary, while under illumination
and projection, before being succeeded by the next. Essentially,
Armat applied to his projector the same principle of intermittent
motion as was exemplified by the Edison camera. Both mechanisms
thus were founded on the persistence of vision: the fact that the
human eye does not work quickly enough actually to see the space
between pictures, and during this space holds an after-image of the
previous picture which it blends with the succeeding one. Armat's
principle was to become the foundation for the later technology
of motion picture presentation.

Lacking facilities to exploit his invention, or to manufacture
it commercially, Armat tried to interest Frank R. Gammon and

Norman C. Raff, who managed Edison's kinetoscope business. "We
have heard of many screen machines," they informed him, "but
even Mr. Edison has not been able to perfect one." Though the
outlook was not encouraging, he took his machine to West Orange
and demonstrated it to Edison, Gammon and Raff. "Mr. Edison
didn't think too much about it at first," Armat recalled when he
was in his eightieth year. "But he agreed to manufacture the
machine, and he reluctantly agreed to have it known as Edison's
vitascope after Gammon and Raff convinced him that the machine
would be easier to sell if it bore his name." Arrangements were
soon made to combine Armat's patents with others held by Edison.
Armat consented to "stay in the background" and let Edison take
public credit for his invention. So when motion pictures were
first offered in a theater, at Koster and Bial's, Edison occupied a
box while Armat, in the primitive projection booth, operated the
vitascope.

On the fiftieth anniversary of that occasion, Armat was interviewed by Thomas K. Pryor, Washington correspondent of the
New York *Times*. He felt no resentment at his failure to achieve
fame as the inventor of the device which, with the Edison camera,
had given birth to a major American industry that had become
one of the most powerful social agencies of the twentieth century.
He had done very well in life, and thought he had a sense of
proportion. After all, he had only given the movies a start; others,
later, had improved on his work tremendously. But his eyes
sparkled as he described the memorable night at Koster and Bial's.
The little film, *Sea Waves*, wasn't a good picture, but it was exciting, for nobody, ever before, had seen a lifelike ocean in a theater.
It had "started a panicky commotion among those up front," he
recalled, as the sea came rushing toward them. And Armat still
remembered how the audience "went wild" and cheered when
they saw the life-size shadow of Annabelle dancing, there before
them, on the screen.

2 The Comet That Became Only a Tail

The enthusiasm of their first audience made the new living
pictures a sensation widely reported by the press. Vaudeville

theaters throughout the land, eager to feature them, stormed the
Edison Company, and soon the newly formed Biograph Company,
for projection equipment and films. In the autumn of 1896, as the
savage, bitter presidential contest between Major William Mc-
Kinley and William Jennings Bryan entered its decisive phase,
the wonderful new medium invaded politics. At his palatial
Olympia Music Hall on Longacre Square, in New York, Oscar
Hammerstein presented a film showing a parade for the Republican candidate in his home town of Canton, Ohio, and another
of the Major taken in the privacy of his residence. Throngs packed
the theater for this unique privilege of participating in the personal life of an eminent man. But although partisan spirit ran
high, and many cheered or hissed McKinley, they all but forgot
him a moment later. For they saw the Empire State Express
rounding a curve, speeding down the tracks, rushing headlong
toward them, its huge engine finally seeming to crash into their
very faces. Women shrieked in terror. A gasp of relief rose in the
darkened theater as the peril passed. Pictures such as this, exhibited in the cities from coast to coast, held audiences spellbound,
and for a time rivaled the appeal of celebrated vaudeville head-
liners.

Americans remote from the nation's capital could nevertheless
attend President McKinley's inauguration. Those who had never
been in New York City could visit Madison Square while a
blizzard was falling. They could see Boston's new horseless fire
department in action. When the Spanish-American War broke
out, they could thrill to *Tearing Down the Spanish Flag*, happily
unaware that the hand which snatched it from the pole, and ran
up the Stars and Stripes, had performed this glorious feat in a New
York loft building. Assured by the press that "the camera does not
lie," and often receiving the exhibitor's pledge that subjects were
neither "posed" nor "faked," they did not doubt the authenticity
of *The Campaign in Cuba*. This patriotic series showed *Landing
Under Fire, The Battle of San Juan Hill* and *Our Flag Is There
to Stay!* Everything might have been spoiled by the knowledge
that these epic events had been photographed on the suburban soil
of New Jersey.

Only the prosperous urban middle class patronized the vaudeville theaters. For several years they delighted in the brief, flickering dance of shadows across the screen. The true source of their
pleasure was not the subjects that they saw, but the unfamiliar
effect which these subjects produced: "life motion, realism, photographed from nature so true to life as to force the observers to
believe that they are viewing the reality and not the reproduc-
tion." But gradually, as the novelty of seeing living pictures wore
off, the potency of their illusion diminished. The technique of
picture-making did not noticeably advance. The kinds of subjects
presented were limited; repetition made them seem monotonous.
The vaudeville audience was a fickle one, and it began to tire of a
novelty that was becoming commonplace. Some managers—especially those in control of the most expensive theaters—concluded
that living pictures were only a passing fad, which now had run
its course, ceased showing them, and sold their projection-
machines. In the cheaper houses, pictures continued to be shown,
but no longer as a feature. They were put at the end of the bill,
so that those who did not wish to see them could leave without
missing any of the show. Soon, the managers came to regard them
as being merely useful in clearing the theater for another audience.
The incredible miracle of science was less esteemed than an inferior animal-act. In the jargon of the theater, it had become a
"chaser."

The great mass of workers who swarmed in the poorer quarters
of American cities had little money to spend on theatrical entertainment; some earned only a dollar a day. For them, the penny
arcade, ablaze with light, noisy and crowded, held a promise of
cheap diversion. A coin dropped into a slot would make the
automatic gypsy nod sagely, and hand out a card with your
fortune. Another coin enabled you to test your skill with the
punching bag, against the certified records of pugilists like
Gentleman Jim Corbett and Bob Fitzsimmons. You could investigate your resistance to electric shock, practice weight-lifting, have
your tintype taken. You could listen to Sousa's marches, and the
latest song hits, on the phonograph. Above all, you could see the
pictures come to life in the kinetoscope. Watching the crowds

lining up to reach these machines, the owners of penny arcades realized that quick profits could be made on screen shows. If they could obtain projection machines, they could remove the rolls of film from the cabinets, paste them together, run them for five or ten minutes, perhaps even for half an hour. The same idea dawned on the showmen whose business it was to carry amusement to the small towns: medicine shows, traveling dime museums, small circuses, the magicians, ventriloquists and acrobats who performed at country fairs. A black-topped tent would serve as a theater; a projection machine and its operator, with enough films, could wheedle big money from the rural trade.

These hardy enterprisers, existing on the disreputable outskirts of the legitimate amusement industry, catering to a public ignored by theatrical magnates like the Frohmans and masters of vaudeville like B. F. Keith, saw commercial possibilities in the novelty that was being discarded by high-priced theaters. Some were able to buy second-hand projectors. Others persuaded machine shops to duplicate Edison or Biograph machines. They erected partitions closing off the rear of their arcades, hung a screen at one end, and crowded as many chairs as possible into the remaining space. In these makeshift theaters, holding fewer than one hundred people, they advertised the exhibition of living pictures. At first, the cutsomers of penny arcades were suspicious and skeptical. Many knew that the novelty had caused a sensation in the costly vaudeville theaters. Few associated it with the pictures already visible in the cabinets of the arcade. All of them doubted that the living pictures advertised for a dime were the genuine article. Thomas L. Tally, a former Texas cowboy who owned an arcade in Los Angeles, pondered this shrewd customer resistance. He cut a peep-hole in his partition, and invited patrons to convince themselves that life-size images were moving on the screen in his darkened rear room before parting with their dimes. This expedient produced the desired result. Word of it spread across the country, and it was widely adopted.

Moving pictures soon became the most popular attraction of the penny arcades. The people who crowded into the little showrooms were not, like the patrons of vaudeville houses, familiar with the stage and therefore hard to please. The sheer mystery of motion on the screen enchanted them, and for the first time they experienced the peculiar pleasure of collective excitement in a theater. Images of traffic moving on a street, pugilists boxing, a dancer doing her turn, comedians going through their routine, evoked roars of enthusiasm. The bloom of novelty did not wear off. In the slums of the great Eastern and Middle Western cities there were herded vast immigrant populations. Largely unfamiliar with the English language, they could not read the newspapers, magazines or books. But the living pictures communicated their meanings directly and eloquently. To enjoy them, no command of a new language was essential. They made illiteracy, and ignorance of American customs, seem less shameful; they broke down a painful sense of isolation and ostracism. Dwellers in tenements, workers in sweatshops, could escape the drabness of their environment for a little while, at a price within their means. They could learn about their adopted country, see the water come tumbling over Niagara Falls, the spectacular architecture of the Pan American Exposition at Buffalo, the funeral of President McKinley, the inauguration of President Theodore Roosevelt. They could participate in little dramatic incidents: a budding courtship interrupted; a chase; a comic altercation between Happy Hooligan, the disreputable tramp, and a smug member of the prosperous classes. In the penny arcades, moving pictures took deep root, both as an agency for information and as a cheap form of entertainment for the masses. In the small rural communities to which they were taken by traveling showmen, they met equally responsive audiences. A broad popular foundation was being laid for a major industry, as well as a social instrument of incalculable power.

An embryonic industry was already taking shape. It was hampered by scarcity of equipment, vexed by the perpetual threat of litigation, had no precedents to follow. It had accidentally discovered an entirely new body of consumers, immensely numerous, but of dubious permanence. The earliest producers, skeptical about the remote future, wasted no effort on long-range plans. For the Edison Company, motion pictures were only a side line. Never-

theless, Edison claimed basic patents and asserted that these were
infringed by any camera or projector other than its own. The
equipment of the Biograph Company had been designed with this
claim in mind; since it differed from Edison's, the company relied
on the validity of its patents. Biograph was unique in having
obtained financial backing from banking interests. To protect
their investment, they placed a representative in the company:
Jeremiah J. Kennedy, an engineer previously associated with large
industrial enterprises. Both Edison and Biograph sold or rented
projection machines; neither would release cameras. They intended to keep the making of motion pictures to themselves.

But other men had determined to break into this new field.
Shortly after Edison's vitascope had been introduced at Koster and
Bial's, the New York *World* sent a representative to interview the
inventor. The task was assigned to James Stuart Blackton, a tall,
handsome, ingratiating young artist. Blackton earned his living in
the lecture lyceums, giving "chalk talks" which he illustrated with
pictures drawn in view of the audience. When not thus engaged,
he produced illustrated feature articles for newspapers. On his visit
to West Orange, he succeeded in interesting Edison, who ordered
the making of a film entitled, *Blackton, the "World" Cartoonist.*
Furthermore, Edison offered to sell him a projector, with a supply
of films, for eight hundred dollars. Blackton discussed this opportunity with Albert Edward Smith, another public entertainer.
Together they managed to scrape up the money, bought the outfit,
and set off on the road. Showing pictures proved to be profitable,
and they surmised that making them might produce an even larger
revenue. But, since cameras were unobtainable, this golden prospect seemed beyond reach.

Presently, Smith learned that the basic principles of the projector and camera were identical. Why not convert their projector
into a camera? Having an aptitude for mechanics and an interest
in invention, Smith began working on the problems of transformation. The experiment turned out successfully, and he later went
on to devise improvements in cameras and projection machines.
Meanwhile, equipped with a practicable camera, Blackton and
Smith needed more money to begin operations. They consulted

William Rock, proprietor of a Harlem billiard parlor. During the summer months, Rock sometimes added to his income by taking traveling side-shows on tour; he, too, had been successful with the living pictures. The three men pooled their equipment and resources. With a capital of some three thousand dollars, they formed the Vitagraph Company to produce and sell pictures. Soon becoming proficient photographers, Blackton and Smith began making brief films of street parades, prize fights, and simple dramatic episodes that could be staged, at little expense, in the loft they had rented for business headquarters. From the very outset, their venture prospered, and it soon became a formidable competitor of Edison and Biograph.

Blackton was to become a major figure in the new field, winning early celebrity both as producer and director. Within a comparatively few years, he was a millionaire. He bought a costly estate on Long Island, and became the neighbor of Theodore Roosevelt and J. P. Morgan. Taking up the sport of yachting, he was invited to join two exclusive clubs, and was presently the "commodore" of both; the title, in which he rejoiced, proved valuable for publicity. His consuming desire for social recognition was probably aggravated by the disesteem for the source of his wealth that prevailed among the well bred. By conservative financiers "picture business" was regarded as a fly-by-night affair. By people of taste, its products were avoided with disdain. The raffish crowd who conducted the business were invisible to anyone stationed near the barrier that protected gentlefolk from unseemly associations. Blackton's eagerness for admission to the sacred citadel became a permanent aspiration of the film world. This was to be fulfilled, before the middle of the century, by the emergence of café society, where new wealth acquired prestige by association with vintage names, and inheritors of seasoned wealth escaped boredom in intimacy with the last surviving exponents of glamor on earth. Of this institution, Blackton himself was a precursor. His active career in pictures outlasted that of nearly every other pioneer. His fortune was swept away by the Great Depression, and he went on Federal relief as director of a film project in Los Angeles. When he died, some years later, he had been earning a

meager livelihood doing odd jobs for Hollywood studios, long
forgotten by the public and scarcely known by the giant industry
he had helped to found.

In the early years of the century, other men as ambitious as
Blackton, with equally slender resources, followed in the wake of
Vitagraph. Sigmund Lubin, in Philadelphia, had been a peddler
of optical goods and novelties at county fairs, and now operated
several penny arcades in addition to a small retail shop. With C.
Francis Jenkins, who had worked with Thomas Armat, Lubin
was soon manufacturing cameras and projectors, trading in films,
developing them in his own laboratories, exhibiting them and
finally also producing them. In Chicago, George K. Spoor, operator
of a newsstand, joined Max Aronson, a vaudeville actor who
adopted the name G. M. Anderson, in forming the Essanay Company. It was not long before they hit upon the notion of transfer-
ring to the screen some elements of the currently popular Wild
West Shows. Films showing pursuits had an irresistible appeal.
Why not add trick horsemanship, Indians, cowboys? Though not
an expert horseman—he invented the use of a "double" for stars
in the performance of hazardous exploits—Anderson, as "Broncho
Billy," won a nation-wide audience; he was the daredevil cowboy
of early "westerns" which, for many years, he ground out at the
rate of one every week. Westerns and other thrillers were also the
specialty of William Selig who, having abandoned the upholstery
trade to manage a traveling minstrel show, turned to the lucrative
business of making films in Chicago. Selig soon gave American
boyhood an idol for emulation. This was Tom Mix, who dazzled
audiences by his brilliant horsemanship and dauntless heroism.
He had abandoned a similar job with the Miller Brothers' 101
Ranch and Wild West Show to perform his feats of daring for the
camera. And it was to this organization that he quietly returned
when, after two decades of international fame, his popularity
waned and he vanished from the screen.

To the owners of penny arcades, the overwhelming success of
the pictures shown in their dark back rooms came as a surprise,
and raised a disturbing problem. Most of them had expected the
vogue to peter out, as in the vaudeville theaters; they had merely

hoped to clean up on it while it lasted. But interest in the arcade machines was evaporating; the crowds seemed only to want the pictures, ignoring all other attractions while they waited for admission. Out in Los Angeles, in 1902, Thomas L. Tally took the bold step of discarding his machines, and converting his whole arcade into a hall for the showing of pictures. He named it "The Electric Theater," and after its success caused him to open a second hall, other arcade proprietors began following his lead. Three years later, in McKeesport, Pennsylvania, there appeared the real progenitor of all future movie theaters.

This was the creation of two brothers-in-law who, having obtained a French projector eight years earlier, had introduced pictures to Pittsburgh and the nearby industrial towns. Both John P. Harris and Harry Davis, unlike most other exhibitors, had worked with "legitimate" theatrical enterprises, and it was this experience that they put to use when they determined to remodel a store in McKeesport for the showing of pictures. Being shrewd showmen, they set out to make the store look as much like an actual theater as possible. They gave it a colorful, arresting, recessed front. They added glamor by decorating the interior and having a pianist furnish musical accompaniment for the pictures. They announced that the hall would open for business at eight in the morning; that the twenty-minute program would be continuously repeated until midnight; that admission would cost only five cents. Then, with masterly intuition, they coined a name for their theater which combined the suggestions of cheapness and grandeur. The name sped across the continent, was adopted by the public as the term defining a picture-house, and thus entered the American language as a new noun. The name was "Nickelodeon."

The "Nickelodeon," with its cheap admission, its music, its colorful interior that produced an effect of luxury, was an instantaneous success. From morning till midnight its ninety-six seats were constantly filled, and on some days several hundred patrons would pay admission for the privilege of standing at the rear of the auditorium. Box-office receipts soon exceeded a thousand dollars a week. Word of this sure-fire means to quick money traveled swiftly. Throughout the United States, there was a frantic effort to rent vacant stores and convert them into picture-shows. Pittsburgh, within a year, had one hundred nickelodeons. In New York, where the Board of Aldermen designated them as "common shows" for which a license fee of only twenty-five dollars was charged, as compared with a fee of five hundred for a theater, licenses were issued at the rate of one a day. Similar conditions obtained in Chicago, Boston, Philadelphia, Detroit, Los Angeles—in every city from coast to coast. Within three years, the nation had some eight to ten thousand nickelodeons, and—as the earliest picture-trade publication reported—"if the nickel delirium continues to maintain its hold, there will be in a few years more of these cheap amusement places than saloons."

They dotted the foreign quarters, the slums, the poorer shopping streets. The well-to-do, having no reason to penetrate these neighborhoods, seldom saw or heard of them. Above their recessed fronts, as dusk fell, electric lights bravely flaunted such appealing names as "The Family" and "The Cosy," or such invitations to fantasy and romance as "The Jewel" and "Bijou Dream." The recessed front served as a crude lobby, made space for a ticket-booth and ticket-taker, was plastered with vivid posters suggesting the excitement, adventure and beauty that five cents would buy. The nickels rattled down like hailstones as workingmen and their families crowded into the lobbies, overflowed in long patient lines on the street. Inside, the program lasted from twenty minutes to an hour: a brief melodrama or chase; a comedy; a news picture or travel picture; a glimpse of dancers or acrobats. Between films, the projectionist inserted "hand-colored" slides of popular songs, the pianist pounded out their melodies, and the whole audience sang. "The Hottentot Love Song"; "Love Me and The World Is Mine"; "Waltz Me Around Again, Willie"; "I'm Afraid to Go Home in the Dark"; "School-Days"; "Laddie Boy"; "I Wish I Had a Girl"; "You Splash Me and I'll Splash You." And, nearly always, there would be a slide of handsome Donald Brian, holding Ethel Jackson in his arms, which set everyone to singing the new, lilting, "Merry Widow Waltz."

Far too often, in the middle of a picture, the projectionist inserted a slide reading, "One Minute, Please!" This indicated a break in the film, or trouble with the machine. Everyone began stamping in unison. If the necessary repair required a little time, there were slides advertising the stores of local tradesmen, and announcing future programs. The audience, impatient for a renewal of illusion, whistled and shouted. Youngsters carrying trays piled with peanuts, candy, popcorn and soda-pop rushed up and down the aisles, crying their wares. Presently the machine resumed its sputtering, and the screen came alive again. There was a ripple of applause, a fluttering sigh of contentment. Then silence, broken by the crackling of peanut shells and popcorn, the whimpering of a frightened child. In the fetid darkness, tired men and women forgot the hardships of poverty. For this was happiness. This was the Promised Land.

3   The Merchants of Dreams

When the owners of penny arcades first began to show pictures, they had to buy these outright from the manufacturers. Since frequent changes of program were necessary, they traded their pictures among themselves. In this haphazard, inefficient way of doing business, a number of men saw an opportunity to make money. A middleman, or jobber of pictures, could serve both manufacturers and exhibitors. Buying films from the manufacturer, he could rent them out to exhibitors, charging each of them far less than the cost of the film, yet making a large profit on every picture before it had run its course. Exhibitors could afford to change their programs more frequently, thus increasing their patronage. This, in turn, would create a demand for more new pictures. The jobber could deal directly with all manufacturers, guarantee to buy their entire output at prices higher than had formerly been paid by the exhibitors, and so distribute a variety of films to his customers. By the time the first nickelodeons were opened, there were more than one hundred film "exchanges" operating in thirty-five of the largest American cities.

The men who hurried to open nickelodeons, as the boom swept across the country, came from the same economic class as their patrons. They were owners of small retail businesses—cheap lunchrooms, candy or cigar stores, corner drug stores. They were garment workers, fur-cutters, salesmen of low-priced goods. Seeing a vacant store, and deciding that the neighborhood would support another picture house, they might persuade a friend or two to share the venture; a house could be opened for business on a thousand dollars, or even less. Many of the nickelodeons were family enterprises: mother and daughter sold tickets; father, as manager, took them at the door; a son ran the projection machine; the younger children peddled refreshments. The nickelodeon owners were genuinely representative of the public they served. Because their preferences were also those of their patrons, they knew what kinds of pictures were likely to prove most popular. When they selected programs from catalogues issued by the manufacturers and exchanges, their personal tastes served as a reliable guide. If a picture, when shown, aroused unusual enthusiasm, they hastened to obtain others like it. If an audience, leaving the nickelodeon, complained about any picture, the owners passed this verdict on to their exchange, and thereafter refused to show films in any way resembling the one that had displeased. By interpreting the wants and prejudices of their public, its inarticulate hopes and dreams, the owners of nickelodeons helped to shape the content, and fix the patterns, of the films which manufacturers were turning out.

A few of them were presently to exercise an even more direct and decisive influence on the nature of American films. They were men whose native shrewdness advanced them quickly, though they had little formal education; who learned as they went; who were driven—either by insatiable ambition, or mere circumstance—to undertake the actual making of pictures. There was William Fox, who grew up in a rear tenement on New York's lower East Side. Fox left school at the age of eleven, to help support a large family. He peddled candy in Central Park until he was old enough to secure work in a garment factory. Long years of privation took him into the ranks of the Socialist Party, but after saving his first hundred dollars he renounced socialism. While still at the factory bench, he invested in a penny arcade; as this prospered, he banked his share of the profits. When he had amassed sixteen hundred dollars, he quit the garment trade to open a nickelodeon. After a few years, he owned a chain of fifteen small picture houses, and branched into the exchange business also.

There was Marcus Loew, who was employed as a furrier when he, too, put money into a penny arcade in New York and was astonished by his quick profits. Presently he opened a nickelodeon, then another, on the lower East Side. He met the popular actor, David Warfield, whom he interested by prophesying that the pictures were bound to become a great industry. Warfield carried this prediction to his manager, the theatrical producer, David Belasco; both decided to help Loew expand his business. Loew took in a partner, and set out to acquire a chain of theaters. His partner was Adolph Zukor, a small, quiet man whose sad eyes and gentle expression masked a flintlike character. Zukor had come to the United States from Hungary at the age of sixteen, found work as an upholsterer at a salary of two dollars a week, later became a furrier, then one of several partners in a penny arcade. When Zukor joined Loew, he owned two or three nickelodeons. Together, the two men made money rapidly. Presently, Zukor withdrew from the partnership, and bought a picture house on Fourteenth Street at Union Square. Loew went on to accumulate more and more theaters; eventually, they stretched across the country. Zukor, studying his audiences on Fourteenth Street, concluded that the public would soon want pictures superior to those which he was showing. He began to dream of making pictures that were different; longer, maybe; somehow like the plays that drew crowds into the theaters on Broadway.

In a Wisconsin town the manager of a clothing store, Carl Laemmle, had long cherished an ambition to go into business for himself. He thought he would do better in a large city and went to Chicago to find out about opportunities there. Far out on the city's west side, he saw a vacant store. It had formerly housed a picture show, and when Laemmle inquired about renting it, the landlord offered to include the previous tenant's screen and chairs. Laemmle, he suggested, could open a nickelodeon in short order. As much alarmed as allured by this notion, the retailer talked it over with a business acquaintance, Robert

Cochrane, who made his living by writing and illustrating advertisements for clothing merchants. Cochrane urged Laemmle to undertake the venture. So Laemmle opened his nickelodeon, applied to it the same merchandising methods that he had previously used, and met with such success that he soon acquired additional theaters. Presently, taking Cochrane as his assistant, he also organized an exchange.

Nobody foresaw that men like Fox, Loew, Zukor and Laemmle were to become, within a very few years, absolute masters of industrial empires as vast and powerful as those which, far earlier, had been founded on oil, beef, sugar and tobacco. The possibilities of erecting such grandiose economic structures had been exhausted. Hostility to those which existed had risen to a peak; under public pressure, the Federal government had already begun to attack monopolies and trusts. America's most distinguished writers, most conscientious journalists; its social theorists, reformers, progressive politicians; many of its spiritual leaders and secular philosophers—all these were pointing to the shrinking opportunity and deteriorating existence available to the common man. Even the common men who were breaking into a cheap, shabby business scarcely understood, as yet, that it was to open a new area of opportunity as dazzling, as golden, as any of the old.

Conditions in the new industry were chaotic. Ruthless competition and an increasing demand for pictures gave rise to various dishonest practices. Manufacturers of pictures were now charging prices based upon fees for every showing of their films. Exchanges resorted to "duping." Having secured a film, they had a negative made from it; from the negative they reproduced prints which they distributed as originals, thereby cheating the manufacturer. Exhibitors devised a scheme to defraud both exchanges and manufacturers. A number of picture houses under one ownership, or merely associated for purposes of fraud, rented a picture for a single theater, then arranged their schedules so that a messenger on a bicycle could race the film from one house to another, until all had shown it. The cash value of priority in showing films was obvious; by paying premiums for this privilege, an exhibitor could often put competitors out of business and acquire their theaters. Owners of chains were in a position to demand rebates, and other special privileges, which frequently enabled them to crush smaller operators. The commercial underworld of cheap movie houses was governed by the economic principle of dog eat dog.

Among the manufacturers of pictures, open warfare prevailed. Each of the major companies held patents covering improvements to cameras and projection machines. But the Edison Company, claiming the priority of its own patents, had instituted lawsuits against all the others. Meanwhile, collectively, these companies had not been able to keep the field to themselves. Men resolved to invade it were importing European cameras, or having American ones illegally counterfeited, and setting up as producers; their operations enabled distributors to profit handsomely by playing one manufacturer against the others. Three years after the first nickelodeon appeared, the field of production was wide open. It promised to become incalculably profitable—especially if it could be brought under monopoly control.

The effort to form a monopoly was undertaken by Jeremiah J. Kennedy, the retired engineer and iron-handed businessman whom bankers had placed in the Biograph Company to protect their investment. He brought together seven domestic and two foreign manufacturers, and a distributor who controlled various valuable rights, and persuaded them to pool their patents. The resulting combination was named the Motion Picture Patents Company, and its legal control of equipment and processes appeared to be so complete that pictures could not be photographed, processed or exhibited without its consent. Each of the ten members were licensed to make pictures under all the pooled patents; no additional licenses were to be issued. In the field of production, the new corporation seemingly held an impregnable monopoly.

It moved promptly to extend this to the distribution and exhibition of pictures. It formed the General Film Company, which bought up fifty-nine major exchanges throughout the country, all of which were forbidden to distribute any pictures except those made by members of the trust. To regulate exhibitors, General Film imposed a weekly tax of two dollars on all theaters. This covered a franchise to use authorized projectors, and to rent films manufactured by members of the trust. Theaters were classified, and paid a weekly fee of from fifteen to one hundred and twenty-five dollars for a daily change of program. The showing of "outlaw" pictures—made by manufacturers not members of the trust—was forbidden, and was punished by confiscation of projectors and loss of franchise. Thus a bottleneck was created through which, it appeared, only trust pictures would be permitted to reach the public. By virtue of their monopoly, and rising public demand, the trust producers were under no compulsion to improve the quality of their product; the public would take what it got—and like it.

Rebellious opposition to monopoly control developed swiftly. Although ten thousand small exhibitors signed up with the trust, all were infuriated by the tax which it imposed on their business; an undercover traffic in illicit projectors and "outlaw" films was soon flourishing. Both William Fox and Carl Laemmle, proprietors of many theaters and prosperous exchanges, determined to fight the trust. Both refused to sell their exchanges to the combine, or submit to the theater tax. Both, in order to supply their houses with pictures, became independent or "outlaw" producers of films. Fox brought suit against the combine under the Sherman Anti-Trust Law, and this eventually brought about its dissolution. Within three years after the trust's formation, ten well-organized manufacturers of pictures were providing it with formidable competition. While the trust attempted to standardize the pictures of its members, these truculent independents were seeking to gain a market through inventiveness, originality and improved quality.

Meanwhile, the bitter conflict that raged over the movie world resembled, in its violence, the warfare waged by Rockefeller in the early days of Standard Oil; by Gould and Vanderbilt over the Erie Railroad; by Capone or Dutch Schultz against rival liquor barons in the future era of prohibition. Jeremiah J. Kennedy set up an elaborate espionage system, and employed a strong-arm gang to raid unlicensed theaters and exchanges which managed to secure films made by the trust; to smash illicit projection machines and destroy outlaw films found in licensed theaters. Independent producers, in order to protect their cameras and personnel while pictures were being made—usually "on the run"—hired armed guards, and built up private militias. But Kennedy introduced his squads into their premises. Taking jobs as "extras," they smashed cameras and provoked riots. There were midnight raids on hideout laboratories; mysterious chemical accidents occurred that destroyed costly negatives. For independent manufacturers, the vicinity of New York City—heretofore the center of production—became too dangerous. Several years before the trust was formed William Selig, making westerns in Chicago, and harried by Edison litigation, had taken his company to Los Angeles, near enough to the Mexican border to provide ease of escape from injunctions and subpoenas. Selig had been taken into the trust, but the independent manufacturers began thinking of the city in the Far West. There, behind a stout board fence enclosing a platform stage, with sentinels constantly on the watch, they might be able to proceed with their work unmolested by violence. If dubious strangers approached, work could be quickly suspended; the precious cameras could be hustled into a motor car for a dash across the border into Mexico, where officers of the United States courts were unwelcome and without authority.

The discovery of Hollywood—perhaps as momentous as the discovery of America itself—was about to be made.

CHAPTER II

Where Is It Now,
the Glory and the Dream?

1 Cinderella in the Kitchen

Nobody, at first, detected the possibility of using living pictures to tell a story. Yet, once recognized, this possibility became the source of their power, the assurance of their permanence, and the reason for a development as inevitable as it was spectacular. The simple fact that, as a form of drama, the new medium could produce effects impossible to achieve on the stage—this fact had results that were to touch the lives of all Americans. It tremendously increased the commercial value of motion pictures as a commodity. By so doing, it made them subject to the forces of economic competition. Competition rapidly brought about technical improvement, as well as notable advances in craftsmanship. Both of these immensely enlarged the audience. Because motion pictures gradually conquered an almost universal public, they became a social force of potentially incalculable capacity for good or evil. The scientific toy which Edison invented and casually tossed aside held consequences so profound and so far-reaching that, a half century later, they could not be accurately estimated. All these consequences flowed from the ability of motion pictures to tell a story—any kind of story—vividly, dramatically and completely; more effectively than stories had ever been told before.

The first man to recognize that a story could be told on film, and to realize that motion pictures offered unlimited opportunities, was a Frenchman. George Melies, a caricaturist, professional magician and part-time actor, experimented on the streets of Paris with a movie-camera, accidentally discovered the trick of double exposure, and went on to devise other "magical" effects. He began working with professional actors, added costumes and scenery to his equipment, turned to literature for his subjects, and told his stories by photographing a series of pre-arranged scenes—carefully devised, adequately rehearsed, and set in a logical sequence. When Melies' films—all of them fantasies— reached the United States at the turn of the century, their success was sensational. American manufacturers promptly "duped" them; none attempted to imitate Melies' films, apply his methods, or adopt his innovations.

But Melies' films deeply impressed Edwin S. Porter, a photographer for the Edison Company. Porter had joined the Edison staff in 1896. A skilled mechanic, he was drawn to the laboratories by a love of machinery which also attracted him to the new horseless carriage, not yet a business proposition. For the new living pictures, Porter felt no particular enthusiasm; he was as dubious of their future as their inventor. With the rush of business precipitated by the success of the vitascope, he was set to work as a cameraman. For six years, like everyone else in the industry, he ground out pictures of news events, vaudeville turns and comic episodes. In the light of this routine experience, the films of George Melies had the impact of a revelation. Porter immediately

determined to try his hand at telling a story in pictures. The experiment would be cheaper if he could compose the story from
pictures already taken—but to do this he would have to cut the
old films and rearrange them in a different order; and to make
his story clear, he would probably have to insert some new shots.
Thus, a purely economic exigency led Porter to discover the principle of editing that was to become basic to the craft of making
movies.

In the Edison stock room, Porter found a large number of
films showing fire departments in action. Aware of their popularity, he decided to base his story on a fire. His film, *The Life of
an American Fireman,* showed the rescue of a woman and child
from a burning building by a fire company whose chief, when
awakened by the alarm, had been dreaming of precisely this crisis.
Released in 1903, before the first nickelodeon was opened, this
film reached only a limited audience. But it excited them more
than any picture they had previously seen, and its success justified
Porter's desire to undertake a still more ambitious project. Could
he not turn out a more powerful, thrilling, sensational story if,
instead of merely using old stock films, he planned it in advance,
and took absolutely new pictures for it? Following this intuition,
and lifting his subject from a currently popular melodrama that
was playing on the road, Porter made *The Great Train Robbery,*
a story film which combined the elements of crime, suspense,
pursuit and breathtaking climax. Offered to exhibitors in 1904,
this film reached the market in time to become a feature of the
first program shown by the original Nickelodeon when it opened
in 1905, and for years it was to remain the most frequently repeated attraction in nickelodeons throughout the land. Because
of its immense popularity with the patrons of nickelodeons, and
because of the simultaneous nation-wide boom in these cheap
theaters, many historians later attributed to Porter's first story
film the permanence of movies as mass entertainment.

Its immediate effect was to transform the motion picture, almost
overnight, from a purely reportorial to a dramatic, imaginative
medium, capable of arousing intense emotions; able to influence
the minds and social attitudes of its spectators, shape their desires,

opinions, prejudices and ideals. Though Porter himself was not aware of it, he had invented an instrument more widely com-municative than the printed page, more insidiously persuasive than the spoken word. Edison's competitors, noting that *The Great Train Robbery* had achieved a success even more sensational than any of Melies' fantasies, at once turned to the production of story films. Like Porter's, most of these were photographed on a single reel of film, one thousand feet long, and they ran for only fourteen minutes. But, brief and crude as they were, they pre-cipitated important changes. Their instantaneous success made rapid and increasing output essential. Actors, scenery and cos-tumes were required; manufacturers therefore had to set up "factories" or studios. An incessant flow of stories was requisite; the film writer who invented or adapted plots came into being. Speed of production brought about the division and specialization of tasks; photographing, directing, acting, writing, lighting, de-veloping and cutting pictures presently became separate crafts. The fundamental principle of mass production was being applied, not deliberately, but as an unpremeditated method of meeting an unforeseen demand. At the outset actors, steadily employed and paid a weekly salary like other factory hands, were expected to do odd jobs when not performing for the camera. At Vitagraph, the leading actress, Florence Turner, uncomplainingly sewed costumes during off-hours. But handsome Maurice Costello, one of the earliest screen idols though still anonymous, touched off a rebellion by protesting: "I am an actor and I will act, but I will not build sets and paint scenery." Soon enough, the pressure to speed up output kept actors before the camera, day in, day out.

In its eagerness to turn out story films, the booming industry looked to Porter for leadership. It not only adopted his technical innovations, but imitated the actual content of his pictures. Porter was a man of the people; he had suffered hardship and privation; he had personal experience of poverty and its problems; his early years had nourished a strong resentment of social injustice; his training as a cameraman had taken him into the crowded city streets. All these influences conspired to make him, unlike Melies, a realist, finding his subjects in the world of everyday urban life familiar to his audiences. Ignorant of the new movement toward realism in fiction and the drama, lacking any literary interest or erudition, Porter nevertheless turned out films that were, in effect, a kind of pictorial literature. In their themes, his little dramas resembled the novels of the common life that were being written by Stephen Crane, Jack London and Frank Norris. In their outspoken criticism of defects in the American social order, they had much in common with the "exposures" of such conscientious journalists as Ida Tarbell, Ray Stannard Baker and Lincoln Steffens.

Porter's early pictures opened the way for others which attempted to deal, more or less fearlessly, with a variety of social, economic and political issues. In *The Girl Strike Leader*, a manufacturer's son, working incognito in his father's factory, fell in love with a machine-operator, supported her leadership in a strike, and eventually secured improved working conditions. *The Long Strike* told a love story set against the background of industrial warfare in Chicago. In *How the Cause Was Won*, the son of a wealthy manufacturer, assigned by his father to investigate labor conditions in the factory, became sympathetic to the workers' cause and successfully led them in a strike against his parent, who eventually complied with the union's demands. In *Capital vs. Labor*, a mob of strikers was calmed, during a riot, by a young clergyman who obtained concessions from their employer. In *The Agitator*, a ranch foreman incited his subordinates to demand an equitable division of their employer's profits. *The Convict's Parole*, sponsored by the governor of Oregon, studied the efforts of labor contractors to discredit the parole system; *The Fight for the Right*, sponsored by the National Parole Committee, studied the iniquities of Southern mill owners who employed convict labor to cut production costs. One of the most interesting of these films was *The Governor's Double*, which showed the governor of New York allowing himself to be arrested for burglary in order to investigate prison conditions from within. And there were films bearing such provocative titles as *From the Submerged, Charity, Lily of the Tenements, The Grafters, The Money King, The Reform Candidate, What Shall We Do With Our Old?* In general, the men who made these films were dramatizing the issues that perplexed conscientious and thoughtful Americans who were troubled by the contemporary drift of affairs, who saw the conflict between property rights and human welfare being won by the forces of economic privilege, and who—like the title of one of the pictures—were asking *Why?*

Although the nickelodeons were disdained by the well-to-do and well-bred, few of whom ever saw the pictures that dealt with current social issues, they soon aroused anxiety among the more prosperous classes. Was skepticism about the established order to be tolerated—especially when it was being communicated, through a medium so unprecedentedly inflammatory, to uneducated workingmen and their families who already were too resentful for the comfort of their social superiors? "A set of revolutionists training for the overthrow of the government," *The Christian Leader* declared, "could find no surer means than these exhibitions." The Chicago *Tribune* denounced them for having an "influence wholly vicious," and asserted that it would be only "proper to suppress them at once" on the ground that they were "ministering to the lowest passions of children." Miss Jane Addams, from Hull House, her post of observation among the slum-dwellers of Chicago, immediately protested. The new theaters of the masses, she proposed, should be regulated, not closed. Rightly conducted, she asserted, motion pictures were "a benefit not a menace, especially to the poorer classes." But demands for suppression and censorship gained the support of three groups whose interests had suffered from competition offered by the nickelodeons. These were the clergymen with parishes in the poorer quarters of cities, whose congregations were being depleted; the saloon-owners whose patronage, seduced by the rival attractions of the nickelodeons, was falling off; the owners of small retail businesses, who could not afford to equal the high rents which promoters of nickelodeons were offering for vacant stores. In their assault on the motion pictures, these oddly assorted allies were joined by still another vested interest. Owners of "legitimate" theaters and vaudeville houses, noting an ominous decline in the sale of their cheapest seats, resolved to meet competition by enlisting powerful political forces in the drive to impose censorship.

An opportune provocation to witch-hunting suddenly offered

itself. One summer night, on the roof garden of Madison Square Garden in New York City, a millionaire playboy named Harry Kendall Thaw shot and killed the eminent architect, Stanford White. The murder was a "crime of passion"; its heroine, an artist's model, Evelyn Nesbit, had been White's mistress before becoming Thaw's wife. The subsequent trial of Thaw, bringing to light episodes highly distasteful to the genteel, furnished a field day for the yellow press. As a result, Americans of the humbler classes were afforded a chance to appraise the private morality of two representatives of privilege—of the class that had always been zealously concerned to protect the morals of the poor. The Thaw case inspired the making of a motion picture, *The Great Thaw Trial,* and exhibition of this film in New York City precipitated the storm. Mayor George McClellan, son of Lincoln's celebrated general and rival, acted promptly. He issued an order closing all nickelodeons in the city.

An injunction against enforcement of this order was sought and issued. But officials in other cities, among them Chicago and Providence, Rhode Island, were quick to follow the lead of the mayor of New York. A nation-wide campaign for suppression of the nickelodeons seemed probable. As the agitation began, Charles Sprague Smith, head of the People's Institute of Cooper Union, in New York City, sagely declared that, "There are more things rotten in New York than motion pictures." Producers of pictures mobilized to meet the attack. Over the signature of Carl Laemmle, Robert Cochrane wrote advertisements calling for action looking to mutual protection and defense. The motion-picture trust became apprehensive, and entered into consultations with Charles Sprague Smith. The upshot of these was the establishment of a National Board of Censorship (later to become the National Board of Review) financed by the trust, and administered by the People's Institute, which wished to secure a measure of freedom for the new medium. As an advisory body, equipped with authority by the industry alone, this organization undertook to pass on the respectability of future films, and certify that their subject matter was not inimical to good citizenship. Not content with the safeguard thus provided, several states established official boards of censorship. These boards were to view and judge all motion pictures before licensing them for exhibition. None of the states required similar pre-censorship of stage plays or vaudeville shows, which drew their audiences principally from the middle classes. It therefore seemed possible that their anxiety about the content and effect of motion pictures bore some relation to the economic and social status of those who patronized them. By supporting the crusade for censorship, reformers, social workers, clergymen, philanthropists and politicians had accomplished one result, whether intentional or not. They had made certain that "the struggling art of the common people"—if art it was—would thereafter be supervised by competent and orthodox champions of the established order.

The issue of censorship stemmed directly from the capacity of the motion picture to tell a story more eloquently than any other medium. Time and change were to complicate it with other factors, and it would flare up again and again in the future, remaining, at the middle of the twentieth century, one of the social problems for which Americans had found no satisfactory solution. But the first round in the battle over censorship had an unforeseen effect: it drew the attention of American intellectuals to the motion pictures. In the autumn of 1912, from his comfortable seat in the "Editor's Easy Chair" of *Harper's Magazine*, William Dean Howells discussed the new phenomenon. Earlier that year, Howells' seventy-fifth birthday had been celebrated by a public banquet at which President William Howard Taft was among the many eminent speakers paying tribute to the dean of American writers. Internationally famous, though more honored than read by his countrymen, Howells met with respectful attention when he spoke on public issues.

The moving-picture show, Howells asserted, had become the most universally accepted of modern amusements, and this fact led him to offer a radical suggestion. Why not incorporate this new powerful social force into the American public-school system, using it to dramatize education? Considering this possibility, there were in his mind certain grave problems that confronted Americans, certain recent events—like the bitter, sanguinary

strike of the textile workers in Lawrence, Massachusetts, during
the previous spring, finally won by the I.W.W.—that emphasized
their gravity. "No economic or social fact," Howells wrote, "need
transcend the scope of the public-school picture show. The operations of some giant industry such as coal-mining or iron-smelting,
or some vast cotton mill, with children younger than themselves
tending the machinery, and the directors in their oriental-rugged
and mahogany arm-chaired parlors, could be illustrated for the
entertainment and instruction of the school boys and girls. Strikers
and strike-breakers in a street fight, or the spectacle of policemen
clubbing mothers from a train in which they are trying to send
their little ones out of town beyond the struggling and starving,
would impart an idea of our civilization which no amount of
study could without it." Howells was indulging in irony. But he
was likewise inviting the motion picture to be serious—more
serious than the commercial theater. He was asking it to use its
immense resources, as a responsible artist might be summoned to
use his talents, for the advance of social justice, progress toward
a more equitable society, and the enhancement of life. The attack
on the nickelodeons had already made the manufacturers of pictures wary and timid. The course set by Porter had been largely
abandoned. It was no longer feasible to present on the screen,
realistically and in a contemporary setting, the controversial social
and economic issues which Americans could scarcely ignore in
their daily life. If undertaken at all, the task proposed by Howells
required a new, and quite different, approach.

2 The Old Master

The man who eventually undertook this task had been engaged in
making movies for five years when Howells wrote his article. In
the autumn of 1907, the celebrated matinee-idol, James K.
Hackett, ventured into theatrical production, bringing to the
Columbia Theater in Washington a new play: *A Fool and a Girl*.
In it, the perennial beauty, Fanny Ward, was returning to the
stage after an interval of absence. The author of this romantic
drama of the California hop-fields was an actor; the kind of actor
who found his engagements only with touring companies, never

on Broadway. For professional purposes he had adopted the name Lawrence Griffith. A Kentuckian, proud, sentimental, idealistic and very ambitious, he was determined not to become known by his real name, David Wark Griffith, until he had won fame. But, notwithstanding the prestige of its producer and its star, audiences in the capital were cool to *A Fool and a Girl,* and after a fortnight's run Hackett prudently closed it. It had earned neither money nor fame for its author. Disgruntled, very nearly broke, he went up to New York to look for work.

Griffith was thirty-two years old, and had cherished the dream of becoming a successful, famous playwright from the age of eighteen. He was tall and lean, and he carried himself with a lordly air; not because he was an actor, but because he considered himself an aristocrat and believed himself to be a genius. People usually remembered this effect of assurance, somehow emphasized by his large head, big aquiline nose, wide mouth and long chin. Some of them thought him a man consumed by restless energy, full of ideas, always occupied in trying to work them out. Others thought him rather aloof from the bustling, everyday world, as if his real life was carried on in some interior sphere of calm. Both of these contradictory impressions were true.

His father had been a colonel in the Confederate Army; the family, originally people of means, were ruined by the war. A sensitive, bookish child, Griffith's mind was nourished on tales of the Old South; a land of columned mansions, delicate brave women, gallant gentlemen; a land of chivalrous actions and noble manners; a land of romance. As a boy, he read widely in Victorian poetry and fiction. At the age of sixteen, he went to Louisville to find work; he ran an elevator, did some reporting for a newspaper, clerked in a drygoods store, took a job in a bookshop. He saw his first Broadway play, brought to Louisville by a touring company. Appropriately, it was a dramatization of George Eliot's novel, *Romola*; the heroine's role was played by Julia Marlowe, a talented and beautiful young actress, soon to become one of the great stars of the American stage.

This experience fired Griffith's lifelong ambition to write for the theater. He immediately set to work on a play; he was to continue working on it, at intervals, for nearly a half century. But when a friend assured him that all great playwrights had learned their craft as actors, he left his job in the bookstore to join a traveling stock company. For the next ten years, he barnstormed with various touring companies, writing constantly during his free time, infrequently selling a poem or short story to some magazine. On one of these tours, he was stranded in California. He found work as a hop-picker and, characteristically, began at once to write a play based on this experience. When the play was accepted by Hackett, Griffith knew that he had reached a decisive turning point in his career.

His intuition proved to be correct. But his subsequent course was one that he had not foreseen, nor would he have chosen to follow it if he had. In New York, after the failure of his play, Griffith saw one of the early story films. Being in urgent need of money, he decided to try and sell a story idea to the Edison Company. All the film-makers were pirating plots, so Griffith wrote a brief synopsis of Sardou's famous melodrama, *La Tosca*. Operagoers, that winter, were thronging the Metropolitan to hear Puccini's setting of it interpreted by Emma Eames, Enrico Caruso and Antonio Scotti. At the Edison Company, Griffith saw Edwin S. Porter, who refused his script but offered him a job acting for the camera. To be seen in pictures, as Griffith realized, was to acknowledge that he wasn't good enough for the stage; actors who worked in the movies when "at leisure" tried to conceal their disgraceful employment. But, since he was stone broke, Griffith had no choice. He went to work for Porter. After some months, he learned that the Biograph Company was paying its actors five dollars a day, and often paid as much as fifteen dollars for story suggestions. He applied for a job, and was hired. By this time he had married, and presently his wife, Linda Arvidson, was also taken on as an actress. In addition to turning out picture plots and acting, Griffith continued to write; his poems and short stories began appearing in several major magazines; he carefully kept secret the source of his livelihood.

When, after a year, Biograph offered to promote him to directing pictures, Griffith was extremely dubious. Though pleased by

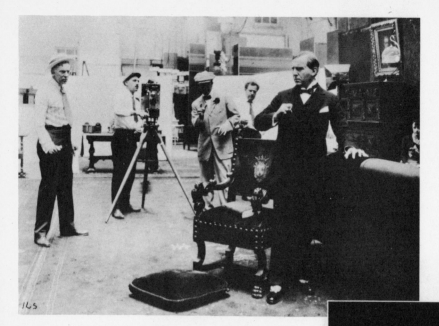

ABOVE: Mr. Blackton Directs E. H. Sothern

LEFT, RIGHT: Between Films These Notices
Would Appear on the Screen

BELOW: A Heartrending Scene from an Early
Biograph Film

PLEASE READ THE
Titles to yourself.
LOUD READING
ANNOYS YOUR
〜 NEIGHBORS 〜

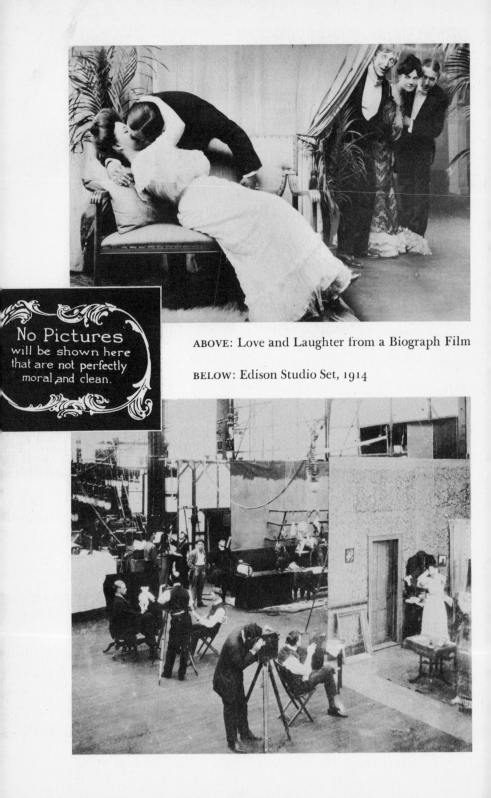

No Pictures will be shown here that are not perfectly moral and clean.

ABOVE: Love and Laughter from a Biograph Film

BELOW: Edison Studio Set, 1914

ABOVE: Ben Turpin and Bronco Billy Anderson

BELOW: Edwin S. Porter,
    The First American to Put Plays on the Screen

Hats Off Pleas

We reserv
the right
to reject
objectionab
persons

ABOVE: D. W. Griffith as an Actor

BELOW: Universal's First Outdoor Studio
in New York

the compliment, he told his wife that he was worried by the prospect of having to tell people that he was working for the films. To his employers, he objected that if he failed as a director, they might not retain him as an actor, and he would be out of work. "If you fall down as a director," they assured him, "you can have your acting job back." Relieved by this promise, Griffith assented. Nevertheless, he undertook his new work reluctantly. He was deeply ashamed of his employment. He had no respect for the canned drama. It excluded poetry and beauty; it rejected the creative imagination. It wasn't an art, or capable of becoming one. Other than money, the only redeeming feature of his job was the slender appeal of its mechanical problems. For Griffith had an experimental turn of mind; he was continually surprising his wife with ideas for improbable inventions which—if only they could be worked out—were bound to make him rich overnight. He began directing pictures in the hope of earning enough money to quit the job quickly; his sole concern was to resume his vocation of writing as soon as possible. Like countless others who were to follow him into the movies with an identical purpose and an equal condescension, he failed to realize his hope. Griffith continued making pictures for nearly a quarter of a century. He won world-wide fame as the "father of the film art" and "king of directors." He made, and lost, a great fortune. Though his prestige never diminished, he was condemned to long inactivity and obscurity. At the end of his life, his feeling about the movies had not changed. He still professed to take a dim view of their merits.

Yet Griffith actually revolutionized the movies. In the pictures which Americans saw at the middle of the century, there was scarcely a single element that he had not either invented, or immensely developed. His innovations in camera technique alone were formidable. They included the close-up, long shot, vista and vignette; the iris-effect, fade-in and fade-out, high- and low-angle shots. Griffith was the first maker of pictures to overcome the frozen immobility of the camera, and move it at will. He originated night photography, and modern methods of lighting. He also added many resources to the technique of story-telling, by making radical experiments in the cutting and editing of his pictures.

Thus, for example, he discovered how to show two or more courses of action occurring in different places, whether simultaneously or not, and keep all threads of a story constantly before his audience. The collective effect of Griffith's many innovations was to extend both the range, and dramatic intensity, of motion pictures. This had an important social result. Within a few years, it multiplied the audience many times. In so doing, it completely changed the character of the public that attended the movies. Griffith not only created the modern movie, but helped to make it a universal entertainment.

He did not foresee this achievement, or deliberately plan it. It was one of the unpredictable consequences of a conflict that always raged within him. He believed that he was a genius, or wanted to believe it. He was proud of the social superiority that his forebears had taken for granted. Yet he saw himself trapped by poverty in an occupation unworthy of an artist, and inadmissible by a gentleman. He was working only for money enough to buy his freedom from detested drudgery. But the more money he made, the more he seemed to need; he squandered it recklessly, perhaps because he could never take it seriously as an end in itself. Since money was the public measure of success, his vanity was nourished by setting a low value on it. Meanwhile, self-reproach kept pace with his mounting success. He scorned himself for not quitting the movies, for being unable to quit them. For what had he surrendered his integrity? Why had he compromised his ideals, abandoned the only aim he genuinely cherished? He had no plausible answers; the questions continued to torment him, sometimes embittering his triumphs. He never completely overcame his contempt for his profession, or the feeling that, for him, success in it was a kind of failure. But the restlessness induced by his conflicting emotions found an outlet in continuous experiment. To shatter the stereotyped formulas that every other maker of pictures accepted as binding; to undertake fearlessly what nobody had ever attempted before: this gave Griffith a perverse satisfaction. It enabled him to give rein to his exorbitant ambition. However obliquely, it expressed his contempt by demonstrating his refusal to be bound by established practice. In a sense, it appeased his uneasy conscience. Each of his experiments was more revolutionary and hazardous than its predecessors, and in time they became more and more costly. So they met with increasing opposition, not only from the technicians who had to execute them, but from the businessmen who were footing the bills. But opposition merely strengthened Griffith's determination to carry them through. He had no respect for the medium in which he was working, but his temperament compelled him to treat it as if it were an art. The result was that he made it one. Yet even world acclaim could not persuade him to believe, wholeheartedly, that this was true.

From the very outset, Griffith's methods proved disconcerting to his associates. His first assignment was a sentimental story of kidnapping, *The Adventures of Dolly*; it was shown at Keith and Proctor's Union Square Theater in New York City on July 14th, 1908, and was liked by audiences throughout the country. Needing a leading man, and not satisfied by any of the actors employed by Biograph, Griffith saw his desired hero in a passer-by on the street, promptly accosted the stranger and hired him. The unknown, Arthur Johnson, soon became one of the earliest of America's anonymous screen idols. The completed film ran to approximately the length of Porter's *The Great Train Robbery*; about two-thirds of a reel. When Griffith had it projected, his cameraman objected that it was too long. Thirty years later the cameraman, G. W. ("Billy") Bitzer, then long famous in the industry because of his subsequent association with Griffith, ruefully recalled this early criticism. "In the light of a completed scenario today," he remarked, "I can readily say that Griffith was years ahead of us." The incident was typical of the opposition provoked by every innovation that he ventured.

Almost immediately, Griffith came into conflict with his superiors on the issue of the kind of story being offered to the public. Simple, obvious melodramas involving a "chase" were the principal staple; Griffith considered them absurd, felt certain that the nickelodeon public would accept something better, but was condemned to grind out several hundred of these naive yarns. In the process, however, he developed methods of increasing their suspense and intensity, and because his pictures were superior to those produced by other companies, they earned substantial profits and won him a measure of freedom. His formula was to put his heroine in a situation of extreme peril, and then effect what soon came to be known by the trade as a "Griffith last-minute rescue." Even in his greatest future pictures, Griffith never completely relinquished this elementary, but powerful, dramatic device. But while turning out these standard products, he also insisted upon trying to use stories that he did not have to despise. As an aspiring playwright, his curiosity about human affairs and social problems was naturally keen; he was an omniverous reader, and the themes which excited him in books seemed capable of presentation on the screen. He made a picture based on a story by Jack London; and, in *A Corner in Wheat*, adapted Frank Norris's novel, *The Pit*, turning that realistic study of speculation on the Chicago Board of Trade into a grim protest against social injustice.

Then, in a series of daring ventures, he brought to the humble patrons of the nickelodeons such masterpieces as Shakespeare's *Taming of the Shrew* and Tolstoy's *Resurrection*; stories by Poe, Maupassant, Fenimore Cooper and Stevenson; poems of Tennyson and Browning. When, after a prolonged struggle with his employers, he secured their consent to film *Pippa Passes*, the New York *Times* reported with amazement that it "is being given in the nickelodeons and Browning is being presented to the average motion picture audiences, who have received it with applause and are asking for more." Soon exasperated by having to confine these serious efforts to one reel, playing for scarcely fourteen minutes, Griffith proposed doubling the length of his pictures. His worried employers forbade it; the public would never accept pictures running for half an hour; they were obviously incapable of such prolonged concentration. In defiance of orders, Griffith proceeded to make *Enoch Arden* in two reels. To punish him, the Biograph Company refused to release the picture as a unit, and issued the two halves separately. After seeing the first reel, audiences everywhere protested; exhibitors were forced to secure both reels and show them in sequence. Against its will, the company had to comply with public demand, and the "long" picture was thus justified.

Delighted by this victory over conservatism, Griffith immediately embarked upon a far more dangerous project. This was a
two-reel "psychological study" of the Darwinian theory of evolution. The cautious businessmen who controlled Biograph were
horrified. Was this appropriate entertainment for the illiterate
masses? But they could not afford to dispense with the maverick
director who, by breaking all established precedents, seemed to
be doubling and trebling their profits. They were not pleased
when Griffith's sober, philosophical picture—dramatizing the
eternal conflict between intelligence and brute force—proved to
be a sensational success. *Man's Ascent* aroused enthusiasm everywhere. "The audience, mechanical Americans fond of crawling on
their stomachs to tinker with their automobiles, are eager over the
evolution of the first weapon from a stick to a hammer," the poet
Vachel Lindsay reported some years later. "They are as full of
curiosity as they could well be over the history of Langley or the
Wright Brothers." But among the magnates of Biograph—the
most respectable and wealthy group in the industry—curiosity
took an anxious tone. Where was all this nonsense going to lead?
Pictures were made and sold by the foot. The business was a mass
production industry, and the product could be made most cheaply
if it was standardized. The trust could make the public accept
whatever it chose to give them. Griffith's insistence upon "better
films" didn't fit into this scheme of operation. It promised to
raise expenses, and who would pay the price? Motion pictures
were—and were bound to remain—a show for the poor and
ignorant. This fact Griffith seemed obstinately determined to
ignore.

He ignored all sound, businesslike procedures. Rapidity of
output was essential, and other directors, taking the brief scripts
prepared for them by writers, went before the camera without
wasting time on any preparation. Not so Griffith. He wouldn't
use a script, in any case. He never had anything written down,
never had a word on paper for any of his pictures; he developed
his stories as he went along. Sometimes, after rehearsing a story all
day, he would chuck it as no good, and begin another. For,
uniquely, he insisted on rehearsing in sequence the scenes of

every picture until each scene dovetailed smoothly into the next, and the acting satisfied him perfectly. He worked out his story by using his actors as if they were chessmen; that was how his wife described it. He always knew precisely what he wanted, and the camera never began to grind until every little detail had been perfected to a degree that satisfied him. But in spite of these idiosyncrasies, his output was enormous; exhibitors clamored for Biograph pictures; and mail began coming into the company from the movie public, praising those which Griffith had directed —a new and surprising phenomenon. At the Biograph factory, housed in an old brownstone mansion on Fourteenth Street, east of Fifth Avenue, the executives didn't know whether to rejoice in having Griffith under contract, or look forward apprehensively to what might come of it. If only he could be relied on to leave well enough alone!

This was precisely what Griffith couldn't do. Things as they were never suited him. Thus, for example, he was always looking about for new actors and actresses. The kind of acting practised on the Broadway stage he considered all wrong for the films. On the screen, the human figure was magnified many times; exaggerated postures and gestures, which the vast distances of a theater made necessary, became ludicrous when enlarged by the projector. Griffith wanted naturalness in acting. For the hard, implacable eye of the camera, he wanted youth and freshness. He began to search for these qualities among the ill-paid youngsters who toured, as he had, with traveling stock companies. He thought they might also prove versatile. For they knew the harsh necessity of playing all kinds of parts persuasively and with conviction; they had to please their unsophisticated audiences, or starve.

One spring morning in 1909, Mrs. Griffith came into the front hall of the factory and noticed a little girl sitting, patiently waiting to see Griffith. She looked to be no more than fourteen. "She wore a plain navy-blue serge suit, a blue-and-white striped lawn shirtwaist, a rolled brim Tuscan straw sailor hat with a dark-blue ribbon bow. About her face, so fresh, so pretty and so gentle, bobbed a dozen or more golden curls—such perfect little curls as I had never seen." So, long afterwards, Mrs. Griffith described the young visitor. Eventually, Griffith appeared, chatted with her, tested her before the camera, and told her to report for work on the following day. He offered to pay her five dollars daily while making her first picture. If the picture turned out well, he'd talk with her about a permanent job. Notwithstanding her youth, she was businesslike, as if applying for acting jobs had become an old story. The arrangement suited her. She agreed to return the next day.

Her name was Gladys Smith, but on the stage she was known as Mary Pickford. She could scarcely remember a time when she hadn't been on the stage. Years earlier, her mother, left a widow with three small children and no money, had found work as an actress. The children traveled everywhere with her, living backstage among actors, unconsciously learning their craft. To add to the family income, Mary Pickford was playing children's roles at the age of five. A veteran trouper at thirteen, she applied to David Belasco for a role in one of his productions, and received it. She had been acting in Belasco companies for three years when she came to see Griffith; most recently she had been with Charlotte Walker in *The Warrens of Virginia*, which had enjoyed a successful run at the Republic Theater in New York. This made her application for work in the pictures somewhat unusual. For if a picture-factory offered you fifty dollars a week, and Belasco offered you half as much, there was no question about which offer you would accept; even if he offered you only ten dollars, you'd be glad to take the job with Belasco.

Griffith gave young Miss Pickford a part in *The Violin Maker of Cremona*, and after finishing the picture engaged her permanently, at a weekly salary of twenty-five dollars, to play three days every week. Acting children's roles, or young girls, she produced an effect of great sweetness and charm; she was "cute," as they said. In many of her pictures, Griffith gave her the character name of "Little Mary." One of the early ones was remembered long afterwards, because of the people associated with it. This was *The New York Hat*, in which a young actor named Lionel Barrymore also appeared. The story had been submitted by a Los Angeles schoolgirl, and Biograph had paid fifteen dollars for it.

4

Thus encouraged, Anita Loos continued writing for the films; many years later, her satirical novel, *Gentlemen Prefer Blondes,* delighted readers the world over. Another early Pickford picture, *The Little Teacher,* brought twenty or more letters daily to the Biograph Company. The writers, enchanted by the child actress, asked for the name of "Little Mary" or "the girl with the long curls." These letters went into the waste-basket unanswered; Biograph refused to reveal the names of its actors and actresses. The term "fan mail" hadn't yet been invented, but the business executives at Biograph took a dim view of this novel correspondence; public recognition might inspire the young actress to demand more money, and would certainly inflate her self-esteem.

Having seen some of the pictures made in California by the fugitive independents, Griffith was seized by a desire to exploit its picturesque backgrounds. In the winter of 1910, he took a company of Biograph players—including Mary Pickford—to Los Angeles, and set up a temporary studio on the outskirts of the city. To feature Mary Pickford, he devised a story, *The Thread of Destiny,* which used the San Gabriel Mission as a romantic setting. He also featured her in *Ramona,* which Biograph advertised as the most costly picture ever made—a claim partly warranted by the fact that Griffith had paid the unprecedented fee of one hundred dollars to film Helen Hunt Jackson's novel. These pictures established the young actress—still anonymous to her public—as the most popular of all players with motion-picture audiences. The other pictures which Griffith made in California were principally based on historical subjects. He had become eager to interpret, for twentieth-century Americans, an American past of which many of them were either ignorant or forgetful. But the contemporary social scene also fascinated him. Oil had recently been discovered; a migration to the new California fields had begun. In two films, Griffith attempted to record the surge of pioneers, from all parts of the country, to this latest frontier Eldorado.

Five years after he began making pictures, Griffith's prestige in the booming industry was unrivaled. By 1913, he was acknowledged to be the most original and successful maker of pictures in the country, the director whose work attracted the largest box-office receipts. Then, with disconcerting swiftness, he saw his prestige undermined. Ironically, his temporary eclipse was brought about by the triumph of causes which he had long advocated: the use of more significant and powerful stories; the making of longer and more spectacular films. European producers, less subject than Griffith to the control of conservative businessmen, and appealing—so it was argued—to a more enlightened, discriminating public, had accomplished what he had been forbidden to attempt. They had created spectacular "feature pictures," and when some of these were imported and exhibited in the United States, their effect was sensational. In dimension, splendor and dramatic force, these foreign films exceeded anything previously shown. They made news in the American press, and people went to see them again and again. The most celebrated was a nine-reel photoplay of the novel *Quo Vadis?* It had been made in Italy, and it combined a sacred story with the sensual excitement of an arena scene featuring a nude girl on the back of a bull. This attractive tribute to early Christian martyrdom drew gasps from the orthodox; it seemed a novel approach to religious edification; but a blending of piety with shock gave the film an irresistible appeal. It was first presented in the Astor Theater on Broadway, in New York, a "legitimate" playhouse, and subsequently sent on tour as a "special attraction" in other theaters dedicated to the spoken drama; and, at advanced prices, it siphoned patronage away from the movie houses.

Learning about *Quo Vadis?* before it reached the public, and embittered by the restrictions which had prevented him from being first in this field, Griffith set to work at furious speed on a four-reel spectacle, *Judith of Bethulia*, apparently without the consent of his employers. Nothing so massive or pretentious had been undertaken in the United States, and Griffith hoped for an overwhelming triumph. But the trust, now dominated by Biograph, had refused to alter its booking system and distribute the new feature pictures. When Griffith completed his film, it was withheld for one year and then released, not as a "special attraction," but as a unit of the trust's standard weekly output, which exhibitors received as part of the service for which they paid an inclusive fee. Although popular with audiences, its extravagant cost made it, under these conditions, a financial failure. Convinced by this that Griffith's projects were not commercially practicable, the trust ignored popular demand for longer and better pictures —and, as a result, was soon eliminated from business. But, even before the release of *Judith*, Griffith had quarreled with his employers, left Biograph, and gone to work, temporarily, with a newly formed company. His object was to earn money enough to make pictures as he chose, unhampered by the restrictions of cautious financiers.

In August, 1914, as war broke out in Europe, Griffith began work, for the first time, in absolute independence. The picture he undertook to make was eventually titled *The Birth of a Nation*. It was destined to have consequences more varied, far-reaching and significant than any that Griffith could possibly have foreseen. It caused riots in the United States, inflamed sectional prejudices, exasperated the always precarious relations of Negroes and whites. It inspired a revival of the infamous Ku Klux Klan, which ten years later, with a reputed membership of five million Americans in all sections of the country, became a powerful force in the nation's politics and was to continue, until the middle of the century, as an organization dedicated to lawless "justice" and barbarism—itself, apparently, beyond reach of the law. Revealing the tremendous social impact of which the motion picture is capable, *The Birth of a Nation* invited Americans to consider whether makers of pictures are to be held accountable for their use of a medium of communication so readily comprehensible, potentially suggestive and universally accessible. More people, throughout the world, saw this picture than had read any one book other than the Bible. At the middle of the century, it remained the most popular and profitable film ever made. Its earnings, by then, were estimated at approximately fifty millions of dollars. And, thirty-five years after Griffith completed it, its social influence had not diminished. Occasional screenings of the picture provoked angry protest, and revived the acrimonious controversy touched off by its initial release. In the interest of social justice and civil rights, the Film Library of the Museum of Modern Art in New York City excluded it from the repertory of old films, having cultural, historic and artistic interest, exhibited to the public in the Museum's auditorium. Yet *The Birth of a Nation* revolutionized the making of films in the United States. More than any other agency, it was responsible for that swift, enormous expansion of their audience which was one of the most remarkable phenomena of the twentieth century. To David Wark Griffith, it brought worldwide fame and sudden fortune.

Griffith founded his picture on a novel, *The Clansman*, by the Reverend Thomas Dixon, which had reached a wide audience of readers and subsequently, in dramatic form, duplicated its success in the theater. An ardent Southerner, still resentful at the aftermath of the Lost Cause, Dixon had written a melodrama of the Reconstruction era, representing the members of the Ku Klux Klan as chivalric heroes, and the Northern carpetbaggers, with their Negro associates, as degraded villains. To question the truth or justice of these values did not occur to Griffith; they formed part of his heritage; his picture must therefore communicate and justify them. But Dixon's novel—as literature, it was mediocre and tawdry—kindled his imagination. What he distilled from it was a tale of epic proportions, covering the years immediately preceding the War between the States, the vast panorama of the War itself, and the troubled era that followed the defeat of the Confederacy. He intended to re-create the Old South, vividly show its despoiling, and the vengeance subsequently inflicted; the tragedy of its humiliation by conquerors and former slaves; the rebirth of its honor in the heroic exploits of the Invisible Empire. Such was his program, and he proposed to make his great historical theme explicit in the story of two families, Northern and Southern, linked by friendship; united by double romances; sundered by war; alienated by the conflicting social aims of victors and vanquished; ultimately reconciled when the Northerners accept the necessity for white supremacy in the South. That Griffith, avowedly a champion of the oppressed and underprivileged, passionately defamed his Negro fellow-citizens was perhaps no more remarkable than that the veteran Senator

Thomas E. Watson of Georgia, spokesman for tenant-farmers and mill hands, took the same course. Both conceived themselves to be humanitarians, and both defended the established mores of the environment that had shaped them.

Conceiving his picture on an epic scale—it was to fill twelve reels, more than any picture had ever used—Griffith quietly proceeded without any script, building it experimentally as he went along. Six weeks of continuous, careful rehearsal preceded the camera's first shot. Griffith taught his cast how to act, move and walk for the camera; told them, with respect to every scene, precisely how many feet of film they could use to secure the needed dramatic effect. In this period, too, he substituted an actress for the one originally chosen to play the heroine's role; the change in large part accounted for the picture's eventual success. Hundreds of "extras" were required, arrangements had to be made for their housing and food. Horses had to be procured, and vast quantities of cotton goods to cloak the Klansmen; both were difficult to obtain because of the war in Europe, which was draining away all types of commodities. An enormous acreage had to be rented to stage the great rides and battle scenes. All the responsibilities of management fell on Griffith, and so did the burden of raising money. The movie companies considered his project crazy, and none would finance it. He had estimated the cost of his super-picture at approximately one hundred thousand dollars, enough to pay for ten "feature" pictures. Even after production was actually under way, the need for money became so urgent that all work was stopped while Griffith went to Los Angeles to secure it—from personal friends, local tradesmen, lawyers, anyone whom he could persuade to grant him a loan. Yet despite all difficulties, Griffith—according to "Billy" Bitzer, his cameraman—remained calm; and long afterwards his leading woman remembered that "everything was always under control because he always was." Six months passed before the picture was finally completed. But not a single scene had ever been re-taken; a permanent and unique record in picture-making.

The leading actors in the picture had all worked for Griffith at Biograph. Their names, previously unknown to audiences, were announced on the film of *The Birth of a Nation*, and most of them were soon elevated to stardom. But a peculiar glory suddenly invested the players to whom Griffith assigned the roles of hero and heroine; nothing like it had ever before occurred, on so wide a scale, in the United States. Requests for autographs and photographs poured in on them by the thousands. Unknowingly, they established new patterns of appearance, fashion and behavior. Young men imitated the haircut, the style of collar, the suits and neckties shown in portraits of the "Little Colonel"; they tried to adopt the gentle but superbly gallant manner which, on the screen, made him universally appealing to women. And American girls quickly cultivated a new look. Plumpness, previously in vogue, ceased to be fashionable. For "Elsie Stoneman" was petite, slim, fragile; her golden hair cascaded below her waist; she was demure, wistful, but magnificently courageous. All over the land, young women strained for slenderness; patiently tried to behave like clinging vines, but also suggest a pure white fire of passion; dressed demurely, and practised shaking down their hair for the beguiling, perilous moment yet to come.

The players who aroused this idolatry later found that it exacted its own strange penalty. So far as the public could exercise its compulsion, they were required to perpetuate the ideal images that had captivated the American imagination. The new king of hearts, Henry B. Walthall, was never to escape this stern necessity; when he was supplanted by another type of hero, he disappeared abruptly from the screen, and returned only after many years to play minor roles. He was born in Alabama, of impoverished parents, and was put to work as a child in the cotton fields. The books loaned him by a clergyman uncle took the place of formal schooling, but later he managed to spend six months at Howard College. He served in the Spanish-American War and, after being discharged from the army, went to New York to seek work as an actor. By 1909, when a friend took him to the Biograph Company, Walthall had acquired considerable experience. Griffith hired him at once. Small, slender, with a very expressive face, he proved to be a skillful pantomimist, and Griffith was soon using him for romantic roles—most notably in *Ramona*, with Mary Pickford, and thereafter in a long series of films.

The heroine of *The Birth of a Nation* was to have a far more distinguished and spectacular career than Walthall. The Gish sisters—Lillian and Dorothy—were brought to Griffith in 1912 by their long-time friend, Mary Pickford. Like her, they had been on the stage almost from infancy. Like her, they had had no real childhood. They received their early education in the stuffy dressing rooms of cheap provincial theaters, in jolting day coaches and the rooms of third-class hotels patronized by the touring melodrama companies in which they acted children's roles. They were constantly haunted by fears of the Gerry Society, a philanthropic organization whose commendable object was to prevent the exploiting of children. "Before I could understand what it was all about," Lillian Gish noted long afterwards, "I knew of subterfuges and evasions and tremendous plottings to keep myself and my sister acting, so that the very necessary money might be earned. . . ." Their obscurity kept them safe, and they remained obscure for a simple reason: "When we were ambitious and went into better productions, the plays seemed to fail." But Lillian Gish graduated from a role in *Her First False Step*—which brought audiences "the awe-inspiring rescue of a child from a den of savage African lions"—to the part of a child dancer in the company of Madame Sarah Bernhardt, who in 1905 was making her usual farewell tour of the United States. Some years of formal schooling followed. When Mary Pickford brought the Gish sisters to Griffith, motion pictures were eliminating the melodrama road companies, and they were glad to accept his offer to take them on as extras. Gradually they worked into leading roles; Dorothy in comedy, Lillian in romantic and dramatic parts. Long after both sisters became celebrated stars, Griffith recorded his early impressions of them: "Dorothy was more apt at getting the director's idea than Lillian, quicker to follow it, more easily satisfied with the result. Lillian conceived an ideal and patiently sought to realize it. Genius is like that: the ideal becomes real to it."

During a rehearsal for *The Birth of a Nation*, Lillian Gish was "standing in" for the actress assigned to the heroine's role. Seeing that she perfectly embodied his conception of the part, Griffith impulsively substituted her for the other actress. Her performance of the role more than justified this hasty decision.

For, largely because of it, *The Birth of a Nation* was the first film ever to be taken seriously by sophisticated patrons of the theater, and the first, also, to win praise from the intelligentsia, as they were coming to be called. Almost overnight, *The Birth of a Nation* lifted the socially despised entertainment of the poor to dizzying altitudes of elegance and taste. So far as possible, this result had been carefully prepared for by expert showmanship. First exhibited to the public in Los Angeles, early in February, 1915, under its original title of *The Clansman,* the picture was acknowledged to be in every way epoch-making. As one representative of the industry remarked, it "certainly establishes Griffith as a leader, and it does seem too bad that such a magnificent effort is doomed to financial failure." A print was rushed to New York City to be run off for the censors and a group of guests; the excitement which it aroused led Thomas Dixon to invent its final title. With a masterly sense of publicity, Griffith next had the film shown at the White House—where no motion picture had ever before penetrated—for President Woodrow Wilson, his Cabinet, and their families. Like Griffith, Wilson had been born and bred south of the Mason and Dixon Line, and according to report his verdict on the picture was that "it is like writing history with lightning." Having thus excited public curiosity, Griffith undertook his boldest exploit. Early in March, the picture was offered to the New York public at the Liberty Theater, a "legitimate" playhouse, at prices then prevailing for the spoken drama; orchestra seats costing the incredible sum of two dollars.

Hailed by the press with unrestrained enthusiasm, *The Birth of a Nation* was an immediate and phenomenal success. Critics reported that its effect was to challenge the supremacy of the spoken drama; in purely financial terms, it offered frightening competition to all plays then being performed in New York. With this triumph to his credit, Griffith took the step that was to make his picture a nation-wide sensation. He arranged for it to be shown in Boston, birthplace of the Abolition movement, and traditionally a stronghold of the organized effort to secure civil rights and equality of opportunity for Negro citizens. For a fortnight before the Boston opening, Negro clergymen, teachers and lawyers in Massachusetts violently denounced the film. Public emotion soon reached the boiling point, and on the film's first night a disturbance broke out in front of the theater. It rapidly assumed the proportions of a large-scale race riot; the police were incapable of restoring order, and the Boston fire department was hastily summoned to help disperse the rioters. On the following morning, this outbreak of violence made headlines in the press throughout the United States. The immediate result was to provoke a demand for the picture from all parts of the country; the Boston riot was frequently duplicated elsewhere; and the American people flocked to box-offices, eagerly paying regular stage prices for the privilege of seeing a film capable of inciting such widespread disorder.

Meanwhile, indignation at the social implications of *The Birth of a Nation* developed quickly. President Emeritus Charles W. Eliot of Harvard University condemned it as having "a tendency to perversion of white ideals." From Hull House, in Chicago, Miss Jane Addams announced that she was "painfully exercised over the exhibition." And in the columns of *The Nation* Oswald Garrison Villard—grandson of William Lloyd Garrison, the first Abolitionist—forthrightly denounced it as "a deliberate attempt to humiliate ten million American citizens." More significantly, the Boston branch of the National Association for the Advancement of Colored People published, and widely circulated, a pamphlet entitled *Fighting a Vicious Film; A Record of Protest Against "The Birth of a Nation."* The Association was headed by Moorfield Storey, a Boston patrician and an eminent attorney; seventy-one years old, and long honored both as a reformer and leader of the American bar, Storey exercised a powerful influence in mobilizing Northern sentiment against the picture. Yet Storey was soon to demonstrate that Northern humanitarians were no less capable of ironical inconsistency than Southerners like Griffith and Senator Watson. For despite his vigorous championship of the cause of the Negro, Storey one year later furnished leadership to the forces which bitterly opposed the appointment of Louis D. Brandeis to the Supreme Court—both because Brandeis was a "reformer" and because he was a Jew—and, as the historian Henry Steele Commager pointed out long afterwards, Storey likewise opposed the admission of Jews to Harvard University.

Specifically replying to Storey's attack, Griffith issued a pamphlet provocatively entitled *The Rise and Fall of Free Speech in America*. In this, he argued heatedly for "the freedom of the screen" and "the fundamental rights of expression." Presently, an acrimonious and passionate controversy over these novel issues was being carried on in American newspapers and magazines. Griffith himself, according to Miss Lillian Gish, was deeply hurt by the antagonism that his picture had aroused, and resented the objections urged by its opponents. Privately, he protested that the film portrayed "bad white people as well as bad Negroes," showing that the Negroes were "bad only because the white people made them so." That his picture had inflicted an irreparable damage on ten million citizens, in addition to humiliating them; that it had inflamed and sanctioned vicious prejudices; that it had been capable of so doing only by virtue of its immense power as drama— these facts Griffith could not bring himself to acknowledge. The critics and journalists who acclaimed it as a great work of art were in a scarcely less equivocal position. For the most part they were Americans of sensitive conscience, advocates of civic morality, presumably eager to see a "better life" for all made possible under democratic institutions. Was socially evil influence compatible with high esthetic significance? The complex social and ethical problems which *The Birth of a Nation* projected were to afflict educators, social theorists, the clergy, lawmakers, and motion-picture executives until the middle of the century.

The controversy which his picture had exploded confirmed Griffith's earlier intuition that the American public was ready to accept films undertaking the serious discussion of major social issues. His literary turn of mind predisposed him to seek significant themes, and he perceived that many of the conflicts occurring in an industrial society provided them; but only a genius for the particular medium in which he was working could have suggested reinforcement of the contemporary illustration by parallels from earlier epochs in human history. This was to be his next innovation. Taking as his central subject the evil that the self-righteous have perpetrated throughout the ages, Griffith chose four stories to exemplify it, and during a thirteen-reel film kept their progress almost simultaneously before the eyes of the audience. The four stories thus woven together in *Intolerance* included a contemporary study of the oppression of industrial workers by capitalists; the massacre of Saint Bartholomew in sixteenth-century France; the fall of Babylon; and an apocalyptic version of the life, betrayal and death of Jesus. Into the making of this film, Griffith poured the considerable fortune which its predecessor had brought him; its final cost was to exceed two million dollars. The epic sermon was in production for more than a year. In addition to an imposing cast of principals, sixteen thousand extras were employed; elaborate architectural settings were constructed, and Griffith's Babylon astonished California with city-walls three hundred feet high on which armies could march, and halls so vast that human beings were dwarfed by them. In this respect, the film established the pattern for all subsequent spectacles. To the middle of the century none exceeded it in splendor or massiveness.

Exhibited in the autumn of 1916, *Intolerance* bewildered critics and audiences by its fatiguing complexity; it became an artistic triumph many years after its commercial failure was irretrievable. But certain of its social effects proved to be highly significant. For his contemporary story of the conflict between capital and labor, Griffith had drawn upon material developed at hearings of the Federal Industrial Relations Commission, and represented vividly on the screen precisely the kind of episodes which Howells, in his article four years earlier, had demanded. To the comfortable middle classes who were now attending the movies, the use of this subject-matter proved deeply disturbing. The exploitation of workers by a reputedly philanthropic industrialist; the brutality of strike-breakers; the slaughter of strikers by factory guards and militia—the public had read about such things in their newspapers, even in some current novels. But it was quite another matter to *see* them, compellingly and convincingly represented. It was far worse to see them associated, in

a series of dramatic parallels, with ancient massacres, with the
most sacred of tragedies. So powerful an indictment of the ethics
of the established order was scarcely likely to please its bene-
ficiaries. Then, too, the nation was drifting toward entry into the
European war, and the film eloquently urged the cause of peace.
Opposition to *Intolerance* increased; in many cities, the film was
banned. Not long afterwards, Nikolai Lenin would arrange to
have the picture toured throughout Soviet Russia, where it was
to be exhibited continuously for a decade. Meanwhile, it had
demonstrated the high potency of the motion picture as a medium
of propaganda. The lesson was quickly understood by the British
and American governments. At the invitation of David Lloyd
George and Lord Beaverbrook, Griffith took a company of players
to England, then to the battlefields of France and Belgium, to
make propaganda pictures.

Possibly an expiation of the harm done by *The Birth of a
Nation,* Griffith undertook, after his return to the United States,
a picture which made a passionate appeal for the application of
the Christian ideal to interracial relations. It also argued power-
fully for the principle of non-resistance to force. The nation,
emerging victoriously from a World War, was about to suffer a
total collapse of moral idealism. In these circumstances, the overwhelming success of the picture was astonishing. For its mood
was unrelentingly tragic, and its subject was the persistence of
exalted ideals in those whom society disinherits and casts aside.
Yet *Broken Blossoms* swept over the United States on a tide of
acclaim, and soon afterwards was being shown throughout the
world. Griffith had undertaken to make a series of pictures for
Adolph Zukor, each budgeted at a quarter of a million dollars.
It is said that when Griffith ran off *Broken Blossoms* for his employer, Zukor remarked that Griffith might as well have deliberately robbed him of this sum as spend it as he had on the picture.
Incensed, Griffith promptly borrowed the sum, repaid Zukor, and
took the picture off his hands. The anecdote illustrated a dissension between industrialists and the indispensable showmen who
made their products that was to become permanently characteristic of the movie business.

In a variety of ways, the reception of *Broken Blossoms* revealed the importance of motion pictures in American society, and the significant influence that they were capable of exercising on the national culture. When the film was released, in 1919, only a decade and a half had elapsed since the production of the first story film; barely five years had passed since the movies, breaking out of the nickelodeons, ceased being an entertainment acceptable only to the poor and ignorant. Now, *Broken Blossoms* was being introduced to the public as the initial offering of a "repertory season" of Griffith's pictures at the George M. Cohan Theater on Broadway. That its audience should include the prosperous and cultivated minority of Americans who habitually attended the spoken drama was taken for granted. The picture was not specifically addressed to them. It was offered on the somewhat remarkable premise that all social stratifications, all distinctions of relative wealth, culture and sophistication, could profitably be ignored by purveyors of the new entertainment; that, indeed, the motion picture had already welded all diverse groups composing the nation into an audience democratically unified and homogeneous. A repertory season of pictures indicated the dignity claimed by the new medium; the fact that so novel a venture could be made commercially profitable indicated the vast changes which had come over the audience.

A contemporary report asserts that, at its first showing, "everyone was overwhelmed" by the acting of the principal players in *Broken Blossoms*: Lillian Gish, Richard Barthelmess and Donald Crisp. Its impact persuaded the ordinarily sedate *Literary Digest* to announce the birth of a "new art . . . as important as music and poetry;" and the conservative New York *Times* to declare that this new art had already yielded "a masterpiece." The film, so breathless critics testified, made "an eloquent and decisive flight beyond the speaking stage"; it seemed that "the screen jumped five years" into an illimitable future of progress that now could be reasonably anticipated.

Even more notably, *Broken Blossoms* demonstrated that the literary shapers of current American culture, far from influencing the new American art, were themselves being profoundly influenced by it. The widely read critic, George Jean Nathan, for example, who kept the middle classes in touch with the intellectual life, was presently moved to discourse on Miss Gish's method of "always playing, as it were, behind a veil of silver chiffon," and to explain to the public that her "particular genius . . . lies in making the definite charmingly indefinite." Writing his novel, *Jurgen,* even before the film was presented, James Branch Cabell had portrayed the young actress in the guise of Queen Helen, "the delight of gods and men." Three years later, Joseph Hergesheimer was likewise to portray her, as the heroine of his novel, *Cytherea*; and in an often-quoted article, he described her as possessing "the qualities which, in a Golden Age, would hold an army about the walls of a city for seven years." Hergesheimer recorded his desire to write a motion picture in which she might appear "like the April moon, a thing for all young men to dream about forever . . . the fragrant April moon of men's hopes." This ambition was not to be gratified. But that one of the more distinguished novelists of the day regarded it as practically capable of fulfillment, showed how significantly the new medium of the films was kindling the imaginations of American creative writers. It was a medium that would not only give them an incomparably larger audience, but enable them to achieve effects impossible to fiction; and many writers, over the years, would attempt to borrow from the films certain devices appropriate to fiction, yet never before attempted.

Few screen stars moved the intelligentsia to open worship; Miss Gish, Charles Chaplin, and later, Miss Greta Garbo were notable for inspiring cults among the intellectuals. But adoration of the stars by the public was becoming a social phenomenon new to American life, and destined to produce extraordinary results. In 1910, the Biograph Company had refused any reply to letters requesting them to identify "Little Mary." But in May, 1919, as *Broken Blossoms* was being released, the magazine *Photoplay* issued statistics covering the young religion of celluloid. Three thousand letters, nearly all addressed to stars, were reaching the major studios every day. No less than one-quarter of a million dollars was being spent every year on correspondence between

motion-picture celebrities and their fans. This required the
services of more than eighty secretaries, whose annual wages
aggregated ninety thousand dollars. And the cost of photographs
dispensed in this ritual of devotion had already risen to seventy-
five thousand dollars. The new art, as these facts suggested, had
likewise become a major industry.

This, in part, explained the subsequent declining influence of
David Wark Griffith. He could not accommodate himself to the
ways of big business. And big business saw little commercial value
in his qualities of independence and daring, his originality and
quest of novelty and need to experiment. Moreover, the times,
for him, were out of joint. The mood of the American people
underwent an abrupt change. In the era of normalcy, prohibition,
jazz and the post-war boom, they had scant patience with his
interest in social issues and literary themes. He continued, for a
decade, to make pictures with diminishing success. Then, after the
onset of the Great Depression, he quietly abandoned a battle long
since lost. And thereafter he sank into embittered obscurity.

CHAPTER III

The Gods Arrive

1 Goldilocks and the Bears

Not long after Griffith had returned from his first expedition to California, in 1910, Mrs. Charlotte Pickford came to see him at the Biograph Company. The demand for "Little Mary's" pictures was steadily increasing, and no matter how many she made the exhibitors continued to write in, asking for more. Mrs. Pickford quietly proposed that her daughter's salary be doubled. Griffith offered a substantial increase. "Remember," he said, "I made her." The argument did not impress Mrs. Pickford. "Little Mary" had been offered a contract at double her current wages; she would now accept it. "You'll be sorry, some day," Mrs. Pickford remarked, though she could hardly have foreseen that this was the opening engagement of a ten years' war that would radically alter the infant industry.

So young Miss Pickford transferred her valuable services to Carl Laemmle. Not only was he willing to double her earnings; he proposed to elevate her from anonymity to stardom. With the skillful assistance of Robert Cochrane, he had already performed the same feat for another player, in an exploit that set a permanent pattern for the industry. Having lured away from the trust Miss Florence Lawrence—known to the public only as "the Biograph Girl"—he cast about for some appropriate means of publicizing his new and popular actress. One day, the press of St. Louis, Missouri, reported the death of Miss Lawrence—whom, quite naturally, they identified professionally—in a streetcar accident. Immediately afterwards, Laemmle published advertisements denouncing this "blackest and at the same time silliest lie" as a false rumor spread by the trust. Later, he announced that to disprove the falsehood, Miss Lawrence, accompanied by her leading man, King Baggott, would visit the city—where, by a remarkable coincidence, her latest film was to be exhibited. When, in March, 1910, the two players descended from their train, an excited mob awaited them; long afterwards, Laemmle was to recall that hospitable Americans "demonstrated their affection by tearing the buttons off Florence Lawrence's coat, the trimmings from her hat, the hat from her head." In this felicitous parturition, the first screen star was born; the event was memorable also for being the initial example of a "personal appearance tour." The hazards of public affection were to increase enormously with time, and before another two decades had passed would reach a point where death itself could not defend the mortal sheath of a favorite star from the riotous attentions of grief-stricken enthusiasts.

In the case of Miss Pickford, elevation to stardom required little assistance from the arts of ballyhoo; it was sufficient merely to tell the public her name. Now able to identify her, they took a proprietary attitude to this cynosure of girlish goodness, and presently Miss Pickford was making pictures at the rate of twenty a year, all tailored to exploit those qualities specifically extolled by her ardent admirers. The wise counsel of the playwright William C. De Mille—she had played the role of Betty Warren in his *The Warrens of Virginia*—appeared to be disproved. He had pleaded with her not to throw her future career into the ashcan by burying herself in a cheap form of amusement. He had warned her that there would never be any real money in acting for galloping tintypes. He had reminded her that the stage gave her an opportunity to become known to thousands of people. But she was a stubborn little thing; she declared that she knew what she was doing. De Mille privately surmised that her decision presaged the end of little Mary Pickford; she would never be heard of again. He felt extremely sorry for her—and it certainly did not occur to him that in three more years he, too, would follow her inauspicious course.

Little Miss Pickford was earning as much money as she could hope to earn on the stage, and was already known to more people than had ever seen a play. But when David Belasco offered to feature her in *A Good Little Devil*, during the winter of 1913, she accepted with alacrity. As soon as the play opened, the effect of her popularity with the masses became evident in the ornate, dimly-lit temple of the drama where America's most revered producer unveiled his offerings to the public. People who had never entered the Belasco Theater before, people who might not have dared to enter it had they wished to, stood in patient lines, waiting to buy tickets, willing to pay far more than they could afford for the privilege of seeing her in person. Notwithstanding her considerable success on the stage, Miss Pickford's return to the theater proved to be only temporary. For an odd combination of circumstances had made it possible for a twenty-year-old girl to earn more money in a year than most Americans hoped to accumulate in a lifetime.

To the production of these circumstances three factors had somewhat improbably contributed. One was the obdurate conservatism of a group of outstandingly successful American businessmen. A second was the financial difficulties of an aging, world-famous French tragedienne. A third was the prophetic intuition that had visited the proprietor of a nickelodeon on Fourteenth

Street. Constantly studying the audiences at his Comedy Theater, Adolph Zukor had become convinced of their desire for better pictures. Both the trust and the independents were turning out two-reel films; Zukor believed that the public would pay for feature pictures of five reels and longer, and that if these were introduced they would soon dominate the theatres. But when he discussed this with other men in the trade, they assured him that his notion was a crazy one. Even his former partner, Marcus Loew, could see no merit in it.

Eventually, Zukor decided to risk his savings in the manufacture of feature films. If the General Film Company—the trust—could be persuaded to release his pictures through its distributors, though quite separately from the trust standard program, his venture might be successful from the outset. Over a long period, he made weekly calls at General Film's headquarters, hoping to present his scheme to one of the august magnates who controlled its policies. Finally, a subordinate promised to bring his proposal to the attention of Jeremiah J. Kennedy, president of the corporation. Zukor was requested to wait until a directors' meeting terminated, and he sat humbly, through a long afternoon, awaiting the hoped-for audience. When the meeting broke up, and Kennedy and his associates appeared, the subordinate explained Zukor's project and his request. Kennedy asked his partners whether they wished to talk with the obscure little nickelodeon proprietor. One of them remarked, with a laugh, that if Zukor persisted in carrying out his plan, he "would soon be back making buttonholes." The others agreed. The audience was not granted.

Meanwhile, in Paris, Madame Sarah Bernhardt, aged sixty-seven and as usual in need of money, had consented to make a four-reel photoplay, *Queen Elizabeth*. The American rights to this film were offered to Zukor, and he consulted the theatrical manager, Daniel Frohman, who advised him to buy them. In subsequent conversations, Zukor outlined his project of making feature films; Frohman was impressed. Zukor then suggested the daring idea of filming successful Broadway plays with the stars playing their stage roles; backed by the prestige of Daniel Frohman's name, these pictures would probably achieve a nation-wide success. The Famous Players Company, born of this concept, began its career by distributing the Bernhardt film, which proved so profitable that Zukor was able to proceed as an independent producer of features. Soon afterwards a group of distributors, persuaded that the novelty of feature pictures would drive shorter ones out of the market, formed the Paramount Pictures Corporation to finance the making of features by qualified producers. The new corporation immediately arranged to finance and distribute Zukor's entire output.

Presently, Zukor announced the addition of Mary Pickford to his roster of players; she was to make twenty pictures within a year, at a weekly salary of one thousand dollars. This fee, startling enough in itself, was made sensational by the developments to which Zukor's series of maneuvers had given rise. For the force of competition had made it necessary for other producers, however unwillingly, to follow his lead. Independents, even certain members of the trust, had hastily negotiated alliances with prominent theatrical managers. A rush to acquire the services of celebrated stars of the stage had, for the time, reduced the value of mere screen players. The costly features announced or projected were to exploit only these eminent personalities. Clearly Miss Pickford's prestige was not comparable to that of Mrs. Minnie Maddern Fiske, or Miss Marie Doro, or Miss Billie Burke. Could Zukor hope to present her as the equal in fame of James K. Hackett, whom he had starred in *The Prisoner of Zenda*? Obviously not. Under the new dispensation, her pictures could only be what the trade now described as "Class B"—standard, run-of-the-mill products. Since this was the case, why pay her so fabulous a sum?

But this, too, was one of Zukor's masterly intuitions. He had conceived his raid on Broadway as a temporary expedient. He realized that it would establish him, spectacularly and swiftly, in the forefront of producers. As a means of popularizing feature pictures, it could not be excelled. But he had no delusions about the permanent popularity of stage celebrities on the screen. He foresaw that the motion-picture audience would eventually nominate its own stars. When stage luminaries ceased being a novelty, their appeal would probably evaporate. The choices of movie fans would be determined only by what gave them pleasure, and they would feel no obligation to be pleased by the favorites of a sophisticated minority in the large cities. In engaging Mary Pickford, Zukor was sagaciously looking to the future. She had been the most popular of players with patrons of the nickelodeons. By skillful exploitation, he thought he could make her a star of the first magnitude, appealing to the common denominator of public taste.

The decision yielded extraordinary results. For a period of years, they influenced the thinking, the day-by-day attitude to life, the inarticulate hopes of many millions of citizens. For Miss Pickford came to be the deputy of American conscience and aspiration. She represented Main Street, the plain people. The views of Main Street were not shaped by the speculations of philosophers and the pronouncements of social theorists. The conduct of Main Street was not altered by a shifting of the winds of doctrine. For those who dwelt there—whether physically, or only mentally— Miss Pickford phrased a concept of what life ought to be like, and they recognized it as their own. She demonstrated conclusively that whatever ought to be, could be. On screens throughout the land, she lived out for them experiences which might yet become their personal adventure, or that of their children. She showed how the application of a few simple principles would bring this adventure to success. She proved that the beliefs which Main Street wished to cherish were genuinely true. Life, she declared, is what you want to make it. And the faith of the plain people was invigorated, their confidence in their personal destinies was enhanced. Stimulated by Mary Pickford's persuasive example, they could readily accept the circumstances of today, since the promise of tomorrow was illimitable.

At the age of twenty, and already married (her husband was the actor Owen Moore), Miss Pickford's ambition was to play mature roles. Golden-blonde, rosebud-lipped, dewy-eyed, she appeared to be a predestined heroine of sentimental romances. Probably any producer other than Zukor would have devised for her pictures in which she could impersonate young love. But he chose to cast her as youth about to slip into adolescence. She was slim and petite. She could create the physical illusion of this indeterminate age. Mentally, said the writer Will Irwin, who later discussed her career with Miss Pickford and Zukor, it was as if her harsh early experiences "had mixed up inextricably her childhood and maturity."

As things turned out, Zukor's decision proved to be a stroke of genius. For, on the screen, Mary Pickford's child-like quality had the effect of insulating her from all gross forms of experience, all sordid ambitions and desires. It translated her, so to speak, into a fairytale world where innocence was wisdom, and exercised a reliable magic. She embodied the present warrant for all dreams about the future. Men could delight in the child without shame, foreseeing that they would fall in love with the woman she must inevitably become. "America's Sweetheart," an astute press-agent subsequently named her. The term suggested how irresistibly she led people's thoughts and feelings away from immediate reality, fixing them upon all that might come to be. For millions of Americans, she was an eloquent symbol of anticipation; a child evangelist who preached that the Promised Land, the more abundant life, awaited everyone around the next corner, and that the power to reach it was already theirs. The titles of Mary Pickford's pictures usually gave a clue to their nature: *Cinderella, Amarilly of Clothes-line Alley, Tess of the Storm Country, The Poor Little Rich Girl, The Foundling, Pollyanna, Rebecca of Sunnybrook Farm, Daddy Long Legs, A Dawn of Tomorrow,* to mention but a few. They summed up the great democratic fable of the rise from rags to riches, but showed that this ascent was possible only to the pure in heart, whose aim was grace, not the wealth and high estate that grace materialized. They were not unlike the exhortations of Dr. Russell H. Conwell, Orison Swett Marden and Ralph Waldo Trine. But, essentially, the Pickford films were a series of parables that expounded Miss Pickford's heartening gospel. And what American of the time did not, in his secret heart, accept it; did not, on the whole, profess to live by it?

Certainly, from the very outset, the success of her films suggested that Miss Pickford was being adopted by the nation. The Paramount salesmen put this in practical terms: "As long as we have Mary on the program, we can wrap everything around her neck."

In these circumstances was she not worth more money? Miss Pickford's mother thought so; the young actress did not dispute parental wisdom; the salesmen's report showed that, in order to obtain her films, exhibitors were gladly taking the entire Paramount output. But to pay her more money required a drastic change in the established sales system. So the Pickford films were withdrawn from the standard Paramount program, and sold separately, as a series, at higher prices. Exhibitors protested, but were powerless; their patrons demanded Miss Pickford. In January, 1915, Zukor made a new contract with her, to run for a year. During this period she would make only ten pictures, half as many as before; she would be paid two thousand dollars weekly, or twice as much; she would also receive one half the profits earned by her pictures. Before this contract expired, it became evident that her ability to crowd the theaters was absolutely unique. Should it not be appropriately rewarded? Miss Pickford's mother suggested that her daughter might be persuaded to accept a new contract, if she were paid one thousand dollars every day in the year.

There was, perhaps, a mild irony in this situation. Did Miss Pickford's incredible capital value demonstrate the practical efficacy of the gospel expounded by her pictures? Or was it merely a proof of the automatic operation of economic law? At the age of twenty-three, this guileless young woman—the child-like heroine of a national fairy tale—had become one of the most valuable commercial properties in the world. The American people were paying some hundred and seventy-five millions of dollars a year to watch the galloping tintypes; and she was the magnet that drew more money to ticket windows than any other star. The triumphant success of Zukor's intuition recoiled on him unpleasantly. His creation had turned into his Nemesis. Obviously, he couldn't afford to let her go, yet it seemed scarcely likely that he could afford to keep her. Miss Pickford was now the industry's principal asset. A business representing investments of several hundred millions of dollars, giving employment to one hundred thousand people, appeared to be balanced on the whim of one American girl.

Four years had changed Zukor's circumstances almost as remarkably as Miss Pickford's. The obscure little nickelodeon owner to whom the trust magnates refused an audience had already put the trust out of business. He had become a magnate in his own right. In a series of rapid moves, Zukor absorbed one of his principal competitors, bought control of Paramount, and now headed a twenty-five-million-dollar combination. He was the largest producer and distributor of pictures in the industry, but this preeminence did not satisfy him. His object now was to make himself, as it were, a trust; to achieve a monopolistic position. His plan was a simple one. Everything depended on the public, for they dominated the theaters. But the stars dominated the public, and by effecting what Wall Street called a "corner" in stars, Zukor hoped to dominate both the public and the industry. That this scheme would rouse opposition by the theater-owners was inevitable; but that they could successfully rebel Zukor thought unlikely. His principal source of anxiety was the competition of other producers for stars. Even while he was negotiating with Miss Pickford, the Mutual Film Company announced that it had acquired a rising comedian, Charles Chaplin, by guaranteeing him six hundred and seventy thousand dollars for one year's work. Zukor hastily came to terms with Miss Pickford. He formed a separate corporation to produce and distribute her pictures. She would make only four during the year; would be paid ten thousand dollars every week; would receive one half of the profits earned by her films. Her probable annual income would approximate one million dollars—making her the most highly salaried employe in the world. Acting, traditionally one of the most precarious of professions, had suddenly become the most remunerative of all.

Zukor's new arrangement with Miss Pickford produced consternation throughout the industry. It trebled the price of her pictures to exhibitors; they could only show Pickford films profitably if they increased the price of admission to their theaters. Would the public pay twenty-five cents, or in some instances thirty-five, for a seat in a movie house? Forced to this hazardous experiment, exhibitors received a lesson in the mysterious psychology of infatuation. The public paid, without complaint. But a movement of rebellion soon developed. It was initiated by Thomas L. Tally, the former cowboy who had opened, in Los Angeles, the first of all movie theaters. Now rich, prominent and powerful, Tally, with other exhibitors, formed a corporation, First National, to manufacture, distribute and show its own pictures—to excel and boycott those produced by Zukor. The new company announced that it would pay the largest salaries in the industry, and thus obtain the greatest stars. It began operations by negotiating with Miss Pickford, and the arrangement which it proposed promised to double the income she was receiving from Zukor.

Zukor now found himself in an intolerable situation. Other stars, less popular than Miss Pickford but still essential to him, had followed her lead, demanded more money, and received it. The astonishing development of the system he had created threatened, in its success, to destroy him; steadily mounting salaries to stars must inevitably bankrupt any producer who played the game to its conclusion. One of his new directors, Cecil B. De Mille, solved the predicament. De Mille believed that profitable pictures could be based on good stories, instead of great stars. On this assumption he had made two, with comparatively unknown players, costing approximately one-third the amount of any Pickford picture; both had earned as much money as Miss Pickford's films usually yielded. De Mille proposed that Zukor abandon the competition for her services, and inaugurate the making of "all-star" pictures—a disingenuous term for films without any stars. If the pictures proved to be successful, their unknown players would become box-office names, and so could be elevated to true stardom. On this principle, Zukor would achieve absolute independence from the tyranny of established stars; he could always create new ones as required, in somewhat the fashion that automobile manufacturers introduced annual new models that superseded those of the previous year. The all-star, non-star incubator provided a method of indefinite extensibility. The project appealed as much to Zukor's opportunism as to his financial astuteness. He resolved to try it out; until its success with the public was established beyond doubt, he would retain most of his stars. But he would let Miss Pickford go.

Although reconciled to the loss of his greatest star, Zukor could not endure the prospect of seeing her join the forces of First

Directed by
    D. W. Griffith.

ABOVE:
A Corner in Wheat.
    1909.

RIGHT:
The Birth of a Nation

BELOW:
The Feast of Belchazar
    from Intolerance

LEFT: Richard Barthelmess and Lillian Gish in *Broken Blossoms*

BELOW: D. W. Griffith Interviews Lillian Gish

OPPOSITE PAGE:
LEFT: Mary Pickford in Her Pre-Movie Days

RIGHT: Charlie Chaplin, Mary Pickford and Douglas Fairbanks

BELOW: America's Sweetheart

ABOVE: Mary Pickford in *Pollyanna*

BELOW: The Keystone Cops

ABOVE: Sennett and His Celebrated Bathing Beauties

BELOW: Custard Pies Were Made for Throwing

ABOVE: Pearl White in
The Perils of Pauline

RIGHT: Theda Bara Plays the
Vampire in *A Fool There Was*

BELOW: Theda Bara —
Fatally Alluring

OPPOSITE PAGE:
ABOVE: Charlie Chaplin in an
Early One-Reeler

BELOW: Charlie Chaplin in
Sunnyside. 1919

ABOVE: To a Fate
Worse Than Death.
Rudolph Valentino in
The Sheik

RIGHT: A Million
Hearts Beat Faster

BELOW: The Funeral
of Rudolph Valentino

National; this new and dangerous competitor had recently acquired Charles Chaplin, and the addition of Miss Pickford would lift it beyond possible rivalry. In a final melancholy conference, Zukor attempted one of his most grandiose gestures. "You've worked very hard for years. Why don't you take a vacation?" he suggested, paternally. "If you will stop making pictures for five years, I will give you two hundred and fifty thousand dollars."

The lovely eyes may have dimmed, the world-enchanting curls may have trembled; but decision was swift. "Oh, I couldn't do that, Mr. Zukor," said Miss Pickford. "I love pictures, and I'm just a girl. I couldn't quit now."

For she was not only America's sweetheart now but, in effect, a national institution. When, a year earlier, the United States had thrown its might into the war, that the world might be made safe for democracy, Miss Pickford had made country-wide tours, speaking for the Liberty Loans; she had made a picture to expose German savagery; and even now there were, "somewhere in France," six hundred American youths in uniform, wearing about their necks golden lockets containing her portrait—the boys she had adopted, whom she kept supplied with chocolate and cigarettes, to whom she represented, symbolically, a righteous cause and a beloved homeland.

So Miss Pickford went on her way to new employers. But even as she went a bright young man, scarcely older than she, was dreaming up a method of making infatuated Americans offer still larger tribute on her altars. Benjamin P. Schulberg, formerly general sales manager for Zukor, conceived the project of bringing together, under a single corporate roof, Miss Pickford, Charles Chaplin, the rising star Douglas Fairbanks and David Wark Griffith, now at the pinnacle of his fame. Under Schulberg's plan, these four would become their own employers. They would act as their own producers, receiving the profits formerly taken by the companies for which they worked; they would also share in the returns of distributing their collective output. The signal merit of this plan, commercially, was the unique nature of the product. Exhibitors throughout the land would be helpless. However reluctantly, they would have to pay any price that United Artists demanded for the pictures made by so peerless, so dazzling a constellation of idols. As a source of financial revenue, idolatry appeared to be inexhaustible.

At First National, where she was said to be receiving somewhat less than two million dollars for making four pictures, Miss Pickford had ample time for meditation.

One year later, Goldilocks moved again.

2   Custard, Cops and Pratfalls

While Miss Pickford was inspiring Americans with a vision of what life ought to be like, another specialist in public education was teaching them to laugh at life as it actually was. During the five years immediately preceding the nation's entry into the First World War, the Keystone comedies of Mack Sennett invited Americans to look at their civilization, and dared them to say that it was not ridiculous. William Dean Howells had observed, somewhat earlier, that "In America, life is not yet a joke with us, even when it is grotesque and shameful, as it so often is, for we think we can make it right when we choose." Americans still thought they could make life right when they chose to, as Miss Pickford's reign so eloquently proved; but under Sennett's tuition they began to realize how grotesque it often was.

Born in Canada and baptized Michael Sinnott, Sennett had been on the stage for some years when he joined the Biograph Company as an actor, shortly before Griffith's arrival there. Usually cast in dramatic roles, it was not until Griffith began directing pictures that his talent as a comedian was recognized. Griffith one day assigned him a minor comic part, and his performance made the picture a success with nickelodeon audiences. In his next picture, he was once again cast in a serious role, but the public, now identifying him as a comedian, began laughing as soon as they saw him, and thereafter he was restricted to comic parts. Sennett was a tireless student of Griffith's innovations; if he had no other reason to be present when Griffith was directing, he undertook to move the heavy camera about as needed. His associates afterwards remembered that Sennett often sought to persuade Griffith to make a comedy picture about policemen, and that Griffith always refused. They were inclined to attribute to this early repression and discouragement the extreme violence of the Keystone cop comedies which subsequently made Sennett famous.

In 1910, Sennett was given his first chance to direct a picture, and nearly four decades later he recalled that a misadventure taught him one of the camera tricks that he was soon to exploit as a laugh-maker. Working on a very small budget, and with an inexperienced cameraman, he was shooting an outdoor picture at Fort Lee, New Jersey, across the Hudson from New York. In order to save film, the cameraman cranked as slowly as possible; when the picture was projected, "there was a blur of jerky figures whizzing across the screen as if jet-propelled." Thus, accidentally, Sennett learned that fast-motion pictures are made by running film through the camera at a very slow speed, and that to make pictures in slow-motion you speed up the camera. Notwithstanding his disastrous first attempt, Sennett continued to direct pictures for Biograph, and acquired considerable prestige in the industry. In 1912, Adam Kessel and Charles O. Bauman—two former race-track bookmakers who had entered the picture business and were distributing their wares through the Mutual Film Company— hired Sennett to make comedy films. They would likewise be remembered because, one year later, they added to his roster of players an unknown English pantomimist named Charles Spencer Chaplin.

For the next five years, Sennett turned out a one-reel or two-reel comedy every week. In them, he blended burlesque, extravaganza, fantasy and satire, and brought these to bear on the current American scene. He chose to treat the elements of social life to which society, by common consent, agreed to attach a solemn importance. He then proceeded to reveal, either the hypocrisy of society's attitude, or the fundamental absurdity of whatever it professed to exalt. Americans, for example, pretended to be law-abiding; insisted that their society exemplified equal justice under the law; professed to hold officers of justice and the law in high esteem. Sennett's pictures suggested that his imbecile, ludicrous Keystone cops represented the profound and unacknowledged

contempt which Americans felt both for the law and those whom
they paid to enforce it. The fruit of this contempt, he intimated,
was the unbridled violence, criminality and chicanery that operated freely in the society portrayed by his pictures. In a sense,
Sennett was expressing satirically, in the broadest farce, the moral
indictment that was likewise being drawn by the muckraking staff
of *McClure's Magazine*, by such disenchanted observers of the
American underworld as Josiah Flynt, by such earnest, passionate
reformers as Judge Ben B. Lindsey, whose sober exposures of the
seamy side of American life probably did not reach Sennett's
audience. But in his pictures they were confronted by a flagrant
discrepancy between the principles in which they professed to
believe and the practices which they condoned and cultivated.
American democracy, as Sennett portrayed it, was a cockeyed
affair.

He poked vigorous fun at all the conventionally established
values of the day. To become rich and respectable was everyone's
secret ambition. In Sennett's pictures it was principally the respected pompous representatives of worldly success who met the
humiliations of pratfalls, and learned the lethal uses of a custard
pie—that appetizing symbol of the domestic achievements of
mother or the little woman. If Miss Pickford expressed the
commonly venerated American girl as innocent, idealistic, untouched by sordid circumstances but still vanquishing them,
Sennett's females illustrated a more jaundiced view. His celebrated
bathing beauties—one of them, Miss Gloria Swanson, was to
become a great star—were as dumb as they were handsome, and
the usual object of their affections was not an alluring hero but
some ugly, obese specimen whose only merit was his bankroll. The
cult of innocence met with rough treatment in Sennett's major
ingénue, Miss Mabel Normand, whose trusting ways continually
got her into trouble. The national myth of romantic love as the
foundation of all happiness fared little better. The wooing
American male, as Sennett saw him, was likely to be represented
by cross-eyed lugubrious Ben Turpin, monumental Roscoe "Fatty"
Arbuckle, or soulful idiotic Hank Mann.

Throughout the country, thousands of business establishments displayed the injunction that time is money; Americans cherished the conviction that high pressure makes for efficiency. But Sennett's hilarious mile-a-minute chases merely indicated that the faster you went the less you accomplished. The nation was beginning to affirm the singular merit of sheer quantity. (At Harvard University, somewhat earlier, President Eliot, meeting Professor George Santayana on the campus, asked how his classes were getting on. The professor replied that they were getting on well, seemed to be keen and intelligent. Said President Eliot, impatiently, "I meant, *what is the number* of students in your classes.") Sennett multiplied everything enormously: cops, guns and bullets, machines, criminals, pretty girls—the result was a maniacal confusion. And to a people beginning to be convinced that ownership of an automobile was supremely important, Sennett's Model-T Ford, hurtling over obstacles, dashing through rivers and lakes, collapsing houses and vehicles, only to blow up in a mighty sulphurous explosion—this, too, offered a sardonic commentary.

That the magnificent, audacious nonsense of Sennett's films reflected a skeptical view of the national life was probably not as apparent to contemporary audiences as to later critics. But that the king of laughs was an astute and acid judge of American mores is evident from his definition of comedy. "You will find your idea for a motion-picture comedy either in sex or crime," he told an interviewer. "These two fields are the great feeding grounds of funny ideas." To serious-minded citizens, regarding the drift of American life with some anxiety, the implications of this novel doctrine were scarcely reassuring.

3 Sadpants

In 1910 Fred Karno, the English producer of pantomimes and music-hall turns, sent a company of his players to the United States. For three years, in an act entitled *A Night in an English Music Hall,* they toured American vaudeville theaters from coast to coast. Part of the fun was furnished by an elegant drunkard, in formal attire, who from a stage box persistently interrupted the act, to the great delight of audiences. The slim, short, derisive spectator was played by a youth named Charles Spencer Chaplin, who thought himself exceedingly well-off on a salary of sixty dollars a week.

This was a good income to be earning at the age of twenty-one, and Chaplin's poverty-stricken childhood freighted it with suggestions of respectability and social approval. He had always been an outsider, hungrily looking at the inaccessible delights enjoyed by the privileged and prosperous. The son of obscure music-hall singers, his father had died when he was three years old, and soon afterwards his mother, ill and without means of support, put him in an almshouse. This transfer to incarceration from the freedom of mean streets in a London slum left a deep impression on the boy's mind; he felt it to be a disgrace, and he knew that gruelling poverty had been its cause. One incident, which he recounted long after becoming world famous, showed the effect of this experience on his view of life. On Christmas, a table was spread with bags of candy, picture books and other small gifts for the children, who formed in line to pass it and receive their bounty. Chaplin, aged seven, had fixed his heart on a big, fat, red apple—the largest one he had ever seen. The line moved, until at last he was fifth from the table; then a matron pounced on him, removed him from the line and told him, brutally, that he would receive no present; this was his punishment for some minor infraction of rules. "I have always found that red apple of happiness just within reach of my hand," Chaplin told the writer, Benjamin De Casseres, in 1920, "when some invisible presence or force drags me away just as I am about to grab it." In one or another form, this conviction was to pervade the best of Chaplin's pictures.

After his mother's recovery and return to the stage, Chaplin was taken out of the almshouse and put to work as a child actor in the companies with which she toured. At thirteen he was one of a group of juvenile dancers and singers known as the Eight Lancashire Lads. Soon afterwards, he determined to break into the legitimate theater. In 1905, when he was sixteen, he played the role of a Cockney page-boy in a one-act Sherlock Holmes playlet which the American star, William Gillette, used as a curtain-raiser for *Clarice*, the comedy in which he was being presented at the

Duke of York's Theater. Though Chaplin scored a success with
critics and audiences, he could secure no other parts; he was too
old for boys' roles and not sufficiently mature to play an adult. He
therefore joined Fred Karno's pantomime troupe as an apprentice,
and during the following five years acquired the technique, and
much of the material, that made his early films outstanding.

At the Orpheum Theater in New York City, Adam Kessel saw
A Night in an English Music Hall, was impressed by the performance of the comic, heckling drunk in the box, and sent for the
unknown player, to whom he offered a salary of one hundred and
fifty dollars a week for a year's work in Mack Sennett's Keystone
comedies. However much tempted by the money, Chaplin was
extremely dubious. It seemed foolish to abandon the stage for
pictures; most actors still considered that the transfer entailed a
loss of prestige. And the pictures might not be an appropriate
medium for his type of pantomime. If he failed to make good, he
would be stranded in a strange country. In the end he was persuaded to sign a contract, and crossed the continent with golden
visions of becoming a romantic actor. When told that his first role
was that of a man with a limp and a backache trying to carry a
trunk, and also balance a coal scuttle on his head while climbing a
greasy ladder, Chaplin was indignant. He refused to undertake
the role; but the prospect of a long, fruitless trip back to Broadway
subsequently convinced him that "It was a good plan to try
anything once." This was in December, 1913, and Chaplin never
thereafter quit the films.

His early work with Sennett was not happy. The master of
slapstick wanted broad exaggeration, whirlwind action; Chaplin's
method of pantomime was deliberate, relied upon understatement
for its effects. It was not until he talked Sennett into letting him
act in his own way, and direct his own pictures, that Chaplin
scored his first success. Meanwhile, having noticed that his costumes and make-up in no way distinguished him from Sennett's
other comedians, Chaplin proceeded to create the absurd, pathetic
little tramp-dandy in whose guise he soon would wriggle helplessly
to world fame. His patched shoes and enormous trousers were
twice too large. His frayed cutaway coat, chequered waistcoat, and

bowler hat were all too small. His wistful aspiration to elegance
was apparent in his cropped mustache, his jaunty handling of a
bamboo cane, the crumpled rag of a handkerchief that extruded
from his breast-pocket, the tattered carnation which he sported
as a boutonnière. Altogether, he represented the social outcast's
yearning for a larger life, nourished only on day-dreams and
togged out in booty snatched from ashcans.

In his Keystone pictures, Chaplin was little more than a comic,
suggestive figure; often a mere target for custard pies. Confronted
by the majesty of the law, or any physically superior force, he
trembled in fear. Plunged always into situations that rob the
individual of his self-respect and make him ridiculous to others,
the little tramp pretended that nothing unusual was happening
and became obstinately intent on preserving his personal dignity.
But audiences everywhere roared with laughter at his antics, his
funny walk, the eloquent shrug with which he indicated that,
however incomprehensible the vicissitudes of life may be, one
must somehow make the best of them. In his year with Keytsone,
Chaplin appeared in thirty-five pictures, and fan mail flooded the
studio. Before long, the press remarked that the Chaplin "shorts"
were more popular with the public than many of the new, pretentious feature films. He signed a new contract with Essanay, the
company headed by "Broncho Billy" Anderson and George K.
Spoor. This permitted him to choose his own stories and direct
his pictures; it also paid him twelve hundred and fifty dollars
each week for a year's work. But before the contract had run its
course, the Mutual Film Company offered him a total of six
hundred and seventy thousand dollars for his services the following
year. And while he was still working for Mutual, the First National
group announced that he would presently transfer to them for a
sum said to be in excess of one million dollars.

In little more than three years, the unknown vaudeville actor
became the most universally beloved personality of the screen.
Miss Pickford was his sole rival in compensation. But Chaplin's
audiences included segments of the public whose allegiance she
never won. He was the delight of American children. Parents
made the privilege of attending his pictures a reward for good

behavior, and withheld it as a disciplinary measure of punishment. At the other end of the scale, he became a cult among the intellectuals. Mrs. Minnie Maddern Fiske, the most "highbrow" actress of the day, paid tribute to his arresting art in *Harper's Weekly*. The social significance of his pictures excited the editors of *The New Republic*, a new liberal weekly of considerable influence, and Chaplin became, as was said at the time, "the pet of philosophers." Columnists like Heywood Broun and critics of the drama like Percy Hammond wrote of him enthusiastically and often. But perhaps even more important than his conquests of children and the intelligentsia was his phenomenal appeal for urban Americans of both the middle and lower classes. Main Street adored him only less than Miss Pickford. But the cities which received her pictures coolly turned out in force for his.

Like Finley Peter Dunne's "Mr. Dooley" some years earlier, Chaplin's sad little tramp resembled a plumb line that passed through all the layered strata of the American social order. Both were daring creations and, despite their dissimilarity, they had one element in common. Dooley came of the despised immigrant class and practised the disreputable trade of barkeeping. Chaplin's tramp was even further removed from respectability. He led his precarious existence outside the boundaries of society, and his frustrations were the result of his unwillingness, or inability, to conform to its rules. Both characters were untouched by the authority of convention, and that of traditional social dogmas. They refused to be awed by wealth or prestige. They would not be deluded by shams or hypocrisies. With equal impudence, they rejected the standards of value imposed by the established order to assure its own maintenance. What they offered the American people was a report on society from the vantage point of ostracized dissent.

As soon as Chaplin was released from restrictions he began to experiment with satire, and feel his way toward the social criticism that became so pronounced in the films which he made between the two World Wars. His first gesture of independence was to make a film called *His New Job*, which made fun of himself and his public. It gently ridiculed the current worship of movie stars by

elevating Chaplin's tramp, with dizzying speed, from the humble
circumstances of a laborer's helper to the golden fortunes of a
popular idol. Then, in *The Tramp,* he brought his perennial hero
into full relief. The tramp was an outcast, but nevertheless a free
individual. He tried to win approval and material success by
sacrificing his liberty and conforming to the accepted code. Failing
in this, the audience saw him—as it was to see him again and
again in the future—wandering dejectedly, alone, down an endless
road. Suddenly, with a shrug of his shoulders, he flipped up his
heels and ambled gaily off toward the horizon, resigned to his
solitude but prizing his independence. In other early films, Chaplin
satirized the national love of sports, the stupidities of the law, the
high and unwarranted respect accorded to financiers and industrial
tycoons. With sly malice he suggested, in a picture called *Work,*
that most Americans, instead of working so that they may live, are
compelled by social pressures to live for work alone. The film
suggested that society offers them the illusive hope of future
leisure, but so arranges their existence that their sole leisure
occurs in daydreams that never will be realized.

Increasing acclaim and prestige strengthened Chaplin's desire
to give his pictures greater significance. An intensifying seriousness
of purpose became evident in his work. "My pictures have always
been for the underdog," he was to explain many years later. "They
have always tried to create pity. I think pity is a great attribute
of civilization. Without it we have no civilization." Evocation
of pity for the weak, outcast, the socially disinherited and underprivileged became a dominant motive with him. His little tramp
was transformed into a champion of the oppressed. In *Easy Street,*
as a reformed derelict, he joined the police force and liberated a
slum neighborhood from the toughs who had terrorized it. In
The Immigrant, Chaplin ironically contrasted a view of the Statue
of Liberty with one of the steerage passengers who gazed at it,
confined and herded together, penned as if they were cattle and
not human beings. To Chaplin, the inherent dignity of the individual, and his fundamental right to pursue happiness in his
own way, seemed supremely important. He saw both being cur-
tailed by social forces so complex that the individual could no
longer understand them, so powerful that he could no longer

resist them. This was the burden of *A Dog's Life*, in which the tramp, with his canine pet, strove for the right to think and live independently, and escaped the various forms of regimentation imposed by society by quietly paying—in poverty, discredit and loneliness—the price extorted for individual freedom. The life of the common man, Chaplin implied, was little more propitious than that of a stray cur—yet everyone, by tolerance, sympathy and kindliness, could make it easier to bear.

In *Shoulder Arms*, which Chaplin made after the United States entered the First World War, he once again spoke for the "underdog"; this time, the army private. Advised by his friends to delay its release because of its "bad taste," he finally permitted it to reach the screen shortly before the Armistice, and it became the most successful of his pictures up to that time. The picture was filled with biting satire on war itself, and on the humiliations and hardships of the average soldier's existence; chiefly, it stressed the indignity of being reduced to the condition of an anonymous integer in a vast aggregation. All of Chaplin's hatred for a regimented society found vent in this comic portrayal of the most completely regimented group in the American social order. Yet this picture nowhere met with greater favor than among the American army, for whom it was screened in canteens, hospitals and rest camps across the Atlantic as well as in the United States. They recognized that it captured the essence of the average enlisted man's wartime experience as he himself understood it. But they realized, also, that it did something more. For, more poignantly than any of his previous pictures, it expressed Chaplin's strong conviction that, whatever his circumstances, genuine happiness always remained within reach of the common man. However oppressed or humiliated, however lacking in the material possessions that secured a position of consequence in society, to be happy he need only find harmony within himself. In the world of his imagination and thought, he could achieve the dignity of which his environment deprived him. He could then laugh at circumstance, at the sorry figure he presented to the outward scene. Armored by his self-respect, he could contentedly dream of the coming of a better day.

It was, no doubt, the unexpected, extraordinary success of

Shoulder Arms that, in the post-war era, changed Charles Chaplin, transforming the gentle, sentimental satirist into a powerful and eloquent critic of the American social scene.

4 Ladies in Trouble

Meanwhile, William Selig had been pondering what appeared to be a sound commercial notion. The publication of serial stories brought magazines and newspapers a continuous sale; readers, having enjoyed the first installment, would repeat their purchase of the publication until the story had run to its conclusion. Why should not the same principle be applied to motion pictures— especially since the result would be to bring people back, week after week, to their neighborhood theaters? And would not the attraction of serial pictures be enhanced by having the stories published simultaneously as newspaper features? Selig submitted this project to the Chicago *Tribune*, which only five years earlier had proposed to abolish the nickelodeons. In December, 1913, the *Tribune* began publication of *The Adventures of Kathlyn*, and the first installment of this hair-raising serial, starring handsome Kathlyn Williams, came to the screen. Week after week, with incomparable adroitness and agility, Miss Williams escaped from disaster with her honor unsullied and her body unblemished, only to be plunged, before the end of the picture, into a situation even more dreadful—and be left there, in misery and despair, until, in the next installment, her ingenuity would once again achieve her liberation. Only the most sour of critics, like Vachel Lindsay, eager to have the motion picture interpret "the largest conceivable ideas that come within the range of the plastic arts," would assert flatly that "Kathlyn had no especial adventures." Over the nation, audiences did not agree. For presently serial films achieved a wide popularity, especially with the groups that had formerly patronized the nickelodeons.

The most successful of these thrillers was, unquestionably, *The Perils of Pauline*, played by Pearl White, Paul Panzer and Crane Wilbur, which began its long unfolding on the screen early in 1914, and was simultaneously syndicated to an eager public in the newspapers of William Randolph Hearst. Almost overnight, it lifted Miss White, who until then had been an obscure player in slapstick comedies, into a blazing limelight of celebrity; shortly afterwards, her fan mail would reach the alarming total of ten thousand letters every week. Sophisticated Americans, sensitive to the grotesque improbabilities of this sensational thriller, dismissed it as irrelevant and ridiculous. They were wrong. For it was a kind of allegory, a translation into fanciful terms of a social situation that had developed from the changing status of American women. The drift of women into industry that had begun before the turn of the century was now at full flood. Women had become wage-earners, but by greatly increasing the labor pool, they had depressed their own compensation. In competition with men, their only economic claim to acceptance was the simple fact that they received less pay. In 1914, when *The Perils of Pauline* came to the screen, nearly half of the nonprofessional women wage-earners above the age of sixteen were receiving less than six dollars a week; nearly three-quarters were receiving less than eight. Economists asserted that seven dollars was necessary for bare subsistence, and more than eight was needed to furnish a living wage. In these circumstances was it remarkable that Miss White, from week to week pitting her wits against the malevolence of men, should seem, to hard-pressed factory workers and salesgirls, to be living out on the higher plane of romantic allegory the hazardous adventure of their own lives?

Heaven would protect the working girl, the popular song asserted, but in her weekly encounter with a hostile world, in her hairbreadth escapes from a doom worse than death, Miss White relied less on providence than on common sense, resourcefulness, determination and physical vigor. A girl's best friend is herself, was the moral of her story; and who could know how many equally harassed young women took courage from the perpetual triumph of her exemplary assurance? For, as Miss White subsequently explained, the perils she endured and overcame often struck terror in her heart. "In the first three episodes I had to play tennis, which I could not. I had to take a flight in an airplane, which I didn't like much, because it was supposed to crash to the ground in a wreck. Then I had to drive a motor car through water, fire and sand. This also didn't sound reasonable. Then I had to go to sea in a yacht, which was all right, only that I was to jump overboard just as the boat was blown up by the villain, and I couldn't swim. Then I was to be in a captive balloon—but oh! the villain was to cut the rope and I was to go sailing about for a while, then drop an anchor, which was to catch in a tree, and I was to descend some two hundred and fifty feet on this, reaching a cliff on the side of a mountain. . . ." What wonder that Miss White reflected: "The picture business is certainly not one of ease and comfort, and I think I can modestly say that my lot is just a little bit harder than most of the others in the profession, because I'm always doing some new stunt and nursing a lot of cuts, bruises and sprains in consequence."

Miss White was able to play her screen role with admirable conviction, and if she became the heroine of the underpaid women workers it was perhaps because of this persuasiveness. She was the better able to translate their lives into allegory for having, quite literally, anticipated their experiences. And, in her later career, she was to show them how far an underprivileged American girl might go in this world—if she chose to. She was born and spent her childhood in a country town in Missouri; her family were very poor. Known in the neighborhood as a tomboy, and disapproved, her favorite recreation was performing on a trapeze. At the age of fourteen, she ran away with a traveling circus, which paid her eight dollars a week and board; a bad fall soon brought her circus career to an end. Returning home, she went to work in a printing establishment, but the monotony of her job oppressed her, and presently she ran away again, with a barnstorming troupe in which she played small parts. Eager to win recognition, she attempted a song-and-dance turn between the acts, in Natchez, Mississippi. Southern chivalry was in decline; the audience pelted her with rotten eggs. Stranded in Charleston, South Carolina, she took a job as stewardess on a boat bound for Cuba, jumped ship in Havana, and worked as an entertainer in a café. When she had earned enough money to buy steerage passage to Buenos Aires, she set off once more, landing in that city on her seventeenth birthday. She worked there until she could afford to ship back to New Orleans, and make her way home.

With what seems singular optimism, her father apprenticed her to a dressmaker. Respectable toil did not long detain her; she ran away with a touring stock company. As an actress, Miss White was no genius; before long, she was ignominiously discharged. She tried to get jobs on Broadway, without success, joined a small-town stock company, and was advised, by a friendly member of the troupe, that she would probably do better in motion pictures —the nickelodeon audiences were less critical. She found a job playing one-reel pictures which paid her thirty dollars a week. Her first sight of herself on the screen so destroyed her illusion of her beauty that, in grief, she disappeared for several days. But, sensibly remembering that a girl must eat, homely or not, she returned to her job. Thereafter, she floated from one picture factory to another, playing any roles that offered.

By the summer of 1913, her bank account showed a balance of six thousand dollars, more money than she had ever dreamed of possessing. So she sailed for England, first class, on the fashionable *S. S. Olympic,* and during the voyage met a friendly officer of the British Army who invited her, after their arrival, to luncheon in his London home. The elegance of his establishment impressed her; she was gratified by being the only feminine guest; she was flattered by the presence of Lord Kitchener, invited to meet her. But, seated at table, she was paralyzed by fright. The footmen in livery, the bewildering battery of forks, knives and spoons, the elevated conversation which she didn't understand, intensified her sense of inadequacy. "Gentlemen," said Miss White, with a prophetic forecast of *The Perils of Pauline,* "I am sorry, so very sorry, that I stayed here to wreck your luncheon. To be truthful, I am all wrong, I am absolutely bewildered by the whole surroundings. I don't know what all this collection of knives and forks means. Your gang of servants make me nervous. I don't know when to eat, what to eat, or how to eat it; in other words, I'm sunk, and there is no use trying to bluff it out." From that moment forward, she enjoyed a spectacular social success.

When, after seven months of holiday on the Continent—she managed to win nine thousand dollars at the roulette tables of Monte Carlo, and promptly spent it all on an elaborate Paris wardrobe—she returned home, *The Perils of Pauline,* and fame, awaited her. She played many other serials and, nine years later, having amassed the comfortable fortune of two million dollars, she retired from the screen. It was then, however, that her second career opened. Migrating to France, she maintained a home in Paris and an elaborate villa in Rambouillet, where she lived and entertained fastidiously. The little dressmaker's apprentice, the unsuccessful actress, the lowly slapstick comedian of early films who a decade before had been distracted by the multiple mystery of knives and forks, now kept a racing stable and was the center of a fashionable international set. People who had never heard of "the lady daredevil of the fillums" knew Pearl White, the fabulous American who inaugurated the Parisian vogue for colored wigs, whose whims created fads, whose presence in a nightclub with her retinue assured its success.

Occasionally, her old love of the theater disputed her enjoyment of the larger life. She made infrequent appearances in French music halls, and once went to London to be featured in a revue. As was her custom, now, she made this journey in the grand manner. Crossing the English Channel, a whole deck was reserved for her use. She was taken to London on a special train bearing large signs that read "Pearl White's Special." At the station, a fleet of motor cars was drawn up, all labelled, "Awaiting arrival of Pearl White's Special." But Londoners, mildly puzzled, merely asked who Pearl White was, and nobody seemed to know. A year before her death, Miss White paid a visit of state to Hollywood. Three studios, remembering that her name on a theater poster had once drawn crowds to the box-office, offered to promote a return to the screen. "Why should I?" Miss White retorted. "I have plenty of money. I'm happy now. Why should I come to Hollywood? Do I look crazy?"

To this Hollywood had no ready answer; Miss White had tactlessly expressed what far too many of its elite felt, yet never dared to say. But Hollywood, like the rest of the country, was often swept by nostalgia for the past, for the remote times when life had been more agreeable, less perplexing, when skies were sunnier and the future implied promise rather than misgivings. This was its mood in 1947, when it made a film about Pearl White:

The Perils of Pauline. Miss White herself might have been astonished by the degree of honor to which the tribute attested. For, to impersonate her before a generation to which even her name was probably unknown, Hollywood had chosen one of its most popular stars, Miss Betty Hutton, whose alluring image was indelibly fixed on the national consciousness by magazines, newspapers and the ubiquitous billboards of the American landscape. Oldsters who remembered Miss White went to see the film in sentimental piety. Though still young enough to respond to Miss Hutton's attractions, their emotions were mixed.

Hadn't there been more to the girl than *that*?

5 Sex Was Sultry

In the pleasant days before the First World War, advertisements in magazines and newspapers furnished, as always, a reliable guide to the nation's mores. You would have noticed that the ladies who chastely displayed lingerie suggested a cosy domesticity. Sweethearts they might be, but they were indubitably wives and mothers in the future, and not the conditional, tense. Rouge, used only by actresses and fancy women, was not advertised. Rice powder was offered discreetly. Feminine readers did not need to be told that, properly applied, it would be imperceptible. Scents were principally floral. They were intended to gratify a desire for luxury, not to bait a mantrap. The clean-cut, rugged young men who displayed the latest fashions in collars and other wearing apparel likewise illustrated the pattern of aspiration that society had devised for the well-bred girl. Handsome though they were, these young men had the look of good providers, pleasing to prospective fathers-in-law. The day had not yet come when they would exemplify an irresistible temptation to casual surrender. American mores were the expression of a whaleboned morality, and most decent folk preferred to leave one of its major premises unstated. Sex was a signpost pointing to the altar and the stork. Nobody, foresaw that it was to become a social pastime.

Sex was introduced to the motion pictures by earnest reformers, in the guise of vice. As the second decade of the century opened, and women poured into industrial centers in search of jobs, the civic conscience of Americans was profoundly shocked by one social result of economic progress: an increase in prostitution. The Rockefeller Foundation issued a melancholy report on "white slavery." In New York City, District Attorney Charles Whitman—later to be Governor of the state—exposed and prosecuted a "vice trust." Under the leadership of prominent citizens, various organizations were formed to crusade against the abhorrent evil and remedy the unsavory conditions which enabled it to flourish. On this wave of civic reform, a film was made dealing with white slavery, allegedly dramatizing the facts already made public. Sanctioned by the Board of Censorship in New York, explicitly approved by the District Attorney, and supported by leading reform organizations, *Traffic in Souls,* a six-reel feature picture, was first shown at Weber's Theater, in New York City, during the autumn of 1913; soon was being exhibited by twenty-eight picture houses in the metropolitan area; and was presently drawing crowds to theaters throughout the country. Its sponsors had every reason to be satisfied with the success of this venture in public education. And the motion-picture industry continued to co-operate with agencies of social welfare; the sensational and highly profitable sermon was quickly repeated in a series of similar pictures. Yet, had they foreseen the ultimate consequences of their sanction, the zealous reformers who brought sex to the screen might have withheld their approval. For the mores of the American people were soon to undergo a drastic change. In the revolution that flamed over the United States, destroying the authority of old traditions, transforming morals and manners, the movies were to play a decisive part.

The earliest portent of this revolution issued from the fertile imagination of William Fox, who—probably unwittingly—adapted to the screen a technique of moral teaching that had been brought to its most eloquent efficacy in the sermons of Jonathan Edwards. Sin is a universal malady, the world is full of snares and temptations, yet mankind must aspire to virtue; and the more alluring the temptations resisted, the greater the merit of man's moral victory. So Edwards felt, in the eighteenth century, and painted, in all their lurid, deceptive beauty, the evils that perpetually solicit the souls of men. Modern improvements should have made the glittering exhortations of William Fox even more forcefully dissuasive than the sermons of Edwards. But cynics, ignoring their moral motive, condemned them as a depraving influence. Could Fox justly be blamed because the American people were more impressed by the delights of sin than by its inevitable punishment? Why strive to preach the gospel of puritanism, when by so doing you aroused the hostility of all puritans? Yet Fox's missionary ardor was not to be discouraged. In three years he turned out no less than forty pictorial admonitions to virtue. All of them conclusively demonstrated—by means of a wanton siren—that the wages of sin is death. Not the least remarkable of their effects was a transient contribution to the American language. The word "vamp," chiefly associated with footwear, suffered a change in anatomical emphasis and practically lost its pedal connotation. Almost overnight, it became a fatiguingly common noun and a regrettably active verb. This disturbance in the popular vocabulary reflected certain novelties that were being added to the repertory of acceptable behavior. They were introduced by Miss Theda Bara, who every month on the screen furnished spectacular evidence of man's corruptible nature.

In her public function, as the incentive to a higher moral life, Miss Bara was a more memorable creation than any of the sermons she illustrated. She was, so to speak, an industrial product, as artfully designed to whet popular appetite as any automobile. A brilliant staff of experts gave her a personality, equipped her with a legend, and made the nation aware of her with so stupefying a campaign of publicity that it might appropriately have been described as a barrage. The drum-fire began early in 1915, with the release of her first picture, *A Fool There Was*, based on Rudyard Kipling's poem, "The Vampire," and showing the ability of a conscienceless female to wreck the lives of men by a calculated use of her sensual charms. White-faced, with brooding, heavy-lidded eyes, and a dark cloud of hair, her colubrine body sheathed in low-cut gowns of glistening satin, Miss Bara was exotic, voluptuous and—in the picture—irresistibly though fatally alluring. She typified the power that can be exercised by a woman adept in sensuality, coldly selfish, bent upon luxury and the satisfaction of her physical passions. She opened fresh vistas to decorous American matrons, and introduced some disturbing notions into the domestic attitudes of the American male.

Presently her photograph—sometimes with a skull, or crystal ball; sometimes with a skeleton stretched at her feet—was featured by newspapers and magazines throughout the country. So was her story. For Miss Bara, it appeared, was the actual embodiment of her screen role. Had she not been born on the sands of the Sahara, the daughter of a French painter and his Arabian mistress? Bara was merely an anagram of Arab; Theda, an anagram of death. In childhood, this deadly Arab girl had been shunned by her schoolmates, for she was known to possess dangerous occult powers which she did not hesitate to use. She was unfathomably wicked, disastrously poisonous; the wedding march and cradle were singularly lacking in attraction for her. Arrangements were made for her to meet representatives of the press at the Blackstone Hotel, in Chicago. The city's film censor declined an invitation to attend; his colleagues throughout the country frequently objected to her pictures. Pallid, languid, black-clad, Miss Bara received in a darkened parlor draped in black and red, heavy with the perfume of tuberoses and incense. When the last caller had departed, she ordered all the windows opened. "Give me air," she gasped. It was, perhaps, a not unnatural request for a circumspect American girl whose name was Theodosia Goodman, who had been born in Cincinnati to a respectable tailor and his wife, and who had been working as an occasional extra in films when she was casually chosen to become the vicarious, shadowy fulfillment of desires never before publicly acknowledged.

As a symbol of masculine desire, and therefore a model for feminine emulation, Miss Bara's ascendancy did not last long. Its brevity merely registered the force of her impact on American imaginations; she sophisticated them so rapidly that she made her own type obsolete. But in three years of hard, and often repetitious, effort she did much to soften the whalebones that kept morality rigid, and to undermine the conventions that protected it. Because of her, the "baby-vamp" became a problem to parents and a nocturnal hazard to collegians. In millions of American homes the fumes of incense came to signify, not the presence of mosquitoes, but the anticipated arrival of a male caller. The undershot "Bara-look" was either an ominous hint of danger, or a half-explicit promise of pleasure, depending upon the degree of emancipation achieved by the female who practised it. For a while, feminine ambulation was slithery, and feminine posture languorous. An exotic pallor was cultivated by the most robust; necklines dropped alarmingly; and in a sudden wave of black that crossed the land, nubile girlhood appeared to be adopting universal mourning. For Miss Bara made voluptuousness a common American commodity, as accessible as chewing gum. And when this had been done, the old order was exposed to successful assault.

But its final overthrow required the co-operation of American men. To enlist this, a hero was needed. And was it not only just that, having shaped herself according to the presumptive desires of men, woman should now turn a critical eye on the supposedly seething sex? By now, she had worked out a new pattern of aspiration. She had learned from Miss Bara that she could win power by exercising a cultivated sensuality. Her immediate problem was to find men who understood what this implied, and were capable of responding appropriately. She was no longer satisfied to consider the male merely as prospective husband, provider and potential parent. She didn't think that presiding over the narrow domestic margin of his existence promised her a full life. She looked at the current American man, and decided that she wanted a different type. All unconscious of what was in store for him, the male took to grumbling about feminine unrest. It was in 1921, shortly after youth returned from the World War, that the movies furnished American women with an image of their needs. He proved to be devastatingly provocative. And the overwhelming force of feminine adulation compelled the questing American male, however reluctantly, to study him as a model and profit by the lesson if he could.

Rudolph Valentino did not have that good-provider look which, so few years earlier, had been the unique criterion of masculine charm. His peculiar attraction had little to do with the promise of economic security; it produced insecurity in quite another department. Valentino, as H. L. Mencken said, was "cat-nip for women." His first film, *The Four Horsemen of the Apocalypse,* made this sensationally obvious. Dark, handsome in an exotic fashion, his sideburns, passionate air and Latin gallantry, his grace in dancing the tango, his sophisticated way of making love—all these quickened the pulses of innumerable women, and instantaneously set the new standard for masculine sex-appeal. The term itself was coined to account for his prodigious effect, and it indicated how far the revolution in American mores had proceeded.

Like Miss Bara, Valentino had been casually chosen for his high destiny. Unlike her, he required no legend to launch him; he soon found it impossible to avoid the perpetual limelight of publicity. He came from Italy to the United States in 1913, seeking work as a gardener, and failed to find it. It was said that he worked as a bus-boy, a waiter, a barber; this he denied. During the vogue of exhibition dancing in cabarets, as nightclubs were then called, he served as partner to Miss Bonnie Glass and Miss Joan Sawyer, two popular performers. He progressed to minor roles on the stage, eventually drifted to Hollywood, and occasionally found equally minor roles in the movies. Married to a screen actress while still unknown, he was divorced by her soon after his swift success. His too-prompt remarriage was presently to involve him in transient, but widely publicized, difficulties with the law. It was the first alliance between Hollywood and old wealth; his bride, professionally known as a writer under her pseudonym of Natacha Rambova, was the step-daughter of Richard Hudnut, a millionaire manufacturer of cosmetics. Miss Rambova subsequently divorced Valentino, but after his death she published a book about him which revealed the unsuspected fact that he possessed occult powers as a medium and clairvoyant. Could these dark resources have contributed to his hypnotic influence from the screen? Apparently not; for at the height of his celebrity, Valentino produced a volume of verse, *Day Dreams,* which communicated to an adoring public his views on love, passion, kisses and kindred topics. His views did not indicate any need for co-operation by mystical forces.

Always playing romantic roles, Valentino made a series of phenomenally successful pictures. His fan mail broke all records in the industry. Valentino fan-clubs sprang up in every city throughout the country. Though harassed husbands discoursed unkindly about the American woman's queer preference for a "lounge-lizard" or "gigolo," this preference soon began to yield results. Barbers reported a growing vogue for sideburns. Manufacturers of hair tonic learned that the demand for good, old-fashioned bay rum had evaporated. A huge business suddenly developed in pomades that would keep men's hair sleek and shiny. Teachers of ballroom dancing were made prosperous by the glamor with which Valentino had invested the tango; connubial pressure added mastery of this complicated footwork to the ordinary hazards confronting the American businessman. In an editorial aggressively titled "Pink Powder Puffs," the Chicago *Tribune* accused Valentino of responsibility for the American male's new, disgraceful habit of applying powder to his face after shaving. Valentino denied the charge, and challenged the anonymous writer of the editorial to a duel; when that unfortunate person refused to disclose his identity, the great star declared that his honor had been satisfied, and the ominous issue was dropped. Meanwhile, in every American community, under the tremendous compulsion of feminine idolatry, young Americans were trying to make themselves over in the image of an image. The drugstore cowboy painfully sought to become a sheik.

Five years after his ascent to fame, Rudolph Valentino died in New York City. His body was taken to lie in state at a Broadway "funeral parlor." Publicity representatives of this establishment, and of the dead star, furnished the press liberal assistance in reporting this melancholy item of news. The result was a crowd which stretched for eleven blocks along Broadway. A street riot occurred in which scores of people were injured; mounted police had to charge into the unruly mob. A seemingly endless procession of curious men and grief-stricken women filed past Valentino's bier. He had been heavily in debt when he died. But so unique was his appeal that it forced Hollwood to shatter a precedent. Unreleased pictures that he had made were brought to the screen after his death; they wiped out his debts and produced a six-hundred-thousand-dollar balance to the credit of his estate. The historian Frederick Lewis Allen, reporting Valentino's obsequies as a phenomenon characteristic of American life in the nineteen-twenties, recorded the regret of high-minded citizens that the death of Charles William Eliot, president-emeritus of Harvard, which occurred at about the same time as Valentino's, had caused no comparably spectacular lamentations. Yet, in his own way, had not Valentino also civilized and educated the young American male?

Certainly the American woman and the American girl seemed to think he had. Three years after his death, a touching and revealing volume was published: *What the Fans Think of Rudy Valentino*. One of the tributes, written by a woman in Colfax, Illinois, may have spoken for a large segment of American womanhood. "He thrilled them all, yes, all, I say. The great, the humble, the rich, the poor. His charms brought joy to many a maid, and taught a courteous gallantry to our youths. He filled vain dreams of many wives, and made a lover of many a commonplace man. . . . He created an ideal for men to live up to. He made some better."

Twenty years after his death, Valentino fan-clubs continued to exist in the United States. The memory of an image had not yet been exorcised from the hearts of women already middle-aged, perhaps even old.

6   Behind the Screen

When, in 1913, it became obvious that the screens of the nation were to be permanently dominated by feature films, a serious problem confronted owners of picture houses. Their profits had been based on short programs, and a rapid turnover of audiences; the new long films radically altered this situation. One solution to the problem would be to offset reduced turnover by a sharp increase in the seating capacity of theaters. This experiment was presently undertaken by Mitchell L. Mark, a veteran of the penny arcade era who had built up a chain of houses in Western New York. He startled the industry by beginning construction of the Strand Theater, on Broadway, in New York City—a vast auditorium capable of seating nearly three thousand people. It departed significantly from standard theater design by eliminating the socially humiliating gallery, and placed its audiences on two levels, in an orchestra and balcony. Opened in the spring of 1914, the new theater—it offered a weekly change of program and played five shows daily—was immediately successful. Its example was therefore widely imitated. Within two years, approximately twenty-one thousand newly built, or largely remodelled, picture houses were completed throughout the country. The nickelodeons, suddenly made obsolete, soon disappeared entirely.

In the larger cities, they were replaced by palaces like the Strand. These achieved new heights of ostentation and luxury: ornate lobbies, elaborate lounging rooms, enormous crystal chandeliers, richly decorated walls and ceilings, costly carpets and comfortable seats, large orchestras directed by popular conductors, cathedral organs. Neighborhood theaters eliminated a few of the more expensive features, and reduced the elaboration, but attempted to preserve the effect of luxury. And even on the country's Main Streets, simpler versions of the metropolitan palaces soon became the standard index of an up-and-coming town, as useful for purposes of community boosting as the local chapter of Rotary. The arresting new "temples of the silent drama" conferred on the motion pictures an ultimate accolade of respectability, surrounding them with an atmosphere of grandeur which proclaimed them to be no longer an entertainment for the poor and ignorant. For their patronage, these temples depended on the nation's populous and prosperous middle classes. The picture-going public was thus enormously expanded.

This expansion of the public had significant results. The industry realized that it had notably raised the cultural level of audiences. To be successful, it was obvious that pictures must appeal to a standard of taste more worldly, discriminating and perhaps intelligent than they had previously been required to meet. Nobody could accurately measure the degree of sophistication represented by the new audience; for a time, the industry was able to rely only on a method of trial and error; since costs of production had risen enormously, economic caution tended to restrain experiment. More than ever, it appeared probable that the character and content of pictures would be determined by businessmen with large investments at stake, and interested mainly in securing an assured return on them. Yet certain forces operated in the opposite direction. Expansion of the public, by immensely increasing the financial rewards of success, attracted new producers of pictures into the industry. Their arrival intensified competition for the public's favor. And this keenness of competition brought about qualitative improvements which otherwise might have been longer postponed. By exercising its final authority through the box-office, the public itself took a hand in shaping developments, and though often it appeared not to know what it wanted, its disinclinations were usually made obvious.

Behind the screen, and more powerful than the godlike stars who were actually their puppets, stood the businessmen who produced pictures and the showmen who created them. Though their attitudes toward their product were divergent, neither could prosper without the other. Businessmen, engaged in a mass-production industry, with quantity of output essential for large-scale operations, naturally wished to standardize their product so far as possible. Stars were one means of standardization, and the reduction of picture content to a few simple types—melodramas, romances, comedies, westerns and others—offered another. By combining both, pictures that were stereotyped in theme, plot and direction could be turned out on a wholesale scale. In so far as the views of businessmen prevailed, "formula pictures" became the industry's principal product. But to these views, showmen opposed as much resistance as possible. Gifted with an intuitive sense of audience reaction, they were aware that standardization could operate only within definable limits. Novelty and originality were prime requisites; the product must be kept responsive to fluctuations in public tastes and interests. Showmen felt that, under highly competitive conditions, success was more likely to be achieved by daring experiment than by standardization and the repetition of stereotyped formulas. These divergent attitudes —the conservative and the radical—represented the extremes of tendency within the industry. In those producing units which achieved permanence over the years, they were usually harmonized by a dominant personality; a businessman with a pronounced flair for showmanship.

Because of the importance of motion pictures as a social and cultural force in American life, and because of the power which they exercised through their control of the medium, these men were far more significant as shapers of the national civilization than was usually recognized. What American of his time enjoyed an influence greater than that of William Fox, for example? This former garment worker, former nickelodeon owner, at the height of his spectacular career dominated enterprises said to represent an investment of between four and five hundred millions of dollars. They included eight hundred theaters in the United States alone, as well as the production unit which kept these supplied with pictures. Fox retained an autocratic mastery over the policies and activities of his extraordinary profit-making machine; the pictures that bore his name were the product of his personal tastes, convictions, interests and view of life. "I always bragged of the fact," he told the novelist Upton Sinclair, "that no second of those contained in the twenty-four hours ever passed but that the name of William Fox was on the screen, being exhibited in some theater, in some part of the world." The remark indicated the scope of his potential ability to influence the habits and opinions of masses of people, to profoundly affect their outlook on life and their ways of living.

To the American people, men like Fox were chiefly remarkable because their careers demonstrated the persistence of untrammeled opportunity in twentieth-century American society. Social reformers, theorists, writers of fiction might assert that the gateway of opportunity had been forever closed to the common man; the rise of men like Fox and Zukor from poverty to power explicitly denied it. Yet surely more remarkable than their material achievements was the fact that they and others like them became architects of the culture which, by the middle of the century, was nourishing an overwhelming majority of the citizens of the United States. For the movies were not only the recreation most universally patronized by Americans. The movies were, even more importantly, a major source of their ideas about life and the world in general. For this reason, the influence of makers of pictures upon public opinion, the mores, the values to which American society gave its allegiance, probably far exceeded that of such eminent contemporaries as, for example, the philosopher John Dewey, the jurists Oliver Wendell Holmes and Louis D. Brandeis, the social reformer Jane Addams, or the novelists Theodore Dreiser and Sinclair Lewis.

Few of these unacknowledged architects of American culture had themselves enjoyed the advantage of extended formal education. Lewis J. Selznick, whose career was meteoric, comparatively brief, but significant in the development of pictures, was the son of Russian immigrants. He spent his childhood in the slums of New York's lower East Side. Quitting school as soon as possible, he took a job sweeping the floors of a jewelry store. In time he advanced to the position of salesman, eventually bought the store, and was a moderately prosperous merchant when he determined to enter the motion-picture business. Calling at the Universal Pictures Corporation, he found its offices in a state of siege during a battle for control by rival factions led by Patrick A. Powers and Carl Laemmle. "This was duck soup for me," Selznick afterwards recalled. ". . . I knew what I was after, so I appointed myself to a job, picked out a nice office, and went in and took it. This got by with bells on. People came in and talked to me about everything that was going on, and pretty soon I knew all about it." While the legal battle for control of the company raged, Selznick assumed the post of its general manager, shrewdly relying on the probability that no one in authority would question his appointment to it. The ruse worked. When Laemmle eventually ousted the rival faction, he discharged Selznick. But Selznick had acquired sufficient experience of the business to form a company of his own. This was in 1914. Three years later, testifying before a Congressional committee that was investigating the industry, Selznick asserted that "less brains are necessary in the motion picture business than any other." As evidence for this cynical opinion, he offered the fact that, having founded a company with one thousand dollars in actual capital, he had realized a profit of one hundred and five thousand dollars within ten weeks.

Of movie magnates, Samuel Goldwyn had the longest career and one of the most distinguished, and he enjoyed a wide celebrity for more than three decades. He was born in the ghetto of Warsaw, Poland; his name was Samuel Goldfish. At the age of eleven he ran away from home, begged his way across Germany, and a year later was heaving coal in an English blacksmith shop. Finally reaching the United States, he entered the glove-making industry; at the age of thirty-three, he was chief sales executive for a prominent manufacturer. In 1913, with his brother-in-law, Jesse Lasky, the playwright, Cecil B. De Mille, and a theatrical lawyer named Arthur S. Friend, Goldwyn formed a company to produce a feature picture of the stage play, *The Squaw Man*. De Mille had been associated with David Belasco; Lasky, originally a cornetist, had become a producer of vaudeville acts, then had tried to launch in New York a European type of music hall and restaurant which failed disastrously. Goldwyn, having no theatrical experience whatever, at first concentrated on selling the pictures which the new company turned out—with such success that, at the end of three years, when the company was merged with Adolph Zukor's Famous Players, its original capital of thirty thousand dollars had reputedly been expanded to four millions. Goldwyn presently left the merger, formed another company, and still later became an independent producer.

His widely publicized solecisms kept Goldwyn constantly before the American people. Some of them, exquisitely apt, passed into the language: "Include me out"; "A verbal contract isn't worth the paper it's written on"; "They're always biting the hand that lays the golden egg"; "In two words, Im possible." But they did scant justice to the mind of the man of whom Bernard Shaw once said, after Goldwyn had fruitlessly tried to persuade him to write a scenario, "There is only one difference between Mr. Goldwyn and myself. Whereas he is interested in art, I am interested in money." For Goldwyn was neither ignorant nor uneducated; the historian Roger Butterfield described him as "a highly cultivated man of many and diverse talents." And that he

was interested in art was evident, not only from the high proportion of significant pictures which he produced, and his tireless
efforts to secure the services of distinguished writers, but from his
insistence upon quality as he understood it. He scrapped a picture
that had cost nearly nine hundred thousand dollars, because it
failed to satisfy him, and remade it. "I am a rebel," he said of
himself. "I defy every convention. I make a picture to please me—
if it pleases me there is a good chance that it will please other
people. But it has to please me first." But if this appeared to
indicate a certain complacency, perhaps a degree of arrogance
natural to a man who, having landed in the United States as a
penniless immigrant, achieved both fame and fortune, the impression was offset by another remark of Goldwyn's. Shortly after
one of his pictures had been acclaimed as the best ever made by
any American producer, he was asked whether he would be able
to rest content upon that achievement. "It is not good enough
to be good," he said.

Less conspicuously in the limelight than Goldwyn, his contemporary Louis B. Mayer rose from circumstances almost equally
humble to a position of greater industrial eminence. Mayer was
a small businessman in Haverhill, Massachusetts, when he invested in a nickelodeon; eventually, he was made chief executive
of the Metro-Goldwyn-Mayer studio. Under his direction, it
became the most profitable unit in the industry, the studio of
highest repute in Hollywood, and was said to command the largest
and brightest galaxy of creative talent engaged in the production
of motion pictures. The most highly paid employee in the entire
industry, Mayer was considered its dominant personality. An
industrialist primarily, and conservative by temperament, he regarded motion pictures as entertainment and was little given to
complicating them by the intrusion of controversial issues.

Of the younger producers, Irving Thalberg and Darryl F.
Zanuck were probably the most outstanding. Thalberg, originally
employed as a secretary to Carl Laemmle, was put in charge of
the Universal Studios at the age of twenty-four, and his success
there made him known as the "boy wonder" of the industry.
Shortly afterward, he became assistant to Louis B. Mayer, under

whom he assumed direct charge of production at the Metro-Goldwyn-Mayer studio. Thalberg showed little inclination to treat, on the screen, any debatable aspects of American life. Yet his talent was considerable; he turned out a long series of pictures which were held to be as successful artistically as they were commercially; he was regarded as a pacemaker for the industry, and an important contributor to the advance of the motion picture during this period. It was generally believed that F. Scott Fitzgerald used Thalberg as a model for the central character of *The Last Tycoon*, his unfinished novel of Hollywood life. Unlike Thalberg, Zanuck founded his reputation on a cycle of pictures that exposed, with unprecedented realism, the national disgrace of gang rule and its alliance with corrupt politicians during the prohibition era. Zanuck's pictures, which aroused public feeling to a high pitch, were supposed to have led the Federal government to initiate prosecution of Al Capone, and other "public enemies" under the income-tax laws. And, in bringing to the screen John Steinbeck's *The Grapes of Wrath*, Zanuck laid down another challenge to the industry to deal honestly and courageously with the major social issues confronting Americans—a challenge as powerful as that issued, so many years earlier, by Porter and Griffith.

CHAPTER IV

The Mink Feedbag and
the Diamond Fishbowl

1 Quiet Suburb

Shortly after Edison's vitascope was introduced at Koster and
Bial's, H. H. Wilcox and his wife, residents of Los Angeles, purchased one hundred and twenty acres of land some eight miles
northwest of that city. They subdivided this tract into blocks,
cut roads through it, planted pepper trees along these vacant
thoroughfares, and hopefully named their suburban development
Hollywood. A post office, established in the vicinity in 1897, made
this name official. The Pacific Ocean lay a dozen miles to the west
of the new community, which was bordered on the north by the
Santa Monica Mountains, later to become known as Hollywood
Hills. When, in 1910, the region was annexed by the city of Los

Angeles, it was still thinly settled. Two main roads ran westward to the sea. They had been ambitiously named Hollywood and Sunset Boulevards, and the latter was the favorite route of city dwellers who wanted to reach the beaches of Santa Monica. Along both boulevards lay scattered wooden bungalows, ranch houses, groves of orange and lemon trees and open fields.

By 1910, several independent producers of pictures were using Los Angeles as a base for winter operations, to escape the racketeering squads and legal proceedings of the trust. Colonel William Selig, the first to travel westward, had been taken into the trust; but, having found Los Angeles a more favorable location than Chicago, he built a permanent studio two miles northwest of the center of the city. That same year, David Wark Griffith made the first of his annual expeditions to California for the Biograph Company. He rented quarters in downtown Los Angeles for a studio, but was compelled by circumstances to make his first picture in Hollywood. This film, *In Old California,* was a costume romance with many outdoor scenes, and the downtown studio was too remote from open country for Griffith to have his actors and actresses make up and dress there.

The Hollywood Hotel, a low, rambling structure with wide porches and a large garden, had been built as a quiet winter resort for sedate people. It was the only hotel between the city and the ocean, and Griffith persuaded the proprietor to allow the players to dress in some unoccupied rooms. When the company emerged in makeup and Spanish finery, hotel guests lolling on the front porch were scandalized. The players drove off in their automobiles to the foothills, only to be followed by a deputation from the hotel. For a while, these uninvited spectators remained quiet and well behaved. But when Griffith directed Miss Marion Leonard, as the beautiful Spanish heroine, and Frank Grandin, as her handsome young suitor, in a dramatic love scene, they broke into outraged protest. Such goings-on were intolerable, and should not be permitted. A vigorous dispute occurred, in which the respectable hotel guests made no attempt to conceal their low opinion of movie actors. As the first instance of Hollywood's resentment, it proved to be prophetic.

Staid residents of the suburb were notably lacking in enthusiasm for the roving bands of actors and actresses who began invading their community. One year after Griffith's first visit, the Nestor Film Company of Bayonne, New Jersey, rented a disused roadside tavern at the corner of Sunset Boulevard and Gower Street, and built an outdoor stage on the adjoining vacant lot. There, at any hour of the day, decent passers-by were likely to be appalled by the antics of painted women, and men garbed as Indians, cowboys, or prospectors. Other companies followed. Here and there, great barnlike structures arose on unrestricted property, to the consternation of elderly retired folk who had built residences near by. Roads were roped off to stage automobile accidents. Private homes were used, often without the consent of their owners, as backgrounds for elopements, or even more reprehensible episodes of domestic drama. Armies in uniform marched down Hollywood Boulevard behind an automobile in which a man was grinding a camera. Out in the hilly Silver Lake district, Griffith, in 1912, worked on *The Massacre*, a re-enactment of General Custer's last stand, with hundreds of cavalrymen and masses of Indians; this noisy, dusty pageant, destructive of peace, alarmed everyone. To Godfearing citizens, the movie-camps, as they were called, seemed dens of iniquity. For the disreputable players—undoubtedly of loose morals—gave further scandal by working on Sundays. The community was united in its desire to be rid of them.

Chance, which had brought the unwelcome invasion, intervened again. In New York, the Jesse L. Lasky Feature Play Company had determined to send Cecil B. De Mille out west to make *The Squaw Man*, with Dustin Farnum as its star. Lasky, a native of California, had once visited Flagstaff, Arizona. Recalling its picturesque topography, its reputedly perpetual sunshine, and the Indians he had seen standing about the railroad station, he thought it an ideal location for the projected film. De Mille was instructed to proceed to Flagstaff with his star and company, and begin work. When he stepped off the train, the town was invisible under a raging blizzard, and not a single Indian was to be found in the station. De Mille climbed back on the train, and took his players to the end of the line at Los Angeles. A few days later, he telegraphed his partners in New York asking authorization to rent a barn, for the modest sum of seventy dollars a month, in an unknown spot called Hollywood. He was told to rent it on a month-to-month basis, and get on with his picture. The barn stood near the intersection of Sunset Boulevard and Vine Street, a quarter still sufficiently rural for the coyotes to come down from the hills at night and prowl around it. To discourage their visits, De Mille shot several, and nailed the skins to the façade of his makeshift studio.

It was the success of the first three pictures which De Mille turned out, in rapid sequence, that irrevocably determined the future of Hollywood. Shortly afterwards, the Lasky company, in the full flush of prosperity, bought acreage at the corner of Sunset Boulevard and Vine Street, and built a permanent studio. It was the finest plant as yet erected, with a series of one-story buildings for offices and dressing rooms, a massive glass-covered structure for the taking of indoor pictures, a large open-air stage, and a lot covered with outdoor sets. Scarcely a dozen years later, this studio was to be abandoned. The land which had been bought for approximately five thousand dollars had advanced in value to many hundreds of thousands, and it became the site of business buildings, hotels, apartment houses and theaters.

In 1915, two years after De Mille's arrival, Carl Laemmle built Universal City, in San Fernando Valley, backed by the slopes of Cahuenga Peak and the Los Angeles River. This was an even more ostentatious project than the Lasky studios. Its offices were designed in the mission style, and surrounding them were forty-two acres of buildings, gardens, outdoor sets, corrals and parade grounds. The ceremonies connected with the inauguration of Universal City brought the name of Hollywood before the nation for the first time. For, with his usual flair for publicity, Laemmle had issued a press story that appeared in nearly every newspaper throughout the land. The Secretary of the Navy, it asserted, had ordered the Pacific fleet to proceed up the Los Angeles River and fire a salute to the new metropolis of the films. So little was the district known to non-residents, that editors everywhere ignored one minor fact: no ship could make its way up the river. With only less fanfare, Thomas H. Ince, that same year, deserted "Ince-ville" at Santa Monica, and built a handsome studio at Culver City, midway between Los Angeles and the Pacific. The main executive building of this establishment improved on Laemmle's local mission style; it was a replica of George Washington's home at Mount Vernon.

Thus, very early, was born the inspired Hollywood architecture that, in time, would flower into real-estate offices shaped like sphinx heads, restaurants resembling derby hats, and soft-drink parlors in the guise of immense ice-cream cones. And the crowds that thronged Hollywood Boulevard at noontime compelled a startled attention. Bathing beauties, extras in evening attire, Indians in full war regalia, Orientals, Biblical characters poured out from near-by studios to snatch a hasty luncheon before returning to the impatient cameras. As the nation's press and the fan magazines spread word of this perpetual public vaudeville, Hollywood became a tourist's playground. Movie-mad girls from all parts of the country began streaming into the celluloid paradise where fame and fortune were so easily to be won. This new migration rose to a flood during the nineteen-twenties, when fifty thousand arrivals resulted in a "girl problem" very unlike any to which the term had ever been applied. And the more eccentric products of show business gravitated toward this spectacular market: midgets, animal acts, jugglers and acrobats, circus freaks, high-wire artists, snake charmers, exhibition dancers. One and all, they identified themselves with the motion-picture industry. Conventional folk viewed the raffish, swarming hordes with profound aversion. There were districts of Los Angeles, Hollywood and Beverly Hills where no "movie people" could rent or purchase homes; an effort was made, William C. De Mille asserted, to keep them "segregated like a leper colony."

While the movies were mushrooming in Hollywood, next-door Los Angeles was striking two additional bonanzas. Oil, first discovered at Long Beach, was being located at various other points in the vicinity; the phenomena of the gold rush began to duplicate themselves. And the city was likewise reaping the fruits of a long, stentorian advertising campaign to attract new residents. Directed largely to the elderly and middle-aged, vaunting a climate eternally springlike, and a life of ease for those possessed of moderate means, the campaign brought armies of settlers from the Middle West, with visions of a bungalow shaded by palms, and an orange tree to furnish the breakfast fruit. Promotions in real estate rivaled those in oil. The city sprawled out in all directions, seeming to grow overnight; its population would more than double in ten years. Los Angeles was a boom town as well as a haven of rest, a capital of quick fortune and a continuous holiday. Speculators and promoters, oil riggers, retired farmers with their wives, professional gamblers, race-track touts, women of easy virtue, all flocked there. So did revivalists, diviners, astrologers, apostles of occult faiths, mental healers, swamis, numerologists, analysts of handwriting, professors of homemade cults: self-appointed saviors of the lonely and troubled who were seeking miracles not yielded by the climate. In 1917, having crossed the continent in a battered jalopy, the unknown Aimee Semple McPherson arrived in Los Angeles penniless. Five years later, she opened her vast Angelus Temple where, at every service, five thousand people succumbed to the delirium of God-intoxication. After a fashion, Sister Aimee symbolized the land of illusion that lay between Pershing Square and the Pacific. For she, too, fused economics and ecstasy, showmanship and salvation, carnival and contrition.

2 Lurid Legend

As the chromium-and-rhinestone era of normalcy opened, millions of Americans were beginning to find a pattern for their aspirations in the charmed life of Hollywood. This was almost inevitable. For, collectively, the film makers had already perfected one of the most remarkable publicity machines ever devised. It operated more continuously and efficiently than any assembly line in Detroit. Its products were distributed to the American people through the daily press (Hollywood was news); the Sunday supplements (Hollywood was romance); the magazines of national circulation (Hollywood was success stories and extraordinary personalities); the fan magazines (Hollywood was an Olympus whose gods must have their Homer).

To captivate the public, every story that issued from the citadel of fantasy had to surpass its predecessors. So the Hollywood publicity machine was geared to an interminable crescendo of fireworks. Looking back at the results, in 1949, when the industry had attained a weary, worried maturity, the producer Dore Schary considered them disadvantageous. "Hollywood is a good example of how misunderstood a place can get," he said. "The mental picture of Hollywood is that it is the capital of screwballism, full of actors either chasing other actors' wives or divorcing their own, of maniac directors and goof-off actresses, of writers surveying their swimming pools and muttering about Art. Though the picture is wrong, it is partly Hollywood's own fault that it exists. In the beginning, many years ago, we made it exist because we thought it was good showmanship. We displayed the roaring tigers and the girl with three heads on Main Street, just as the small circus does today. It sold tickets."

But, being designed for mass consumption, this circus-parade legend tacitly observed certain rules of decorum. It exploited idiosyncrasy, and suggested discreet forms of unconventionality. It did not condone impropriety, whisper of immorality, or acknowledge the existence of what the great American public might be supposed to regard as sin. For these were the days before the private morality of President Harding, his Cabinet and his cronies had become a subject of cynical gossip. Impropriety, immorality and sin were beginning to be represented on the screen, but the private lives of those engaged in portraying them were supposed to be innocent of major transgressions. Already, an embattled elder generation had launched an attack on the film makers. Clergymen, reformers, educators and women's clubs throughout the land were angrily protesting against jazz-age pictures that treated sex with the skeptical freedom so reprehensibly being cultivated by American youth. So when some prominent members of Hollywood's elite began behaving as if real life resembled life as portrayed on the screen, a series of scandals aroused widespread indignation.

In 1920, Miss Mary Pickford purchased a home in Nevada and announced her intention of becoming a resident of the state. After the interval required by law, she applied for, and received, a divorce from Owen Moore. Shortly thereafter, she married Douglas Fairbanks in California. This union of the nation's most idolized players aroused criticism only among the most implacably righteous. Though both had dissolved previous marriages, divorce was sanctioned by the mores, and thousands of otherwise reputable citizens had passed through the national uncoupling station at Reno without provoking a continental scandal. But clamor filled the land when the Attorney General of Nevada, after the Pickford-Fairbanks wedding, threatened to annul the Pickford-Moore divorce on the ground that Miss Pickford had not been a bona-fide resident of the state. Only cynical Americans concluded, from the fact that this charge was soon quietly dropped, that Nevada's Attorney General had deliberately used two world-famous people as a means of publicizing his state's most profitable industry.

Scarcely had this sensation died down when the unpleasant case of Roscoe Arbuckle erupted in headlines. "Fatty" Arbuckle, who had begun his wage-earning as a plumber's helper, was reputedly being paid a quarter of a million dollars annually as a screen star. His popularity as a comedian was exceeded only by Charles Chaplin and Harold Lloyd; his brand of humor was especially appealing to children. A flamboyant, free-spending type in private life, Arbuckle was apparently given to indulging in what Americans were beginning to call "wild parties." Notoriety first descended on him in the summer of 1921, when the Attorney General of Massachusetts brought action for the removal of one of his subordinates in connection with a "hush fund" put up by certain film magnates who, some years earlier, had honored Arbuckle with a wild party in Boston and its environs. Two months after this unfavorable publicity, Arbuckle went on holiday to San Francisco. In his hotel suite, one evening, he entertained a group of friends. They were joined by two young women, one of whom died the next day under circumstances that suggested mistreatment by Arbuckle. (The cause of death was later asserted to be a chronic illness.) In due course, Arbuckle surrendered to the police; was indicted on a charge of manslaughter; was subsequently found not guilty. Meanwhile, the spinners of yellow journalism extracted from the scandal its last ounce of discreditable suggestion. In the stories of Hollywood that they put out, "Beautiful maidens were ruined, oceans of alcohol were consumed, and hints of the most horrible forms of debauchery were indicated." Though legally cleared of guilt, Arbuckle sank under overwhelming obloquy. His unreleased pictures were scrapped, and he was never permitted to return to the screen.

While the Arbuckle case was still before the public, an English director, William Deane Taylor, was murdered in his Los Angeles bungalow. Investigation by the police broke a story of traffic in narcotics and "dope." In it figured two popular film stars: Miss Mary Miles Minter, said to have been in love with Taylor; Miss Mabel Normand, with whom he was reported to have been in love. It was brought out that Taylor had warned a "dope" peddler to discontinue his visits to the studio, and refrain from selling narcotics to any actresses; the warning had been disregarded, and Taylor thrashed the peddler. Thus, the public learned that addiction to drugs could be added to the list of Hollywood's iniquities, and this fact appeared to be confirmed, shortly afterwards, by the death through "dope" of Wallace Reid, one of the screen's leading stars. Then, in Paris, during a holiday with her husband, Jack Pickford, Miss Olive Thomas committed suicide. A widely admired beauty, Miss Thomas had been translated to screen stardom from the Ziegfeld *Follies*; it appeared that she had taken her life in an access of despondency, as might any anonymous citizen; but this melancholy fact somehow contributed to the public's impression of Hollywood depravity.

When Hollywood scandal ran short, the yellow press proceeded to manufacture it. Ladies of professional unchastity, who had registered as extras in order to evade the California vagrancy law, gave feature writers an opportunity to report that "three beautiful film stars were arrested in a bawdy house" or that "beautiful film star causes shooting affair at wild gin party." As a result, every star, player, director and magnate presently came under public suspicion. The blanket indictment of Hollywood idols was quite as extravagant as the prior undiscriminating adulation.

In an effort to lift itself from public disrepute, the industry resorted to stern measures. Producers hired detectives to investigate the personal lives of their employees. Exhaustive inquisition failed to substantiate charges of widespread immorality and depravity. A few screen players disappeared from the scene; others received warnings to amend their conduct. Studio executives inserted "morals clauses" in their contracts, enabling them to dismiss anyone suspected or accused of dereliction. Central bureaus were established to regulate casting practices; ladies of elastic virtue were excluded from the rolls of extras. In a film entitled *Hollywood*, some fifty stars contributed to a satirical portrait of the city of illusion; its serious motive was to discourage the pilgrimage of aspiring girls, by warning them of their meager chances for employment. After a time, the public conscience of the nation was satisfied, and attack on the morals and manners of Hollywood ceased.

"Good behavior . . . was enforced in general by the merciless lens of the movie camera, which invariably records the tell-tale lines left by vice, bad habits, or even such carelessness as overeating." So wrote Benjamin B. Hampton, one of the earlier historians of the motion-picture industry. "Ambition and business prudence have made the Los Angeles movie colony a class of careful people who hesitate before doing anything that may reduce their earning power." But Hampton did not foresee that the area of conduct requiring prudent hesitation would steadily diminish. Hollywood, which became a major source of changes in the nation's mores, was itself affected by the modifications it inspired. Over the years, the range of permissible deviation available to celluloid deities expanded continuously.

Thus, by the nineteen-forties, domestic scandal, however sensational, no longer ruined a star's career, but was more likely to enhance the star's fame and popularity. So asserted Leo C. Rosten, who had subjected the life of Hollywood to the same kind of sociological study that the Lynds applied to Muncie, Indiana. The practices of Hollywood's brightest luminaries, as reported by the press, suggested only one conclusion. This was that the American middle classes had become skeptical of the moral code which they professed to support. For they actually favored its transgression by their current idols.

They were, for example, romantically thrilled by the costly nuptials of Miss Lana Turner and Robert Topping. Miss Turner, at the age of twenty-seven, was reputedly earning an annual salary of two hundred and twenty-six thousand dollars; she had been married and divorced three times previously. Topping, heir to a tin-plate fortune, had enjoyed an equal diversity of matrimony. The public's pleasure in their widely publicized union was increased by the announcement that Topping's recently detached wife, Miss Arline Judge, also a screen favorite, was about to take her sixth husband. A picture featuring Robert Mitchum, a popular young star, was released while he was serving a jail sentence for indulgence in the forbidden pleasures of marijuana; the picture proved to be an outstanding success. The eccentric antics of Errol Flynn, another current idol, which involved him in legal difficulties with ladies, seemed only to increase his appeal for feminine audiences. And when the nation's most celebrated "pin-up girl," Miss Rita Hayworth, made a prodigally annotated tour of Europe with the son of an Oriental potentate who had neglected to free himself from a prior matrimonial commitment, the caprice did not noticeably diminish that universal effervescence of passion which it was Miss Hayworth's peculiar ability to generate.

All this suggested that the inhabitants of Middletown and Main Street had charged the celestial residents of Hollywood with a ritualistic office. Upon them fell the duty of violating the canons which still, in theory, were regarded as binding upon ordinary mortals. It was their obligation—disguised as a privilege—to provide for anonymous millions the vicarious experience of illicit delights. The way of the transgressor might, indeed, be hard; but who were better fitted to pursue it than the gods themselves? In Hollywood, those who endured temptation with the least resistance seemed most likely to receive the crown of life.

3   Imitation of Life

It was during the nineteen-twenties that the new elite of the movies finally displaced, in the imaginations of the American people, an older elite of industrial wealth. While the palaces of Newport were being abandoned to caretakers, and the mansions of Fifth Avenue were being demolished, social authority passed to Hollywood. Thereafter, it was to exercise a predominant influence on fashion, manners, morals and the complex art of civilized living.

In one ironical respect, the situation of the new arbiters was unlike that of their predecessors. In Newport, and on Fifth Avenue, wealth had been a weapon indispensable to those who fought to win social power. In Hollywood, social prestige was an instrument essential to those determined to win wealth. Mrs. Astor's fortune was not augmented by her acknowledged dominion over "society," although this raised her to eminence in the estimation of the American people, and persuaded them of the infallibility of her dictates. But the fortunes of a great Hollywood star were determined by her ascent in popular prestige. For her, therefore, the exercise of social power—the ability to impose on an infatuated public her preferences in fashion and decor, her decrees concerning manners and the amenities of living—was something more than the satisfaction of personal vanity. It also seemed to be an urgent economic necessity. The lady had conducted social life, not as an art, but as a competitive amateur sport. The Hollywood star usually conducted it, with whatever grace she found possible, as one phase of a professional career.

The obvious financial value of prestige gave Hollywood, like Newport before it, the character of an ornate arena. From the very outset, social life in the new American Olympus assumed the same fiercely competitive cast that it had, a generation earlier, in the Valhalla of the displaced gods. The environs of the celluloid paradise soon began to bristle with architectural rivalries as notable as those of Bellevue Avenue. At the reputed cost of more than one million dollars, the comedian Harold Lloyd erected a memorial to sudden fortune renowned for "its terraces and gardens and cascading fountains, its swimming pool and tennis courts." But when John Barrymore designed his residence— which he afterwards described as a Chinese tenement, a kind of nightmare—he installed no less than three swimming pools. He embellished his modest retreat with furnishings gathered from all over the world, and included among its conveniences a bowling green, skeet range, an English taproom, an elaborate music room and lodgings for twelve servants.

On the gardens, parks and lawns that surrounded two estates, Cecil B. De Mille was reported to have lavished a quarter of a million dollars. In the Beverly Hills residence of Winfield Sheehan, guests were said to dine on golden dishes and drink from golden goblets. Sheehan, originally a reporter attached to police headquarters, in New York City, had recruited William Fox's private militia during the trust gang-wars, had risen to executive administration of the Fox studios, and was married to Maria Jeritza, a former star of grand opera. The exotic personality of Rudolph Valentino achieved expression in "Falcon's Lair," a hilltop den remarkable for its black-painted interior walls and mourning-draped windows. But Miss Lilyan Tashman spectacularly reversed this whim. A recognized authority on matters pertaining to fashion, Miss Tashman ordained an all-white drawing room, and for it imported the first white piano that Hollywood had ever seen. By festooning the arresting object with blue satin ribbon, she "earned a reputation for great chic."

But, however splendid, none of these establishments could vie, in social authority, with those of the feminine rulers whose supremacy everyone acknowledged, and the boundaries of whose respective dominions were subject to dispute only by each other. For the celluloid constellation revolved about twin luminaries, equally though differently majestic, and in Hollywood they occupied positions exactly comparable to those formerly held, at Newport, by Mrs. Astor and Mrs. Stuyvesant Fish. Superior to all professional exigencies, requiring no augmentation of fortune, Miss Mary Pickford and Miss Marion Davies alone were enabled to value power merely as an ornament, and prestige as a personal satisfaction delightful in itself. Uniquely emancipated from the many sordid compulsions to which all lesser divinities were subject, it was scarcely remarkable that they were also uniquely exalted.

With Douglas Fairbanks, Miss Pickford held court at "Pickfair," a massive gray residence set high in the hills, its park and gardens enclosed by great walls. This was Hollywood's most august social tribunal, and its atmosphere suggested the remoteness and exclusiveness traditionally associated with royalty. An invitation to dine at "Pickfair" was an accolade, the local equivalent of a command to Buckingham Palace. It was long believed that Fairbanks' annual trips to Europe were made for the purpose of arranging "Pickfair's" official calendar for the ensuing year, by fixing precise dates for the sojourns of visiting nobility. Entertainment there was stately, formal, quiet in tone. Protocol established a high rank for representatives of literature and the arts, so native as well as foreign celebrities usually described "Pickfair" as their first intellectual oasis in Hollywood's glittering Sahara. As the diversity of her occupations indicated, their hostess possessed resources of energy in excess of the demands of her high station. For Miss Pickford was not content with the fame she had won as an actress, or with the regal role to which this committed her. She went on to acquire mastery of the complexities of finance and business. Still later, after the breakup of her marriage to Fairbanks, she sought another outlet in writing. In addition to a novel, she published two expositions of her personal philosophy, and these were touching because they revealed the degree to which fame and power and prestige had failed to yield personal fulfillment. "Unlike most women," she confessed ruefully in one of them, "I have never been able to work out my intimate problems in private. I have to do it in front of the whole world, for the world knows what is happening to me professionally, domestically and personally almost as soon as I do myself." In Hollywood, the major goal of ambition sometimes turned out to be a major punishment.

Yet, as the career of Miss Marion Davies showed, the compulsion of ambition continued long after its most obvious rewards had been achieved and far exceeded. The power and wealth of

William Randolph Hearst made Miss Davies a screen star; they could not make her a great actress. But Miss Davies indefatigably went on making pictures when neither her prestige nor fortune could possibly be enhanced by any popular acclaim of her talents. On the social life of the Hollywood pantheon she exercised an influence equal to Miss Pickford's, but very different in kind. An invitation to "Pickfair" certified that you had arrived, that your professional achievement placed you among the elect. An invitation to Miss Davies' mansion assured you that, whether you had arrived or not, you were considered socially diverting. For, like Mrs. Fish, though with far greater good nature, Miss Davies conspired to bring about the defeat of dullness. In the process, she managed to create a tradition of entertainment that survived rather as a legend than as a reality. Until the retired radio tycoon, A. Atwater Kent, settled in Hollywood to pyramid its frivolities as he had formerly multiplied industrial units, nobody was able to approximate the precedents set by Miss Davies.

The pillared Georgian mansion which Miss Davies built on the ocean front at Santa Monica probably surpassed, in costliness and splendor, all other Hollywood residences. It furnished an appropriate setting for her inclination to large-scale hospitality. It enabled her to achieve the most populous, spectacular and unconventional social ceremonies that the land of fantasy had witnessed. This establishment contained some ninety rooms, and its exterior paraphernalia included, besides gardens, tennis courts and other commonplace aids to relaxation, two swimming pools. One of these, eighty feet long, and filled with salt water from the disparaged Pacific Ocean a few yards away, was traversed by a marble bridge imported from Italy. The interior of the mansion reflected a cult of the baroque which was likewise exemplified by Hearst's castle at San Simeon. There were three dining rooms, a banquet hall, two bars, an immense drawing room, a private movie theater. Many of these baronial halls had been transported from Europe to be set up, intact, at Santa Monica. The drawing room, an eighteenth-century masterpiece with a ceiling in fourteen-carat gold leaf, came from the Hertfordshire castle of the Earl of Essex. The basement bar was a sixteenth-century taproom from Surrey, complete to the handmade nails and wooden pegs which held together its massive oak walls and floors. The furnishings and decorations, throughout, were worthy of their setting. In its accumulated treasures, the mansion resembled a museum. Such house guests as George Bernard Shaw, Winston Churchill and the Duke of Kent were said to have been greatly impressed by the marvels that surrounded them. But it was not the presence of these eminent visitors that Hollywood found most memorable. It was, rather, the occasion when Miss Davies had "tossed a circus shindig with a merry-go-round on the tennis courts."

Perhaps because nobody else could hope to equal the domiciliary grandeur achieved by Miss Davies, the cult of architectural ostentation presently lapsed. It was superseded by one of costly simplicity. Among Miss Davies' neighbors at Santa Monica were Miss Norma Shearer and her husband, the producer, Irving Thalberg. Their residence was considered a showplace, and it was described, perhaps not too literally, as "a provincial French cottage." But the uses of disciplined austerity as a means of conspicuous display were necessarily limited. In time, therefore, competition in prestige was shifted to other fields of activity.

What Hollywood prestige signified in the non-celluloid world was once innocently illustrated by Miss Shearer, then at the height of her fame. Miss Shearer's social power was evident, for her example had revolutionized the coiffure of American women during a whole season. But it was to receive even more eloquent confirmation. To Miss Elsa Maxwell, she dispatched a telegram of invitation: "Elsa Baby, expecting you on the eleventh." Miss Maxwell was herself a celebrated party-giver, a leader of café society, a seasoned and intrepid collector of celebrities on two continents. In her newspaper column she quoted Miss Shearer's telegram, and made a comment on it. "You haven't lived in vain," Miss Maxwell testified, "if Norma Shearer calls you 'Baby.'" The meaning of failure to achieve prestige, or its loss, was probably clearer to Hollywood itself than to the outside world. The movie colony could scarcely fail to notice the loneliness, in mid-career, of Miss Clara Bow; it was said that night after night she sat in her kitchen, playing poker with her cook, maid and secretary. Everyone understood the situation described by an elderly, but still reasonably successful actor who, returning from his studio on a day when there had been a call for extras, remarked that, "Some of those people used to be my friends." And the plight of Richard Arlen enforced a moral lesson. For twenty-five years, Arlen had been "a big wheel in movietown; then he slid down in a hurry." The cause of his swift descent was the fact that he had acted in "B" pictures. This, he discovered, was "the kiss of death"; thereafter no producer thought him worthy of stardom in an "A" picture. Following three years of unemployment, Arlen finally received a small part in an "A" picture—and accepted it, gratefully. For it indicated a very slight revival of his collapsed prestige.

Fame and income were the major determinants of social standing in Hollywood, and since both were subject to sudden and spectacular fluctuations, it followed that the social scene exhibited both a greater instability and a narrower stratification than anywhere else. The ultimate criterion of success was financial, but the standard of actual success could not be fixed. In a community where it was possible to earn more than three hundred thousand dollars a year, not even the person who made it was impressed by an income of fifty thousand. Yet the actor or actress who made more than three hundred thousand dollars one year might conceivably find difficulty in securing any contract for the following one. These conditions accounted for some of the more characteristic phenomena of the Hollywood social scene. "After years of listening we can tell the calibre of our callers by how many times they have to shift gears on our hill inside the yard," Will Rogers wrote humorously. "When they make it on high without a shift, we go to the door. On a one-shift noise, we let the maids go—I mean the maid. And on a complete stall, why, everybody ducks and no one is at home."

But the principle thus jocularly stated was seriously applied. At the apex of the Hollywood social pyramid, according to William C. De Mille, were a group of six or eight overlords; they virtually determined who should or should not work in pictures. Attendance at their Sunday cocktail parties—"where nothing is talked but shop and nothing is played but cards" was obligatory, and their stories found "an appreciation seldom accorded to other illustrious raconteurs." Reigning hostesses selected their guests with respect to current financial ratings. The presence of a slipping reputation or a failure would prove embarrassing to everyone. For actors and actresses were known by the company they kept; they moved only with those of approximately the same income level; to associate with people in a lower financial bracket would inevitably result in loss of prestige. Essentially, snobbery was a form of professional self-protection. After the premiere of *A Woman of Paris*, in which he was featured for the first time, Adolphe Menjou, as he left the theater, saw Harold Lloyd seated in his car, and received a smile of congratulation. "It was one of the big thrills of my life," he recalled in his autobiography, twenty-five years later, "for I was not intimately acquainted with Lloyd, and this recognition from one of Hollywood's great stars meant that Menjou had arrived." Even in the community's favored public restaurants and nightclubs, the stern rule of financial rating was applied to the seating of professional guests, and an experienced observer, glancing at the crowd assembled in a fashionable luncheon rendezvous, could accurately gauge the degree of prestige attaching—on that particular day—to anyone present; it was almost mathematically expressed in terms of distance from the most valued location.

As a means of inflating prestige, Hollywood stars did not disdain the exploitation of idiosyncrasy, or even mere caprice. The process was hazardous, but sometimes yielded extraordinarily favorable results. Thus, in *It Happened One Night*, Clark Gable disrobed; the audience saw that he was not wearing an undershirt. The men's underwear industry soon went into a tailspin, and within a year its business declined by fifty percent. So far as Hollywood was concerned, this regrettable social effect supplied convincing evidence of the star's social power, and its financial implications were obvious. Not equally successful, however, was the venture of a well-known actress. As a birthday gift to her husband, an actor of less effulgent fame, she commissioned an interior decorator to refurbish the stable of his polo ponies. Whatever its charms for the ponies, this generous tribute of connubial affection did not notably advance the status of either donor or recipient. When the beautiful Miss Dolores Del Rio was the screen's most popular *femme fatale*—at the not despicable salary of nine thousand dollars a week—she maintained her prestige by justifying a legend that her rivals found inimitable. She permitted gossip to circulate that, because of her, a duel was to be fought. It was said that she would drink only from a gold chalice, and that this had to be brought to the set whenever she was engaged in making a picture. Her exquisite complexion was attributed to a favorite salad of rose petals and orchid leaves. On her frequent European holidays, she was accompanied by a miniature menagerie that included a Russian wolfhound, a German dachshund, an English pointer, an Irish setter and a St. Bernard. Besides all this, Miss Del Rio arrested attention by the elegance and individuality of her attire and jewels. The consequences of so much earnest effort inspired high respect for her professional sagacity.

Casual improvisation, however, sometimes produced equally notable results. At the "premiere" of a new picture, Mrs. Darryl Zanuck appeared in high-heeled white sandals, a light summer frock, and a white fox cape. This ensemble drew a public reproof from Mrs. Emily Post, authority on etiquette, who took a dim view of Hollywood's influence on decorum. Mrs. Post's acid comments provoked a reply by Miss Constance Bennett who published, in *Liberty*, an eloquent defense of Hollywood's independence in rejecting the manners cultivated by New York's inelastic inner circle. In the course of her article, Miss Bennett pointed out that summer nights in California were often chilly, and that Mrs. Zanuck's furs, far from being an example of "distressing unsuitability" as Mrs. Post declared, were merely a sensible precaution. This journalistic feud, which reached millions of readers, was apparently without effect on either combatant. Nevertheless, it precipitated a nation-wide vogue for "summer furs" that alarmed husbands, astonished the trappers of the far north, and certainly would have elevated Mrs. Zanuck to a higher pedestal in Hollywood's pantheon had she not already occupied one of the very highest that it contained. For to Hollywood, the exercise of social power by remote control was never without economic significance. Everyone recalled how Miss Marlene Dietrich's repute had been reinvigorated when her new addiction to slacks persuaded American women of all ages and sizes to adopt them. Still later, everyone was impressed by the new distinction that came to Miss Veronica Lake when the United States officially took cognizance of her hairdo. Miss Lake habitually wore her hair very long over one eye, and Federal authorities invited her, at the outset of the Second World War, to change her coiffure, lest imitation by girls working in defense plants lead to widespread accidents. Miss Lake immediately complied; the inconvenience, if any, was, so to speak, its own compensation.

According to their temperaments, Americans read about Hollywood parties either with envy or exasperation. "You don't give parties to enjoy yourselves, but to advance yourselves," a young bachelor had remarked, in the heyday of Newport's glory. In Hollywood, this was an observation which nobody troubled to make; since everyone knew it to be true, common decency suggested that the unsavory truth be ignored, so far as possible. The obligation to pretend that hospitality was spontaneous, and without other motive than pleasure; and the equal obligation to pretend that enjoyment was genuine, and that acceptance implied no more than its anticipation—these could be discharged with greater grace in Hollywood than elsewhere; to simulate, convincingly, emotions that one did not feel was the vocation of nearly everyone concerned. Yet, occasionally, the exquisite mask of delight slipped, and a brief glimpse of the naked truth disconcerted all, as when Miss Bette Davis confessed to an interviewer that she had never drunk liquor before coming to Hollywood, and explained, unguardedly, "I had to do *something* to enjoy those parties." This exposed a reality. No matter how irksome the prospect of attendance, no matter how certain the ennui to be suffered, to decline an invitation from one's peers or superiors was unthinkable. For absence might be attributed to omission or exclusion, and the sensitive register of prestige would begin to fall. Yet who, in the old days, would have declined an invitation to dine with Mrs. Astor?

The most elaborate revels were, for a time, great costume balls such as those periodically offered by Miss Marion Davies, or at a later date by the Basil Rathbones who, according to Leo C. Rosten, had "hacked their way with steely resolve" to leadership of the very smartest circle. As at Newport, far earlier, these were a natural result of narrow social stratification: they furnished an escape for the members of a group who knew each other almost too well to find continuous pleasure in meeting. They likewise had advantages as a business investment for, being the most expensive of festivities, they demonstrated, in the indisputable terms of conspicuous waste, both the income that could afford them and the prestige which this income rated. Less ambitious ceremonies followed the patterns that prevailed in other metropolitan centers: dinner parties, whether large and formal or small and intimate; cocktail parties, entertainments that were "original" according to an established formula for originality that admitted the bizarre but precluded the unconventional. "The Hollywood of today," William C. De Mille reported at the end of the nineteen-thirties, "is popularly supposed to be a community of unconventionality, of individualism and of general personal freedom; just a gay, carefree lot of youngsters having a perpetual good time. But a glance beneath the surfaces of the gaiety soon convinces a careful observer that in Hollywood, as in other places, conformity rules with an iron hand." Actually, it was scarcely necessary to penetrate beneath the surface. Nothing more completely revealed the rule of conformity than the nature of the gaiety that was designed to alleviate it.

The showing of new pictures was a standard diversion; all producers had projection equipment in their homes, and some of the less exalted also. Cards, charades and other infantile games were notably popular. In this, Hollywood differed little from Muncie, Indiana, where—so the Lynds found—an evening of bridge was "the supreme hostess technique" because social conversation presented the greater risk of being liable "to run on the rocks of monotony, vacuousness, gossip or outright antagonisms." Bridge, said the Lynds, was a universal social solvent, "an unparalleled device for an urban world that wants to avoid issues, to keep things impersonal, to enjoy people without laying oneself open or committing oneself to them, and to have fun in the process." It was precisely this function that successive game fads served in Hollywood. Conversation, there, ran to shop-talk; not talk about the movies in any of their larger aspects, but about the making of movies. It also ran, coincidentally, to personal gossip, "a disguised and sanctioned form of slander" which provided a socially acceptable outlet for inadmissible envy or frustration.

Hollywood long remembered a party given by Countess Dorothy di Frasso, who impishly scattered dictaphones at strategic points under the furniture in her drawing room. "The upshot was that best friends heard their supposedly best friends commenting caustically on their clothes, boy friends and pecadilloes—all of which was highly amusing to the hostess, but spread social havoc among the hapless victims." Countess di Frasso was not a professional member of the movie colony; she was an illustrious visitor. Miss Louella O. Parsons, who recorded this instance of lamentable social originality, could never persuade herself that the Countess had been deliberately malicious.

The Countess, like many another Hollywood hostess and guest, may only have been bored. Yet did her effortful diversion prove anything not long familiar to everyone? William C. De Mille remarked the evanescence of motion-picture loyalties. In the general competition for personal power and individual advantage it was sometimes unavoidable that, in reaching for a pal's hand, one found that one had the pal by the throat. "After all, business is business; the show must go on," De Mille observed sagely, "and it is part of the higher unselfishness to prevent a friend from being in a position to do us harm and thus cause him to suffer the torture of self-reproach." Miss Constance Bennett summed up the situation, even less obliquely, in a general deduction. Hollywood, she contended, was predisposed to appreciate only persons of influence who might be of professional assistance.

Many of the peculiarities of Hollywood—and not only its notorious partiality for informal attire—stemmed from a primary circumstance of its existence. Actresses reported for work early in the morning wearing the full nocturnal regalia of furs, decolletage and jewels; actors often passed their laborious days in the armor of white tie and tails; and the emotions that they were paid to express were, by most other Americans, considered to be night-time, and not daylight, reactions to experience. If life in Holly-wood had a somewhat topsy-turvy quality, did not this, in part, account for it? And, since so much of the professional activity of the movie colony was a form of pure fabrication, was it any wonder that life in Hollywood often seemed less like life itself than the imitation of it?

Certainly actual life, in the capital of illusion, sometimes had the odd attribute of being more like a movie than any movie ever made. Yet to exaggerate its quality of topsy-turviness, or irrelevance to reality as most Americans understood reality, was easy. For Hollywood also reflected, although with unique inten-sity, many of the conditions that prevailed throughout twentieth-century America. Its preoccupation with material goals and consequent uneasy conscience; its pervasive economic insecurity and wild oscillations of fortune; its incapacity to fix a standard of success that would insure contentment and leave the spirit free for nobler purposes than those conceived by an ambition to win larger income, greater power, and wider prestige—could any American deny their existence in his own community, or fail to recognize them as shaping, to some degree, his personal hopes and fears and actions?

Some years before Hollywood was colonized, Henry Adams had pointed out that "The American wasted money more reck-lessly than anyone ever did before; he spent more to less purpose than any extravagant court aristocracy; he had no sense of relative values and knew not what to do with his money when he got it, except use it to make more, or throw it away." Hollywood had done little to educate Americans in a more socially valuable use of the money to the earning of which they sacrificed so large a proportion of their lives. It had merely emphasized an ancient lesson: that money purchased prestige, and that prestige earned still more money; and that, in these circumstances, conspicuous waste might prove to be a profitable investment. "Riches used in this way are of course indispensable to the man of prestige, but neither he nor anyone else is concerned with the reckoning of possessions, but with the ceremonial roles which he has taken. A 'valuable' family, in native parlance, is always a family which owns permanent fetishes, and a man of importance is one who has undertaken many ceremonial roles." In these sentences, the eminent anthropologist, Dr. Ruth Benedict, was not considering the civilization of Hollywood. Her subject was the culture of the Pueblo Indians of the Southwest.

4 | The Dithermythers

When, in 1936, Pius XI issued a papal encyclical on the subject of motion pictures, the importance of Hollywood to the twentieth-century world was vividly illustrated. Other evidence was not lacking. Nearly four hundred journalists were assigned to report the news of the film capital for the American and foreign press, a number exceeded only by those assigned to Washington and New York City. Yet the copy they turned out did not suffice to appease worldwide curiosity. It was supplemented by twenty-two magazines devoted to motion pictures; in 1948, these had more than six million readers. And in the United States, millions of eager fans turned on their radios to hear, direct from Hollywood, the weekly reports of several noted columnists whose daily budgets of intimate gossip were featured by newspapers throughout the country and abroad.

By the middle of the century two of these columnists had become, in effect, national institutions. On the air, and in the press, they commanded audiences of incredible size. The newspaper columns of Miss Louella O. Parsons were said to reach thirty million people; those of Miss Hedda Hopper, twenty-three million. Clearly, they ranked among the most widely read writers of all time. That they were probably among the most powerful women in the world was less obvious. Their influence on the life and work of Hollywood was subtle, profound and perhaps incalculable. In the metropolis of fantasy they occupied the exalted station—and enjoyed the privileges—of dowager empresses. Without accredited office, they were nevertheless autocrats. Their decrees were respected, their displeasure was feared, and even the greatest personages found it desirable to propitiate them. That they were deadly rivals increased the hazards of rendering an expected and acceptable homage.

Americans who read their columns and listened to their programs on the radio seldom realized that Miss Parsons and Miss Hopper were remarkable social phenomena; that they were, indeed, concentrations of power almost without precedent and certainly without parallel. In part, this power derived from the size of their audiences, which made their diverting specialty indispensable to the industry. In part, it derived from the nature of that specialty, which supposedly enabled them to affect the industry, for better or worse, through its most vulnerable factor. Gossip, as practised by Miss Parsons and Miss Hopper, was big business erected on an ancient local nuisance. They preserved the artless insouciance of the village tattler. But they told the world.

To understand the high value set on their favor, it was necessary only to consider the reasons why they were presumed capable of conferring benefits and inflicting damage. The American motion-picture industry was capitalized at more than two billion, six hundred million dollars. It employed upwards of two hundred thousand people, and its annual payroll exceeded five hundred and thirty-three millions of dollars. In the United States, its products were seen, in eighteen thousand theaters, by an estimated ninety million people every week. In foreign lands, they were shown in some sixty-eight thousand theaters, having an estimated weekly attendance of one hundred and forty-five million people. One peculiarity distinguished this vast economic mechanism from all other industries of comparable magnitude. Its assets of highest worth were human beings—most notably, stars and directors. On these persons, the industry staked its huge investments. And their appeal for the public was largely determined by a single intangible factor: their current prestige. It was precisely at this sensitive point that the power of Miss Parsons and Miss Hopper could be felt most acutely. For they were credited with the ability to create and destroy prestige. It was frequently asserted that they were capable of making or breaking actresses, actors and directors. Whether or not their authority actually extended to these awesome limits was, from a practical point of view, irrelevant. The presumption that it did was quite sufficient to justify anxiety. The permanent benignity of even the most benevolent despot can never be taken for granted. That either Miss Parsons or Miss Hopper could be relied on to remain universally and continuously magnanimous, did not happen to be among Hollywood's favorite illusions.

As public personalities in their own right, almost as colorful, and certainly as rich in idiosyncrasies as any of the stars about whom they chattered, Miss Parsons and Miss Hopper were frequently written about by other journalists. These accounts were usually frivolous in tone, and sometimes patronizing in attitude; they seldom indicated the extraordinary competence of the columnists in their special field. Both were engaged in filling the demand of a vast undifferentiated public for intimate and unusual news of an elite. This demand was probably as old as organized society itself; the village gossip had been a journalist even before the first village newspaper was founded; when the movies became mass entertainment, the village expanded to include the world. The secret of Miss Parsons' and Miss Hopper's outstanding success was their remarkable resemblance to James Boswell. For, like Boswell in respect to Dr. Johnson, they cherished a conviction of the primacy in the universe of Hollywood and whatever went on there. To them, the movies and the people engaged in making movies were central, supremely absorbing subjects of human interest, having an importance that overrode that of wars, catastrophes, political convulsions, or any other competing disturbances in the world's affairs. They both had an implacable appetite for detail, a terrifying microscopic vision, and a genius for divination sometimes regarded as more fertile than accurate. To the fine art of disclosure they both brought such gusto, exuberance and breathless excitement as to leave their public stunned by the impact of revelation rather than concerned about the truth of its content. It was precisely so, and with an identical effect, that the Delphic oracle uttered her mysterious pronouncements.

Miss Parsons, a native of Illinois, had worked for the Essanay company before, in 1914, she inaugurated for the Chicago *Record*

Herald the nation's first movie gossip column. Later appointed press agent for William Randolph Hearst's motion-picture enterprises, she was eventually given the task of turning out a daily Hollywood column for the Hearst press. Plump, dark-haired, hazel-eyed, with "an expression of blank bewilderment that no longer fools anybody," Miss Parsons was described as a damply sentimental woman at heart, for whom her friendships were almost sacred; and it was reported that she once put the number of her friends at three hundred and twelve. But neither her affectionate nature nor her conviviality—she was an indefatigable party-giver and party-goer—blinded her universal Hollywood acquaintance to the fact that she was a determined, resourceful collector of news and gossip which, she insisted, must be given to her alone, and withheld from all other columnists. Since Miss Hopper made the same exaction, Hollywood nominally distributed its "scoops" equally to the two sibyls, and followed the same meticulous protocol in social matters, to the point of carefully seating them, on ceremonial occasions, equidistant from the guest of honor.

In her task of gathering news, Miss Parsons was assisted by a secretary, an assistant reviewer, a young woman reporter who covered the Hollywood restaurants, and a "leg-man" whose function that term adequately described. But the most intimate tid-bits she garnered herself. She composed her columns in the blue-and-maroon study of her Beverly Hills home, working every day from ten in the morning until half-past one, when the day's prose lyric was put on a teletype for distribution to newspapers throughout the world. In the process of composition, Miss Parsons usually talked over three telephones simultaneously; this, she averred, was a talent with her. The victims of her interrogation seldom failed to agree. What escaped Miss Parsons' lively attention could be dismissed as of negligible interest in the field of private life susceptible of public dissemination.

It was an index of her power that Miss Mary Pickford first confided to Miss Parsons the momentous story of her parting from Douglas Fairbanks. This Miss Parsons regarded as the biggest "scoop" she ever received, and the press considered it the biggest story ever to break from Hollywood. With due appreciation of its journalistic value, Miss Parsons kept it, as she said, "exclusively exclusive" by withholding it until the exact hour when the Hearst press could score a world-beat in putting it on the wires. Another index of her power appeared when, in 1934, she launched Hollywood as a broadcasting center with a program called *Hollywood Hotel*. During the three years that she acted as its mistress of ceremonies, she invited Hollywood stars, whose services were reckoned as having a value of two million dollars, to make guest appearances without remuneration. It was reported that only one failed to comply with her request; this rebellious soul was Miss Greta Garbo. But perhaps the most arresting indication of Miss Parsons' power was the alleged rule that her copy could not be edited, altered or corrected. To any other journalist—familiar with the solecisms, vagaries and aberrations of the dithermyther style which was her personal invention—this rule definitely placed her, as a power, beyond competition, perhaps even beyond envy.

Miss Parsons' trademark was the style of her columns; Miss Hopper's was that of her hats, which were as eccentric in their way as her colleague's prose. She was a collector and wearer of weird headgear; on one occasion she suggested to her radio audience that they design and send her some nice, new hats; she received sixty-five thousand. The daughter of Quakers and a native of Pennsylvania, Miss Hopper ran away from home at the age of seventeen to go on the stage, achieved a modest success in musical comedy, entered the movies as an actress in 1915, and became the fifth wife of the celebrated comedian, De Wolfe Hopper. For many years one of the screen's best-dressed actresses, and a successful player of sophisticated roles, she eventually retired and made her debut as a columnist by reporting Hollywood news on a radio program. Two years later, she was put under contract by a newspaper syndicate which advised her, after some study, that her columns were too kindly in their comment on Hollywood personalities, and would fail of success. Miss Hopper managed to subdue her native kindliness. Success followed rapidly.

A handsome, dashing blonde whose personality, appearance and legend fascinated the public, Miss Hopper had acquired an expert sense of showmanship during her long career as an actress.

A "personal appearance tour" which took her barnstorming across the continent turned out to be more successful than those of many stars. In her radio broadcasts, and in her published columns, she made skillful use of a headlong, racy, offhand manner that produced an effect of suspense. She, too, gathered much of her material by telephone; there were said to be five lines in her Beverly Hills home. She maintained an office in Hollywood, with a staff of assistants, and dictated her columns there every morning, sometimes turning out two or three in a few hours. In her quasi-private capacity, Miss Hopper served as one of Hollywood's official hostesses to distinguished visitors, who therefore never failed to view a parade of the colony's brightest luminaries. Her vast erudition in the secret mythology of the film capital, so it was said, exempted her from the necessity, sometimes felt by autocrats, of defining obedience as duty.

The chief competitor of the two sybils, on the air and in print, was Jimmie Fidler, who went to Hollywood after serving an enlistment in the Marine Corps during the First World War. His intention was to become a screen actor, but his success was not notable and he turned to the profession of publicity agent. Like Miss Hopper, he began his career of reporting on the radio, and became a syndicated columnist for newspapers only after he secured a large audience of listeners. No less censorious of the manners and private lives of Hollywood's elite than his two eminent colleagues, Fidler also reserved the use of an additional whiplash: he specialized in the previewing of pictures about to be released, and his critical comments were not invariably productive of pleasure. Another major syndicated columnist, Sidney Skolsky, took a more humorous and ironical view of the follies of Hollywood than most of his colleagues, and devoted his efforts chiefly to scraping away the lacquer of glamor which tradition had applied to the community. But those who swam bravely about in the diamond fishbowl had also to consider the effect of their conduct on a local disciplinarian whose castigation was especially to be feared. The column of Miss Edith Gwynn appeared in the *Hollywood Reporter*, the industry's most authoritative trade paper, and its barbed revelations, because they were designed for intramural rather than nation-wide consumption, held explosive possibilities exceeded by none. Miss Gwynn was quoted as acknowledging that "everything I hear goes in one ear and out the column." This, in a community remarkable for its ability to dispense with acoustical equipment, held implications which nobody could afford to ignore.

Readers of the columnists presumably enjoyed the occasional denigration of their idols; readers of the magazines published for motion picture fans did not. These copiously illustrated, lushly written productions were ruled by the creed of Panglossism and dedicated to the maintenance of a myth. In their pages, Hollywood appeared as an immaculate mirage; all the brothers were valiant, and all the sisters virtuous. The text of the fan magazines bore no discernible relation either to the gossip industriously reported by the major columnists, or to the more sensational items which appeared in the news columns of the nation's press. Every month, the fan magazines offered beguiling studies of love, glamor, wealth, immense prestige, gratifying security and idyllic happiness. Marriage, in these reassuring accounts, resembled perpetual courtship; romance—the prenuptial condition of all stars—was as elegantly stylized as a minuet. Here, treated with excited solemnity, were to be found the chronicles of mutual infatuation that had been painstakingly engineered by studio publicity departments: one set, subjected to realistic analysis by Leo C. Rosten, indicated that during a single year four major male stars had been "engaged in a libidinal round robin" with four equally distinguished female stars employed by the same studio. But readers of fan magazines apparently did not question the authenticity of these transient lyrical excursions; and one editor described them, illuminatingly, as "inverse statements of frustration." Nor did they regard with any dubiety the legend of rags-to-riches which consecrated Hollywood's official faith in the great god Luck. For every fan knew that, scarcely a twelve-month before their sudden Olympian splendor, one star had been an elevator operator in a Chicago department store, another a manicurist, a third a theater-usher and a fourth a saxophone player. Occasionally the great tycoons wondered whether the sustained organ-note of their publicity experts and the fan magazines was not, indeed, being overworked. In 1948, the industry began producing a series of short films intended to dispel the illusion of romance that surrounded its activities, and portray them as a species of hard, serious work.

Very probably such efforts would have little effect on the permanent high temperature of devout fans, whose fever found an outlet in the correspondence columns of the magazines, and in the mail which they addressed to their favorite stars. After reading all the fan mail received during one month at a single studio for one male and one female star, Rosten drew a sobering conclusion. "There is a pronounced desire to make the fantasy of movie experience less of a fantasy and more of a reality," he reported. "There are many efforts to support a conception that the star is a personal friend. Many fans offer elaborate details about their life, family, work and hopes, and urge the star to reciprocate with similar information. A small proportion of the letters are pathological in content and make pathological requests." The socially significant fact, however, was that ninety-six percent of this mail originated with writers less than twenty-one years of age, and fifty-three percent of it came from children under the age of thirteen.

Whether or not the influence of the dithermythers was socially beneficent remained open to question. But that it ran deep into the currents of American life was obvious. Cities competed for the premieres of well-publicized pictures, proclaimed civic holidays on the day of their release, organized festivities for the coincidental visits of their stars. Hordes of autograph hunters beseiged the hotels of stars on personal appearance tours, or merely on holiday. And the frenzied hubbub that surrounded them did not lapse at continental frontiers. For the illusion of Hollywood was a worldwide export. As the year 1949 opened, and the stability of the civilized world was threatened by a cold war between its two major powers, the screen actor Tyrone Power and the film starlet Miss Linda Christian honored the city of Rome with the celebration of their nuptials. According to the august New York Times, which devoted considerable space to a cabled report of the ceremony, thousands of bobby-soxers rushed the police to break into the church, and the solemnities were muffled by the din of a riot in adjacent streets. "Mounted carabineri in full-dress uniforms," the *Times* recorded, "had been out since early morning to handle the crowds and motorized police were obliged to charge battalions of women bent upon gaining admission to the church of Santa Francesca Romana at all costs."

In view of this evidence, who dared question the basic assumption of such eminent authorities as Miss Parsons and Miss Hopper —the final supremacy of Hollywood in the life of the twentieth century?

5   Unquiet City

In general, the myriad disciples of the dithermythers believed Hollywood to be an Arcadia of marble swimming pools, Lucullan feasts, gold-plated station wagons, ubiquitous beauty and universal romance. Certain other Americans had formed different concepts. In his unfinished novel, *The Last Tycoon,* F. Scott Fitzgerald portrayed the film capital as a monstrous, corrupt force, deliberately imposing on American society standards and attitudes that would enable big business to perpetuate its dominion over the national life. A younger novelist, Budd Schulberg, furnished an acid profile of the city in *What Makes Sammy Run?* This set forth the saga of a Hollywood big-shot, and studied the society that yielded him its great rewards. In Sammy, an exponent of jungle ethics, readers were invited to examine "a blueprint of a way of life that was paying dividends in America in the first half of the twentieth century." The darker realities of Arcadia, suggested in these fictional studies, were likewise reflected in *Hollywood,* the sociological study made, under the auspices of the Carnegie and Rockefeller Foundations, by Leo C. Rosten and a staff of investigators.

Americans sometimes forgot that Hollywood was a major national center of industrial production. It was afflicted by the same tensions and conflicts as South Chicago or Detroit. The issues of labor organization and collective bargaining, which produced violent strife in the steel and automobile industries, penetrated to the motion-picture studios. The public was astonished by the spectacle of great stars—recipients of fabulous salaries—joining a labor union, more politely described as a "guild," and threatening an industry-wide strike. It suggested the emergence, in American society, of a new class of millionaire proletarians. But the position of these screen favorites, in relation to the executives for whom they worked, was exactly that of labor to management. Whatever their wages, they were merely hired employees, compelled to sell their services in a market where, as individuals, they stood at a disadvantage. The objectives of greater security, improved working conditions, the curbing of an arbitrary exercise of power by management, and the right to bargain collectively through representatives of their own choosing—these were as significant to workers in the film industry as to those in steel plants, or on automotive assembly lines. And the great stars were merely spearheads for lowlier colleagues. Actors, directors, writers, and other contributors to the making of pictures organized in occupational unions, or guilds, in order to achieve these objectives. In so doing, and for identical protective purposes, they followed the course taken, far earlier, by technicians, mechanics and other specialized workers whose craft unions had won recognition from the industry. The unionization of talent, however, was bitterly opposed by management, and success was not easily attained. The prospects for stable and peaceful industrial relations seemed no more certain in Hollywood than anywhere else in the country.

And Hollywood was not only beset by internal strife. It was likewise perpetually subject to external pressures that sometimes were ominously threatening. The fact that its products reached a world-wide audience brought them under the critical scrutiny of foreign governments, agencies of the United States Government, religious groups, the official spokesmen of various businesses and professions, and other similar organs of collective pressure. Each of these attempted to impose on the making of pictures an obedience to its own special purposes. (Glass-blowers protested the showing of canned beer; can manufacturers objected to emphasis on bottled beverages; the Newspaper Guild was aggrieved by the types of reporter represented on the screen; public carriers wanted all forms of accident avoided, as destructive of public

ABOVE: Clara Bow in *Man Trap*

BELOW:

Cecil B. De Mille Takes *The Squaw Man* Company out on Location

ABOVE AND AT RIGHT: Hollywood Before and After

LEFT:
Lasky, Zukor, Goldwyn, De Mille and Kauffmann

BELOW: The Inspired Architecture of Hollywood

RIGHT:
    Marion Davies' Ninety-
Room Home on the Beach

BELOW: Marlene Dietrich
        Starts the Day

BELOW: Charles Laughton and
        Hedda Hopper

RIGHT: Arrest on the Picket Line

BELOW AT RIGHT:
"A Stately Pleasure-Dome." The
Paramount Theatre, New York

OPPOSITE PAGE:
ABOVE: It Was Pictures Like This
       That Led to Censorship

BELOW:
Cleopatra — Played by Claudette
Colbert — Is Immortalized by
              Cecil B. De Mille

TOP: Fanny Brice in the Vitaphone Talking Picture, *My Man*

CENTER: Gloria Swanson and
Elinor Glyn

RIGHT: Gloria Swanson and Her
Husband, the Marquis

LEFT: Charlie Chaplin in
                Modern Times

CENTER:
        The First Animated Cartoon
Made by J. Stuart Blackton in 1906

BELOW: *The River:*
        A Documentary of 1937

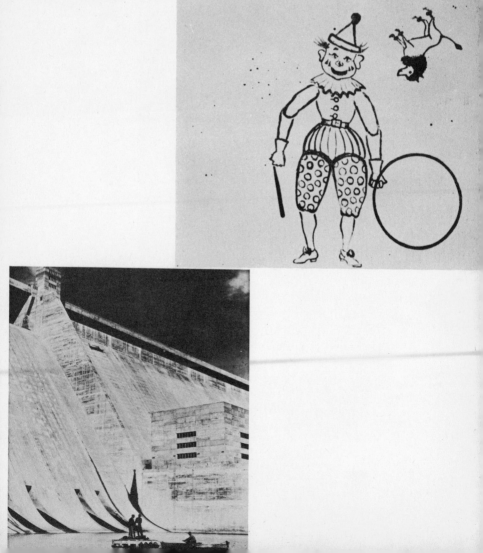

A Modern Studio

confidence; the National Billiard Association demanded that the showing of low-grade pool rooms be discontinued.)

In the foreign field, the industry was especially vulnerable, because a large proportion of its profits was derived from markets abroad. It was heavily penalized for its success. The fact that audiences abroad preferred American pictures to those made by their own producers led certain countries to impose quotas on the importation of American films. So the products of Hollywood became a major concern of American diplomacy. But commercial restrictions were not the only form of pressure exercised from abroad. Through the threat of boycott, by way of reprisal, foreign nations were able to apply a powerful censorship to the content of American pictures. The most spectacular instance of this censorship occurred when plans for the production of Sinclair Lewis's anti-Fascist novel, *It Can't Happen Here,* were abandoned lest the picture give offense to Adolf Hitler and Benito Mussolini.

Equally, the objectives of American foreign policy operated as a form of pressure on Hollywood. At the end of the Second World War, the State Department embarked upon an effort to spread the gospel of democracy in Europe through fair and honest presentation of the American way of life. In these circumstances it was determined not to release abroad such films as *The Grapes of Wrath* and *Tobacco Road,* because they "might be used as propaganda against the United States." These pictures, dealing with dispossessed segments of the nation's population, would inevitably give foreign spectators a distorted concept of American society, and thus embarrass operations of the State Department. But, could Hollywood, without retreating into pure escapism, concern itself exclusively with the romantic idealization of American life?

That powerful official groups in the United States were bent upon imposing their will on Hollywood became clear during, and after, the Second World War. The production of certain anti-Fascist pictures, before Pearl Harbor, led to a Senate investigation of alleged "war propaganda disseminated by the motion-picture industry." The industry invited Wendell Willkie to represent it at the senatorial hearings, and Willkie made a ringing assertion of

the right of the industry to freedom of expression, a right fundamental to a medium of mass communication. Even earlier, Martin
Dies, chairman of the House un-American Activities Committee, had made sensational charges that American films were being
made a vehicle for Communist propaganda. Dies failed to substantiate these charges, but they were revived, after the war, by J.
Parnell Thomas, then head of the committee, and a series of
hearings were held which rocked the nation with controversy.

These events indicated the degree to which Hollywood could
be made a convenient scapegoat for the purposes of political
pressure groups within the United States. It was permanently
exposed to sensational attack, and the crusades of politicians like
Dies and Thomas need never be substantiated by proof; their
purpose was served by publicity. In these circumstances, it appeared likely that Hollywood—traditionally cautious in its treatment of controversial social problems—would be tempted to
retreat further into a policy of abstention. The immensity of its
economic stakes made it peculiarly accessible to rule by fear. But
if it accepted the rule of fear, it would merely fail to discharge its
obligations—as the possessor of a medium of mass communication
—to those functions of public information and enlightenment
which, in a democratic society, it should be expected to serve.
Freedom of expression for the screen, in terms comparable to that
of the press and radio, had always been in jeopardy, and seemed
likely to remain so.

At the middle of the century, Hollywood bore little resemblance to Arcadia. It seemed rather like a citadel under siege,
bereft of the sense of security, anxiously on the defensive, un-
certain of its future. It had the look of an unquiet city.

CHAPTER V

We Have Changed All That

1 While Fashion's Brightest Arts Decoy

In the year 1920, the operations of a diminutive, slim Italian in the city of Boston, Massachusetts, heralded a new era in American life. An ex-convict, a former laborer, clerk, fruit peddler and waiter, he had set himself up as an importer when visions of grandeur came to him at his offices in School Street. His altruism was extreme. For he offered to make anyone and everyone rich; if not overnight, within a few weeks. Who could resist investment, with a guaranteed return of fifty percent in forty-five days? Many did not. So presently the cry of Charles Ponzi rang over the land: "Double your money in ninety days."

This benefactor of humanity, so he declared, had found an infallible formula for the spontaneous generation of wealth. By using international postal reply coupons to engage in large-scale transactions in foreign exchange, he could make Americans rich, and nobody the poorer. Money flowed in on him so torrentially that it couldn't be banked quickly enough. Day after day, the cash-boxes in his offices were stuffed with currency, then the drawers of the desks, finally the waste-baskets, until these in turn overflowed onto the floor. Businessmen, farmers, laborers, widows, the aged, the very young—they all sent him their savings: fifteen millions of dollars within a few months. Crowds cheered Ponzi in the streets of Boston. And, for a while, he paid off as promised. Then the iridescent bubble burst. Ponzi had been using incoming funds to pay off earlier investors, merely robbing Peter to pay Paul. But his scheme prefigured the shape of things to come. For this was the era of Harding and high living; prohibition and pleasure; sex and the saxophone. It was the age of beautiful nonsense, of the long, lovely, swelling boom that was never going to come to an end. This was normalcy.

The visions that had tormented the Boston fruit peddler and his credulous client soon began swarming across the nation's screens. For it was obvious that the proper uses of the new prosperity required an informed expounder. Now that Americans were at last free to pursue happiness, should they not be furnished with an image of their quarry? The age demanded a qualified arbiter and pundit. Hollywood provided him, in the person of Cecil Blount De Mille. Nearing his fortieth year, stocky, bald, pugnacious, and every inch a showman, De Mille became almost as widely known for his idiosyncrasies as his films. He was the first director to use a megaphone and, still later, a loudspeaker. His predilection for shirts that were open at the throat initiated a Hollywood vogue that was to spread across the nation and endure for three decades. On the set, he always wore puttees; they had been indispensable when, a few years earlier, he was shooting pictures in the desert. But his fad established them as insignia of rank; and his brother, William C. De Mille, later was moved to wonder whether Hollywood's veneration of directorial puttees did not emphasize the wrong end of all directors.

In a sense, De Mille could be reckoned as the Ward McAllister of the times; the self-appointed mentor of anxious wealth, inviting instruction in an appropriate way of life, and—to enjoy this fully—requiring assurance that it was, beyond doubt, in the highest degree superlative. McAllister, the paunchy, pompous cousin of Julia Ward Howe, had been the accredited chamberlain of Mrs. William Astor; the autocrat of drawing rooms in New York and Newport; but he had limited his school of the more perfect life to an enrollment of four hundred carefully chosen novices. In a period of lambrequins, fringe and gilt, he had applied to social amenities all the decorative exuberance of a Victorian upholsterer. De Mille's classes could be estimated only in millions. His registration far exceeded the wildest dreams that afflicted any correspondence school. Yet his function was precisely that of the forgotten McAllister, and his methods were almost identical.

The cornucopia of plenty, tilting over the nation during the World War, had balanced at a novel angle and for a decade would pour its paper-golden stream over most Americans. There was a sudden dissatisfaction with old ways of conducting existence. The accent was now on youth, and the bobbed-haired, short-skirted flapper, with her male partner, the raccoon-coated sheik, led the national pilgrimage to an improbable holy city. Women had stopped buying cotton underclothes. Salesgirls, stenographers and factory workers were adopting the silk lingerie and stockings previously monopolized by the rich. In five years, the number of automobile owners nearly doubled, rising from eight to more than fifteen million. New resorts, country clubs, night spots, real-estate developments were springing up everywhere, and luxuries were in demand throughout the country. Women of the protected classes were turning to careers outside the home. As a result, the bungalow and kitchenette flat became popular. Delicatessen stores were the major source of urban home-cooking. But people in cities dined out, and when they didn't go to a favorite "speak," you might find them in restaurants whose signs flaunted the comforting assurance that "Mom's in the Kitchen." Most other Mamas were likely to be red-hot. In 1914, only one couple of every ten dissolved their union by divorce; fifteen years later, the rate had reached one of every six. The old social order—at its inaccessible peak, rigid, exclusive and aristocratic—was speedily crumbling. There was, everywhere, an intense curiosity about wealth, about the manner of life cultivated by the rich, about all the things that money could buy. There was a widespread interest in etiquette, social amenities, the standards of fashion, beauty, diversion of the non-existent Medici whom Americans thought they admired. And there flourished an immense, insatiable, largely ungratified pre-occupation with sex. A democracy that had suddenly achieved prosperity without precedent, a prosperity that surpassed hope and challenged belief, was asking for a pattern to follow.

In the films that were to make him famous, De Mille provided instruction as well as delight; he taught by pleasing. His themes were two—money, its uses and by-products; and sex. His formula was to avoid life in the raw, and to serve it *sous cloche*, piping hot, stewed in the most costly butter and sauced in the richest cream. The United States portrayed in his pictures was the America of the future as his audience wished to conceive it. De Mille's America was a society surfeited with luxuries, domiciled in exotic surroundings, equipped with a morality more flexible than rubber, to which boredom was a sin, excitement a necessity, and romance —in the guise of a perpetual search for the embodiments of "it" (a manifold unity deduced by Mrs. Elinor Glyn)—the favorite avocation of both sexes.

For, as De Mille reminded his fellow-citizens, "the ruined woman is as out of style as the Victorian who used to faint." He saw to it that the indestructible woman who presided over his brave new world enjoyed suitable surroundings. Her bathroom ceased to be a purely functional utility. In eleven of his pictures, De Mille transformed it into a place of esthetic resort, with settings that established fresh standards for American domestic architecture. De Mille also converted her bedroom into a boudoir, divorcing it from familiar and literal associations with sleep. Largely because of him, the verb itself, as used by Americans, shed all suggestions of dormancy, and took on enchantingly active implications. The De Mille boudoir became a chapel for the celebration of rites authorized by custom, but still accounted irregular by the law and the church. The De Mille heroine always had a sumptuous drawing room. Its principal use was as a way-station for the performance of devotions that were preliminary, propitiatory and pleasant. To encourage the shy, and accelerate the masterful male, it sometimes contained an absolute novelty: a portable bar.

While redesigning the American home, De Mille did not neglect the attire of its mistress. Not only did he introduce new fashions; he revolutionized their diffusion. Previously, the fashion shows of Paris and New York had been restricted to the elect, and strict controls withheld their novelties from the popular market until after they had ceased to be new. But De Mille changed all that. Invading the citadels of privilege, he lured to the Paramount studios eminent creators of style, renowned bootmakers, coiffeurs, milliners; a staff of accredited experts able to produce the lingerie, frocks, hats, furs, slippers and accessories formerly available only to the very wealthy. Then, he incorporated the fashion show into his photoplays, using his most attractive actresses as models. Under his dispensation, the woman on Main Street needed only to go to her local picture house to see displays far more elaborate than those offered on the Rue de la Paix, or Fifty-seventh Street, and equally authentic. De Mille thus made Hollywood a new source of fashion; and, since the screen could promulgate its dictates quickly, Hollywood was soon influencing the attire of women throughout the world.

For his demonstrations of the new decorum, De Mille chose titles as provocative as the views of life that they dispensed: *Don't Change Your Husband, Why Change Your Wife?, Male and Female, Forbidden Fruit, Saturday Night, The Golden Bed,* were typical. They were persuasive lessons in morals, aspirations, decor and deportment, showing Americans not only what they ought to want, but how to go about getting everything that was coming to them. They left unrepresented only the economic foundation, and final achievement, of the purposes they illustrated—and audiences, fortunately, could take the one for granted while dreaming about the other. All of De Mille's pictures professed to deal with "problems." But whatever the nature of their issues, these superheated dramas encouraged a hopeful conclusion about the national life. No impassable social and economic abyss separated the jerry-built suburban bungalow, or kitchenette flat, from the opulent Park Avenue penthouse. Here today, and there tomorrow; while riding the breathtaking escalator of fortune, two events were almost certain to occur. The little woman would meet her soul-mate, a man capable of understanding and fulfilling her need for love; and he would remarkably resemble Thomas Meighan. The man, meanwhile, would come upon a lively counterfeit of Miss Gloria Swanson, willing to undertake his further education and perhaps even the manicuring of his soul. She would be seductive, worldly-wise and a trifle disillusioned, dashing, and very costly. She was bound to be "leading her own life" under the dual inspirations of her impetuous heart and cool, practical mind. She would be a creature all platinum and pearls—a perennial invitation, an indefatigable torch-bearer of advancing culture. Such were the phantoms that rose on the horizons of American hope.

That De Mille's gospel profoundly impressed his countrymen was evident, not only from the extraordinary popularity of his pictures, but from their widespread imitation by other studios. But nothing more clearly revealed its impact on the American mind and heart than the fortunes of a rival gospel: that of Miss Mary Pickford. After joining the United Artists constellation in 1919, Miss Pickford, now her own producer, was free to indulge her old desire to play mature roles. She soon undertook one in *Dorothy Vernon*, a costume romance founded on an old novel by Charles Major. The picture "didn't click" with audiences. Was this only because her adorers refused to permit her to grow up? She had made herself a symbol of eternal youth; her admirers felt, when they saw her playing adult roles, that they too were advancing in years, and they resented the implied accusation of middle age: this was one explanation of Miss Pickford's waning popularity. Yet, how could the innocent idealism of Mary Pickford's philosophy compete with the doctrine of bigger-and-betterism so persuasively set forth by De Mille? She herself lamented its inadequacy to the times. "In the epidemic of hair-cutting that has swept the country, I am one of the few who have escaped," she wrote, in 1927, in the *Pictorial Review*. "It has been a hard-fought battle, and the problem has occupied many of my waking and sleeping hours. I say 'sleeping' because it often intrudes itself into my dreams. . . . Sometimes it is a dreadful nightmare, when I feel the cold shears at the back of my neck, and see my curls fall one by one at my feet, useless, lifeless things to be packed away in tissue paper with other outworn treasures. . . . My curls have become so identified with me that they have almost become a trade-mark . . . a symbol, and I think that shorn of them I should become almost as Samson after his unfortunate meeting with Delilah. . . ." But, with an ironical fitness, Miss Pickford submitted to the shears in the first year of the Great Depression. And when she played *Coquette* and *Kiki*—two girls who were anything but nice—it became obvious that the gospel of Pollyanna had gone down to final defeat, that the victory of sex-à-la-mode was complete.

De Mille, meanwhile, had been considering the eventual salvation of his countrymen. After his secular evangels had been widely imitated, he made *The Ten Commandments*, which prefaced a contemporary story with a screen version of the Book of Exodus. During the filming of this spectacle, Theodore Roberts and James Neil, in Biblical costume and makeup, waited for a promised conference with De Mille. Finally overcome by exhaustion, they sent him a message: "Just say that Moses and Aaron are waiting to see God." Perhaps it was a memory of this levity that made De Mille draw up, for all players in *The King of Kings* —a celluloid equivalent of Bruce Barton's *The Man Nobody Knows*—one of the most remarkable contracts ever issued in Hollywood. Under its provisions, the players guaranteed that their conduct in private life would be exemplary during the filming of the picture, and for one year after its release. As William C. De Mille afterwards explained, "It would never do to have the Virgin Mary getting a divorce, or St. John cutting up in a nightclub."

At the middle of the century, Cecil B. De Mille was still an active force in Hollywood. For thirty years he had exercised a powerful influence on the making of motion pictures, and so, on the thoughts, hopes and habits of Americans. One lesson he had deeply impressed on both Hollywood and the nation. It was illustrated in an anecdote about Samuel Goldwyn told by the columnist Earl Wilson. In 1949, the Italian director Roberto Rossellini visited Hollywood. Rossellini had made, with amateur actors, at little expense, stark and tragic pictures of post-war life in Italy which, when released in the United States, were widely acclaimed. They proved also to be highly profitable, and Goldwyn —according to Wilson—asked Rossellini to explain his secret. "It's simplicity," said the Italian director. "I don't use Big Names, I don't use lights. I don't use makeup. I don't use scenery." But Goldwyn had a question. "What's new about that? I did that forty years ago, when I was broke."

The obligation to lavishness, the avoidance of simplicity, were one of the major contributions of Cecil B. De Mille. He taught Hollywood, and the nation, how not to feel poor.

2   The Object All Sublime

The overwhelming popular success of De Mille's pictures inspired Hollywood to produce a cycle of "society dramas." Many of these showed little respect for the institution of marriage; most of them examined sex from viewpoints notably lacking in solemnity. Two German directors brought to the American screen a European sophistication that made light of traditional native taboos. Erich von Stroheim's *Blind Husbands, The Devil's Passkey* and *Foolish Wives* were cynical in their treatment of the ancient sanctities. Ernest Lubitsch's *Kiss Me Again, Forbidden Paradise* and *The Marriage Circle* reported indulgently on the casual infidelities of the socially elect. Presently, one picture bluntly inquired, *Is Matrimony a Failure?* Another pertinently asked, *Why Be Good?* Americans who wished to consult the oracles of Hollywood on these topics received further information in such films as *Mad Love, Flaming Youth, The Beautiful and Damned.*

During the year 1925, the sociologists Robert S. Lynd and Helen Merrell Lynd studied the culture of Muncie, Indiana. In *Middletown*, they made public certain facts about the movies in that city. There were nine picture theaters which, during one month, drew an attendance approximately four and one half times as large as the total population. During one week, films entitled *The Daring Years, Sinners in Silk, Women Who Give* and *The Price She Paid* competed for public attention. They quoted a press account of the Sunday first showing of a new picture: "Sheiks and their 'shebas' . . . sat without a movement or a whisper through the presentation. . . . It was a real exhibition of love-making and the youths and maidens . . . who thought they knew something about the art found that they still had a great deal to learn." And no wonder. For, as the Lynds remarked, quoting the advertisement of a locally featured film, this was a culture dealing with "the things you've always wanted to do and never dared."

But Hollywood's transvaluation of values assumed to be eternal did not meet with universal approval. Clergymen, educators, clubwomen and reformers joined in a savage attack which thoroughly frightened the film magnates. Resolutions condemning sinfulness and immorality in pictures were passed by the Southern Baptist Conference, the Central Conference of American Rabbis, Roman Catholic, Episcopalian, Methodist and Christian Endeavor organizations, and the General Federation of Women's Clubs. One hundred bills providing for the censorship of pictures were introduced in the legislatures of thirty-seven states during the year 1921, and were defeated in thirty-three.

In December of that year, two representatives of the film industry journeyed to Washington as envoys to Will H. Hays, chairman of the Republican National Committee which had conducted Senator Warren G. Harding's successful campaign for the presidency, and subsequently Postmaster General in Harding's cabinet. The film magnates invited Hayes to become "leader of the industry" at an annual salary of one hundred thousand dollars. Hays afterwards related that on Christmas morning, while his son and two nephews were putting on cowboy suits which they had found beneath the tree, he overheard an argument about which one of them, in an ensuing game, was to represent Bill Hart, the popular cowboy star. At that moment, he recalled the familiar words, "Out of the mouths of babes and sucklings . . ." Was not the proffered post a challenge, a duty? Describing this touching scene nearly a quarter of a century later, Raymond Moley observed that, "Tears still come to his eyes when he tells that he stood up, then, in the shadow of the Christmas tree, and silently repeated the vow of St. Paul: 'And this I do.'" Indeed, Hays did so well as president of the Motion Picture Producers and Distributors of America that his salary was later increased by fifty percent.

Hays took office as czar, or overlord, of the motion-picture industry in January, 1922, and remained in office for twenty-three years, eventually being succeeded by Eric Johnston, former president of the United States Chamber of Commerce. Small, wiry, intensely energetic, Hays was a favorite subject for caricaturists because of his pronouncedly large ears and his three-inch-high stiffly starched collars. But journalists who had closely followed his career rated him as a genius in practical politics. As a young Indiana lawyer, he had become party chairman of his county, then of the state. At the age of thirty-eight, national chairman of the Republican Party, he had been largely responsible both for its financial prosperity and its electoral victory. In *Washington Close-Ups*, the journalist Edward G. Lowry described Hays as "an articulate emotionalist if ever there was one; a politician to his fingertips and a strong josher; a real handshaker and elbow-massager." His friend Raymond Moley, when writing the history of Hays' overlordship, remarked that, "Even back in 1922, Hays always had carrots in his pocket for the donkey." This facility in vegetable suasion was reinforced by an aptitude for the kind of rhetoric which, by many of his countrymen, was accounted a unique index of profound truth. "We must have toward that sacred thing, the mind of a child," Hays declared shortly after taking office, "toward that clean and virgin thing, that unmarked slate—we must have toward that the same sense of responsibility, the same care about the impressions made upon it, that the best teacher or the best clergyman, the most inspired teacher of youth would have." Who, indeed, could ask more of Hollywood than this?

The organization over which Hays presided—soon popularly known as "the Hays office"—was, in function, a trade association.

Its announced major objects were four. It wished to insure, for the industry, freedom "from the deadening hand of governmental interference through political censorship." In order to achieve this freedom, it proposed to establish an increasing measure of self-regulation by the industry. In the public, it wished to arouse increased interest and understanding that would ultimately result in a rising level of taste for better pictures. And, within the industry, it hoped to bring about improved relations among producing companies, and between the great groups of producers, distributors and exhibitors.

In 1930, Hays secured the technical adoption, by producers holding membership in his organization, of a "production code" designed to govern the morals of motion pictures. This code had been drafted by Martin Quigley, publisher of motion picture trade papers and magazines, and the Reverend Daniel J. Lord, S. J., professor of dramatics at the University of St. Louis. It set forth certain fundamental principles to be followed, and a series of specific prohibitions to be observed, in the making of motion pictures. Members of the Motion Picture Producers and Distributors of America were pledged to obedience to this code. But, since no practicable method of enforcing its provisions had been devised, it remained largely inoperative.

Meanwhile, the movies were being coldly scrutinized by a group of academic experts in social studies. Under the auspices of The Payne Fund, these educators had organized the Motion Picture Research Council, and had set up a program of investigation. It was estimated that some thirty million boys and girls under the age of twenty-one visited the nation's movie houses every week. The kind of nurture that they were receiving seemed, to the professors of sociology, education and related subjects, a matter of grave social importance. The studies which they undertook were intended to analyze the content of motion pictures and determine, so far as possible, the nature of their influence on youth.

Publication of the Payne Fund Studies began in 1933; the factual findings and general conclusions which they reported were widely publicized and provoked resentment in large segments of the population. Statistical analysis indicated that crime, sex and love (the distinction, in itself, appeared to be significant) furnished the themes of nearly three-quarters of the pictures being exhibited. These pictures placed a disproportionate emphasis on the lives and environment of ultra-wealthy, leisured social groups. The privileged folk who figured in them were represented as leading a violent existence; some four hundred and fifty crimes were either committed or attempted in the pictures. Their goals in life were predominantly selfish; only nine percent were actuated by motives likely to benefit society at large. Statistical calculation indicated that winning another's love was a major preoccupation of seventy percent of the characters. Yet marriage for love was the ambition of only slightly more than one-third. So far as youth was concerned, the Payne Fund investigators concluded that the patterns of conduct offered for emulation by the movies tended mainly to encourage anti-social behavior.

To reply to the challenge of the Payne Fund Studies, the motion-picture industry chose Raymond Moley, former professor of public law at Columbia University, and one of President Franklin D. Roosevelt's early advisers. Moley's book, *Are We Movie-Made?* was based, as he acknowledged, on *Art and Prudence*, a philosophical study by Mortimer Adler. As a result the movie-makers of Hollywood were in the peculiar position of finally relying, for their defence, on a medieval saint of whom probably not many of them had ever heard. For Adler, professor of the philosophy of law at Chicago University, had based his book on the teachings of the French Catholic philosopher, Jacques Maritain, and these were derived from the works of St. Thomas Aquinas. Adler and Moley asserted that the Payne Fund Studies were of no practical value, since "The findings of social science are no better than the common opinions of men about the same matter." Scientific research was not capable of establishing any real connection between conduct as represented in the movies, and conduct as practised in everyday life. The ideal to be followed by movie-makers was "the general subordination of the popular arts to prudence"—an ideal which Moley contended could be best realized by entrusting the supervision of motion pictures to those charged with administration of the production code, who could secure the co-operation of representatives of the churches, schools, and welfare agencies. "All of this," Moley urged, "results in a pooling of private efforts in a constructive way—a method vastly superior in effectiveness to the efforts of government through censorship or other forms of repressive action."

To William C. De Mille, however, this theoretical discussion appeared to ignore a practical situation faced by makers of movies. After a successful career as a playwright, he had spent twenty years in Hollywood writing and directing photoplays, and he asserted that the American people, when buying their tickets for the movies, were paying for enjoyment, not for mental and spiritual benefit. "If a show is only moral and cultural, educational and artistic," he declared, "the mass of our fellow citizens will treat it as though it were rat poison. If it is entertaining, they will throng to it though it may lack all other virtues. The function of the stage and screen alike is first, last and all the time, to entertain. Educational and artistic values are unobjectionable, but not at all fundamental or even necessary." Whether or not De Mille correctly interpreted the will of the American people, he seemed to speak accurately for Hollywood's understanding of it.

It was not discussion, but action in the form of a threatened boycott, that led the Motion Picture Producers and Distributors of America to impose a measure of self-regulation on the industry. In 1934, the bishops of the Roman Catholic Church organized a nation-wide Legion of Decency for the purpose of protecting members of their communion, especially children, against the influence of "immoral" pictures. Those who joined the Legion were required to pledge their intention to boycott any film listed as offensive by the clerical authorities of their diocese. Within a few months, the Legion enrolled a membership of several millions. The crusade thus initiated was publicly approved by leaders of other faiths, and the Federal Council of the Churches of Christ in America issued a warning to Hollywood that, if reform was not undertaken, it would do all in its power to bring about Federal censorship. The upshot was an agreement by the Hays office rigorously to enforce the production code.

On July 1, 1934, the internal censorship of motion pictures began under a system that was to continue in force at the middle of the century. It was effected by the Production Code Administration, soon to become known by the name of its Director, Joseph I. Breen, as the "Breen Office." Producers belonging to the Hays organization agreed not to release, distribute, or exhibit any picture—whether made by them, or by independent producers distributing through their facilities—unless the picture had received a certificate of approval signed by the Director of the Production Code Administration, and displayed its official seal. The penalty for contravention was a fine of twenty-five thousand dollars. The services of the Breen Office were made available to all producers of pictures, whether or not members of the Hays organization, and as the scheme worked out, more than ninety-five percent of all motion pictures made in the United States were subjected to the censorship of Breen and his subordinates.

The production code stated three general principles. (1) "No picture shall be produced which will lower the moral standards of those who see it. Hence the sympathy of the audience shall never be thrown to the side of crime, wrongdoing, evil or sin." (2) "Correct standards of life, subject only to the requirements of drama and entertainment, shall be presented." (3) "Law, natural or human, shall not be ridiculed, nor shall sympathy be created for its violation." The specific provisions and prohibitions of the code covered fifteen subjects. These were: crimes against the law; sex; vulgarity; obscenity; profanity; costume; dances; religion; locations; national feelings; titles; repellent subjects; and special regulations on crime, costume and cruelty to animals. By 1947, over sixteen thousand films had received the certificate of approval of the Breen office, and its decisions had been codified in more than nine hundred and fifty categories to furnish applicable precedents.

But notwithstanding this vast apparatus for the preservation of an absolute morality, morality itself remained a largely relative subject. Thus, for example, according to Joseph I. Breen, it was "not uncommon for the Production Code Administration to find out who are being cast in certain parts before judgment is given as to the acceptability of the script." The reason for this, as Breen explained, was the universal star-worship of American youth, which inclined young spectators of pictures to identify themselves with the parts played by their idols, and thereafter, at least subconsciously, strive to live accordingly. In the nature of things, "a well-known, an admired, a glamorous star leaves a greater, a deeper, a more lasting and potentially a more beneficial—or more harmful—impression than an average or ordinary actor." It was, therefore, in Breen's judgment, "reasonable and legitimate not to allow too much latitude to leading stars in the portrayal of sin. So true is this, that at times the acceptability of a scene may rightly depend, not so much on what transpires, as on who is playing the role."

The way in which this moral relativism actually worked out could be deduced from two examples cited by Martin Quigley, of films released just prior to the organization of the Breen office. One was *Riptide,* starring Miss Norma Shearer, a glamorous and widely beloved actress who, during the course of the picture, committed a casual adultery. The story was objectionable, according to Quigley, "principally because of the depiction of the popular star in a role of casual attitude toward infidelity on the grounds of the pattern of conduct toward which this conduct inclines an audience." Presumably, the picture might have been found less objectionable had the role been played by an actress of minor consequence, inferior attraction, and the object of little idolatry.

On the other hand, *I'm No Angel,* which starred Miss Mae West, an actress of quite different appeal than Miss Shearer, was disapproved for reasons equally deriving from the public personality of the player. It was condemned by Quigley as "a vehicle for a notorious characterization of a scarlet woman whose amatory instincts are confined exclusively to the physical" and was held to be morally objectionable "because specifically its sportive wisecracking tends to create tolerance if not acceptance of things essentially evil." Since in all of her pictures Miss West played only one type of role—the hard, brassy, cynical, wise-cracking, uninhibited woman with a roving eye and an inalterably rising temperature—it was clear that nothing could be done to bring

her within the moral boundaries of the production code. Shortly
after the Breen office came into existence, and at the peak of her
popularity with movie audiences, Miss West disappeared from the
nation's screens.

Hollywood's effort to bridge a gap between the moral restrictions imposed by the Breen office, and the mores of the movie-
going public, sometimes resulted in humorous expedients on
which the censors apparently cast a benevolent eye. Such was the
"sign language" described, in 1949, by the columnist Sidney
Skolsky, a device for making explicit actions which could not be
represented, or thoughts that could not be verbally expressed.
Skolsky cited, as an example, a scene played by Miss Susan Hay-
ward and Richard Conte. "Richard had just brought Susan home
after an evening at night clubs. She stands in a dimly-lighted,
luxurious living room, and he's at the door. Not a word is spoken.
Conte takes hold of the door knob to go, and it's then that she lets
her fur jacket slip off her shoulders and fall to the floor, revealing
her in a black, low-cut evening dress. That's the 'sign' which
means, 'I want you to stay.' Conte knows this, takes off his coat,
and stays."

It was Skolsky's opinion that audiences, too, would understand
the "sign"—for Hollywood, notwithstanding the censors, had
educated the movie-goers, to the degree that when Miss Betty
Grable took off a shoe, the audience understood this as a "sign"
indicating a more thorough disrobing than the Breen office permitted. Yet the necessity for these subterfuges indicated an increasing disparity between the moral assumptions of the Breen office
and those which actually governed American life. By the middle
of the century, none of the original provisions of the production
code had been dropped, but many of them appeared to be obsolete. "Some of the restrictions are as inappropriate as the bathing
suits of 1927 would be on the beaches of today," asserted Dr. Ruth
A. Inglis, author of a book on *Freedom of the Movies* and associate
professor of sociology at the University of Washington. "If the
screen is to have anything to do with the world of reality, it cannot
be shackled by rules that are insensitive to changing moral and
social values." A contradictory view was expressed by Geoffrey

Shurlock, assistant to Joseph I. Breen. "The basic moral aspects of the code seem fundamental for all time," he stated. "History proves that sound morals remain constant through the centuries." This was a dogmatic assertion which many historians, anthropologists and perhaps even some moralists might question, and which the practice of Hollywood itself did not consistently support. But it did not invite attack at the box-office.

3 Kings Are Pawns

During the gay and gorgeous nineteen-twenties, Cecil B. De Mille was teaching Americans to be satisfied only with films whose makers could point proudly to the expenditure of one million dollars. A new criterion of excellence and beauty gained ascendancy; the worth of anything could be reckoned in terms of its costliness. One event demonstrated the authority of this new value. In 1927, the Model-T Ford passed into history. Mother was having her face lifted, and under the ubiquitous permanent-waving machine was busily knitting copies of those fabulously expensive, little Chanel sweaters that she saw on the screen—and friendly, familial Lizzie went on her way to join aspidistras, corsets and the obsolete one-dollar bill.

The cellulords of Hollywood, as Leo C. Rosten was later to call them, were meanwhile engaged in a battle that revived, on the industrial scene, the kind of savage warfare practised, forty years earlier, by such tycoons as John D. Rockefeller and Andrew Carnegie in their determination to achieve monopolistic status. The new autocrats were the humble independents of the previous decade, who had rebelled against the magnates of the General Film trust. Now, such men as Adolph Zukor, Carl Laemmle, William Fox and Marcus Loew were themselves masters of vast empires, commanding resources that rivaled those of the oil-kings, the steel-princes and the pork-barons. For Wall Street was pouring its billions into the industry: Kuhn, Loeb and Company, Halsey, Stuart and Company, the du Ponts and others were furnishing the life-blood of empire, strife and conquest. Competition took the form of making ever "bigger and better" pictures. Since these had to be forced upon a captious public by the arts of prestige, the possession of "first-run theaters," where the prestige of films was established, became a matter of overwhelming strategic importance. It was Adolph Zukor's plan, for example, to exclude the films of his rivals from the screen by acquiring as many first-run houses as possible in key cities, and to this end—like Rockefeller so long before—he sent out emissaries who became known as the "wrecking crew" and "dynamite gang" to force theater-owners either to use his pictures exclusively or, by threatening to erect more magnificent houses in adjacent locations, to surrender their properties.

In the orgy of theater-building that this warfare precipitated, the new cult of costliness as beauty became a potent weapon. The favor of hundreds of millions of Joe Doakeses was the prize at stake. Not only must Joe Doakes be shown pictures constantly more lavish and extravagant; he must also be stunned into preliminary anesthesia by the splendor of the temples in which they were first shown. For a few hours he must be made to feel that he entered, by natural right, into a palace more spacious than Versailles, more ornately improbable than the Newport chateau of any nabob of the gilded age; that this stupefying miracle of fantasy genuinely belonged to him; that because it had been created only for his pleasure, he was, indeed, more powerful than any king. In Chicago, to please Joe Doakes, Barney Balaban and Samuel Katz, who had begun their careers as ushers and pianists in nickelodeons, built with the assistance of John Herz, the taxicab king, and other capitalists, the sumptuous Central Park, Riviera, and Oriental theaters, which made the lately opened Strand, in New York, seem a monument of old-fashioned simplicity. In Hollywood itself, the enterprising Sid Grauman erected Egyptian and Chinese tributes to the common man which surpassed, in their wonders, any spectacles conceivably to be projected on their screens. In the lobby of one of them, eternally etched upon concrete, were the footprints of the public's most venerated idols; and even the humblest citizen could stand where once Charles Chaplin had trod, or Mary Pickford, or whatever other divinity he worshipped.

Nothing was more characteristic of American civilization, in the public aspects of private desire, than this new architecture of tangible illusion, dedicated to the vending of a universal daydream. It reached a memorable pinnacle in the autumn of 1926 when Adolph Zukor, who fourteen years earlier had owned a shabby picture house on Fourteenth Street, opened the mammoth Paramount Theater in New York City. The Fifth Avenue mansions of millionaires were passing into the hands of the wreckers; Henry Ford was angrily protesting the seduction of sensible, frugal Americans by gadgets, streamlining and chromium plate; but the Paramount, a stately pleasure-dome of magic casements, was the costliest theater yet built. The skyscraper that housed it represented an outlay of seventeen millions of dollars. The shrine itself had absorbed three millions.

You entered a massive domed lobby, with a semi-circular colonnade of strikingly veined marbles, supported on a black and gold base one story high. From this, you passed into the Hall of Nations, one wall of which was formed by stones collected from thirty-seven different countries, identified on a set of bronze tablets. The Grand Hall came next, one hundred and fifty feet in length, forty feet wide and fifty feet high, its dome supported by huge marble columns, with an immense, ornate marble stairway at one end. Beyond was the vast auditorium, seating approximately four thousand people, a French Renaissance marvel of ivory, rose-red, turquoise blue and gold, with fountains at either side of the proscenium glowing under the shifting play of multi-colored lights.

But this was not all. For there were more than a dozen lounging rooms where the public might enjoy a cultivated leisure amidst paintings collected by a defunct Vanderbilt. Each of these rendezvous bore a name, so that people wishing to meet could designate a preferred locus of impatience. Thus, in the basement, there was the superb Elizabethan Room, paneled in walnut, illuminated by bronze brackets embellished with figures in porcelain each representing a fashion of feminine coiffure from the time of the Virgin Queen to that of the unchastened flapper. Elsewhere, there were the Peacock Promenade, the Tea Gallery for refreshment, the Chinoiserie sacred to feminine cigarettes. There were

the Club Room, the Hunting Room, the Jade Room, the Powder
Box, the Marie Antoinette Room, the Empire and Colonial
Rooms, the Music Room where chamber concerts were played
by a string orchestra. In the auditorium, of course, a picture was
being screened— (with exquisite irony, the film chosen to open
the Paramount was titled *God Gave Me Twenty Cents*)—and the
complex magnificence of this setting was somehow requisite to its
eventual success.

But amidst the manifold delights of theaters like the Paramount, every American could enjoy the sense of regality, blissfully
unaware that this extravagant wooing of his favor showed him to
be a pawn in Hollywood's imperial struggle for power. Oddly
enough, the lords of Hollywood were as bemused as their public.
Blinded by their visions of dominion, their expanding empires,
the gold and marble and crystal of their rising temple-playhouses,
the former upstarts whose radical innovations had been scornfully
rejected by the magnates of the Trust were now, in their turn,
as unreceptive to novelty as their predecessors. So when a revolutionary improvement was offered to them, the monarchs of the
screen turned it down.

4 "The time has come," the Walrus said

When Thomas Edison invented the kinetoscope, he planned to
unite it in a single cabinet with his phonograph, and give the
public a picture that both moved and uttered sounds. Though
Edison lost interest in his toy, other inventors resolutely attempted
to synchronize motion and sound. As early as 1910, Eugene Lauste
developed a crude sound-picture in which the sounds were registered directly on the film. Three years later, Elias Reis perfected
an improved method of accomplishing the same result. In 1922,
when radio broadcasting was beginning to captivate the imagination of Americans, Lee De Forest, inventor of the audion tube
that had made long-range broadcasting possible, returned from
Germany with the announcement that his experiments in making
talking pictures had finally been consummated in the "phonofilm."

His invention, De Forest claimed, perfectly synchronized

sound and images on the same film. He had succeeded in translating sound waves into light waves, registering them on film; and he
had perfected a device which, synchronized with the projection
machine, would re-translate them into sound, amplifying them
for all to hear. A new era was about to dawn for motion pictures,
he prophesied. It would see "introduction of all the dramatic art
of the spoken drama into the movies—the end of the movie actor
who has nothing but a good 'camera face'." It would mean the
end of the director with a megaphone, who would have to learn
a method of directing in sign language. In small towns, people
would hear music with picture plays—music played by the finest
orchestras of New York. The use of dialogue would do away with
explanatory titles; where the dramatic action required reinforcement, the actors could speak. His phonofilm, said De Forest,
would "add brains to the movies."

De Forest's first phonofilms were exhibited to New York audiences at the Rivoli Theater, in the spring of 1923, without provoking extraordinary enthusiasm. Meanwhile other inventors
were working toward the same goal. Theodore W. Case had
perfected certain electronic devices; had then been associated for
a time with De Forest, and later continued independent experiments. Finally joining William Fox, he developed a sound track
on film which he named the "movietone." At the laboratories of
Electric Research Products, Inc., a subsidiary of the Western
Electric Company, engineers worked out a system of synchronizing
movie-films and talking-machine disks which they named the
"vitaphone." The new Radio Corporation of America had developed a "photophone." But to all of these, as to De Forest's
phonofilm, the magnates of Hollywood were majestically indifferent. The innovation would prove to be, at best, a temporary
fad. It would disorganize established procedures and methods of
production. Why should prudent businessmen jeopardize their
safe situation and swelling profits?

The vitaphone was finally offered to Warner Brothers, then
a minor firm dangerously close to bankruptcy; they took it on
immediately. In 1926, both the Warners and Fox brought short
sound-pictures to the screen by the vitaphone and movietone

systems. In the following year, the Warners produced the first
feature film with dialogue and music: *The Jazz Singer,* with Al
Jolson as its star. The sensational success of this novelty doomed
the old silent picture, after another two years, to follow the
Model-T on the road to the graveyard. And, as a result, an im-
memorial feud between the dynasties of Morgan and Rockefeller
reached into the motion-picture industry through a patent war.
For the House of Morgan dominated the American Telephone
and Telegraph Company, which controlled the Western Electric
Company. And the House of Rockefeller dominated the General
Electric Company, which controlled the Radio Corporation of
America. Both giant corporations found their appetites for profit
whetted by the prospect of enormous revenues to be obtained
from the use of electronic equipment in the manufacture and
exhibition of talkies. The intensity of their determination became
evident in the swift elimination of William Fox from his own
great enterprises. Under the sovereignty of titans, there was no
room for Fox's form of absolute monarchy; he had become
economically obsolete. The brief war of the Morgan and Rockefeller dynasties for patent control was concluded by the formation
of a patents pool in the profits of which their corporate instruments shared. Thus, Hollywood was drawn into the vast network
of "communities of interest," interlocking directorates, inter-
corporate ownerships and common banking controls through
which the titans and their allies exercised dominion over the
American economic order.

The great magnates of Hollywood, so impressive to the public
in their supposedly absolute power, became, in fact, mere deputies
of overlords far more illustrious and potent. Within a very few
years Spyros Skouras, one of the newest tycoons in the industry,
would define the conditions of existence imposed upon it by these
remote, invisible, but absolute potentates: "For we are no longer
fighting each other, nor is there any longer such a thing as competition, but establishing solidarity or perishing." This would have
rejoiced the elder J. P. Morgan, long since in his grave; for it
expressed the ideal of economic order which he had sought to
impose on American society. It would likewise have delighted the

elder John D. Rockefeller, more recently garnered to his eternal life. For had he not once proclaimed economic death as the most expedient remedy for economic competition?

By 1929, the overwhelming public demand for talking pictures produced a revolutionary overturn of affairs in Hollywood. For the new medium required thorough revision of every technical procedure that contributed to the making of photoplays. To thousands of the lesser personnel engaged in the industry, the resulting changes brought personal tragedy. The microphone abruptly terminated the professional careers of "visually lovely girls who talked through their noses; silent heroines with adenoids or squeaky, tinny voices; young women who could no longer play society girls because of Kansas intonations; splendid young heroes whose enunciation was lingual goulash; strong he-men of the open spaces whose vocal efforts sounded like the wood thrush calling to its mate."

The microphone invaded the American Olympus and annihilated many of the major deities. Great foreign stars like Miss Pola Negri, Emil Jannings and Conrad Veidt were unceremoniously returned to Europe. The "It girl," Miss Clara Bow, blazing exemplar of the insouciance of flaming youth, was suddenly extinguished; for now carefree passion had to crackle audibly as well as burn. Miss Gloria Swanson and Miss Norma Talmadge, who for nearly a decade had disciplined the American woman to ways of worldliness, ceased to function as cynosures of that elegance which is the fruit of varied experience. Miss June Caprice, whose name indicated the amiably ingenuous nature of her whimsicality, faded from view. Miss Clara Kimball Young, beautiful victim of the malignity of men in a score of tearful melodramas, whose lovely eyes were insured by Lloyds of London for one hundred and fifty thousand dollars, retired to private life; long afterwards, she would return to the screen as a player of "bit parts." But the pathetic effect of revolution was most evident in the case of John Gilbert, the current "great lover" of the screen. In 1929, to the cardiac acceleration of American womanhood, he co-starred with the glamorous Miss Greta Garbo in *A Woman of Affairs,* founded on Michael Arlen's lurid novel, *The Green Hat.* It was his last

triumph. Soon afterwards, the fan-world was shocked by the news
✝ of his suicide. His contract had not been renewed, it was said,
because his high-pitched, fluty voice was irremediable.

The American people soon learned to take talking pictures
for granted, and quickly forgot that there had ever been a time
when pictures were silent. Yet a number of social effects could
be traced to the new element. Now that the screen could speak,
it had to have something to say. From 1929 onward, the best
photoplays assumed, to an increasing degree, the responsibilities
of a kind of dramatic literature, and furnished the public food
for thought as well as amusement. In translating to the screen the
more important works of current fiction and drama, they brought
within the reflective range of a far wider audience than ever
before many topics that were receiving the serious intellectual
consideration of creative minds. The talkies likewise, by force of
example, did much to standardize the speech of Americans; to
produce a norm of conversational etiquette; to enrich the available vocabulary of pungent colloquialisms; to shape the prevailing
decorum of social intercourse, always more influenced by verbal
than ocular illustration. And, for a large segment of the American
public without access to metropolitan centers of entertainment,
they made available the resources of gaiety enjoyed by urban
sophisticates. Plainville no longer languished enviously for want
of such amenities as the Stork Club. To Main Street there were
brought girl-and-tune shows more arresting, costly and prodigally
rich in stars, more overpowering in the populousness and pulchri-
tude of their chorus lines than any that had ever been devised for
Broadway by Florenz Ziegfeld, Earl Carroll or George White.
Only pedants and prudes found fault with these ministrations.
To others, it seemed that they were diffusing a genuine element of
the living national culture.

5   Aphrodite and the Boys Downtown

In its moments of greatest timidity, Hollywood asserted that it
was engaged only in purveying "pure entertainment." Serious
students of its product found this term ambiguous. For no
motion picture could be made wholly empty of meaningful con-

tent. And none could be screened without effects on the audiences exposed to it. Although scientists had failed to develop methods for accurately appraising these effects, there was little dispute about their basis. Those Americans who went to the movies in search of nothing more than recreation and escape, were rewarded only to the extent that the films furnished something more. The condition of escape was temporary detachment from personal existence. And this was achieved when spectators became absorbed in the events and characters portrayed on the screen. Few adult Americans, in all probability, accepted the stories told on the screen as literal substitutes for reality. Yet they participated in them, imaginatively. And it seemed that their participation was likely to be most active and intense when the stories in some way gave meaning to their own lives—expressed their interests, problems and aspirations. In so far as the movies thus recorded the inarticulate, or unacknowledged, private experience of Americans, they furnished a relevant commentary on certain aspects of the national civilization.

One of the most striking aspects was revealed by the emphasis which motion pictures put upon love. This emphasis became noticeable as soon as the movies emerged from the nickelodeons. By the middle of the century, what was called "romantic love" had been a major theme of the films for more than three decades. Judged by its quantitative weight in the movies, it appeared to be the dominant value genuinely cherished by American society. It was likewise a constant value: over the years, the movies represented it, almost invariably, as the most desirable of all objectives in life. Less important, by far, were material success; the satisfactions to be derived from work; personal integration in a social group through friendships or participation in community affairs; the approbation of one's fellows; the attaining of a spiritually satisfying place in the world. For the American woman, to the degree that the screen represented her, all these were secondary to fulfillment through love. But if this objective remained constant, the ways of achieving it varied significantly. In the types of heroine who succeeded one another on the screen, there was to be found a record of the images acceptable to American women as illustrations of successful achievement—and, therefore, as models to be imitated.

The heroine most appealing to women as the First World War drew to a close was portrayed by the Russian actress, Mme. Alla Nazimova. Having won fame on the stage as an interpreter of the plays of Henrik Ibsen, she brought to the screen an embodiment of dissatisfaction and revolt. For this, Hollywood paid her the record salary of thirteen thousand dollars a week. Slender, very pale, dark-haired, she had a large, expressive mouth and deep, burning eyes. On the screen, she wore gowns that accentuated what was described as her "exotic look." She also possessed a "bizarre quality" later to be defined, more prosaically, as neurotic. The woman portrayed by Mme. Nazimova possessed reserves of passion untapped by her environment. She knew herself to be exquisitely sensitive, potentially creative, and intellectually far superior to the people by whom she was surrounded. How could she be content in a humdrum home? How could she be satisfied by a husband engrossed in business, exasperating to her finer sensibilities, unappealing to the inward volcanic turmoil that signified her frustrated capacity to love? In a series of pictures, Mme. Nazimova expressed—as feminine audiences translated it— a rebellious discontent with middle-class monotony, matrimonial dullness, the narrow orbit of kitchen, nursery and evenings at the bridge table. She opened vistas on a wider sphere of influence, and a more agreeably exhausting repertory of experience. When the American husband returned home to find his wife clad in an alluring, clinging hostess-gown, smoking a cigarette through a long, fragile holder, and nervously tapping one golden-slippered foot on the floor beneath her chaise-longue, he could be absolutely certain of one thing. Her mind was not on him.

The heroine projected by Mme. Nazimova brooded resentfully on possibilities of rebellion and escape. Her immediate successors slammed the door on convention before they came to the screen. Both were shaped by the masterful mind of Mrs. Elinor Glyn, author of *Three Weeks* and other tropical novels, who in the nineteen-twenties was Hollywood's sybilline authority on the glorification of romance. She had come there with the philanthropic purpose of "helping to spread the ideals and the atmosphere of romance and glamor into the humblest homes." This was easier said than done. To her horror, Mrs. Glyn discovered that American men simply could not make love. Not even the leading screen actors had any idea how to do it. Screen tests of handsome young film stars were shown to her for approval, and she found their amorous performances lamentable. To her, they seemed like woolly lambs; she wanted actors who, before the camera, would treat the actresses playing their sweethearts quite differently than those who were playing their sisters and aunts. Thus Mrs. Glyn verified, in melancholy fact, the basis of the protest registered in the photoplays enacted by Mme. Nazimova. But, with perseverance and skill, Mrs. Glyn managed to train some American actors to surmount their native disabilities.

The two heroine-types that Mrs. Glyn ushered to the screen were widely imitated. "I wanted to stir up in the cold hearts of the thousands of little, fluffy, gold-digging American girls," she afterwards confessed, "a desire for greater joys in life than are to be found in candy boxes and car rides and fur coats; a desire to be loved as European women are loved; and as a result, a desire to give as well as to receive." To spread her gospel of the higher generosity, she evolved the "It girl" and the adroit, experienced free lance. But, once launched, the "It girl" got out of her creator's hands. Exploited by social forces that even Mrs. Glyn could not control, she turned out to be quite unlike what that somewhat naive lady had intended. Yet, for nearly a decade, the perspectives of American girlhood were defined by the stories of F. Scott Fitzgerald and the screen plays of Miss Clara Bow. In Miss Bow, the emergent flapper found her predestined model, pointing to such novelties as a boyish figure, short skirts, step-ins, chain smoking, a vanity case of precious metal with flask to match, necking, petting parties and the single standard. The "It girl" streamlined the technique of conquest. She was merely a continuous sexual provocation. With her, the higher generosity functioned almost as indiscriminately—and efficiently—as the concealed mechanism of a coin-box telephone. Her imitators wore their chastity as casually as their opened, flapping galoshes, their rolled stockings, and their exuberant fondness for jazz. Romance in a roadster was the unique vocation of the "It girl." This was even further simplified by her votaries. It became sex in a sedan.

The more mature free-lance introduced by Mrs. Glyn survived, as a pattern for imitation, until the Great Depression, although she passed through a series of minor transformations. These transformations affected neither her essential nature, her philosophy, nor her technique. They were imposed by the various actresses who most notably portrayed her on the screen. This suggested that it was usually the actress herself, rather than the character she portrayed, who achieved acceptability as a model; the pattern, at any particular moment, was invested with the special qualities of appeal peculiar to the public personality of its current exemplar. Thus the imaginations of feminine movie-goers may not have been stirred as deeply by the type that staked everything on love, as they were by the inseparable legends that attached to Miss Gloria Swanson, Miss Constance Bennett, Miss Tallulah Bankhead, or Miss Greta Garbo.

As the pupil of Mrs. Glyn, Miss Swanson could be considered the classic example of the worldly-wise, proficient and adventurous free-lance in love. Personal legend, in her case, enormously reinforced the gospel of her photoplays. For, more convincingly than any character she portrayed, she herself illustrated the possibility that a simple American girl might achieve fame, fortune, immense influence, and an assured position in the great world—yet fulfill the dictates of her imperious, unsatisfied heart. The daughter of an army officer, born in Chicago, she had entered the Essanay studios there as an extra at the age of sixteen, had later appeared as one of Mack Sennett's bathing beauties, and had progressed to stardom in the De Mille "society" pictures, an oddly haughty figure, yet flamboyant and overdressed. Then she re-created her public personality, emerging as a formal, cool woman whose dignity was paralyzing, and the elegance of whose attire was impeccable: so the dithermythers of the day described her. Twice married and divorced, she took as her third husband the Marquis de la Falaise de Coudray. "When Gloria Swanson lies in her golden bathtub, a tired woman of almost thirty, she must realize at sight of her golden plumbing that she is a success. For only the successful can achieve bathrooms of black marble, hidden soft lights, and basins of gold." So wrote Miss Allene Talmey in the year 1927, in a portrait not entirely laudatory. She went on to specify that Miss Swanson's living expenses ran to ten thousand dollars a month; that, besides her Hollywood home, she maintained a penthouse in New York and a country estate on the Hudson; that she employed four secretaries, a press agent, and various other professional servitors. But, observed Miss Talmey, "her screen sparkle and gaiety vanished when off the screen, leaving her a quiet, weary person, with hair soft and dark, a husky voice, blue almond-shaped eyes, and a manner so reserved that it embarrasses those meeting her for the first time."

Miss Swanson shaped the classic stereotype of the disillusioned, neurotic, passion-driven woman bent upon a "free life," and showed that its persuasiveness was enhanced by an identification of personal legend with the character as portrayed on the screen. Later actresses could scarcely improve on this formula; they merely varied it. Miss Constance Bennett—who married the Marquis de la Falaise de Coudray after Miss Swanson divorced him—divested the type of some of her formidable dignity. Miss Tallulah Bankhead gave her a hoydenish quality, befitting one who, at a masked ball in London attended by royalty, was reputed to have been seen turning perfect cartwheels around the room; a personage who, in general, behaved like a lonely cyclone. Miss Greta Garbo brought to the role of siren an air of enigmatic detachment, of mystery. This was natural, perhaps, for, as Miss Mary Margaret McBride described her, she was "the woman nobody knows, the woman everybody wants to know." But Miss Garbo's later pictures indicated that the type was coming upon evil days; in them, she no longer played the siren as a contemporary figure, but as one revived from a romantic, bygone era. For the prosperity of the siren, as a type, depended upon the susceptibility of men to the dangerous attraction of sin. And, in the United States, the sense of sin was rapidly diminishing. During the Great Depression, women were welcome to a "free life" if they wanted it; public conscience no longer made an issue of sexual liberty; illicit adventure ceased to be mysteriously exciting; and, suddenly, the siren became as much an anachronism as the vamp.

The change was heralded on the screen in 1931 when, in *The Public Enemy*, an early gangster film, James Cagney squashed a grapefruit on the face of one girl, and hit another on the jaw. These examples of a new decorum brought forward a new type of screen hero: tough, aggressive, unsentimental, coldly appraising of the sexual attractions of women, not in the least inclined to "romance." Was the national daydream itself subject to the force of economic determinism? In the era of prosperity, feminine votaries of love displayed on the screen represented, in general, the American woman's concepts of what she would like to be like; and none of these concepts seemed to be influenced by the established preferences of the American man, against which they were, in a sense, a protest. But the new heroine-type produced by the era of hard times was tailored to conform precisely to the prevailing taste of men. The "platinum-blonde" hair and pleasing curves of Miss Jean Harlow broke all of Hollywood's glamor records during the nineteen-thirties. It was the men, not the women, of the United States who adored her, and by their overwhelming approval established her as a type for women to imitate, however reluctantly. Essentially, the girl portrayed by Miss Harlow expressed the American male's boredom with the traditional concept of "romance"; with the doctrine that fulfillment in love is a primary objective in life; and perhaps also with the restless discontent and implied superiority of the American woman. For this girl was earthy, humorous, hard-boiled. She made no pretensions to culture or refinement. For her, sex and love were by no means inseparable, and she mocked at prudery and puritanism, at fastidiousness and pretentiousness. Brought up in a fiercely competitive world, without advantages or protection, she had learned to defend herself adequately and to value, at their specific practical worth, the goods she might hope to secure. Warmhearted, gay, gaudy, her lack of subtlety and deviousness amounted to a kind of honesty—and to anxious businessmen, during the Great Depression, she seemed entirely desirable.

Yet the businessman had never lacked his spokesman on the

screen, and except for Rudolph Valentino, none of the interminable procession of great lovers had ever equalled in popularity two major exponents of American humor and common sense. In his early films, made at the time of the First World War, Douglas Fairbanks represented all young democratic Americans, quick-thinking, fast-acting, self reliant and self-made. Ridiculing all fashionable affectations, Fairbanks preached the gospel of pep, the merits of clean living, the obligation to take everything with a smile, the claims of traditional decencies. Many of his silent photoplays were written by Anita Loos and John Emerson, who inserted comment that had a wise-cracking, whimsical humor typically native, and appropriate to Fairbanks's brash and bouncing personality on the screen. Again and again, in his pictures, Fairbanks demonstrated how ambition, alertness, daring and perpetual hustle would inevitably bring a young American to success, rewarding him both with the fortune he hoped for and the girl of his choice. This was a national myth that, to some skeptics among his countrymen, seemed rather threadbare, but his own happy belief in it enabled Fairbanks to persuade audiences of its enduring truth. So seriously did he come to be taken in his function of advocate that when he turned to the production of extravaganzas, some years later, he was reproached as if derelict in a duty. Edison, remarked the film-historian Terry Ramsaye, "devoted his life to machines intended to make thinking unnecessary for the masses. Fairbanks is devoting his to pictures calculated to keep their minds off the fact that they do not think."

Like Fairbanks, Will Rogers came to be the object of national idolatry. In foreign lands, where he traveled widely in his later years, he was regarded as an unofficial American ambassador, a spokesman not for the government but the people of the United States; he inherited, as it were, the mantle of Mark Twain. But it was not as an actor in motion pictures that he gained this unique distinction. The worldwide popularity of his films derived from his prestige as a humorist and commentator on current affairs, and from his personality which, like his humor, reflected attributes historically associated with the American spirit.

Born in 1879 in Oklahoma—then the Indian Territory—

Rogers was of partly Indian ancestry. His schooling was irregular; he once remarked he had "studied the fourth reader for ten years." At the age of fourteen, he was riding range for his father as top cowhand and steer-roper. When his father gave him a herd of cattle, he drove them to Galveston, Texas, sold them, and sailed for South America, where he intended to start a ranch on the American system. But he was swindled out of his money, and shipped on a cattle boat to South Africa. There, the Boer War was in progress, and he enlisted in the Boer army. When he returned to the United States, he secured a job as trick rider with a Wild West show, later drifted into vaudeville, and in 1913 entered the Ziegfeld *Follies*, in which he achieved celebrity as a monologist. In familiar cowboy garb, chewing gum and spinning his lariat as he spoke with a characteristic drawl, Rogers delivered a shrewd, pithy commentary on the news of the day. Some years later, he began writing a brief daily feature along the same lines which was syndicated throughout the nation.

Asked, at one time, for the secret of his success, Rogers replied that "t'aint no secret—just gum and gumption." But this was a very modest appraisal. For Rogers' humor stemmed from the American tradition exemplified by Mark Twain and Finley Peter Dunne. Its salty, colloquial drollery was directed to shattering shams and pretenses, and it often implied rebuke of the condition from which it evoked laughter. "If we must sin," he remarked at the height of lawlessness under prohibition, "let's sin quick, and don't let it be a long, lingering sinning." Rogers seldom failed to make explicit his personal faith that the foundations of American democracy were truth, justice and tolerance, but there was a measure of indictment in such a verdict as, "We are a nation that runs in spite of and not on account of our Government." Elected mayor of Beverly Hills, then the residence of Hollywood's wealthiest elite, he announced: "I'm for the common people, and as Beverly Hills has no common people, I can't help but make good." Of an illness that had brought him to the operating table, Rogers later wrote: "Will Hays had just been out here and spent the day with us. Now I don't lay the illness directly on to him, but a continual listening to the merits of the Movies and the

Republican Party will sometimes react disastrously on a previously ailing stomach."

Unlike Mark Twain, Rogers was content to think of himself merely as a humorist. "A comedian can only last," he said, "until he takes himself serious or his audience takes him serious, and I don't want either one of them to happen to me until I'm dead—if then." But, in point of fact, his audience did take him seriously. He served as the deputy of their consciences, as a kind of accredited national moralist who would keep steadily before them the democratic creed to which their faith was pledged, and who would expose to them the follies and abuses and delusions that corrupted their social practice. On the screen, usually cast in some transparent disguise of his own personality, he seemed to speak for the honest purposes and enduring realistic idealism of the plain people.

The pictures made by Fairbanks and Rogers, in which romantic love occupied a position of secondary interest, were outside the mainstream of Hollywood's typical product. As the century reached its midpoint, in the bulk of American motion pictures fulfillment through love continued to be represented as the major value to be gained in living. At that time, an analysis of the content of representative current films was made by Dr. Martha Wolfenstein, a psychologist, and Dr. Nathan Leites, a specialist in political science. In its treatment of love, they found, Hollywood was attempting to combine the appeal of the conventional and the unconventional in a single relationship. Romance began in an unconventional meeting, usually a pickup. The heroine appeared to be a "bad" girl; this was what initially attracted the hero, for her presumptive badness was the element that made her sexually exciting. Only after he had been completely subjugated did the heroine permit him to discover that she was not bad, but good, and therefore worthy of marriage. The "good-bad" girl, these investigators suggested, was a new phenomenon in the motion picture, but not one lacking a counterpart in American life. She was the product of a culture in which the ideal of monogamy persisted, but in which sheltered innocence had ceased to be sexually desirable. She fulfilled the American's "uncompromising demand to have everything" in a society where "the belief that you can eat your cake and have it still seems strong."

Another student of the films, Dr. Hortense Powdermaker, professor of anthropology at Queens College, drew attention to a significant fact. "In an increasing number of contemporary movies, the setting of the story is married life, with a beautiful, rich, neurotic heroine threatened by a loss of love object. Her response to this usually takes an extreme form, such as alcoholism or murder." Dr. Powdermaker surmised that adult audiences would recognize this as a flagrant distortion of reality, but she offered it as a characteristic example indicating that Hollywood's portrayal of love had very little psychological validity. The probable social consequences of this defect were obvious, and not salutary. For, under conditions of urban life, Americans were becoming increasingly lonely because their contacts tended to be more and more impersonal; they spent their lives surrounded by strangers; their need for personal relationships was acute, and often desperate. Love, therefore, had the status of a major problem. Did not the movies, by making love carry the entire weight of living, both exaggerate the problem and, for most people, also make it seem unsolvable?

How far the obsessive cult of love had been taken over from the movies into American life was clear from the unique position occupied, at the end of the nineteen-forties, by Miss Rita Hayworth, the nation's leading exponent of the "good-bad" heroine. During the Second World War, Miss Hayworth had been overwhelmingly the favorite "pin-up girl" of the American armed forces. She was said to receive six thousand poems and prayers every week from American men; the number of mere letters that reached her was not disclosed. When Operation Crossroads took place at Bikini Atoll in 1946, "Her picture was reverently and symbolically pasted to an atomic bomb while the world's scientific and military minds anxiously awaited one of the greatest destructive explosions mankind had yet contrived"; and the bomb then discharged was christened *Gilda*, after her latest photoplay. Women were following Miss Hayworth's changes of appearance with absorbed concentration. They were modeling their clothes on hers, imitating her undulant walk and her coiffure, adopting her makeup and trying to reshape their contours to a closer approximation of her figure, in a resolute effort to resemble her, if that happy outcome was possible. To the critic Winthrop Sergeant, who wrote an article about Miss Hayworth for *Life*, all these phenomena suggested that she had acquired the status of a religious institution. "It has remained for Americans of the hard-boiled twentieth century," he noted, "to enthrone Aphrodite as the supreme deity of their popular religion, to portray her rather dubious machinations as the most exalting and satisfying of human experiences, and to subscribe with unquestioning faith to her incessant litany that sex is the most important thing in the world."

And this, when you came down to it, seemed to be all that the movies had found to say, during three decades, on the subject of love.

6 A Comedy to Those That Think

But these same years brought proof that the motion picture could rise to more significant purposes than mere prattle about romance. In the opinion of many Americans, it did this most notably in the films made by two masters of fantasy. The pictures of Charles Chaplin and Walt Disney furnished eloquent commentaries on certain aspects of the life of the times.

In *The Kid*, which he produced in 1920 with five-year-old Jackie Coogan as his co-star, Chaplin devised an allegory from the hopes and realities of the dawning post-war era. The picture related the story of Chaplin's tramp and the abandoned child whom he involuntarily rescued. The society in which they lived was committed to an economy of abundance. It was potentially capable of yielding a decent life to all its members. But the tramp and the child were social outcasts. They roomed in a squalid slum court. They were able to exist only by means of a desperate ruse; the child broke windows with rocks, and the tramp appeared as an itinerant glazier to mend them. To the hardships of existence they opposed the power of imagination; one saw the tramp, for example, fastidiously removing his fingerless gloves to choose a butt from the sardine can that served him for cigarette case. And the tramp persistently cherished the vision of a better life so easily attainable by society, yet so needlessly ignored. The vision was made vivid in a dream, with the slum court transformed into fairyland, and its wretched inhabitants flying about happily, having sprouted wings on their shabby clothes. That the picture had a happy ending in no sense diminished the irony that made it a forceful criticism of society.

"The whole of humanity, seen from the angles of the comic imagination, are Charlie Chaplins," said Chaplin in 1920. "In my antics, my clothes, my horseplay, my illogical movements and comic pathos I show mankind itself as it must look to spectators Higher Up, if there be any who are looking at this Charivari on earth." This view of human affairs emerged sharply in *The Gold Rush*, Chaplin's commentary on the nation's passion for wealth during the era of Coolidge prosperity. "Nothing fails like success," he had told an interviewer who asked him how it felt to be a millionaire after having known the most grueling poverty. In *The Gold Rush* he applied this insight to the headlong pursuit of riches engaging most Americans. The little tramp, become a prospector, was surrounded by men concerned only with outsmarting their fellows and finding gold. Uniquely among them, he had a heart; he cared for human relationships; his responses to life were generous. But at the moment of striking gold, he found himself suddenly and miserably alone. The joys of wealth were illusory, Chaplin showed, and he intimated his disbelief in the reality of Coolidge prosperity; for the prospector's cabin was shown rocking perilously on the very edge of a precipice, beneath which there was a bottomless abyss.

This prophecy, unheeded in 1925, was already confirmed in 1931, when Chaplin released *City Lights*, which opened ironically with the unveiling of a statue to "Peace and Prosperity" on which the tramp was discovered happily asleep. This, perhaps, was Chaplin's retort to President Hoover and the banking tycoons who kept airily announcing that prosperity would soon return. Later in the film he attempted to rescue an inebriated and desperate banker from suicide in the river. Almost drowning himself, he finally pulled out the would-be suicide, then threw out his chest and urged the stronger man to revive his courage and fortitude. There could be little doubt that in this scene Chaplin was attempting to counsel the nation.

In 1936, Chaplin brought forward *Modern Times*, announcing it as "the story of industry, of individual enterprise—humanity crusading in the pursuit of happiness." But this definition of purpose proved to be wholly ironical. The picture was a withering indictment of a social order and an industrial system which, in Chaplin's opinion, doomed the masses to a form of existence intolerable to human beings. The picture opened with a herd of sheep·rushing down a runway to slaughter; there followed a mass of workers surging out of a subway to enter a factory. In the huge mechanized plant Chaplin, one of the workers, tightened bolts as they passed on an endless conveyor belt. To facilitate a speed-up, the magnate owner installed a mechanical feeder. Chaplin's hideous encounter with this device, and his glimpse of a fellow-worker inextricably jammed in another immense machine, revealed his indignation at a mass-production system which subordinated men to mechanical processes. The monotony and regimentation of his job, in the picture, finally drove Chaplin insane. After escaping from the factory, he went through adventures that displayed the extreme contrasts of an American city during the Great Depression: the Hoovervilles, the luxurious department stores and nightclubs, the streets crowded by jobless and hungry workers, the hospitals, the jails where alone there was some semblance of peace and security. Essentially, the picture expressed Chaplin's profound resentment of a social order in which speed-ups, oppression, unemployment, starvation, riots and crime were characteristic and tolerated phenomena; in which men, like unsuspecting sheep, were hustled relentlessly toward death for the advantage of an impersonal system to which human life no longer had any value.

In 1940, with *The Great Dictator*, Chaplin uttered a powerful denunciation of totalitarianism, and an equally powerful plea to its victims not to despair, not to give themselves to men who sought to enslave humanity, but to unite however possible in the

hope of a future democracy. After the Second World War had
ended, Chaplin released *Monsieur Verdoux,* a picture, so he declared, "intended to create a pity for all humanity under certain
drastic circumstances." He acknowledged that its satire was very
bitter, but thought that the times were bitter also. The picture
expressed his conviction "that our contemporary civilization is
making mass murderers of us." Relatively few Americans saw
Monsieur Verdoux. A wave of anti-Communist sentiment was
sweeping over the nation, and among certain powerful pressure
groups Chaplin had become an object of suspicion. "I am not a
Communist," he asserted during a mass interview in New York
City. "My patriotism has never been to one country, one class, but
to the whole world." And then Chaplin—a small, white-haired
man nearing his sixtieth year—added, as if in explanation of his
picture: "As you get older, you aren't content to go along always
in the same line. You want to get excited before you do something.
I suppose it's my indulgence to put messages in my movies." To
many, it seemed that his principal message had been a plea for the
rights of the individual in a world increasingly disposed to over-
ride them.

Chaplin's only peer in the realm of fantasy was Walt Disney,
who rose to fame in 1928 with an animated comic strip featuring
the engaging character Mickey Mouse. In the two following decades, Disney peopled the screens of the world with a whole
menagerie, of whom Donald Duck, Pluto and the Goof became the
most popular. Unlike Chaplin, Disney explicitly denied that his
pictures contained any message. Yet *The Three Little Pigs,* appearing shortly after President Franklin D. Roosevelt had declared
that "the only thing we have to fear is fear itself," was understood
by the American people as a summons to build a house so strong
that the wolves of hunger and fear could be kept outside, and at
a safe distance. The picture's theme song—"Who's Afraid of the
Big, Bad Wolf?"—became, at the time, an anthem of courage and
hope for the whole nation. As Disney's subsequent pictures
quickly followed one another to the screen, the resemblance of the
world which they portrayed to the world of twentieth-century
reality grew more marked.

For Disney's animal world was one in which violence, conflict, ruthless physical force and utter desperation were normal, accepted elements of experience. It was a world in which kind-heartedness was associated with brutality; in which contempt for the weak prevailed; in which conscience had become a kind of stupidity. Mickey Mouse succeeded in astutely outwitting his adversaries, but usually he battered them down in the process of reaching his goal; he alone, in this curiously hard and hostile world, illustrated positive achievement. Donald Duck, with his explosive temper, his impotent rages and exasperated protest, showed the confusion to which it was capable of reducing the unqualified and hapless individual. This was a society in which aggression paid out, inhumanity was practical, and power, being right, was always admirable. Disney made audiences roar with laughter by endowing such inanimate objects as steam-shovels and rocking chairs with human emotions. Was he not depicting a world in which scientists would speculate about the analogies between electronic "thinking machines" and the human brain? His pictures were pure fantasy, and almost pure fable, but what they reported about twentieth-century existence afforded little warrant for optimism or complacency. That they seemed so funny to so many Americans was, in itself, socially significant. It indicated the extent to which a mood of disillusion had overtaken the nation. It testified that an old faith was in temporary eclipse, and that a traditional dream had, for the time, ceased to be potent.

Chaplin and Disney were independent producers. Owning their own businesses, both were able to dictate policy without reference to the opinions of others. In making their films, as they frequently testified, they took no account of the supposed tastes of the public, or of the commercial maxim that it is better to get while the getting is good. All this may have contributed to the acknowledged superiority of their pictures. At the middle of the century, no other maker of movies had produced a body of work as sustained and coherent as Disney's, or equal to Chaplin's in the significance of its social criticism.

But Hollywood's commercial output of pictures showed a long roster of films that dealt honestly with problems of American life, and that even undertook to portray the seamier aspects of the American scene. From *The Crowd*, in 1928, to *The Best Years of Our Lives* in 1946, *Call Northside 777* and *The Snake Pit* in 1948, and *Knock On Any Door* in 1949, scarcely a year had passed without the release of at least one picture that attempted an intelligent evaluation of some segment of the American social order. The comparative triviality of Hollywood's typical product continued to furnish a subject for critical attack from many quarters. Yet the peculiar and seemingly irrational circumstances that governed the making of pictures made prevailing inconsequence less remarkable than occasional excellence. There was abundant evidence that Hollywood could surpass mediocrity when it chose to; could do far better than it usually did. Had it not brought to the screen *Fury* and *I Am a Fugitive From a Chain Gang; Dodsworth; Arrowsmith* and *The Late George Apley; Citizen Kane* and *The Grapes of Wrath; The Miracle of Morgan's Creek* and *Mr. Deeds Goes to Town; Gentleman's Agreement* and *Crossfire?* The appeal of such films as these appeared to require some correction of Hollywood's favorite assumption. As defined by Martin Quigley, this was "that millions of people, immersed in the drabness and disappointment of their daily lives, go to the movie theater to revel for a while in ornate display, in dreams of easily and pleasantly won success, to revel even in sentimental sprees."

Hollywood may have set its sights too low.

7   Not Just for Fun

It was not only through the so-called "entertainment film" that motion pictures exercised a social influence. Films were also used to report news; to expound a theme and convey ideas; as an instrument of propaganda by special interests; as an instrument for industrial and military training, and as an accepted resource in public education.

Newsreels, which originated during the infancy of the motion picture, took on greatly increased importance with the arrival of sound. The addition of explanatory text, spoken by a commentator, notably enhanced the interest, power and persuasiveness of a pictorial record. As a result, camera journalists were sent all over the world to photograph "spot news" events. Occasionally, they were also enabled to record the important pronouncements of eminent personages concerned with either domestic or international affairs. In general, however, a preponderant share of the footage of newsreels was devoted to sports, fashions, displays of pretty girls, views of parades and public ceremonies, accidents and disasters. Such subjects were considered "safe" by producers because they involved no controversial problems. A more limited coverage was given to events which related to political, economic or social issues currently in dispute. In this sphere, the impartiality of the newsreels was taken for granted by many of the public, under the same presumption of objectivity which they applied to the reporting of news by the press.

Producers of newsreels could, and sometimes did, "slant" the news which their films reported. A notable instance occurred when in 1937 pictures of the so-called Memorial Day "massacre" near the South Chicago shops of the Republic Steel Company were suppressed; in this incident, Chicago police had fired on pickets, killing ten people and wounding forty. Another instance occurred, later in the same year, when the United States gunboat *Panay* was bombed by the Japanese in the Yangtze River; according to the columnist Walter Winchell, although editorial writers failed to become hysterical, "The newsreel narrators put on the big jingo act." The mere cutting or editing of films made it possible for producers of newsreels to influence the audience's opinion, and this possibility was enormously extended by the spoken commentary which accompanied the pictures shown. The devices of dramatic emphasis available to producers of "entertainment films" were equally at the disposal of producers of newsreels. Thus movie journalists, even more effectively than their brethren of the press, were able, if they chose, to manipulate the news for partisan purposes. An important innovation in the making of newsreels was put forward in 1934, when the *March of Time* films took as their subject a single topic, or issue, currently before the public, and by re-enacting the principal events connected with it, presented a pictorial, dramatic essay in history. *The March of Time*

films were intended to furnish interpretation, not merely a report
of fact, and could therefore be considered the screen equivalent
of a magazine article. In them, for the first time, a serious effort
was made to use the powerful resources of the motion picture for
the acknowledged purpose of molding, as well as enlightening,
public opinion in the field of current affairs.

The documentary film, in general, applied the dramatic and
narrative methods of the fictional motion picture to purely factual
material. Its purpose was the study of a problem or theme, and to
the degree that it was used mainly for the dissemination of ideas,
the documentary film enabled the motion picture to undertake a
function previously restricted to literary exposition in non-
fictional books. The inventor, or "father," of the documentary
film was Robert J. Flaherty, an explorer, who in 1920 was bound
on an expedition to the Eskimo country of Northern Canada. The
fur-trading firm of Revillon Freres engaged Flaherty to make a
film of Eskimo life in the vicinity of one of their Hudson's Bay
trading posts, intending to use it for purposes of publicity.
Flaherty had no previous experience as a director or producer of
motion pictures, but *Nanook of the North,* the film which he
made to carry out this project in public relations, opened a new
range of possibilities to the medium. In *Nanook,* as in all his
subsequent films, Flaherty concentrated on the theme of man's
conflict with his physical environment, his effort to subdue nature
to the purposes of economic livelihood and social organization.
Discarding dramatic plot and fictional development, *Nanook of
the North* portrayed with realism the incessant struggle for existence of Eskimos in a land where the procurement of adequate
food supplies was always problematical, and always the price of
survival.

The phenomenal success of *Nanook,* when released in motion-
picture theaters in 1922, caused Hollywood to send Flaherty three
times to the South Pacific, where he made *Moana of the South Seas,*
a record of the life of a Samoan community, *White Shadows in
the South Seas* and *Tabu.* Thereafter, he made other important
films under British auspices, but he produced no documentary
picture with an American locale until 1948, when his *Louisiana*

Story won wide acclaim. This picture, made for an unidentified oil company, dealt with the invasion by oil-riggers, with their immense drilling derricks, of the sparsely populated bayous where Cajun fishermen and trappers existed untouched by industrial civilization. Like *Nanook, Louisiana Story* was a project in public relations. Its object was to persuade the American people that oil is the product, not of an impersonal industrial colossus, but of the labor, fortitude and daring of common men. But as Flaherty made the picture, it illustrated his favorite social thesis that mankind is a single community which ought to be united by the purpose of securing a better life for all.

That the documentary film provided a powerful new instrument for stimulating public consideration of social problems became evident during the nineteen-thirties. Under the auspices of the Federal Resettlement Administration, Pare Lorentz produced two films that eloquently presented issues which affected the whole nation, and illustrated the solutions undertaken by the national government. In *The Plow That Broke the Plains*, the problem of soil erosion, and the need for measures of conservation, tragically demonstrated by the "black blizzard" that had brought catastrophe to the prairie states, were expounded simply and forcibly. Another film, *The River,* dealt with the need for flood control and portrayed the work of the Tennessee Valley Authority. Similarly, though without government sponsorship, Robert Stebbins made *People of the Cumberland*, portraying the emergence of isolated descendants of pioneers from poverty and social stagnation; and Ralph Steiner in *The City* dealt with the need for far-sighted urban planning.

Entry of the United States into the Second World War greatly expanded the social use of documentary films. Frank Capra, an outstanding Hollywood director, made *War Comes to America,* a skillful re-editing of newsreels. The United States Army produced *Let There Be Light*, which dealt with the important problem of psychoneuroses, and *Swinging into Step,* a report on new methods of prosthesis. Both of these, inviting compassion for crippled soldiers, actually held profound implications for American society under conditions of peace, since the understanding which they urged was equally applicable to the victims of industrial accidents and the patients in mental wards of civilian hospitals. For the overseas branch of the Office of War Information, which released them in foreign countries, there were made three notable documentary films. How citizens of the United States elect their government was shown in *Tuesday in November*; an operation of the United States Department of Health was vividly shown in *Capital Story*; and the prevention of epidemics was studied in *The Pale Horseman*. In order to bring the human cost of war home to American civilians, the War Department issued a number of remarkable documentary films, of which *The Battle of San Pietro, The True Glory* and *To the Shores of Iwo Jima* were representative examples.

By the end of the war, the practicable use of documentary films in social education had been amply demonstrated. In the judgment of Iris Barry, Curator of the Museum of Modern Art Film Library in New York City, "Our society needs this instrument in peacetime to help the man in the street grasp the complexities of the world in which he votes, extend his horizon, supplement his education." It remained to be seen whether or not the instrument would be used for these purposes, and under what sponsorship.

The documentary film, originally conceived as an extension of the public-relations methods available to industrial enterprises, was likewise capable of being used by special interests as a means of directing and controlling public opinion. During the Great Depression, when the American people had turned against the leadership of its conservative business community, and had elected a government committed to large-scale social experiment, a concerted effort was made by big industry to "sell business to the public." This campaign was subjected to critical analysis by S. H. Walker and Paul Sklar in a series of articles written for *Harper's Magazine*. The role of documentary films, they found, was especially significant. The National Association of Manufacturers made films that were exhibited in four thousand theaters, reaching an audience of six million people. It likewise produced films to be shown, by large-scale employers of labor, before their workers.

Among the great industrial units engaging in the production of propaganda films were the United States Steel Corporation, the General Motors Corporation, the Westinghouse Electric and Manufacturing Company, and the du Pont chemical interests. Some of their films secured presentation in theaters, others before non-theatrical audiences. The Young Men's Christian Association operated a Motion Picture Bureau "for the benefit of American industry" which offered a "guaranteed distribution of advertising films." This service reached some twenty-five thousand non-theatrical exhibitors having a total audience estimated at twelve million people. Almost half of these exhibitors were schools, high schools, universities, and adult-education classes. Similarly, the American Museum of Natural History in New York circulated industrial films to audiences that totalled more than eleven million people, including the membership of fourteen hundred schools. Through such facilities as these, and by means of the documentary film, American corporations were enabled, as the National Association of Manufacturers declared, to meet "with sound facts the falsehoods and half-truths that imperil the American system."

In the field of industrial training the motion picture was well established by the nineteen-thirties. But its use was greatly extended during the Second World War, when films were employed as an integral part of the process of fitting some twenty million workers for unfamiliar tasks in war production. Films were likewise used to train approximately fifteen million members of the armed forces in a variety of essential skills: "whether to load and fire a tommy gun, improvise a bridge, deliver a baby, compute altitude, butcher meat, or overcome malaria, fire or fear." The Navy Department reported that, "Men learn more, remember longer, and show more interest in learning when training films are used than when more traditional methods are employed. Films tend to standardize training, shorten training time, and make instruction more practical." And that the motion picture was beginning to revolutionize methods of public education in the United States was evident from the fact that in the period between 1926 and 1947 there had occurred a seventy-fold increase in the number of sound-equipped projectors used in the public schools.

By 1947, American public schools were using fifteen thousand projectors to show silent pictures, and thirty-five thousand projectors to show pictures with verbal commentary or musical accompaniment. The role played in the school system by educational films was defined by Floyde E. Brooker, of the United States Office of Education: "The motion picture can free the classroom from the experiences of here and now, and can make all the past, and all the present, and all the phenomena that lie beyond the ken of the senses contribute to the learning of the students."

8   Curtain Call for a Titan

In Hollywood, during the spring of 1948, you might sometimes have seen a tall, lean, lordly-featured man strolling along Hollywood Boulevard, stopping to look into shop windows. He wore a wide-brimmed, floppy felt hat, and he carried a cane, but in a city where idiosyncrasy was commonplace, he was not sufficiently neutral to attract attention. So David Wark Griffith, aged seventy-three and long forgotten, moved unrecognized through the pedestrian traffic of the city he had helped to create.

He lived in a modest hotel one block from the crossroads of filmdom at Hollywood and Vine, where his room overlooked the heart of the city. But his existence was practically unnoticed. Griffith apparently cherished his isolation; he refused to answer his telephone, and did not collect the mail that had accumulated for him. He had made no motion picture in seventeen years.

One afternoon, he granted an interview to Ezra Goodman, for the New York newspaper, *PM*. It was his ambition, he said, to see a stage production of *The Treadmill*, the play he had been working on for more than half a century. It was a play about the earth and solar system, with the theme of eternal recurrence, and it told that the universe was foredoomed to annihilation, being of the essence of dust. It was a story of the beginning of life to the ending of life, but perhaps too beautiful and too good for anyone to see.

There had been no improvement in movies since the old days, Griffith declared. Forty years earlier, he had made pictures from the poems of Browning and Keats; but nobody would dare to do this any longer. "Today they have forgotten movement in the moving picture—it is all still and stale," Griffith said. "The moving picture is beautiful, the moving of wind on beautiful trees is more beautiful than a painting. Too much today depends on the voice. I love talking pictures properly done. Sometimes the talk is good, often very bad. We have taken beauty and exchanged it for stilted voices."

And, as if to emphasize his verdict, Griffith summed it up in a single pregnant sentence. "In my arrogant belief," he asserted, "we have lost beauty."

On a hot day at the end of July, three hundred members of Hollywood's motion picture colony turned out to attend the funeral of the genius whom they had rewarded with years of ingratitude. At the services, they were rebuked for the neglect, the obscurity, the tragic frustration that had embittered his later life.

For as one eulogist put it, there had been no solution for David Wark Griffith but a kind of frenzied beating on the barred doors.

PART TWO

The horseless car-

riage makes good

CHAPTER I

Get a Horse

1 Eve of an Epoch

On Thanksgiving eve, 1895, Chicago was having a snowstorm. As the night drew on, you could see great drifts piling up in the streets. Prosperous citizens decided to get out their horses and cutters early in the morning. Nobody wanted to miss the fun. For, after a postponement of some weeks, the absurd event was finally coming off, and a heavy snowfall was bound to make it even more ludicrous.

All Chicago knew about it, of course—the *Times-Herald* had seen to that. Most readers were bewildered. The paper held sound opinions on nearly all subjects. Its publisher, H. H. Kohlsaat, had amassed his wealth in business. Yet this affair was a flagrant departure from common sense. Through his paper, Kohlsaat was sponsoring a contest for self-propelled vehicles. The "motocycles," as the *Times-Herald* called them, were to run from Jackson Park to Evanston and back—more than fifty miles! For this impossible feat, the deluded publisher had offered a total of five thousand dollars in prizes.

The bait had certainly attracted some very queer fish. Cranks and tinkerers from all over the country announced their intention of competing. In all, eighty-eight laid claim to having built some form of "horseless carriage" capable of moving under its own power. Such a contraption could be built, of course. Nine years earlier, one had been demonstrated on the streets of Paris by its inventor, Gottlieb Daimler. In Mannheim, Germany, Carl Benz was working along the same lines. And in France, under Daimler's patents, the firm of Panhard and Levassor was actually manufacturing the costly, dangerous toys. Indeed, they had been raced from Paris to Rouen during the previous year; as a result, wealthy European sportsmen were said to be taking them up as a fad. Recently, Thomas Alva Edison had announced that the horse was now doomed. But this statement was dismissed as the pardonable vagary of a wizard. Sensible, practical-minded Americans knew better. The preposterous things could be built—but why build them? It was obvious that they had no future. Not while roads were what they were, and oats were cheap.

Meanwhile, some of Kohlsaat's self-styled inventors failed to get their machines to Chicago. Others, receiving theirs at the railroad freight yards, were unable to move them to an outlying race track which the *Times-Herald* had rented as headquarters for the contestants. A young man named Hiram Percy Maxim who had come on from Hartford, Connecticut, to see the race, found scattered about in various places throughout the city an astonishing assortment of mechanical monstrosities. There was a bicycle with a direct connected crank from a gasoline engine cylinder on each side. There were enormous wagons that seemed to lack any definite system of propulsion. There was an electric carriage, run by storage batteries. Its steering wheels were in the rear and its driving wheels were in the front; this gave it the slightly disconcerting appearance of running hind end foremost. Its hopeful entrant, a manufacturer of storage batteries in Philadelphia, called the thing an "electrobat," and he had prudently cached, every few miles along the route of the race, relays of charged batteries as replacements for exhausted motive power. Three vehicles were powered by Benz engines, but only one wore its imported carriage. Young Maxim thought it looked like a machine shop on wheels. In his opinion, the best-looking outfit of all was that entered by the Duryea Motor Wagon Company of Springfield, Massachusetts. It was called a "buggyaut" and was actually a horse-buggy, complete even to whip-socket, equipped with a two-cylinder engine.

In a way, Maxim ranked as an expert critic. His father, Hiram Stevens Maxim, was the inventor of the famous Maxim gun; in the years to come, he himself would give the world the racketeer's best friend, the Maxim silencer. But in 1895, a slight, dark-haired, dark-mustached youth in his middle twenties, Hiram Percy Maxim had served for five months as engineer in charge of the new "motor carriage department" of the Pope Manufacturing Company of Hartford, makers of the celebrated Columbia bicycle. The cycle craze was still at its peak, but Colonel Albert A. Pope was a shrewd business man. Though to him it seemed incredible, there might come a time when people would rebel against pedalling, and demand a mechanically propelled device for independent, long-distance travel over the nation's roads.

Should the fickle public ever make this demand, Colonel Pope wanted to be ready to satisfy it. Young Maxim was recommended to him as one who had been experimenting with gasoline engines. Like everyone else, Colonel Pope knew that gasoline was sold in hardware stores by day, in drug stores at night. It was said to remove grease spots from clothing. If exploded in an engine, it was thought capable of releasing tremendous power. But people who fiddled with it were likely to be killed, for it was every bit as temperamental as dynamite. Aware of its murderous nature, Colonel Pope courageously surmounted his instinctive misgivings. He hired Maxim to design and produce the hypothetical Columbia motor carriage.

Maxim hoped to father a sweet-running little gasoline carriage

that would effortlessly skim over rough country roads, up hill and
down dale, its shiny engine contentedly purring somewhere down
below. In August, 1895, he mounted his engine on a light Craw-
ford runabout and—attended by a crowd of cyclists, pedestrians
and drivers of terrified horses—successfully wheedled his embryonic motor carriage for a quarter of a mile in the streets of
Hartford. Nearly forty years later he was to recall that the vehicle
shook, trembled, rattled and clattered; that it spat oil, fire, smoke
and smell. To any person who disliked machinery, and who had
been trained to appreciate the lustrous elegance of fine horse
carriages, it was revolting. Mr. George H. Day, vice-president of
the company, was such a person. He contemplated the noisy,
greasy, mechanical monster with distaste. He could see no place
for it in any civilized scheme of things.

Although Maxim drove it, two months later, to the city line
and back—all of six miles—without disaster, Mr. Day remained
convinced that he was on the wrong track. Maxim could continue
working on a gasoline-powered vehicle, but the projected Columbia was to be an electric carriage. Mr. Day was one of the city's
foremost industrialists, and his views were accepted without
question. An obscure young engineer could privately reject Mr.
Day's judgment as faulty; he could not publicly affirm his own
faith that a great industry would one day be founded on the
gasoline motor vehicle. Yet less than a decade later, he was to see
Mr. Day become president of the Association of Licensed Automobile Manufacturers, whose members built motor cars powered
only by gasoline.

In Chicago, Maxim consorted with the weary, harried and
very dirty men who were spending days and nights underneath, or
half inside, the grotesque wheeled objects that required about
five hours of tinkering for every hour of locomotion. To ride in
one of them was an adventure of the first magnitude, and Maxim
surmised that only courageous men, well equipped with tools,
knowledge and spare parts, who were indifferent to dirt, grease,
smoke and noise, would consider going anywhere in any motor
vehicle as yet built. Like his friend, Charles Brady King, of
Detroit, who also had been trying to build a gasoline carriage,

Maxim was not a contestant in the race. Both were appointed to ride as umpires; Maxim, with the driver of the "electrobat," and King with the driver of one of the Benz carriages. As the snow-storm increased in fury, consternation prevailed among the contestants. On the advice of someone, many began a frantic search for rope and sash cord to wind around their tires. But late in the night all but eleven abandoned hope of entering the race.

2 Not to the Swift

On Thanksgiving morning only six drivers showed up with their vehicles at the starting line in Jackson Park. Despite the intense cold and deep snow, a large crowd had gathered. There were so many family sleighs and speedy cutters present that each racer seemed likely to be trailed, at a discreet distance, by the music of tinkling bells and equine laughter. The hopes of three contestants were speedily dashed. The "electrobat" in which Maxim rode dropped out before reaching its first cached battery replacement; another electric vehicle followed suit; a gasoline carriage gave up the ghost in a snowdrift less than a mile from the start. This left the field to the Duryea "buggyaut," the Benz in which King was riding, and another entered by R. H. Macy and Company, the New York department store, which hoped to secure the American agency for Benz's motor carriages. All three vehicles were delayed by the panic of outraged horses, the hostility of small boys, and the snowdrifts from which their drivers frequently had to extricate them by dismounting and pushing. All three suffered from mechanical breakdowns.

Nevertheless, they succeeded in reaching Evanston and setting out on the return journey. After colliding, successively, with a horse-car, a cutter and a hack, the Macy Benz became an un-manageable wreck in Douglas Park. The driver of the Benz in which King was riding lapsed into unconsciousness on reaching Garfield Boulevard, probably as a result of exposure. Propping him up with one hand, King managed the tiller with the other, and brought the vehicle to the finish line. But the Duryea "buggyaut" had come in a half hour earlier, completing the course of fifty-two miles at an average speed of slightly more than five miles an hour. The first of many gruelling endurance tests for horseless carriages had been won by an American vehicle. His confidence inflated by this vindication, the delighted Kohlsaat immediately put his own reputation in still graver jeopardy. Within five years, he announced, the streets of Chicago would show five horseless carriages for every equipage still in use.

Such unbounded confidence was expressed by only one American other than Kohlsaat, Edison, and the pioneer experimenters. This happy visionary was a New Yorker, E. P. Ingersoll, who had just launched the trade magazine of a still unborn industry. In the first number, he candidly acknowledged that inauguration of the *Horseless Age* might strike some readers as premature. Yet, he declared, "those who have taken the pains to search beneath the surface for the great tendencies of the age see what a giant industry is struggling into being there." To many readers this must have seemed pure hallucination. What, then, could they think of the deductions which Ingersoll drew from the Chicago race? "From the gradual displacement of the horse in business and pleasure will come economy of time and practical money-saving. In cities and in towns the noise and clatter of the streets will be reduced, a priceless boon to the tired nerves of this overwrought generation . . . Streets will be cleaner, jams and blockades less likely to occur, and accidents less frequent, for the horse is not so manageable as a mechanical vehicle."

But an overwrought generation seemed likely to have to endure the weariness of its nerves, the incidence of traffic jams and accidents, and the defilement of its streets by Dobbin for a long time to come. In the summer of 1896, six months after Ingersoll's predictions were published, there was scant indication that they would ever be fulfilled. True, the Patent Office had received more than five hundred applications covering self-propelled vehicles and parts; and so fertile were the imaginations of the eccentrics who filed them that there were said to be some three hundred different kinds of contraptions on their drawing boards. But in the United States, that summer, there were only sixteen horseless carriages in existence and capable of being operated.

Of these, the most widely known was a duplicate of "the

famous Duryea Motor-Wagon or Motor-Cycle" which had won
the Chicago race. Indeed, the happy owner had plastered the
nation's billboards and barns with its picture, alleging it to be
"the identical horseless carriage that won the great race." For even
in his old age P. T. Barnum was a tireless searcher for sensational
novelties, and he had bought a "buggyaut" to add to the wonders
of Barnum and Bailey's Circus. All over the country, it drew
gaping crowds. In the street and circus-ring parades it preceded
the freaks and wild animals, spasmodically coughing and belching
noxious smoke, and many reasonable Americans decided that it
had found its appropriate, perhaps predestined, place.

However, by this time the Duryea marvel had won a second
race as widely publicized as the Chicago event. It was sponsored by
John Brisben Walker, editor and publisher of *The Cosmopolitan*,
and to make it the more impressive he had persuaded three
variously distinguished Americans to serve as judges. The names
of General Nelson A. Miles, Chauncey Depew and John Jacob
Astor should have acted as a powerful antidote to popular
skepticism. For the general was the nation's ranking military man;
Depew was not only an eminent corporation lawyer and president
of the New York Central Railroad, but the most celebrated of
after-dinner speakers; while Astor was, so to speak, the American
Prince of Wales, for his mother had long been the undisputed
ruler of native "society." Under the reflected brilliance of this
triple prestige, the *Cosmopolitan* race was run on Decoration Day,
1896.

The course led from City Hall in New York to the fashionable
Ardsley Country Club in Irvington-on-the-Hudson, and return.
At the club, nearly one thousand guests were assembled to welcome
the arrival of the first horseless carriage; a prize of three thousand
dollars awaited the winner at City Hall. Three Duryea carriages
participated; a Benz was their only competitor. The winner—so
an astonished observer reported—climbed the steepest hills without assistance or delay, and went up a stiff grade with perfect ease.
Indeed, its performance convinced him that horseless carriages
of quality and price suitable for general use must soon be on the
market.

This, in fact, was the ambitious project of the Duryea company, which presently set up a "demonstrator" on Broadway, in New York City, prepared to take orders for future delivery. The "new model" Duryea was persuasively advertised. It was described as being adapted for general use on all kinds of roads in all kinds of weather. It was guaranteed to be noiseless, odorless, free from vibration, perfectly controllable and absolutely safe. It exemplified the indefinable element of style, for it had the handsome lines of a high-grade carriage, but presented a "complete" appearance—not a "carriage-without-a-horse look." Yet this unique combination of utilitarian, functional and esthetic appeal—even when reinforced by the combined impressiveness of a Miles, Depew and Astor—utterly failed to break down the sales resistance of skeptical New Yorkers. The Duryea company built thirteen vehicles before the year was out, but nearly half a century later its surviving member confessed that all sales were made to New England people. Even in a perplexingly changing world the persistence of Yankee idiosyncrasy could be relied on.

CHAPTER II

Some Called Them Crackpots

1 The Springfield Zanies

Although Springfield, Massachusetts, was the birthplace of the
first American car, its builders—the brothers Charles E. and J.
Frank Duryea—were born and brought up on an Illinois farm.
Charles, the elder by six years, was both inventive and imaginative.
At seventeen, never having seen a bicycle, he succeeded in constructing one. Two years later, in an essay written for the grad-
uation exercises of his class, he predicted that, "The humming of
flying machines will be music over all lands, and Europe will be
but a half day's journey." In 1882, this was scarcely the kind of
notion which enterprising Middle Western capitalists were likely

to favor, so Charles Duryea found work, successively, as a carpenter, blacksmith, millwright and machinist. By 1890, at the age of twenty-seven, he was established in the bicycle business in Chicopee, Massachusetts, where his younger brother, Frank, was employed as a toolmaker. In the summer of the following year the brothers did some reading on the subject of gas engines, and in an English book they found an illustration of the four-cycle compression engine designed by the German inventor, N. Otto. The project of using this engine to power a vehicle was conceived by Charles, and to it he devoted all his leisure hours. He completed his drawings early in 1892, and during March of that year managed to persuade a local businessman, Erwin F. Markham, to become the first American investor in an automotive enterprise. According to the historic contract, Markham put up one thousand dollars to be spent in "constructing the first of the above-mentioned mechanically-propelled road vehicles, and in otherwise developing said invention." Thus assured of capital, Charles promptly engaged Frank to help in the work of actual construction.

The subsequent course of events was afterwards to become a savagely disputed issue. In middle age, personal misfortune embittered Charles Duryea. More than anything else, he wished to have sole credit as the designer of America's first automobile, and up to his death in 1938 he tirelessly asserted his claim to this credit. Thereafter, his right to recognition was sustained by his son. But Frank Duryea, surviving Charles, was deeply offended by certain statements made by his nephew. Having maintained silence during Charles' lifetime, Frank Duryea published his version of the story of America's first car in 1942, when he was seventy-three years old. In the controversy that developed, the arguments of both sides, set forth in books and pamphlets, were deposited in major libraries throughout the country, and the clamor of the earliest horseless carriage was perpetuated, for future generations, in an acrimonious family feud.

In the autumn of 1892, Charles Duryea moved from Springfield, Massachusetts to Peoria, Illinois, where he again engaged in the bicycle business. According to him, his "buggyaut" received its first road test on April 19th of that year. According to Frank

Duryea, the contract under which Markham agreed to finance its construction was dated March 28th, and "no car—especially the first of its kind in America—could have been built in twenty-two days, ready for operation." The car, Frank Duryea contended, was neither completed nor operated before Charles's departure from Springfield; when moving to Illinois, Charles announced that he must leave the finishing of the "buggyaut" to Frank, whom he had hired to take charge of its actual construction.

Thereafter, Frank Duryea asserted, construction proceeded, and Charles' designs were rigorously followed. But before the car had been completed, its mechanism was seen to be defective, and Frank Duryea persuaded Markham to let him design and build a new engine. Work on it was not finished until the last of August, 1893, when it was installed in the "buggyaut." The vehicle was then removed from the shop, briefly stored in an alley, and hauled by horse to a barn owned by Markham's son-in-law, from which Frank Duryea hoped to drive it on a test run without attracting any observers. On September 22nd, 1893, the *Springfield Evening Union* reported that the "buggyaut" had actually been driven on the road. This test—presumably the first appearance of a motor car on an American road—revealed that the transmission was not efficient, so Frank Duryea designed and installed a gear and clutch transmission giving two speeds and reverse. Thus improved, the vehicle performed successfully on the road in January, 1894. By this time, additional capital was required, but Frank soon discovered that, although the "buggyaut" operated satisfactorily, an inspection of it, with its mechanism down close to the ground and plainly visible, always left a possible investor cold. He therefore began building a second model, with its machinery concealed in the body. This was finished late in 1894, when Charles Duryea visited Springfield, and was given "his first ride in a Duryea car" on the top floor of the building in which it had been constructed.

This second car—which almost a year later Frank Duryea drove to fame in the Chicago race—was constantly operated in and around Springfield during the spring and summer of 1895 for the purpose of attracting further financial investment. Finally, after undertaking an eighteen-mile trip, a promoter enlisted sufficient capital to form the Duryea Motor Wagon Company, the first of its kind in the United States. Both brothers were stockholders and directors, but Frank was appointed engineer in charge of design and construction, and Charles returned to his home in Peoria. After the victory in the Chicago race, Frank built a third model, embodying various improvements, and with it won the *Cosmopolitan* race in New York. He then made further changes in design, and a new Duryea car was completed in October, 1896; one month later, this vehicle was the victor in the English "Liberty Day" race from London to Brighton and return —the first gasoline car of American manufacture to achieve recognition abroad.

By this time, the Duryea brothers were internationally famous, and appeared to be on the threshold of lasting prosperity. But two years later Frank Duryea negotiated the sale of their stock in the Duryea company, and their business association ended. He went on to design and manufacture the Stevens-Duryea car, and retired from the automotive field in 1915. Charles Duryea's subsequent career was far less fortunate. Apparently incapable of keeping abreast of rapid developments in the industry which he had helped to found, Charles steadfastly held to his original project of a vehicle as light as a buggy, and unsuccessfully attempted to build and market three-wheeled motor cars. Failing in this, he turned to writing for automotive trade journals, and gradually sank into what he considered an unmerited obscurity. As an aging and embittered man, he wrote pamphlets to prove that he, alone, deserved credit for the first American automobile. It was his melancholy fate to be all but forgotten by his successors; to have his claims seriously damaged after his death; and to be celebrated, in the end, not as the father but "the apostle of the automobile."

2   The Dragon of Kokomo

While Frank Duryea was working at the "buggyaut," another restless mid-Westerner, unknown to the brothers and ignorant of their project, was seized by the same notion. The fantasy, in his case, sprang from painful experience and urgent practical

ABOVE: Duryea's First Horseless Carriage

BELOW: Barnum & Bailey Display the "Buggyaut"

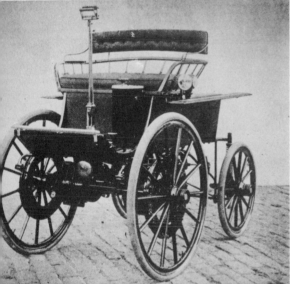

ABOVE: A Home-Made
Steam Wagon. 1893

LEFT: An Electrobat

BELOW: An Early Stevens-
Duryea "Gasoline Wagon"

OPPOSITE PAGE: Duryea's
Second Horseless Carriage.
Winner of the 1895 Race

ABOVE, LEFT:
Elwood Haynes
    and His First Auto

LEFT: Birthplace of the
            Ford Car

ABOVE, RIGHT:
Henry Ford
    with His First Car, 1896

ABOVE:
The Stanley Brothers
    in Their Steamer

CENTER:
Hill Climbing Test
    by an Early Oldsmobile

BELOW:
The Horseless Carriage
    Reaches the Country

OPPOSITE PAGE:
R. E. Olds
Takes President Theodore
    Roosevelt for a Ride

need; the prospect of exploiting it commercially did not dawn until later. This procrastination of the profit motive was the more ironical because Elwood G. Haynes was neither a crank nor a tinkerer, but a prosperous businessman. Unlike most of the other automotive pioneers, he had received an excellent education. Specializing in science, he took postgraduate courses at Johns Hopkins and was already launched on his chosen career of teaching when natural gas was discovered in his native state of Indiana. A new industry mushroomed almost overnight, and Haynes abandoned teaching to enter it. At the age of thirty-six he was living in the city of Kokomo; as field superintendent of a natural gas company, his work kept him constantly traveling over rural roads in a buggy. Though otherwise satisfied with his existence, Haynes fretted over the multiple discomforts and inconveniences of his time-consuming expeditions. The desire to eliminate these became obsessive. Not unreasonably, for Haynes was suffering, in an acute form, from the peculiar torments that afflicted all urban residents who ventured to drive or cycle far out into the countryside.

These hardy explorers faced primitive conditions soon after crossing the city line. There, they left behind cobblestoned streets and the stretches of macadam paving that were beginning to replace them; horse-cars and cable-cars and the new electric trolley lines for which enterprising capitalists were securing franchises, often by shady political deals. Once in the open country, adventurous souls found themselves abruptly translated into an earlier era. Throughout the United States, roads were prevailingly wretched: rough and rutted always; deep in mud after the winter thaws, heavily layered in sand and dust all summer. When the nation's expanding railroad system achieved a monopoly of long-distance haulage and travel, turnpikes, like canals, began to be abandoned. Regional roads fell into disuse, except as they served narrowly local needs. Their upkeep was the responsibility of the townships. In general, rural property-owners could pay their road tax in money or, as most preferred to do, work it out whenever the authorities got around to making casual repairs. American farmers were already feeling the hard times which would bring about the prolonged financial depression of the eighteen-nineties and usher in the angry revolt of the Populist party. Aggrieved by low incomes, tight money, the high cost of manufactured goods, the tribute exacted by railroads, bankers and trusts, and rising taxes, they were not in a mood to undertake the additional burden of highway improvements. For how would better roads add to their income?

An incipient "good-roads movement" therefore aroused their opposition, the more savagely, perhaps, because it was sponsored by prosperous city folk whom the farmers regarded as their oppressors. The demand for better roads followed hard upon the appearance of the first "safety-bicycle" in 1887—a novelty which, replacing the high front and low back wheels with two of equal size, was readily mounted, easily pedalled, and far less hazardous to sit. From the very outset, it seduced the imagination of city dwellers; men and women alike thronged to the riding schools that were opened everywhere; special costumes were designed for the new sport; and soon the output of bicycles could not keep pace with the rising popular demand for them. By 1889 Colonel Albert A. Pope, the nation's foremost manufacturer of bicycles, was pleading the cause of better roads, in behalf of better business, before a convention of the National Carriage Builders' Association. Within a few more years, the number of cyclists could be reckoned in the millions and the League of American Wheelmen, organized to represent them, began a militant agitation for nation-wide improvement of highways. The legislature of New Jersey, first to succumb to this pressure, established the principle of granting state aid to develop a network of roads. Other states gradually followed this example. By 1893, the League had carried its campaign to the Federal government. In that year Congress—with a noteworthy blindness to the possibilities of patronage—appropriated ten thousand dollars to set up the Office of Public Roads Inquiries. Under its auspices, qualified experts advised state and township authorities in all matters pertaining to roadbuilding or improvement. The profession of civil engineering seemed due for an expansion, and manufacturers of roadbuilding machinery and materials enjoyed visions of future prosperity.

But rural hostility did not abate. It was, if anything, intensified by the antics of city-slicker cyclists. These were of two breeds:
the "scorchers" who, imitating celebrated professional racers, were
maniacs for speed, and the members of the Century Road Club,
who wore badges laddered with gold bars, each of which certified
to the pedaling of one hundred miles in eighteen hours. Both the
"scorchers" and the "centuries" streamed out through the countryside, crouching over their handlebars, scaring nervous farm
animals and spattering villagers with mud in their demoniac
pursuit of "records." This, surely, was bad enough; but there was
worse to come. For presently the stern public morality of American
farmers received a shattering jolt. Incredibly, there flashed by a
"tandem" bicycle—and for it, one half the motive power was
being furnished by a woman: probably young, necessarily short-
skirted, and therefore obviously abandoned. When, far from home,
these jezebels and their sinful companions begged shelter for the
night, conscience required that they first be turned away; and
the price ultimately set on exposure to moral contamination was
seldom low. It took a long time for the American farmer to admit
that, in the words of a song which swept the nation, Daisy might
look sweet upon the seat of a bicycle built for two.

Therefore, since legislatures were sensitive to the rural vote,
it was not surprising that some, although making appropriations
for road improvement, also passed statutes to regulate unusual
forms of transportation. The advice of Washington experts was
often filed and forgotten. By the turn of the century, Americans
of all ages and both sexes were pedaling ten million bicycles;
three hundred manufacturers were producing them at the rate of
more than a million a year. But their riders presumably endured
physical misery in order to enjoy the delights of exercise and sport.
For when, in 1904, the first census of the nation's highways was
taken, it showed that although the mileage of rural roads totalled
more than two million, only some hundred and fifty thousand
miles were "surfaced" in any form—and less than one hundred
and fifty miles, in all the United States, had any kind of paving.

In 1893, however, conditions were almost certainly worse.
Brooding, unhappily, on the bruises received during his buggy

rides, on the long monotonous hours spent in driving from one gas-well to another, Elwood Haynes dreamed of the comfort and speed which might be attained with a horseless carriage. His scientific training equipped him to understand the principles underlying construction of a motor vehicle. But—again, unlike most other pioneers in this field—he had no aptitude for practical mechanics. So when he had made drawings of the vehicle he wanted, he decided to show them to two brothers who ran a machine shop in Kokomo.

Neither Elmer nor Edgar Apperson knew anything about horseless carriages. But they were expert in their craft and gifted, to an unusual degree, with the mechanical ingenuity common to young Americans of their time. Their rates for work were forty cents an hour. Whatever their private opinion of Haynes' project, they accepted his commission to execute it as imperturbably as if it had been any routine job. They worked on it during slack periods, buying whatever parts were available, themselves making all others. At the end of a year, they had Haynes' horseless carriage ready for him.

Most of the early builders of horseless carriages made their first road tests in secret, usually at night and on unfrequented streets, for misadventures were all too likely, and the ribald jeers of onlookers were inevitable. But Haynes and the Appersons displayed unique courage, perhaps born of blind faith. They not only announced a public demonstration but made certain that it would have the largest possible audience. Independence Day, in 1894 as always, would be celebrated with a parade, a band concert and patriotic oratory before the grand climax of fireworks after nightfall, and from early morning the people of Kokomo were likely to be out on the streets. Shortly before the holiday, Haynes and the Appersons had the horseless carriage hauled to the outskirts of town. On the morning of the Fourth, they prepared it for trial. At length, with Elmer Apperson at the tiller and Haynes beside him on the high seat, the vehicle moved off, its engine patriotically saluting the day with explosive sounds and a trail of smoke. And presently, incredulous townsfolk who lined the route stared wide-eyed at the homemade wonder as it passed, triumphantly charging into Kokomo at the spanking speed of six miles an hour.

3 Try, and Try Again

To other resolute experimenters, accounts of the successes of the Duryeas and Haynes and the Appersons were both a source of envy and an additional incentive. And some of them were soon to enjoy similar triumphs. In Cleveland, Ohio, Alexander Winton, a prosperous manufacturer of bicycles, was hard at work in a corner of his factory. Having earlier served as assistant engineer on an ocean liner, Winton was a competent machinist and, at about the time when Elwood Haynes was making his sketches for a horseless carriage, had succeeded in building a motor-driven bicycle. Dissatisfied with its commercial possibilities, he decided to undertake a four-wheeled vehicle. Completing this in 1896, he was visited with an inspiration. Would it not be far more comfortable to ride in if he equipped it with pneumatic tires like those supplied with his bicycles?

The notion was a happy one, and Winton promptly went to the B. F. Goodrich Company in Akron, which in addition to manufacturing such rubber products as wringer rolls and fire hose did a large business in bicycle tires. His reception might have daunted any less obstinate innovator. Bertram G. Work, superintendent of the plant, and later to become president of the company, was not impressed. Warning Winton that there might never be another demand for similar equipment, he undertook to execute the commission only if Winton agreed to assume all costs which it might involve. A set of four giant tires for Winton's vehicle would probably come to around four hundred dollars. Winton took the plunge. Under Work's direction, the Goodyear plant proceeded to build four outsized, extra-strong, extra-reinforced bicycle tires, adding plies of fabric until they appeared to have sufficient toughness. When finally fitted to Winton's carriage, they were sixteen-ply monsters made of ordinary cross-woven bicycle tire fabric—the first produced for their specific purpose in the United States.

A shrewd businessman with a flair for publicity, Winton was the earliest experimenter, after the Duryeas, to deduce the commercial possibilities of the horseless carriage, and to realize that, if a market was to be established, the merits of the vehicle must be dramatized in some spectacular manner that would arrest public attention. Racing—in which Winton was shortly to become pre-eminent—proved, for a decade or more, to be the most successful means of securing wide publicity. In this, the United States was merely following the pattern established by France, where the motor car was introduced rather as a toy for wealthy sportsmen than as an efficient and reliable mode of transportation adapted to general use. But, although Winton exploited the vogue for racing, he was also the first American to foresee one of the ultimate major uses of the automobile, and to dramatize it for purposes of publicity. In the summer of 1897, having built two more vehicles —one of which he sold, but promptly took back from its dissatisfied purchaser—he organized the Winton Motor Carriage Company and pondered the problem of awakening the nation to its existence. What he needed was both capital and a market for his products, and these needs were inseparable, for without a market he could not hope to secure capital, and without capital he would be unable to develop a market. New York was, obviously, the likeliest place to find both, and the means which Winton employed to stun the jaded metropolis, and through it the nation, had a touch of prophetic genius. Climbing into his car, he left Cleveland on the first of all American cross-country motor tours, and reached New York ten days later. Unfortunately for Winton, this exploit proved to be premature; the momentous trip yielded no sales and attracted no capital; and presently Winton shipped his vehicle back to Cleveland by freight.

Meanwhile, in Detroit, Michigan, Charles Brady King—who had been working on the construction of a motor vehicle since 1894, and as umpire had driven the last miles of the Chicago race—was spurred on to new efforts by the excitement of the Chicago event. "It wasn't money I wanted," he told the journalist Brendan Gill fifty years later. "It was to do things. I was bursting with ideas. Bursting!" Of the original pioneers, King was easily the most inventive and versatile. With the single exception of Elwood Haynes, he was the only one who displayed a strong predilection for scientific research. Haynes, after many years spent as a manufacturer of automobiles, returned to the interests of his youth and made important contributions to the metallurgy of steel and aluminum. King, during some two decades of immersion in industry, found time to develop and patent more than forty varied inventions. Success alone never fully satisfied him, and he was intellectually too restless ever to be completely absorbed by business. Just before the first World War, concluding that spade-work had been finished in the automotive industry, and that the fun was therefore going out of it, he retired—in order to devote himself to art, architecture, music and other avocations which had always claimed his interest.

King's maternal grandmother had been born in Detroit when it was a frontier stockade, and his grandfather operated the first steam ferry between Detroit and Windsor. His father, a veteran of the Mexican War and the War between the States, was an army officer, and King's childhood was spent, largely among scouts and Indians, moving from one far-Western army post to another, often by wagon train. Watching the westward thrust of the railroads, he developed an early interest in transportation, and his first youthful inventions were largely in the field of improved railroad equipment. After two years at Cornell University, King settled in Detroit and presently established himself as a manufacturer of marine engines.

By 1894, King had already begun building his first motor vehicle, a four-cylinder bevel-drive machine. This failed to satisfy him, and he abandoned it without ever trying it on the road. Within the next year, the company he had organized put out a new engine; fifty years later, King described it as the first four-cylinder block engine ever produced. On his return from the Chicago race, he determined to use this engine on a second vehicle. More conversant with foreign achievements in automotive engineering than any other American pioneer, King had probably been impressed by the cars being made in France by Panhard and Levassor. These were a new form of vehicle; having the engine forward, they bore no resemblance whatever to the horse-drawn carriage which Americans were imitating. For his second vehicle, King had designed a new carriage, replacing the tiller with a steering wheel. Had he used this design, King might have been the first American to develop a horseless carriage not haunted by the reproachful ghost of a horse.

But King put his design aside when a firm of carriage builders offered him a body built for experimental trial on a self-propelled vehicle. This had a tiller, and he retained it. He installed his new engine, a foot-operated accelerator, a muffler and tanks for water and gasoline. In several respects, this vehicle was an improvement on any previously produced. It was ready for a road test on March 1, 1896; but, as a precaution against unfavorable publicity, King first drove it several times at night, unseen by anyone. The fact that it actually ran was sufficient justification and, on the evening of March 6th, King drove it along Woodward Avenue in a public demonstration. Next morning, Detroit newspapers excitedly reported the first appearance of a motor car on the streets of the city.

4   Citizen Fixit

While he drove that evening, King recalled long afterwards, a friend followed him about on a bicycle. This absorbed watcher was a slight, wiry, cold-eyed, stern-visaged man who looked older than his thirty-three years; whose thin lips, tightly compressed, gave his expression a touch of defiant obstinacy. The successful performance of King's vehicle may have encouraged Henry Ford, but it must likewise have caused him a sharp pang of envy. The two men had been acquainted for some years. They had been drawn together by their besetting ambition to build practicable self-propelled vehicles. During the winter of 1896, they met frequently in the evenings to discuss their problems, compare progress and exchange ideas. At the time, all the advantages rested with King. He was well grounded in engineering theory, had read widely on the subject of automotive invention, and his reputation as an established and successful marine engineer inspired some confidence in his project. The mechanical resources of his own plant were adequate, and his financial credit enabled him to procure not only whatever materials he needed, but the best of their kind. As a result, his progress was faster than Ford's. More importantly, his vehicle was of considerably more advanced design.

Whereas King was working under conditions propitious to success, the atmosphere that surrounded Ford was heavily saturated with frustration and failure. A born tinkerer whose only known talent was an uncanny aptitude for repairing, and keeping in running order, almost any kind of machinery, his forays into the field of invention had never yielded tangible results. His persistence in making them met with explicit disapproval or, less endurably, with ridicule and a degree of contempt. The son of a farmer in Dearborn, nine miles west of Detroit, he had always detested the farmer's life. From earliest childhood, he was fascinated by machinery; the only toys he ever knew were tools. At thirteen, he was pulling apart old clocks and watches, and putting them together again, somehow making them run. Presently, he was keeping his father's farm equipment in repair, and mending that of the neighbors. At fifteen, after some years of sketchy schooling, he put formal education behind him forever. At sixteen, driven by his passion for mechanical work, he ran away from home and tramped up to Detroit to learn the machinist's trade. His practical-minded father, who wished him to become a farmer, all but gave him up for lost.

At twenty-four, Ford was a journeyman mechanic in Detroit, installing and repairing steam and gasoline engines. Abruptly, he abandoned this congenial life to return to Dearborn and farming; to tempt him back, his father had given him forty acres of woodland and a threshing machine. Young Ford set up a portable sawmill to clear his timber, hired out with his thresher when opportunity offered, and laboriously tried to build, with odds and ends of discarded equipment, a steam locomotive capable of being hitched either to a plow or a road wagon. His attempt was fruitless. Married, now, to the daughter of a neighboring farmer, he was considered an able "fixer," but in every other respect impractical and queer—a grown man who spent his time fiddling with childish contraptions; a foredoomed failure on the land. Perhaps nettled by this local appraisal, certainly more disenchanted than ever with a farmer's life, Ford cast about for some way of escape. The offer of a mechanic's job with the Detroit Edison Company came opportunely. For a twelve-hour day, it paid forty-five dollars a month, more money than he had succeeded in making in Dearborn. With his wife and his tools, Ford returned to Detroit.

Eight years later, in 1896, he had risen to be chief engineer at the Edison plant, and his monthly paycheck stood at one hundred and twenty-five dollars. It looked as if the impractical tinkerer had finally found his proper niche; kindly folk hoped that he might have sufficient common sense to remain in it permanently. His prospects appeared far better than he had any legitimate right to hope. Everyone knew that electricity was going to be the future universal power. The industry was headed for an immense expansion, and Ford was already established on the ground floor.

Meanwhile Ford, like nearly every other American, had read about the Duryeas and their horseless carriage. He could not forget his humiliating failure with the steam-powered traction unit. The spectacular success of the Duryeas with an internal combustion engine started his mind off on a new track. He resolved to build himself a gasoline horseless carriage. For the general construction, transmission and steering gear, he could draw on his experience with the ill-fated steam vehicle. But, with respect to the engine itself, he knew that he would once again have to work from the ground up. Lacking any theoretical knowledge of engineering, he would have to rely exclusively on his proved ability as a mechanic.

In the rear of the two-family house on Bagley Avenue where Ford lived with his wife and small son, there was a brick shed intended for the storage of wood and coal. There he had set up his workshop and now, in his leisure hours, nights and Sundays, he began to struggle with his recalcitrant dream. An expert cyclist, his initial plan—soon discarded—was for a motor bicycle. The projected machine that he presently evolved was a conglomerate of personal souvenirs. The steam car he had failed with, the motorcycle he had abandoned, the engines he had repaired presided over its birth. He called it a "quadricycle." It was to be mounted on bicycle wheels, and a bicycle saddle fastened to the fuel tank would serve for a seat. His tools were crude, and he had to do most of his work by hand. Lack of time to search out the best materials for each part, lack of money to pay for them retarded his progress. His credit at the hardware store did not exceed fifteen dollars, so he made most of his parts from odd bits of scrap metal. But even the irreducible minimum of purchases which he had to make took more money than the family could well spare. "It seemed," Mrs. Ford remarked long afterwards, "as if we would never have any for ourselves." This, at the time, was not her only grievance. For her husband had clamped an experimental engine to the kitchen sink, and on winter nights in 1896 he and Charles King would fuss over it, oblivious of young Edsel, asleep in the adjoining room, and all too likely to be poisoned by gasoline fumes.

Gradually, as the spring of 1896 wore on, the quadricycle approached completion. Money had been found to replace its bicycle saddle with a buggy seat. King, who was already at work improving the engine of his car, contributed two intake valves he no longer needed. Ford had made two cylinders by hand from the exhaust pipe of an old steam engine. He was in a tense mood. He hoped that he was headed in the right direction, occasionally felt sure that he was, sometimes merely wondered whether he was not wasting his time. The old, ominous note of disapproval had once again come to him, this time at the Edison plant. He was highly regarded by his superiors, but word of his experiments had reached Alexander Dow, president of the company. Dow had no objection to experiments as such—if they had anything to do with electricity. That his chief engineer should be devoting himself to gas engines seemed rather worse than a waste of time; it was, in fact, like biting the feeding hand. One day, he offered some pointed advice. "Electricity, yes, that's the coming thing. But gas—no."

The quadricycle would operate at two speeds; ten, and twenty miles an hour. It could be manipulated to turn, which was essential, since Ford had failed to solve the problem of reverse gear, or neglected to provide any, and the machine would move only forward. It would move, and it would stop, but it could not slow down: it had no brakes. Such as it was, the vehicle was ready for a trial on the road one rainy night early in June. Ford always prided himself on the care with which he planned his work in advance, overlooking no contingency and no detail. Many inventors, he asserted years afterwards, failed because they did not distinguish between planning and experimenting; this was not his habit. But when he tried to move his quadricycle out of his workshop, he found that it was too wide to squeeze through the doorway. In a storm of rage and impatience, he seized an ax and knocked away a part of the brick wall. Then, trundling his car out through the hole, he turned the flywheel until the engine started, climbed into the seat, and drove off into the rain.

Now, for the first time, he knew the elation of success, and in a few weeks he was ready to confute his detractors. Taking King along as a passenger, he drove out to Dearborn to show off his quadricycle. When they reached his father's farm, Ford's pride and anticipation were obvious. King was always to remember how old Mr. Ford came out of the house, and silently stared at his son and the vehicle, how some neighbors drifted by and likewise stared, saying nothing. It was plain to King that old Mr. Ford was ashamed of this son whose trivial toy had humiliated him before his friends. It was probably also plain to Henry Ford, who, as King recalled, stood it as long as he could, then turned to King and said, in a heartbroken way, "Come on, Charlie, let's you and me get out of here."

Vindication was presently to come, however, from a higher authority. In August, the annual convention of the Edison electric companies was held at the Oriental Hotel in Manhattan Beach, near Coney Island, then a resort for fashionable New Yorkers. To this gathering, Alexander Dow of the Detroit company took his chief engineer. At the opening afternoon session, the convention heard a discussion of the new field that promised to develop in the charging of storage batteries for electric vehicles. Several manufacturers had already pioneered with these, and the Pope Manufacturing Company of Hartford, having recently tested the Columbia electric carriage designed by Hiram Maxim, was rumored to be in production. The Edison authorities, weighing this evidence, optimistically predicted that electric carriages and cabs would soon be on the streets of every American city, bringing in an enormous revenue from repairs and recharging.

At the dinner which followed this session, Ford was seated, with Dow, Samuel Insull, the presidents of the New York and Boston Edison companies, and some others, at the table presided over by Edison himself. The talk of electric vehicles continued until Dow, perhaps hoping to impart a salutary lesson, told the group that Ford had built a gas car. One day Dow had heard displeasing noises under his office window, had looked out to see a carriage without any horses, and a woman and little boy sitting in it, and presently had watched Ford leave the plant, climb up to the seat, and drive the thing off. Someone asked how Ford made it go; he began to reply, and soon Edison, cupping his deaf ear with his hand, was listening attentively. Places at table were shifted, and Ford was seated beside the wizard. Edison plied Ford with questions. Ford, always better at graphic than verbal description, sketched out his machine with a pencil. When he had finished, Edison brought his fist down on the table with a bang.

"Young man," said the wizard, "that's the thing; you have it. Keep at it. Electric cars must keep near to power stations. The storage battery is too heavy. Steam cars won't do either, for they have to have a boiler and fire. Your car is self-contained—carries its own power plant—no fire, no boiler, no smoke and no steam. You have the thing. Keep at it."

Reporting these words thirty-four years later, Ford acknowledged that the thump of Edison's fist on the table had been worth worlds to him. Until that moment, no man had ever given him any encouragement. Now, suddenly, from the blue, the man whom he considered the world's greatest inventive genius gave Ford his unqualified approval. From boyhood, Ford had idolized Edison. He admired the wizard's inventions and personality; even more, his gift for hard, continuous work and his refusal to recognize the possibility of defeat. But, beyond the sentimental value of his hero's benediction, Ford was quick to perceive its practical significance. The man who knew most in the world about electricity had disqualified it as a source of motive power, had asserted that, for the purpose in view, Ford's gasoline motor was superior to any possible electric motor—it could go long distances, Edison said, and eventually there would be stations on the roads to supply the cars with hydro-carbon. It was the first time that Ford had ever heard this term used for liquid fuel. He could hardly wait for the convention to adjourn, so eager was he to set to work on a second car. Edison had done away with all anxiety that he might be wasting his time.

Back in Detroit, working in his shed whenever his duties at the Edison plant permitted, Ford began to dream of a day when he could give all his time to this major interest. During the next three years, he built two more vehicles. They were much like the first, but lighter in weight; they lacked reverse gear and brakes; they retained the belt drive which—since the belts were satisfactory except in hot weather—he did not abandon for gears until some time later. Meanwhile, like Charles King, he began driving on the streets of Detroit in full daylight. The police refused to permit them to exceed the speed of five miles an hour. Both men were cursed and threatened by teamsters and other drivers of frightened horses; for some time Ford made a practice of having a friend precede him on a bicycle, to warn them of his approach. The two men found that the clatter and smoke of their cars infuriated many pedestrians. A crowd—some of them angry and all of them curious—would collect whenever Ford stopped his machine; if he left it alone for a moment, some bystander would always climb in and try to run it; he took to chaining it to the nearest lamp post whenever he was compelled to leave it unattended in the street. Daunted by the varied risks to which he was exposing himself, he appealed for protection to the mayor of Detroit, and received a special permit authorizing him to continue his expeditions.

5 Blueprint of the Future

Neither King nor Ford, however, was to make Detroit a potential rival of Springfield, Hartford, Kokomo and Cleveland as a center for the manufacture of horseless carriages. This was to be the

achievement of their contemporary, Ransom E. Olds, whose singular vision projected the pattern of an industry, and thus shaped the
economic destiny of a city and a state. Born in Geneva, Ohio,
Olds was early taken by his father to Lansing, the capital of
Michigan. In this quiet little city, scarcely more than a sizeable
village, the older man set up a machine shop. Like other youths
of his generation, Ranny Olds was imaginatively excited by all
forms of machinery; he could scarcely be driven from the shop.
An expert craftsman, he became his father's partner at the age of
twenty-one. The shop had been making a few crude gasoline
engines for farm and marine use; Olds was already determined to
improve them. He dreamed, also, of applying some form of
mechanical power to vehicles, for he was familiar with the carriage
factories that centered in Flint and Lansing. Very shortly, he
succeeded in producing a new type of gasoline engine and, at the
age of twenty-three, early one morning awakened the people of
Lansing with the roar of a primitive three-wheeled, steam-powered
horseless carriage.

Five years later, Olds bought out his father's interest in the
shop, and organized a company to make and market gasoline
engines. But he also continued his experiments with steam-
powered vehicles, and soon produced a four-wheeled model so
remarkable that the *Scientific American* devoted an article to it.
This periodical was read all over the world, and presently Olds'
steamer was bought by a firm in Bombay, India. This extraordinary result convinced him that a practicable horseless carriage
would command a worldwide market; the commercial possibilities, he thought, would be incalculable. "The gasoline engines
were our bread-and-butter business," he remarked long afterwards,
"and most people thought the car was just a toy, but I knew that
the car was the big venture."

Meanwhile, further experiments with steam persuaded him
that boiler troubles and other difficulties would eventually work
against popular adoption of a steamer, and he foresaw the limitations to which an electric car would be subject. He resolved
to put his knowledge of gasoline engines to use. With Frank G.
Clark, whose father owned a carriage factory, Olds worked for

two years in whatever time could be spared from business, and the two men finally built an experimental gasoline car. This was successfully tested in 1897, and in August of that year, with the assistance of local bankers, Olds organized a company to manufacture and sell motor vehicles. At the first meeting of its directors, Olds was authorized "to build one carriage in as nearly perfect a manner as possible and complete it at the earliest possible moment." This vehicle, carrying four people on two forward-facing seats, was produced within a few months.

Having completed his show car, Olds began to ponder the future. His rivals—the Duryeas, Haynes and the Appersons, Winton—had no more grandiose plans than to build a few vehicles at a time as a speculative venture, or solicit orders in advance and then fill them. But Olds' imagination had been fired by the mirage of a mass market. As yet non-existent, it could not be created through a system of unit production, which involved high costs and must necessarily result in high prices. Costs and prices, he realized, could only be reduced by a system of volume production—yet, in the absence of an assured market, the adoption of such a program might quickly lead to bankruptcy. Nevertheless, Olds could not reconcile himself to building only on order, or to the prospect of limited initial production and gradual expansion. He had conceived a large-scale, full-time operation; he could be content with nothing less. And he had a notion that he could apply certain techniques used by the carriage-builders of Flint, the most important manufacturers engaged in this line. They had originally come to Michigan because of its vast, cheap lumber resources, but these had been exhausted. For some time, therefore, instead of building their carriages locally, they had farmed out the making of parts to specialized suppliers who were located nearer to lumber mills, and had trained their own craftsmen in the efficient assembling of these parts, reducing their operation to a putting-together and final finishing of carriages. Olds thought that this method might be useful in achieving quantity production.

For the large factory upon which he had set his heart, Olds knew that Lansing offered inadequate resources. There were not enough skilled machinists there to staff it. There were not enough houses to accommodate those whom he would have to bring in. There was not even enough capital in the town to finance construction of the plant. At the suggestion of his bankers, Olds went east to talk with their connections there, with a view to setting up his plant in Newark, New Jersey. But Eastern capitalists were dubious about the future of horseless carriages; in 1899, Olds' project struck them as a crackpot scheme; they promptly rejected it. Deeply discouraged, Olds returned to Michigan, stopping in Detroit to confer with his principal stockholder. S. L. Smith was an elderly millionaire who had retired from business after making successive fortunes from lumber and copper mines. A native of the free and easy West, accustomed to large hazards, he did not share the prejudice of Eastern capitalists against novelty, or their timidity when confronted by audacious daring. He had two sons whom he wished to set up in business, and Olds' project, which looked to the future, seemed a fine one for young men. Olds readily consented to take them in and Smith put up approximately two hundred thousand dollars to launch the Olds Motor Works.

A factory was built on East Jefferson Avenue in Detroit, the first in the United States to be designed and laid out for the production of motor cars. Olds devised a model to be sold for twelve hundred and fifty dollars, which was fitted with such unusual improvements as a pneumatic clutch, cushion tires and electric push-button starter. But sales were few and slow; the car proved to be too complicated for a public accustomed to tolerant guidance of a friendly creature; and the company lost eighty thousand dollars in its first year. This convinced Olds that success could be achieved only with an extremely simple and relatively cheap machine—a car which anyone could drive, and any local shop could repair. He therefore designed a lightweight, curved-dash runabout, to be priced at six hundred and fifty dollars. One sample was produced, and announced as the "Oldsmobile," taking its name from the recently coined French word "automobile," which the French Academy had just legitimized, after earnest debate, by inclusion in its dictionary. But before any more Oldsmobiles could be produced, the factory was wrecked by fire. All that remained to the company was its single new model car, rescued from the flames by a plucky employee.

This disaster proved to be a catalytic agent which not only hastened success for the company, but in doing so gave the nascent industry its major principles of development. Audacious as always, Olds refused to suspend production until his plant could be rebuilt. Circumstances now forced him to resort to the technique which he had wished to adopt at the outset. He had no alternative but to farm out the making of parts for his car, and concentrate his workers on the job of final assembly. He had already decided to inaugurate volume production with the new car, and obstinately held to this decision. Ruin and recklessness led him to a group of men whose participation in his plans was to exercise a decisive influence on the future of the automobile.

For some of the parts that he required, Olds turned to two brothers, John F. and Horace Dodge, like himself mechanics by trade, who had lately opened their own machine shop. It was their first introduction to the automotive business; four years later, the experience would persuade them to a speculation the results of which were to be felt throughout the world. Meanwhile, Olds wanted no less than two thousand motors built to his design, and in Detroit there was only one plant competent to undertake so unprecedently large an order. By persuading the Leland and Faulconer Manufacturing Company to accept it, Olds drew into the industry a man who was to furnish its second generative principle. Olds himself had conceived the principle of mass production, and understood that its efficient application depended upon the technique of assembly. Henry Martyn Leland made this technique possible by applying the principle of standardization—the manufacture of parts to such extraordinary precision as to make them absolutely interchangeable. Thus, from their accidental collaboration, there was to be born a product having incalculable social effects; an immense, world-girdling industry; and a technology which was to revolutionize modern productive processes.

Leland, a native of Danville, Vermont, was nearing his sixtieth year when Olds' order for motors launched him, unknowingly, on a new career. As a youth, he had been apprenticed to one of the earliest tool works in Massachusetts. Leaving it as a skilled mechanic, he was employed in the Federal arsenal at Springfield during the War between the States, and afterwards moved on to the Colt arms plant. These munitions factories, following the doctrine originally laid down by Eli Whitney, inventor of the cotton gin, had long assembled their weapons from finely machined parts that were approximately interchangeable. Thus Leland had been imbued with the ideal of accurate machine work at a time when industry still accepted the variations resulting from rule-of-thumb methods. During the 1870s and '80s, he was associated with the foremost manufacturers of machine tools in the East, but in 1890 he settled in Detroit and with his son, Wilfred, embarked on the making of machine tools, marine engines and bicycle parts. His plant constantly worked for closer tolerances; as a result, certain of its products, because of their remarkable precision, commanded premiums as high as three times the current market price. Leland not only had the old-fashioned artisan's extreme pride of craft, but an intimate knowledge of the best factory methods so far devised by the new industrial era. He was already a wealthy man, and the volume of business flowing into his plant assured its continued prosperity. But Olds' order for two thousand motors challenged his vanity. It gave him the opportunity for a spectacular demonstration. He accepted it for the purpose of showing his customers and competitors to what delicately fine standards of accuracy a gasoline engine could be built.

The motors which Leland turned out for Olds soon gave the Oldsmobile a unique reputation for reliability, ease of repair, and smooth, efficient performance. Before the year ended, Olds sold four hundred and twenty-five cars, but in his impatience to expand his market, he also sought nation-wide publicity by duplicating Winton's premature exploit. To the second New York automobile show, held in the autumn of 1901, he sent off a curved-dash runabout driven by one of his young testers, Roy D. Chapin, who would later become a power in the industry and one day enter a president's cabinet as Secretary of Commerce. Chapin spent seven and one half days on wretched roads that almost shook his small, light car to pieces. He exhausted an ample supply of spare parts and had to lay up until more could be sent him. Over a part of his journey he was forced to leave the highways and take to the towpath of the Erie Canal, contesting the right of way with teamsters and their mules. But in the end he drove triumphantly down Fifth Avenue to find that his car and his exploit were the talk of the town.

New York was the most populous and wealthiest state in the union, but in 1901 it possessed fewer than one thousand horseless carriages. Yet the feat of a twenty-one-year-old youth in driving from Detroit to the American metropolis so impressed the public that Olds was able to appoint an agent who undertook to sell one thousand cars in New York City alone. Thus encouraged, he pushed on toward larger and larger production; twenty-five hundred cars in 1902; four thousand in 1903; five thousand in 1904. Clearly, the era of quantity manufacture had dawned. In 1905, determined to make America motor-minded, the Olds company sent two cars off on the first transcontinental trip to be attempted by automobiles. They were to make their way from Detroit, over mud roads and cattle trails and mountain passes, to the Lewis and Clark Exposition in Portland, Oregon, and the first to arrive at this destination finished its journey after forty-four days.

The spectacular and adventurous expedition was eagerly followed by newspaper readers throughout the country, and its successful conclusion led Gus Edwards, a noted composer of popular songs, to write one celebrating the automobile. With most of the nation whistling and singing "In My Merry Oldsmobile," its eventual conquest by the new vehicle appeared inevitable. As the future was to show, the Olds factory served as a training school for more than one hundred men who later rose to leadership in the industry. And the meteoric success of Olds' enterprise—which spread its orders for material through the machine shops, carriage works, and supply firms of the region—had the effect of centering the industry itself in the city of Detroit.

6 A Choice, and a Lesson

While Ransom Olds, with the backing of a millionaire, was organizing the enterprise that would soon catapult him to fame, the fortunes of Henry Ford approached a crisis. One after another, he had built three crude cars in his little workshop and, driving them, became a familiar figure on the streets of Detroit. His local notoriety as an "automobileer" drew to him others of that peculiar breed. Now, in the Bagley Avenue kitchen, Charles King was no longer the sole visitor; more often than not he would be joined by Tom Cooper, a former bicycle racer who had saved his money and retired from the track, and Childe Harold Wills, a talented young draftsman and engineer who was on the staff of a company that manufactured adding machines. Wills liked to help Ford with his drawings. Cooper, noting the growing vogue for motor races, dreamed of a car that would really develop speed.

But despite the benediction of Thomas Alva Edison, Ford's leisure time obsession gained no favor with Alexander Dow, president of the Detroit Edison Company. Dow was planning large extensions of the company's service; these would increase Ford's duties, and require his undivided attention. One day in the summer of 1899, Dow sent for Ford and offered him the general superintendency of the company. The promotion carried a single condition: if he accepted it, Ford was to give up his hobby. He could choose between his job and his automobile. Ford had neither personal funds nor immediate prospect of livelihood, but for him no choice existed. It was merely a relief to learn that his wife agreed with him. The car could not be given up; with it, they would have to make or break.

Ford was little given to reading—indeed, the day was to come when his ability to read would be publicly impugned—but, had he read *McClure's* for July, 1899, his decision might have seemed amply justified. For in that authoritative and ordinarily accurate magazine, Ray Stannard Baker, who was sometimes called the greatest reporter in America, was writing of automotive developments in the United States. Though the motor vehicle, he acknowledged, was still in its babyhood, though it had hardly passed the stage of promotion and promise, never before had Yankee genius created an important business interest in so short a time. Five years earlier, there had not been thirty self-propelled carriages in practical use anywhere in the world. But in the first four months of 1899, American companies with the enormous aggregate capital of three hundred and eighty-eight millions of dollars had been organized for the sole purpose of manufacturing these new vehicles. So Baker reported, adding that at least eighty establishments were in prospect, to build two hundred types of vehicle, with nearly half as many methods of propulsion. And who could say there was no market for them? "A motor ambulance is in operation in Chicago; motor trucks are at work in several cities; a motor gun carriage will be ready for army use in the summer. The Santa Fe railroad has ordered a number of horseless coaches for an Arizona mountain route."

Shortly after he left the employ of the Edison plant, Ford was approached by a group of Detroit capitalists who—perhaps fired by the example of sagacious old S. L. Smith—wished to take a speculative flyer in the making and selling of cars. They needed a car to exploit, and the use of a name known at least locally. They invited Ford to join them, offering him both a stock interest and the position of chief engineer at one hundred dollars a month. The salary was less than he had been earning at the Edison plant, but this was the golden opportunity he had been awaiting for so many years. Now he could emerge from the ranks of despised amateur experimenters, and the way was open to unpredictable advancement; designer, manufacturer, industrial leader. He went to work for the Detroit Automobile Company, with a budget of ten thousand dollars for the building of ten cars. Optimistically, the company announced that it would presently offer a fine motor carriage, with power applied to the rear axle and all machinery hidden from sight. Best of all, the company claimed, it had solved the problem of overcoming bad odor by securing perfect combustion.

But Ford, possibly beguiled by Cooper, had fallen victim to the mania for speed, and set himself to developing a high-priced racing car. The company had contracted with the Leland plant to build its motors; all was ready for production to begin. Then Ford became dissatisfied with the "mixer," or carburetor, he had designed, and began experimenting to improve it. Meanwhile, production was stalled. Ten thousand dollars melted away before the first car was assembled. The promoters raised more money. Henry Martyn Leland, apostle of precision manufacture, became increasingly critical of the company's chief engineer. Eventually, having watched eighty-six thousand dollars vanish without yielding any appreciable return, the promoters recognized the wisdom of making a change. Henry Ford was once again out of a job. The problem of perfect combustion had not been solved. To his old reputation for stubbornness, he had added only the bad odor of failure.

The promotors of the Detroit Automobile Company, having ousted Ford and scrapped his car, lacked a product as well as a production manager. Reorganizing as the Cadillac Automobile Company, they founded their enterprise on Leland's reputation. That Leland had been sharply critical of Ford's tinkering methods and imperfect motor was not surprising. He had developed what was undoubtedly the best automobile engine then in existence— and it was not being used. In the course of working on Olds' motor, he had steadily improved its performance and increased its horsepower. Finally, by ever closer machining and the introduction of certain refinements in design, he produced a virtually new engine, three times as powerful as Olds' original motor. But when he took it to Olds, he was dismayed by having it rejected. Olds wanted no further improvements made in his car; he already had all the business he could handle; so radical a change in its power plant would necessitate major changes in the body of the Oldsmobile. Like Ford, long afterwards, Olds assumed that there would be a permanent, increasing demand for a standard, successfully established model. So the new motor which Leland had built for the Oldsmobile went, instead, into the projected Cadillac. Among many other improvements, this car was the first to be equipped with a steering wheel instead of a tiller. The public quickly recognized its superior merits, and soon the Cadillac began to displace the Oldsmobile in popular favor.

In 1906, four years after embarking on the manufacture of automobiles, Leland taught the world a lesson destined to leave indelible effects on the life of men everywhere. Nettled by the obsolescence of men's thinking and standards and taste, he determined to precipitate change. His special grievance was the failure of machine-made American cars to win appropriate recognition. In Europe, they were dismissed as inferior products. In the United States, they lacked the prestige of European cars, still custom-built by expert craftsmen. Everywhere, people continued to believe that quantity production by machine involved the sacrifice of quality. Quality could be achieved only by handwork or—at best—through slow, careful fabrication by skilled craftsmen trained in the versatile use of labor-saving machinery. Mass-production might mean cheapness; but cheapness could only mean inferiority. Quantity and quality were irreconcilable.

Leland hit upon a dramatic method of proving the validity of his principles. To demonstrate the new methods they made possible, he shipped three Cadillac cars to England. Upon arrival at the dockside, these cars were taken over by officials of the Royal Automobile Club. Under their supervision, the cars were torn down, and all their parts thoroughly scrambled. The resulting mass of junk was dumped into an open shed at the Brooklands race track. There, Cadillac mechanics rapidly sorted out the component parts. Then, using only wrenches, hammers, screwdrivers and pliers, they assembled the parts into three cars. These they turned over to the Club's officials, who promptly drove them for five hundred miles on the track. All three cars finished their runs with perfect scores.

As Leland foresaw, this demonstration, widely reported on both sides of the Atlantic, made a profound impression. To the American automobile industry, barely ten years old, it revealed the perspective of the future—the volume manufacture of standardized, dependable cars having interchangeable parts, at a cost cheap enough to make them available to millions of buyers. But the implications of Leland's exploit were destined to reach far beyond the automobile, into nearly every branch of industrial activity. On that English race track, as in an apocalyptic vision, there was foreshadowed the coming of the new messiah—the infinitely duplicated factory designed for mass production, where workers who needed no special skills would, almost automatically, respond to the dictates of machines, attaining a speed and volume of output never before envisaged, yet achieving an accuracy calculable to within one millionth of an inch.

CHAPTER III

Dusters and Devil-Wagons

1 Malice in Newport

New York always liked to be first, but in the hazard of dubious enterprises usually indicated its primacy by proxy. In "society," nobody had ever been so variously first as Mrs. O. H. P. Belmont, who delighted in blazing trails for others to follow. She had pioneered in misalliance, mansion-building, the patronage of social ineligibles, even the practice of divorce in the full view of all Fifth Avenue. But when, in 1897, she imported the first French motor car to reach the United States, she had it sent to Newport.

Dauntless as Mrs. Belmont was, she recognized the limits of

New York's tolerance, and the prospect of being mobbed on Fifth Avenue was one which she preferred not to face. On Bellevue Avenue, the display of her costly, flatulent plaything was unlikely to provoke violence. The natives, long since subdued, might gape, but they would scarcely dare to protest. And the envy of her neighbors—why else, if not to arouse it, had she purchased the contraption?—would issue only in emulation. So in the end she would have the sardonic satisfaction of pointing out to them that, once again, they had followed her expensively but without profit. For the mechanical monster would carry nobody any further than they could already go behind their horses. Whatever their vehicle, the transit of the elect could proceed only from Bellevue Avenue to the termination of the Ocean Drive. Elsewhere, not even Mrs. Belmont could undertake the roads.

But to move more uncomfortably than ever in the same fixed orbit was a novelty. And, by aristocratic parthenogenesis, Mrs. Belmont's firstling soon incubated a numerous, noisy progeny. As a practical means of locomotion, the motor car was little more efficient than a sedan-chair. It was, however, more extravagant to maintain, more elaborately useless, and almost as outlandish. Since this was the case, Mrs. Belmont and that dour social critic Thorstein Veblen might have made the same prediction: among the elect, the motor car was destined to become a "craze." The twenty-six different equipages in the stables of Mrs. John R. Drexel were abruptly made obsolete. The polo ponies and hunters in those of Harry Payne Whitney were temporarily superseded in their master's affections. And the young Vanderbilts—Alfred and William K., junior—seduced from the tooling of four-in-hands by multiple mechanical horsepower, courted more attractively injurious mishaps, at higher speeds, on the old familiar courses.

Within two years, the afternoon carriage parade had been transformed into a procession of motor cars. The Newport correspondent of the New York *Times* reported that the automobile fad was growing daily; nothing that was ever introduced in the national social citadel had so quickly caught "the popular fancy" as the horseless carriage; the company owning and servicing these vehicles had been "compelled to keep its place open day and night"—for, incredibly, there had been a number of nocturnal races around the Ocean Drive by cottagers in their automobiles. In short, the *Times* reported breathlessly, at Newport, if nowhere else in America, the demand for these "smokeless vehicles" still exceeded the available supply. In the circumstances, it was not enough merely to take the air behind an imported and liveried mechanic in a fastidiously appointed imported car. A need had arisen for some equally public, yet more exquisitely competitive, amenity. The problem merited attentive consideration. It received this from imaginations never before successfully challenged—had they not triumphed over ennui with white balls, dinner parties for monkeys, and picnics on the sands served by footmen from gold plate? Providence, as usual, sent a suitable inspiration.

In September of 1899, to celebrate the end of a brilliant season, there was held a parade of florally decorated automobiles. In colorful and perfumed splendor, they moved at a dignified pace to Mrs. Belmont's estate. There, the chatelaine surprised their drivers with an "obstacle park." This proved to be a labyrinthine course, fiendishly spattered with counterfeit hazards of the road; dummy figures apparelled as policemen and pedestrians, equipages with wooden horses. Serenely, the drivers would have to manipulate their vehicles through the maze without brushing against, or toppling over, these incentives to profanity. It was recorded that Colonel John Jacob Astor steered his car—a bower of green and white clematis—"with the same cool-headed dash that distinguished him while serving under fire at Santiago," and that his brilliant example was emulated by Reginald Ronalds, who had been one of Theodore Roosevelt's Rough Riders, and was "now riding to new glories." But Harry Lehr, who had not undergone military discipline in the recent war, while weaving about the course prankishly bowled over every mental hazard as he reached it. After concluding this trial of nerve and skill, the contestants drove their mobile floral bowers to a point outside of Newport, followed by their mechanics in an "automobile ambulance" equipped with tools and spare parts. Having dined, they turned homeward at midnight, when "every vehicle was brilliantly illuminated with countless little glow-lights interspersed among the floral wreaths," so that the cavalcade resembled "a veritable pageant of fairy chariots."

The nation learned with amazement of this fantasy, which implied that the new terror could be tamed, and might eventually prove to be predictably tractable. It was no wonder that E. P. Ingersoll, in his *Horseless Age*, expressed gratitude for the "gracious patronage" of "our American aristocracy." One year later, in the first autumn of the new century, a new and rival publication, *Automobile Topics,* revealed that the motor car had been even more extensively taken up by the world of fashion, and during the summer had played a most important role in the life of Newport and Lenox. Indeed, this oracle announced, "women like Mrs. Stuyvesant Fish, Mrs. Herman Oelrichs, Mrs. William K. Vanderbilt, Jr., and others who are noted for their daring in taking up sports which have the merit of unconventionality, will not be satisfied until they have driven their motor carriages through the city streets." Things had come to a pretty pass, if women were to be permitted to endanger the lives of innocent citizens! And presently the alarm of men at this prospective exorbitance touched off a spirited controversy in the public press. Were women capable of becoming "good chauffeuses?" Or were they not?

For the moment, alarm was premature. The eminent votaries of unconventional sports exercised a commendable restraint. Mrs. Stuyvesant Fish did not apply her cruel wit to the slaughter of anonymous New York pedestrians. It is true that her relative, Mrs. Hamilton Fish, bought one of the elegant, easily operated electrics designed especially for the use of ladies on city streets, and that she chose to master it in the vicinity of her New York residence. The discouraging result of this experiment was long afterwards related by a friend, Edward R. Hewitt, who at the time was addicted to a flame-spouting steamer. Starting her electric in the general direction of Third Avenue, Mrs. Fish had the misfortune to encounter a member of the proletariat bent upon crossing the street. Women were said, by competent authorities, to be all nerves and impulsiveness, and so not to be trusted with any machine. But Mrs. Fish, moving toward a wayward male, displayed

firm purpose and extreme concentration. She knocked him down
and ran over him once going forward. Then, backing her car, she
ran over him again in reverse. Moving forward once more, she
ran over him a third time. Having presently managed to bring her
vehicle to a stop, she dismounted with dignity and returned home
on foot, abandoning the juggernaut where it stood, and forever.
Her victim, meanwhile, had considerately picked himself up and
vanished. For both, presumably, the experience was a foretaste of
the quality of a new era.

When, that same autumn, W. K. Vanderbilt, Jr., decided to
drive his Daimler from Newport to New York, his adventurous
spouse made the journey by train and awaited him—with what
was considered noteworthy composure—at the Waldorf Astoria
Hotel. To most other Americans, if not to her, Vanderbilt's project
seemed quite as hazardous as an expedition to the North Pole. So
his safe arrival was promptly announced by *Automobile Topics*,
which remarked on his "novel appearance," specifying that "he
was attired in leather jacket, large goggles over his eyes, and a
patent leather cap." Like more seasoned explorers, he had not
dispensed with the services of experts, but was accompanied by
his French chauffeur and a footman. To an inquiring world,
Automobile Topics reported that, during his trip, "Mr. Vanderbilt
took no account of miles and hours, for he was delayed by rain and
going much out of his way by not knowing the roads. He thinks
his fastest time was at the rate of about forty miles an hour."

Touring, as Vanderbilt learned on that occasion, was not a
sport but a hardship. Racing, however, was sport. A gentleman
might fittingly encourage it, and possibly even practice it. Within
a very few years, the Vanderbilt Cup Race, annually run on a
one-hundred-mile track, was to become the premier sporting
event of the season. It would lure nearly half a million New
Yorkers from their beds, to set out at midnight for the chilly
darkness of rural Long Island. There, at sunrise, they could watch
goggle-armored men take their lives in their hands, driving like
demons for three hundred miles at a mile a minute. All over the
country, the race aroused frantic excitement for, as the journalist

Walter Prichard Eaton asserted, in gratifying the lust for speed it became the prize shock-producer of history.

Meanwhile, the problem of the newly organized Automobile Club of America was not to produce shocks, but to allay them. Clearly, the populace must be won to tolerance of this new luxury, so far beyond their reach, before gentlemen could safely enjoy it. For, unlike other satisfactions available only to the wealthy, it was inexorably public; and, although this made for added pleasure, the perverse temper of the people gave it an element of disadvantage. This condition was anxiously pondered by George F. Chamberlain, and at the first meeting of the Club, in the autumn of 1899, he proposed the holding of an exhibition in New York City specifically devoted to automobiles. Persuaded by his arguments, the members deputed Albert C. Bostwick to make the necessary arrangements—only to be dismayed, somewhat later, by his temerity in securing Madison Square Garden for the purpose.

But Bostwick was not being as incautious as this arrangement suggested. Evidence of the hostility of the common people was rapidly accumulating. In one California community they had succeeded in passing an ordinance requiring motorists to stop dead within three hundred feet of every approaching horse. In Vermont, they had won a law compelling every motorist to be preceded, at a distance of one-eighth of a mile, by a person of mature age carrying a red flag. Cities throughout the country were officiously regulating the speed at which motorists were entitled to travel: the permissible limit was usually about eight miles. Worse still, motorists were being forbidden the use of city parkways—and where else could a gentleman be expected to take his daily spin? Indeed, this situation was producing dangerous symptoms of revolution, for once among the aristocracy. To win freedom of movement for their pathetically frustrated clan, two self-sacrificing members of the world of fashion—Dave Hennen Morris and Augustus Post—had separately defied the law, braved the wrath of mobs, and cheerfully offered themselves as martyrs to arrest by taking their vehicles into Central Park in New York City. If this example was followed, the entire Four Hundred might soon be found in the Tombs; to Bostwick, the prospect was intolerable. Nor could he approve the palliative of popular fury suggested by one Uriah Smith of Battle Creek, Michigan. This inventive soul, destined to be unjustly forgotten, had designed a horsey horseless carriage, approximately certain to eliminate equine hysteria: its dashboard presented, to any nervous approaching nag, the head and shoulders of a horse—whether stuffed or merely sculptured history does not record.

In determining to hold the first American automobile show in Madison Square Garden, the arena used by Barnum and Bailey and Buffalo Bill, Mr. Bostwick did not intend to apply the old imperial principle of offering circuses to the mob. His purpose was to demonstrate the more remarkable achievements of which the new vehicle was capable when guided by practiced hands. He had laid out in the Garden a circular track one eighth of a mile long and twenty feet wide. On it, contests were held for skilled automobileers, who competed in starting, stopping, turning, and driving between obstacles. To the crowds that thronged the Garden early in November, 1900, these displays of facility—so reminiscent of, yet so different from, the familiar exhibition of horsemanship—proved fascinating. Their import could not be dodged: granted sufficient discipline on the part of its driver, the new mechanical menace would respond with comforting docility. Less antagonistic than before, the crowd examined the booths of the show's fifty-one exhibitors. These offered a wide choice in forms of locomotion. There were no less than nineteen makes of gasoline vehicles, seven of steamers, six of electrics, and two of an odd hybrid class which combined the resources of gasoline and electricity.

2 Henry James Spends a Night Out

Yet a selection among these alternatives offered no promise of finality, as was soon realized by Mrs. Edith Wharton. She had already shown a degree of daring in publicly cultivating the art of fiction, and the trait was presently to reappear in her passion for emancipated circulation. She had lately deserted Newport for a new villa in Lenox, and there—among the earliest of her circle—she determined to set up a motor, as they said. A single motor

The Horse Is Still in the Majority

The Automobile Begins to Come into Its Own

LEFT: Winton Model of 1900   ABOVE: A Rear-Entrance Cadillac, Vintage of 1904

Finish of a 100-Mile Non-Stop Race

FINISH

soon resulted in a series of them, for it was difficult to find one which did not rapidly develop some organic defect, and selling, buying and exchanging had to be carried on continuously, though without appreciable improvement.

Though roads and motors were equally unknown quantities, though the project of a ten-mile run caused as much apprehension as might a journey across Africa, enthusiasts like Mrs. Wharton were not to be deterred, and armed with one of the new guide books that contained carefully drawn gradient maps like fever charts, they spurred their dubious mechanics on to greater and greater feats of distance. Like many another early enthusiast, Mrs. Wharton was a country-lover. Her range of exploration had previously been limited, her imagination tantalized by the mystery beyond the next blue hills. She found an inexhaustible delight in penetrating to the remoter parts of Massachusetts and New Hampshire, discovering derelict villages with Georgian churches and balustraded house-fronts, and investigating slumbrous mountain valleys. From such expeditions she and her guests would return, weary, but laden with a new harvest of beauty, having seen hamlets whose sad inhabitants still lived in conditions not greatly changed from those endured by their ancestors who had fought off the Indians. (She would later write of these folk in her tales, *Ethan Frome* and *Summer*: literary fruits of the motor car.) But before these journeys were concluded, Mrs. Wharton's fortitude was taxed by their invariable concomitant penalties: sticking fast in ruts, having to push the car up hills, to rout out the village blacksmith for repairs, to suffer the jeers of horse-drawn travelers gaily trotting past. One of her house guests, Walter Berry—he was her literary mentor, and lifelong love—wrote to the poet George Cabot Lodge about this novel mixture of pleasure and pain. "Great fun here, we motor every day, and yesterday we did sixty-five miles." Mr. Berry quite correctly underscored the mileage; it was a record.

Sometimes, the expeditions did not turn out so pleasantly. Mrs. Wharton always remembered one occasion when, returning homeward late, her car broke down on a lonely stretch of road; she and her husband and Henry James were forced to dismount, and sit all night by the roadside while the chauffeur grimly went on tinkering. Henry James was visiting the United States for the first time in many years, and looked forward happily to exotic experiences, though he probably did not anticipate making so informal a contact with his native soil as that evening provided. But Mrs. Wharton had adroitly involved him in her new enthusiasm, and his responses to it anticipated several subsequent developments on the national scale. Thus, he set the pattern for the later universal pastime of "going for a drive." During his visit to Lenox, the weather turned extremely hot. James detested heat, and suffered from it; incessant motoring proved to be the sole panacea for his misery. He pleaded for it, asking to be kept in constant motion. He consented to stop on the road only for liquid refreshment; tea on a high hillside, or a cooling drink—if procurable—at some village drugstore. Once, he demanded "something less innocent than Apollinaris," and was enchanted by being served an orange phosphate; though not precisely what he had in mind, he thought it showed a touch of imaginative sophistication. All unwittingly, Henry James was initiating the demand that, long afterwards, would create a new service-industry and dot the American continent with "drive-ins."

The subject of liquid refreshment preoccupied him; this was not only an effect of the heat. For advertisers were already following the adventurous motorist, and billboards extolling a bottled beverage had begun to deface the thin, empty, lonely beauty of the American landscape. One day, catching sight of a fine solitary peak with a vast wooden hotel near its summit, he asked his hostess to identify it. The peak, Mrs. Wharton told him, was called Mount Tom; the barrack-like building which crowned it was, she said in whimsical allusion to Europe, a famous Carthusian monastery. "Yes, where the monks make Moxie," her eminent guest retorted, ironically fulfilling the speculative hopes on which all billboards rested. Henry James' impressions of the new America were not of a kind to gratify the majority of his fellow-citizens, but he foresaw more clearly than they what the automobile was destined to mean in their lives. Forgetful of its treachery in trapping him into a night-long vigil by the roadside, he acknowledged himself converted—by the potent way in which it dealt with so large a country—"to the sense of all the thing may do for one and one may get from it." If he were rich, he confessed to his brother William, he wouldn't hesitate to take up with it. For the automobile, he affirmed emphatically, was "a great transformer of life and of the future."

3   A Spur to Socialism

This prediction seemed, in the year 1905, most unlikely to be fulfilled. For, in the main, the automobile continued to be an ostentatious symbol of wealth. What the plain people learned about it only intensified their smoldering resentment against the idle and predatory rich. The journalism of exposure was getting into its stride. Within the next few years, the crusading articles of the muckrakers would stimulate the people's yearning for social justice, and their determination to obtain it through political action. The automobile offered an obvious and inviting target for attack. It was one of the more conspicuous expressions of arrogant privilege; it exacted menial services from the less prosperous classes; and many of its immediate effects seemed flagrantly detrimental to social welfare. Indeed, as Woodrow Wilson reported from his observation post at Princeton University, nothing had spread socialistic feeling more widely in the United States than the automobile.

This verdict was supported by considerable evidence. Newspapers and magazines described the extravagant fittings of custom-built imported cars: silver-framed mirrors, jeweled or enameled clocks, crystal vases for orchids, filigree bottles for perfume, card-cases in tooled leather or precious metals. In Detroit, a wealthy young bachelor outfitted his motor to suit the whims of the most exigent female companion; it was equipped with receptacles for creams and powders, atomizers, an electric hair-curler and a manicuring set. In New York, a prominent member of the Automobile Club of America had the lamps of his Panhard gold-plated, and each of them bore the club emblem in solid gold, set with rubies. Ladies of fashion could indulge in lap robes made of costly furs, sealskin for daytime use, and ermine for the evening.

When motoring out of town, ladies and gentlemen wore "dusters" and goggles, but the perpetrators of feminine high fashion soon developed appropriately costly models: long, graceful motor coats in charming shades of "Gloria silk," with short capes and not-too-flowing sleeves; and, although the choice of motor chapeaux was acknowledged to be rather bewildering, they all cascaded with veils of chiffon or delicate lace which, tied tightly under the chin, were intended to "frame a pretty face enchantingly," and sometimes did.

By the privileged class it was assumed that the plain people of the country could, in time, be trained to minister to the wants of the new vehicle. A group of residents of New York's fashionable Westchester County, seeking to assure themselves of adequate rescue with a minimum of embarrassment, formed a club to build a chain of gasoline and repair stations, for their exclusive use, along the road to the city. For obvious reasons, their example was not widely imitated, but in the country's larger cities a new institution came into being. The "automobile depot" was the prototype of the later public garage, and was far more pretentious than the old-fashioned livery stable. One, in New York City, combined "a storage and repair department with a general trading depot where machines may be placed on exhibition and sales effected for either individual or manufacturer's account." This establishment stored, maintained and fueled gasoline cars at from twenty-five to forty dollars a month, depending upon their type. It charged, and cared for, electric vehicles at rates ranging from thirty to forty-five dollars. It was also hospitable, at varying fees, to steam cars, quadricycles and tricycles. For an additional payment of five dollars a month, patrons could have their vehicles delivered to their doors.

Schools were likewise set up for the training of mechanics or drivers—the term "chauffeur" did not, as yet, invariably connote the successor of a coachman. It was early realized that this new branch of domestic service required an arresting combination of aptitudes. The ideal was a man who joined, to a professional skill as mysterious as that of a French chef, the decorum and tact which might be expected of a confidential secretary. Recognizing this, perhaps with a degree of skepticism, the Detroit *Saturday Night* suggested that the most satisfactory drivers could probably be recruited from the ranks of former coachmen; these disciplined members of the "servant class" could be relied on to understand "exactly what is expected of them by their masters." However, certain progressive members of the master class dissented from this verdict. In their view, a new field of opportunity was opening for youthful members of the lower orders who had a liking for mechanics. As a result, the New York City Y.M.C.A., co-operating with the Automobile Club of America, opened a school where young men were taught the arts of driving, grooming and repairing motor cars. Every applicant who hoped eventually to obtain a position, the president of the Club sternly asserted, "knows that to succeed he must not only be intelligent, honest and sober, but also a competent mechanic, with the instincts of a gentleman." To the old American formula for success in life, the twentieth century had added one novel ingredient. No Morgan or Vanderbilt or Rockefeller had ever found it necessary to have the instincts of a gentleman in order to get ahead in the world.

The exercise of these instincts, however, was seldom observed by the non-motoring public. Shortly after the turn of the century, fleets of electric hansoms and broughams were put into service as public cabs in New York, Boston, Philadelphia, Chicago and Washington. Hiram Percy Maxim, the designer of these cars, alleged that the worst thugs to be found in New York were selected to operate those plying its streets. A certain want of refinement in the drivers of public conveyances might have been endured, but the conduct of motor enthusiasts precipitated widespread anger. Noting this, in 1904, *The Churchman* reminded its readers that, "In the Paris of 1789 the coaches of the wealthy, arrogantly driven through crowded streets, were at last halted, overturned and the horses cut from them." In free and democratic America, this temperate publication surmised, the wealthy would not be able "to buy with money immunity to offend the social conscience and endanger the public safety." An equally highminded magazine, *The Outlook*, reflected bitterly that in the United States, which called itself a democracy, pedestrians now existed merely on sufferance; they could enjoy a reasonable expectation of life only so long as they did not obtrude themselves on the public highway. Outraged by the homicidal proclivities of the wealthy, the New York *Tribune* predicted that science might presently diagnose motor murder as "a specific form of human perversion and depravity." And the New York *World*, espousing the cause of the common man, denounced the new mobility of the rich. "The automobile," it thundered, "has developed into an expensive luxury for the man who does not need one. It was well named the 'devil wagon.'"

Yet, already, there were indications that the devil wagon had begun making its way into segments of the American community whose reputability might elevate it from general opprobrium. Many physicians had testified that—quite apart from its incidentally lethal misapplications—it constituted an alarming menace to the nation's health. But younger and more progressive members of the profession, recognizing its practical advantages, hopefully adopted it. In the cities most of them, at the outset, made their rounds in sleek electrics, easy to drive and able to make twelve miles an hour. For country doctors, the electric was not practicable; they took to gasoline cars during the summer months, but maintained a horse and buggy to tide them over the frequent periods of breakdown and for use in winter. By 1906, the *Journal of the American Medical Association* was publishing, for the benefit of all its members, the reports of those who had put the automobile to work in their practice. Here and there rural clergymen who served several parishes boldly added the devil wagon to the Lord's stable. At first they incurred extreme disapproval; in time, the prestige of their example softened the prejudice of their flocks. These courageous souls might have been comforted had they foreseen that less than two decades later, in 1924, Warren H. Wilson, a member of the Board of National Missions of the Presbyterian Church, would casually report that "the rural minister who has not a motor is a rare man." The social authority of the medical profession and the clergy was great, but that of the American woman was even greater. And it was she who, perhaps, did most to overcome hostility to the new vehicle—by quietly domesticating it.

4 The Girl and the Car

During the first years of the century, women of the prosperous classes, in cities throughout the land, learned to handle the simple, elegant electric carriages designed for urban use and specifically adapted to their mechanical helplessness. But, although safe, noiseless, immaculately clean and docile, these vehicles did not permit a range of movement comparable to that of the discarded bicycle. Their use was restricted to sedate occasions; to taking the air in pleasant weather, going shopping, paying calls. Restless youth soon came to regard them as the perfect vehicle for their decorous elders. The most imaginative dreamed of challenging both disaster and social disapproval with the swifter, more complex gasoline car. But to translate this dream into action required more than the courage to defy convention. It implied a willingness to lay aside vanity, wear rough clothes that no lady would consent to be seen in, mess about with dirty machinery. It necessitated physical strength, not yet a fashionable attribute for women. Above all, it exacted the acquisition of skills never before cultivated by women, and the ability—universally denied them—to master a subject considered intelligible only to men.

One of the earliest innovators was, quite appropriately, a career woman. Hilda Ward, a painter by profession, bought her first gasoline car in 1906; and, as the dubiously unique exponent of a new female avocation, she published, two years later, *The Girl and the Motor,* a book recounting her experiences for the benefit of possible imitators. Her most trusted male adviser, she recorded in gentle understatement, "seemed to think that, within limits, I might be equal to the job of driving a car, but was not over enthusiastic when I told him I wished to undertake all the care of it as well." Very shortly, Miss Ward understood this lack of enthusiasm. She had been informed that, if she looked her car over and made sure that it was in good shape before starting out, she would theoretically have no trouble on the road. But she rapidly became convinced that there was more difference between theory and practice in motoring than in any other pursuit. Mechanical troubles dogged her wherever she went. Tire blowouts were so frequent that she ceased even to jump at the noise, but instinctively looked for a nice place to pull up at the side of the road. Her profession gave her one notable advantage: "some of my old canvases made lovely patches for the inside of blown-out tubes." But, after two years, her enthusiasm was undiminished. "To this day, as I cruise around the country," she told her feminine readers, "I come upon certain landmarks and say to myself: 'This is where I got my first puncture. That house was where I borrowed water to fill up my radiator when it had leaked out. Along this lovely dusty stretch of road I walked in search of gasoline.'"

Thirty years later, another American woman also wrote a book about the automobile. To realize the changes since Miss Ward's day, one needed only to read its title. For in calling her book *The Car Belongs to Mother*, Mrs. Priscilla Hovey Wright was pointing to a complex of social facts so universal that everyone took it for granted, and an era of such swift industrial advance that nearly everyone had forgotten its genesis. Unlike Miss Ward, Mrs. Wright offered no guidance in mechanical crises; none was needed. Her subject was, so to speak, the etiquette of service. She dealt "with the problems of the matron—and her name is legion— who, with one family car at her disposal, transports her husband to and from trains, her children to school, herself to market, club-members to their homes on unaccepted streets and relatives on their various whims and vagaries." By 1939, the automobile had become an article of utility, no more remarkable than any other. But scientists, economists and historians were still impressed by the tremendous changes it had brought about in the American social order, and President Herbert Hoover's Committee on Social Trends had not exaggerated its significance. "It is probable," this committee reported, "that no invention of such far-reaching importance was ever diffused with such rapidity, or so quickly exerted influences that ramified through the national culture, transforming even habits of thought and language."

CHAPTER IV

The Better Mouse Trap,
the Ogre, and the Baby Giant

1 Explosions in a Bar

To those with a stake in the future of the automobile, the Hotel Ponchartrain in Detroit seemed like the very center of the universe. There, all during a breathless decade, you might have watched history in the making, or heard about it. For in its stately, spacious barroom there congregated, every evening, the men whose hopes were tuned to the sputter of engines, were timed to the revolutions of wheels: inventors and engineers, promoters, racers, builders of cars, makers of parts, designers, owners of machine shops. At the long bar, Peter Drexelius presided. In later years, he was to become one of the leading lawyers of Detroit; and the future held equally unpredictable changes of fortune for many whom he served across the bar. They could come there—men who afterwards were to be millionaires, builders of palaces in fashionable Grosse Pointe—from their dingy boarding houses and drab side-street hotels, and at the cost of a very few cents soon be on terms of familiarity and friendship with other men intent on the same ultimate objective and proceeding, however blindly, toward the same goal.

Thus it came about that the Ponchartrain bar was the place to which every kind of invention, device and contraption was brought, to be shown and demonstrated to an eager audience. Thirty years later, Peter Drexelius remembered that it was a common thing to see four or five men, carrying a heavy piece of machinery, enter the bar, deposit their burden on the floor or a table, and set it in motion. Many a device that was to revolutionize automotive construction had its first public showing under Drexelius' tolerant eye. Tire vulcanizers, rims, valves were exhibited; so were innumerable methods of mounting and dismounting tires. Brakes, steering gears, carburetors, magnetos were closely examined, and their merits vigorously disputed. Drexelius recalled an evening when Albert Champion—recently arrived from France —came to the Ponchartrain with an elaborate electrical set and enthusiastically put his spark plug through its paces. And when the urgent need for a self-starter was generally recognized, the Ponchartrain bar took on the look of a disorderly, diabolical laboratory: electrical starters would spit sparks, air starters emitted shrill whistling noises; mechanical starters would sometimes go off with a bang, showering the crowd with springs and gears. And always the talk ran high—to the frank and free interchange of ideas that obtained, the rapid development of the automobile, during the most eventful decade of its history, was largely due. Sometimes, when Drexelius called the closing hour, and argument was still going on, the disputants would adjourn to John's Night-Owl lunch wagon in Cadillac Square—an institution so closely associated with automotive history that Henry Ford was to preserve it piously, along with Thomas Alva Edison's laboratory, and Charles Proteus Steinmetz's river-cabin, in Greenfield Village.

The ultimate glory that was to overtake John's humble wagon might have seemed little less plausible—to the frequenters of the Ponchartrain bar—than what the future would hold for its preserver. After his ignominious release from the Detroit Automobile Company, Henry Ford made a bold attempt to rehabilitate his reputation. With Wills' and Cooper's assistance, he built a small, light racing car that developed twenty-six horsepower. In the autumn of 1901, Daniel Campau, owner of the Blue Ribbon Race Track in Grosse Pointe, arranged a championship sweepstakes for machines of any weight, over a ten-mile course at his track. The great Alexander Winton, most daring and successful of American racers, was the announced attraction, and so certain did it seem that he would win the contest, as usual, that the prize—a "beautiful punch-bowl set"—had been selected for its appropriateness to display in the bay window of his dining room. On the night before the race, Henry Ford, in leather coat and leather cap, with a pair of goggles shoved above the visor, posted his entry fee for the event.

According to the Detroit *Free Press*, the city's social elite sanctioned automobile racing by turning out *en masse* to see the sweepstakes. Winton's smart, sleek racer, developed from rich experience, was capable of forty horsepower, and during the first seven miles it led Ford's by nearly half a mile. Ford's mechanic, Edward S. ("Spider") Huff, hung far out in his effort to ballast the car, but it swung wide at every turn. As one reporter noted, that Ford was an amateur "was plainly shown by the way he took the curves. At the turns he was compelled to shut off the power entirely, and two-fifths of the time his machine was simply coasting." Suddenly, a great cloud of smoke burst from the rear of Winton's big car, and his mechanic leaned over the sputtering motor, frantically pouring oil on red-hot bearings. Then, as the reporter chronicled, "Ford swept by them as though they were standing still. Down the stretch he came like a demon, and the crowd yelled itself hoarse. In the next three miles Ford increased his lead to fully three-quarters of a mile and won amid great cheering." He had driven the ten-mile course in thirteen minutes, twenty-three and two-fifths seconds. Brash, as always, and ignoring the part played in his victory by Winton's accident, he remarked, "Put Winton in my car and it will beat anything in the country." But, with his victory, "Henry Ford broke into the front ranks of American chauffeurs."

Now track champion of the United States, Ford's prestige as a "speed demon" was helpfully inflated by the *Horseless Age*: one issue chronicled his achievement of a speed of seventy miles an hour over a half-mile course; another made much of a challenge by "the Detroit chauffeur" to race "any foreign mechanic" if the contest were held in the United States. Meanwhile, Ford had no difficulty in finding another group of financial backers prepared to gamble on his ability as a manufacturer. The Henry Ford Company was set up, and within a few months liquidated, having produced no cars, but a crop of bitter recriminations. For the second time, and on the threshold of his fortieth year, Henry Ford had proved himself a discreditable failure in business. Cars were being produced by Olds in Detroit, by Frank Duryea in Massachusetts, by Haynes in Kokomo, by Winton in Cleveland. James Ward Packard was building cars in Warren, Ohio. Edwin Ross Thomas was producing a "flyer" in Buffalo. The Locomobile was being turned out at Westfield, Massachusetts, the Stearns in Cleveland, the Case at Racine, Wisconsin, the Auburn at Auburn, Indiana. And, in Detroit, the crowd at the Ponchartrain bar, writing off the future of Henry Ford, began talking of David Dunbar Buick, who, having invented a method of fixing porcelain on metal—destined, in the end, to transform the American bathroom and kitchen—was now embarking on the manufacture of automobiles. And while Ford's star fell, as it seemed forever, enthusiasm at the Ponchartrain rose at the news that Henry Martyn Leland's Cadillac was soon to be on the market.

2   Future Gold Mine

Once again Ford returned to "experimenting"—and though later he was to assert that he "never thought much of racing," the notion of speed was, in 1902, his nearest approach to a practicable idea. But, then, he always felt that an idea is just an idea; almost anyone could think one up; the thing that counted was developing it into a practical product. His practical product, now, was two racing cars, built with the help of C. H. Wills and Tom Cooper: the "Arrow" and the "999," precisely alike; one-seated affairs with four huge cylinders that developed eighty horsepower in a deafening roar, so that "going over Niagara Falls would have been but a pastime after a ride in one of them." Ford and Cooper tried out the great red "999," which shot flames from its engine when put under speed; neither of them had sufficient courage to race it. But Cooper knew a former bicycle racer who lived on speed. Nothing could go too fast for Barney Oldfield. So, although he had never driven a motor car, Oldfield was sent for to drive the "999" against Alexander Winton and his "Bullet" at the Grosse Pointe track.

As Ford quickly discovered, Oldfield did not know what fear was. Under Ford's and Cooper's instruction, he learned to drive within a week; learned, too, to control the monster whose two-handled tiller drained all the energy of a strong man. The Grosse Pointe track was not adequately banked, nobody knew how much speed the "999" could develop, and the turns of the course might bring death to its driver. As Ford cranked up the car for the three-mile contest, Oldfield, from the driver's seat, cheerfully remarked, "Well, this chariot may kill me, but they will say afterward that I was going like hell when she took me over the bank." He was as good as his word. He never dared to look around; he drove the monster at full speed, without shutting off at the curves; and he won the race by a lead of a full half-mile. In thus launching his own career as the most celebrated "daredevil" of the age, Oldfield likewise succeeded in re-establishing Henry Ford. Long afterwards, he was fond of saying that each of them had made the other. Sometimes he added, with a smile, "But I did much the best job of it."

Among those who watched Oldfield's spectacular performance was Alexander Y. Malcolmson, a prosperous Detroit coal dealer who had been looking for an opportunity to get into the automobile business. He was prepared to risk a modest investment; what he required was a competent designer and engineer, able to turn out a car and free of commitments. The triumphant victory of the "999" persuaded him that Ford was his man, and after some investigation he decided to negotiate for Ford's services. The upshot of their discussions was the organization, early in 1903, of the Ford Motor Company. By now, the industry appeared to be established on a sound basis. During the previous year, Ransom Olds had produced the stupendous total of twenty-five hundred cars, and was announcing an estimated output of four thousand; the National Association of Automobile Manufacturers boasted a membership of one hundred and twelve; and nine thousand cars had been built in the United States during a single year.

The launching of the Ford Motor Company was accomplished in circumstances to which time gave an effect of irony. At the outset, it became obvious that the new venture would require more capital than Malcolmson had foreseen. Ford had little or no money, and his sole effort to attract investment was scarcely encouraging. He went to see his former employer, Alexander Dow; the president of the Detroit Edison Company wished him luck, but flatly declined to risk a dollar in his projected enterprise. So Malcolmson, after siphoning out of his coal business all the cash he dared withdraw, undertook to raise additional funds by pledging his personal credit. His efforts brought ten shareholders into the venture which, capitalized at one hundred thousand dollars, began operations with twenty-eight thousand dollars on hand. Sixteen years later, having meanwhile received millions in dividends, the seven remaining stockholders of the Ford Motor Company were to surrender their shares to Henry Ford for the sum of approximately one hundred and six millions of dollars.

In order to secure a plant without putting up cash, Malcolmson persuaded a carpenter, Albert Strelow, to accept twenty-five shares of stock for the erection of a one-story building behind a shop which he owned on Mack Avenue. The deal hung fire while Strelow wrestled with his prejudice against Ford; two years later, he disposed of his stock for twenty-five thousand dollars which he promptly lost in speculation. Long afterwards, he was reported to have been seen outside the employment office of the Ford plant, in a line of applicants for a laborer's job.

While dickering with Strelow, Malcolmson had approached

John and Horace Dodge, who were making part for Olds in their machine shop, with a view to having them build the new car designed by Ford and Wills. Of the two brothers, John was the more aggressive; he figured most prominently in the negotiations, and in the subsequent relationship of the Dodges to the Ford Motor Company. Astute, tough-minded and high-tempered, he was unimpressed by Ford's previous record, and insisted that any contract be guaranteed by Malcolmson personally. As finally drawn, the contract provided this security and reserved to the Dodges the right to market any cars for which they failed to receive payment. Thus protected, and awarded fifty shares each in the new company, they severed their connection with Olds and proceeded to retool their shop to produce the new car. In 1919, after an acrimonious lawsuit, they surrendered their holdings in the Ford Company for twenty-five millions of dollars.

The arrangement which he made with the Dodges sent Malcolmson to John S. Gray, a manufacturer of confectionery who also was president of a Detroit bank. Gray agreed to make a loan of ten thousand dollars to the company, secured by Malcolmson's personal note; he was awarded one hundred shares of stock, to which he added another five, and as the company's largest investor, was made its president. He died three years later; sixteen years after his death, his heirs received twenty-six and one-quarter million dollars for his holdings in the company.

Having mortgaged his personal credit and the future of his business to establish the new enterprise, Malcolmson now took two steps apparently dictated by his knowledge of Ford's previous failure. They revealed a sense of caution which would presently desert him in the conduct of his own affairs—in 1906, after the first remarkable success of his new company, he decided to promote another automobile; the directors of the Ford company requested his resignation, and he sold out his interest for one hundred and seventy-five thousand dollars. But before the Ford company opened its doors for business, he determined to protect it from any recurrent incompetence on the part of Ford himself. To this end, he installed a personal representative as business manager, and he added his attorneys to its list of shareholders.

The man whom Malcolmson chose as his deputy had, as yet, revealed no strain of genius, though he was destined to play a major role in shaping the fortunes of the Ford concern; to bring about a radical change in American industrial practice; and finally, as Senator from Michigan, to become a political liberal and an implacable guardian of the public interest. James Couzens had received no more formal schooling than Henry Ford. In childhood, he had earned money as a newsboy. At the age of seventeen he was working full time as a car-checker on the Michigan Central Railroad. At the age of thirty, he was Malcolmson's bookkeeper. When Malcolmson proposed moving him over to the new Ford plant, he had amassed nine hundred dollars in savings, and—as he told John W. Anderson, his employer's lawyer—he had determined to invest in the new enterprise all the money he could beg, borrow or steal. He added his own modest savings to the company's capital, then borrowed an additional fifteen hundred dollars on notes endorsed by Malcolmson. Not content with this, he also tried to borrow two hundred dollars from his sister, Rosetta V. Couzens, a teacher in the Detroit public schools. She reluctantly loaned him half the sum he sought, for which he subsequently assigned to her one share of stock, When, sixteen years later, she sold her interest to Henry Ford, her one-hundred-dollar investment had brought her a total return of three hundred and fifty-five thousand dollars. At that time Couzens, who had systematically added to his holdings until he broke with Henry Ford in 1915, received slightly less than thirty millions of dollars for his interest; before his death, and during the Great Depression, he set up a twelve-million-dollar foundation dedicated to the welfare of children everywhere, regardless of race, creed or color.

In this philanthropy he was imitated by Horace H. Rackham who, with his law partner, John W. Anderson, was persuaded to enter the company by Malcolmson. The two attorneys each borrowed five thousand dollars to invest in their client's new enterprise, and each in 1919 received twelve and one half million dollars for their shares. Rackham, a modest and frugal man, devoted much of his wealth to unpublicized philanthropy, and when he died left the bulk of a sixteen-million-dollar estate in trust to be devoted to "the benefiting of humanity." Anderson, who had received a fee of twenty-five dollars for drawing up the papers of incorporation of the new company, appealed to his father, a physician in La Crosse, Wisconsin, for a loan to enable him to buy into it. In outlining the company's set-up and plans, young Anderson reported to his father that the demand for automobiles had become "a perfect craze." Three factories were producing cars in Detroit; all were oversold and could not begin to fill their orders. Malcolmson had already "begun to be deluged with orders" for the new Fordmobile, as it was to be called, although not a single machine had yet been put on the market. The car was in construction at the Dodge shop. Buyers had heard of it, went there to inspect it, and filed their orders. It had likewise been examined by experts "from all over the country," who pronounced it superior to any car as yet designed, and "a sure winner."

Such merits as the car possessed were not, however, entirely due to Henry Ford. Its design owed much to the brilliant and technically proficient mind of C. Harold Wills, for whom Malcolmson had made no place in the organization. Frightened by the prospect of losing Wills' services—the young engineer refused to continue without a stake in the company—Ford proposed a private arrangement whereby Wills would receive approximately ten percent of Ford's personal profits from the enterprise. Since fifty-one percent of the company's stock was held, in equal shares, by Ford and Malcolmson, this offer impressed Wills as an advantageous one. He accepted it; joined the staff under this odd compact; and was soon to be responsible for many of the metallurgical and mechanical features of the car which swept Ford to world-wide fame.

When the Ford Motor Company opened for business, the only manufacturing operation which it carried on was a limited final assembly. The cars, complete except for bodies and wheels, were built in the Dodge brothers' shop, loaded on hay wagons, and delivered to the Ford factory. There, a dozen men and boys, paid a daily wage of one dollar and a half, and supervised by a foreman, put on the bodies, fitted the upholstery, added wheels and tires, and painted the finished cars. The initial model, with tonneau, sold for eight hundred and fifty dollars, and showed a profit of two hundred and forty-six dollars. As Couzens claimed in an early advertisement, it was "built to stand the severest strains" of hills and muddy roads; a "thoroughly practical car at a moderate price." Anderson's optimistic appraisal of the demand for automobiles soon proved to be correct. In the first fifteen months of its existence, the new concern sold seventeen hundred cars— and the directors declared a cash dividend equal to its entire capitalization, of which approximately only one-fourth had been received in actual funds. With the death of Gray, and the retirement of Malcolmson, Ford took over the presidency, and Couzens the financial direction of the company. Meanwhile, in what was to be his last venture as a "speed demon," Ford had brought the company invaluable publicity. Driving his racing "Arrow" on the ice of Lake St. Clair, he established a world's record for speed: one mile in thirty-nine and two-fifths seconds, or a rate of ninety miles an hour. Increased business forced an expansion of plant facilities: the company moved into a new building which was to become obsolete within five years.

During the first five years of its existence, the Ford Motor Company put eight different models of cars on the market in the effort to develop a product having the widest possible sales appeal. The plain people of the United States dismissed the automobile as a luxury far beyond their means. The experts who wrote for the trade magazines agreed that a market for it existed only among the very wealthy and the moderately rich classes. As a result, the trend was increasingly toward the production of large, high-powered, expensive cars made to resemble the European custom-built vehicles favored by the world of fashion. Even Ransom Olds, fighting for his early vision of a mass market, had been defeated. His backers, preferring to concentrate on supplying cars to the prosperous, forced his resignation from the company he had founded, and he was building a new product for a new organization. In these circumstances, it was only natural for Henry Ford to follow the prevailing trend. Three years after putting out his first model at a moderate price in imitation of Olds, he pushed into the luxury trade with cars priced at one and two thousand dollars. Sales fell off sharply; profits were cut by two-thirds. Dismayed by these results, Ford himself ordered a drastic reduction in prices for the following year. The immediate effect was astonishing: although a financial panic overtook the nation in 1907, the Ford Motor Company sold nearly fifteen thousand cars and showed a profit of more than one million dollars.

3   The Universal Car

Already the majority stockholder in the company, Henry Ford was in a position to dictate its policy. The lesson of its recent experience was obvious, but this lesson merely confirmed certain notions which Ford had been pondering for some time. One day, talking with John W. Anderson, he had come out with a radical opinion. The automobile industry, he thought, was getting off on the wrong foot; annual changes of model were the rule, but this was an absurd proposition, for people were going to get out of the habit of buying a new car every year; who would think of buying a new carriage every spring? The way to make cars, Henry Ford told the young lawyer, was to make one like another—"as much alike as pins or matches." The gospel of standardization was not an original one. Henry Martyn Leland had been preaching it and had given it a spectacular demonstration in England. Olds had already carried it into practice. But Ford, in talking with Anderson, outlined a new and profoundly original application. The standardized car he wanted to develop was one cheap enough for every American farmer to buy; simple enough for him to operate and, if necessary, repair himself; sturdy enough to keep going through sand and mud, snow, slush and water, up hills and across fields, over roadless plains. And this was not all. Ford wanted to build a "universal" car—that is, a vehicle whose engine could be applied "universally" on the farm, not only to get the farmer to market, but to run his machinery, saw his wood, perhaps even pump his water. To those, like Anderson, who had not known Ford at Dearborn in his early thirties, chafing at farm work and frustrated in his attempt to invent a steam-powered, all-purpose farm wagon, the concept must have seemed a sudden, whimsical divination. Years afterwards, James Couzens recorded that Ford arrived at the concept impulsively, and without warning insisted upon making it the sole basis of company policy. But Couzens was no more than half right.

For when, one morning in 1909, Henry Ford startled his associates with a dictatorial edict, he was staking everything on the experience of a single year. During the previous season, the company had continued to market its two most successful prior models, but Ford himself had sponsored a new one, and the company had introduced it to compete with them for public favor. Working under Wills' direction, Ford's staff of technicians had designed it to realize, so far as possible, his concept of a "universal" car. It embodied certain improvements in engineering, among them, the use of vanadium steel, which Ford had learned that French manufacturers were employing for increased tensile strength and lightness. Its mechanism was so simple as to be practically fool-proof, and any fool could learn to run it in a few days. It had caught on at once. So Ford abruptly announced that, in the future, the company would build only one model; that its chassis would be precisely the same for all cars; that "any customer can have a car painted any color that he wants so long as it is black." This decision reflected his impatience with "a tendency to keep monkeying with styles and to spoil a good thing by changing it." But it also expressed his conviction that he had succeeded in producing "a car for the great multitude." He proposed to concentrate on this product, and permanently freeze its design.

The Model-T Ford was as undistinguished as a pin or a match; one of the earliest of perennial Ford jokes described it as capable of going anywhere except into society. But what it lacked in beauty it made up in virtue, and homespun Americans, believing that handsome is as handsome does, understood precisely what Ford meant when, a few years later, he declared bluntly that he wouldn't give five cents for all the art in the world. The Model-T, built for performance on the farms and in the small towns of the land, needed no pretensions to elegance, refinement or style, and made none. It was a lowly black box mounted very high on wheels —as functional as a mouse trap, as long-lived and tireless as a maiden aunt, as serenely indifferent to hardships as a saint. It would go where no vehicle had ever gone before, and presently Americans were to learn that it fulfilled the promise of a peculiar bliss: "you can press down on the foot-lever until all the scenery looks alike to you and you have to keep your eyes skinned to count the milestones as they pass." It was one of Henry Ford's most masterly insights to foresee that the further his fellow-citizens traveled, the happier they would be to find themselves in the same place.

Before many years had passed, Americans were speaking of Model-T with the affectionate derision which they reserve for their folk heroes and national cynosures. "Tin Lizzie," they named it, and talked of the "flivver" they planned to buy, or—still later—of the "jalopy" they had lived with so long, acknowledging that there was a dance in the old girl yet. In less than two decades, fifteen million Model-T Fords were to pour out on the American roads, and the fund of folk humor, of jokes and tall tales that accumulated about them indicated, perhaps more impressively than anything else, the profound changes they wrought in the national life. For it was this homely, utilitarian car which, far more than any other, put the whole nation on wheels, made the automobile an indispensable convenience to the common man, and thereby brought about results so far-reaching as to transform American society, civilization and culture. During a whole era, the Model-T seemed the most persuasive symbol of American democracy. It was the car of the people, admitting the humblest citizen on terms of absolute equality with the plutocrat to the new dimension of untrammeled mobility. To the world at large, it announced the fabulous nature of the United States—a land where nearly every man, whatever his condition, could afford to own an automobile; where almost none, in literal fact, could afford not to own one.

Yet Henry Ford, who had projected a car for the great multitude, apparently did not foresee its ultimate consequences, either for the nation or for himself. For twice—in 1908, just after his tentative introduction of the Model-T, and in 1909 shortly after his decision to concentrate on it exclusively—Henry Ford and

James Couzens entered into negotiations for the sale of the Ford Motor Company, and both deals fell through only because the prospective purchaser was unable to meet the terms upon which Ford insisted. Both men, presumably, were tempted by the possibility of reaping quick millions. And both may have been alarmed by another and much darker one. For the company lived under the threat of an ominous lawsuit. If the suit were finally decided against the Ford Motor Company, heavy damages might be assessed against it—and it might even be compelled to go out of business.

4   The Ogre Growls

The suit concerned possible infringement of a patent, generally assumed to be basic for the industry as a whole. The story of this patent was one of the queerest in the history of American industry, though the uses to which it was put exemplified a pattern of economic and financial concentration that became increasingly familiar; the pattern emerged again, for example, in the development of both the movie and the radio. The patent which involved Henry Ford in costly and prolonged litigation had originally been applied for in 1879; fourteen years before the Duryea brothers produced the first American automobile, when Henry Ford, as a lad of sixteen, ran away from his father's farm to become an apprentice mechanic in Detroit. The applicant was George Baldwin Selden, then thirty-two years old, a patent attorney and amateur inventor of Rochester, New York.

Selden came of a prosperous and cultivated family; his father was judge of the Court of Appeals of New York. He received an excellent education, studying at two universities, and taking a year's work in science at Yale's Sheffield School. He was one of the first Americans to become obsessed by the idea of a "road locomotive" not driven by steam. In the early eighteen-seventies, when gasoline became available, he began experimenting with this novel fuel. A two-cycle gasoline engine had been exhibited, in 1876, at the Centennial Exposition in Philadelphia, by George B. Brayton, an Englishman living in Boston, Massachusetts. Using Brayton's engine as his model, Selden designed one during the following year. Three years later, after preparing his claims and specifications, he filed application for a patent covering "the use of the gasoline motor as the propelling force of a road vehicle, and upon the vehicle as a whole."

Selden's application was allowed; but actual issue of a patent was the very last thing that Selden then desired. For the life of a patent was limited to seventeen years, and Selden's investigation of the commercial possibilities of his invention had convinced him that he was far in advance of the times. His problem, therefore, was to keep his application in force until a final patent became profitable. As an attorney specializing in patent cases, he knew precisely how to do this. He merely filed with the Patent Office periodic amendments to his original application, embodying further claims and alleged improvements; this strategy kept the application pending, and the fact that it had been officially "allowed" gave him adequate legal protection. Oddly enough, however, Selden made no attempt to build a car. He was content to nurse along an invention that existed only on paper.

When reports of the Daimler and Benz machines first reached the United States, Selden began negotiating with capitalists to finance a model of his car. He met with the ridicule experienced by all the other pioneers. To one prominent, wealthy manufacturer of Rochester from whom he was trying to secure funds, he remarked that some day horseless carriages would be as numerous on Main Street as vehicles drawn by horses. The prospective backer told Selden he was crazy; presently, he came to be regarded as slightly unbalanced. Nevertheless, over the years, he succeeded in interesting six different promoters, but in each case some mishap occurred that prevented any deal from being consummated. After the news of the Duryea brothers' achievement broke in the American press, Selden realized that commercial development of the motor car would not long be delayed. Having maintained his application in force for more than a decade, he now pressed for the immediate issue of a final patent. No Selden car was in actual existence, but in 1895 a patent was granted broadly covering any gasoline-driven vehicle having a disconnecting device between the engine and the vehicle, and carrying a receptacle for liquid fuel. This patent, if he could enforce it, promised to give Selden a monopoly on the manufacture of automobiles for seventeen years, until 1912.

Shortly afterwards, when it appeared probable that electric vehicles were going to find a ready market in the United States, a group of millionaires decided to take over this new industry. The group was headed by William C. Whitney, Secretary of the Navy under President Cleveland, and it included Anthony F. Brady, P. A. B. Widener of Philadelphia, and Thomas Fortune Ryan. These gentlemen had already made fortunes in the promotion of municipal electric traction systems. Their present purpose was to effect a monopoly of the manufacture of electric carriages, and put fleets of cabs on the streets of the major American cities.

Late in 1899, after William C. Whitney had assumed control of the electric vehicle combination, Selden assigned to it exclusive rights under his patent. By this time the manufacture of gasoline cars had been undertaken by the Duryeas, Haynes, Winton and Olds. Whitney, who had acquired the Selden patent somewhat incidentally, quickly realized its potential value and proposed to enforce it vigorously. He therefore filed suit against Winton. This litigation was carried on until 1903, when the automobile industry appeared to be securely established. The holders of the Selden rights then came forward with a brilliant project. With the sweeping Selden patent as its foundation, they set up the Association of Licensed Automobile Manufacturers, whose members, by paying a royalty on every car sold, received immunity from prosecution for infringement, and the assurance that they might continue in business without legal interference. To this arrangement, Winton and nine other manufacturers immediately subscribed. Other companies, as they entered the business, promptly joined the Association under the threat of suit.

To extreme individualists like Henry Ford and James Couzens, the payment of royalty looked like acquiescence in a private tax on manufacture. In their view, the A. L. A. M. was merely a budding trust, organized by Wall Street financiers for the usual purpose of getting something for nothing. Their mood was therefore not entirely genial when, soon after the Ford Motor Company began operations, they were invited to confer with representatives of the Association at the Russell House in Detroit. The meeting was very brief. A spokesman for the Association outlined the advantages of "getting together for the good of the industry"; remarked that Ford was infringing the Selden patent; proposed that he join the Association, take out a license, and pay the established royalty on his cars. Before Ford could reply, Couzens, whose temper was short and inflexible, shouted, "Selden can take his patent and go to hell with it." An official of the Association, looking pointedly at Ford, said that suit could be brought immediately. "Couzens has answered you," Ford retorted. The official then brought greater pressure to bear: the Association would do everything possible to put Ford out of business. At this, Ford leaped out of his chair, shook his finger at the official in fury, and snarled, "Let them try it!" The conference broke up in disorder.

Early in the autumn of 1903, the threatened suit was brought. The plaintiffs in this action—brought at the request of the Association—were the Electric Vehicle Company, as Selden's assignees, and Selden himself. Fought through two courts, the litigation was to last for eight years. In its course, thirty-six volumes of testimony were taken, and the only example of a Selden car ever built was constructed at great expense, and demonstrated in court. Six years after the suit was begun, the United States Circuit Court handed down a decision upholding the validity of the Selden patent. Its effect was to vest control of the automobile industry, during the lifetime of the patent, in the Electric Vehicle Company, dominated by a group of millionaire promoters. Unless it could be reversed, the outlook for Ford was disastrous. Legal costs, damages and the payment of back royalties might easily reduce him to bankruptcy. And he could be put out of business by the simple expedient of denying him membership in the Association. His lawyers therefore promptly took an appeal. This sent the case to a higher court; but, until a final verdict was handed down, Ford's business would be in jeopardy.

That the outcome of this case would determine the future of the automobile industry was not evident. But it was obvious that, aside from the issue of monopoly control, the case involved conflicting economic theories. Except for Ford, practically all manufacturers of automobiles were members of the Association, and most of them were builders of relatively high-priced cars. They were doing business successfully under a policy of limited production, taking a large profit on every unit sold. Ford's announced program rested on a very different policy. His aim was quantity production. This would reduce the unit-cost of his cars, enabling him to sell them at a low price. The low price would result in volume sales; on these, a large aggregate profit could be made by taking a small profit on every unit sold. It was the belief of the Association that, should Ford succeed in realizing his program, the entire industry would be disorganized. Their conviction that his program could not, in fact, be realized merely increased their animosity. Why should an economic crackpot be permitted to threaten the established order?

During the two years that elapsed before a verdict was reached on Ford's appeal, the parties to the action conducted relentless warfare in the advertising columns of the nation's press. In an effort to force Ford out of business, the Association threatened his prospective customers with eventual prosecution. Ford countered with an offer to post a bond with every car sold, protecting buyers from any financial damages that might result from prosecution. Of approximately eighteen thousand purchasers of Model-T cars who presumably became parties to the case through ownership of a Ford automobile, only fifty ever demanded a Ford bond. The final phases of the litigation were reached after the exposures of the muckrakers had brought about a widespread attack on industrial mergers, trusts, monopolies and combinations of competitors. In this climate of opinion, Ford was widely acclaimed as a champion of the people. In 1911, the Court of Appeals handed down a decision in his favor. It held that the Selden patent was valid, but that Ford had not been guilty of infringement; the patent covered a two-cycle motor, but Ford—and all other American manufacturers—had adopted the four-cycle Otto motor. This decision shattered the patent monopoly beyond repair. Since Selden's patent, though valid, was worthless, no further royalty could be collected from American manufacturers. The tax on production ceased to be operative. In order to prevent any similar litigation in the future, the principal manufacturers of automobiles soon organized to form a patent pool. However unexpected by his former antagonists, nothing could have been more characteristic than Ford's refusal to join them in this defensive alliance.

A decade later, Ford was to look back with satisfaction on the long, troublesome Selden lawsuit. Nothing, he affirmed, had ever advertised his car and company so well. During this litigation, the Ford concern had appeared in the role of an underdog; this had won it the public's sympathy and good will. Although, at the outset, the Association commanded seventy millions of dollars, and the Ford Company not half that many thousands, Henry Ford himself had never been in doubt about the outcome of the case. So he believed, or professed to believe, in 1922; but apparently this exalted confidence had actually been more fitful than he found it convenient to remember.

5   A Giant Is Born

One day in the autumn of 1909, Ford and James Couzens were in New York City, at the Belmont Hotel. Ford, suffering from lumbago, was lying on the floor of their room when the telephone rang and Couzens answered it. After a brief exchange of remarks, Couzens went down to the hotel lobby, and presently returned to the room.

"Billy Durant," he announced, "wants to buy the Ford Motor Company."

"How much will he pay?" asked the invalid.

"Eight million dollars." This was five million more than he had offered one year earlier.

"All right. But—gold on the table," Ford snapped.

"How do you mean that?" Couzens asked, though Ford's terms had been the same the year before.

"I mean cash," said Ford.

On this basis, Couzens began negotiations the following day. Before long, a final agreement was reached. Then Durant put it before his bankers, who had previously consented to finance the transaction. But these gentlemen, upon sober second thought, concluded that the risk was too great. The Ford Motor Company, they informed Durant, was not worth the price asked for it. Nor did Durant succeed in finding any other capitalists willing to invest eight millions of dollars in the purchase of an industrial property soon to become one of the most fabulously profitable in the world. It is very probable that Durant himself queered the deal, in every quarter. For, shortly before, he had irreparably prejudiced J. P. Morgan and Company, the national repository of financial and economic wisdom. In those sacred precincts, he had unfortunately given the impression of being stupid, irresponsible and—even worse—shamelessly impudent.

During the course of a conference with George W. Perkins, one of the Morgan partners, Durant blithely prophesied that the day was coming when three hundred thousand automobiles would be produced and sold annually in the United States. Perkins, it is said, was so exasperated by this frivolity that he got up and left the room. Having thus alienated the august rulers of the capital market, it was almost inevitable that Durant should be regarded with suspicion. Yet, forty years after the collapse of his projected acquisition of the Ford Motor Company, Americans might perhaps concede that Durant, alone of the parties concerned, demonstrated the vision, sagacity and daring upon which —according to its classic oracles—progress under the system of free enterprise ultimately depends.

Spare, small, quiet and soft-spoken, William Crapo Durant dazzled the American people for a generation, and left as his monument an industrial colossus which might continue to affect their lives long after anyone had ceased to remember his name. Four decades after he conceived and created it, The General Motors Corporation was the biggest enterprise in America's biggest industry. Its assets then totalled two and one half billions of dollars, and its prosperity or adversity modified the material well-being of four hundred thousand stockholders. Even more directly concerned were the three hundred and seventy-five thousand people whom it employed. Most of them earned their livelihood in one hundred plants operated by the corporation in fifty-two American cities located in fifteen states; besides these, it owned twenty-six others in foreign lands. General Motors turned out approximately two and one quarter million cars and trucks every year, or two in every five built in the United States. But the automotive industry, which it dominated, was not its sole area of operations. It was likewise deeply involved in the field of aviation. It made Diesel engines for marine and railway use; farm power and lighting plants; electric pumps. It was a leading producer of domestic refrigerators and industrial refrigerating machinery. It manufactured radios, electric fans, vacuum cleaners, quick-drying paints. Under licensing agreements, it drew a large income from the oil industry, which produced a "knock-proof" motor fuel originally developed by General Motors chemists. For the corporation also maintained one of the greatest institutions for scientific and industrial research in the United States. By the middle of the twentieth century the General Motors Corporation had become—in magnitude, wealth and social influence—the most powerful industrial enterprise in the world. More perfectly than any other single feature of the American scene, it exemplified the methods, objectives and achievements of twentieth-century finance capitalism.

William Crapo Durant, who conceived this colossus and brought it into being, died in relative obscurity, without wealth, although during his comet-like passage across the American financial skies he had made many millions of dollars. He possessed nearly all the qualities which most of his compatriots esteemed most highly: boundless ambition, immense energy, audacity, persuasiveness, an inexhaustible talent for circumventing obstacles and transcending failure. The quality which he notably lacked was caution, and its absence from his makeup proved costly. His mild appearance and quiet manner misrepresented him. For Durant thrived on the stresses and tensions, the alarms and excursions and explosive climaxes of heroic drama; these were his nourishment, not his stimulant. Fundamentally, he was an adventurer in the literal sense, like the New Bedford mariners and shipbuilders who were his forebears. During the first two decades of the century, his exploits confounded the discreet and conventional; he played the great American game of business with all the deuces wild, and in his hand.

Born in Boston, Durant was brought up by his grandfather,

Henry H. Crapo, governor of Michigan during the War between the States, and afterwards a major figure in its great lumber industry. Rejecting the opportunity to go to college, young Durant entered his grandfather's lumber mill in the little city of Flint. Before reaching his twenty-first year, he branched into the insurance business; presently, he deserted this for the vehicle industry of which Flint had become the chief center. Having bought, for fifty dollars, the patent rights to an improved road cart, Durant formed a partnership with a young hardware clerk, Josiah Dallas Dort, put the cart into quantity production, and proceeded to develop a nation-wide market for it. With their earnings, the partners then formed the Durant-Dort Carriage Company, which presently rose to leadership in the trade, for Durant's salesmanship made necessary a yearly production of fifty thousand vehicles. This unprecedented output created problems of supply, and Durant met them by setting up subsidiary companies to produce wheels, axles, paint and varnish, and to develop timber reserves in the Northwest. He had already conceived the project of a "vertical trust"—an industrial unit made absolutely self-sufficient by controlling supplies and processes from raw materials to finished product.

A millionaire before he reached his fortieth year, at the turn of the century, Durant began to lose interest in his highly prosperous carriage business; when its major problems had been solved, it ceased yielding him any adventure. But, apparently, the notion of the self-sufficient industrial unit continued to preoccupy his imagination, for he went off to New York City with the intention of making a first-hand study of the stock market. It was in Wall Street, as he knew, that industrial combinations were effected and trusts were built. And it was in New York that an urgent appeal reached him; opening, as he could not foresee, a second and far more adventurous career.

The appeal was one which he could scarcely refuse: it was to save the business community of his home town from imminent financial disaster. David Dunbar Buick, the Detroit manufacturer of plumbers' supplies, had started building automobiles in 1903 with high hopes and no money. Of an inventive turn of mind,

Buick always had remarkably progressive ideas—usually far in advance of the times—but he was lacking in aptitude for business. Shortly after beginning to build his cars, his business was taken over by his major creditors, Frank and Benjamin Briscoe, Jr., manufacturers of sheet metal. But they, in turn, found themselves unable to carry it, and began looking for a purchaser. In Flint, James H. Whiting, the elderly president of the Flint Wagon Works, had become convinced that the automobile was eventually going to put builders of carriages out of business, and had determined to find a car which could be produced in his plant. Automobiles, he surmised, could be put together the way carriages were, and could be sold by the same men who marketed his line of wagons, carts and buggies. Learning that the Buick business was for sale, he formed a company to take it over, moved it to his plant in Flint, and proceeded to borrow heavily from local bankers to finance operations. By 1904, the money raised by loans had been exhausted. Only fifty-three Buick cars had been built and sold; and no further capital could be raised in Flint. Whiting himself was perilously close to bankruptcy, and it was clear that if he were ruined the bankers and many of the business men of Flint would be carried down with him. It was in these circumstances that Durant, as the town's wealthiest citizen, was invited to rescue the business community.

Returning to Flint, Durant's first concern was to assess the merits of the Buick car as a marketable product. He had no technical experience with automobiles, but he learned to drive, and for nearly two months he took the car over a widely varied region lacking any good roads other than a few turnpikes operated by toll companies. Under this gruelling test, Durant learned that the car could survive the mud, sand, stumps and gullies of rural Michigan, and he concluded that it was a saleable product. He took over, and set to work with incredible swiftness. Recapitalizing the moribund company, he set up efficient factory procedures, secured dealers, and raised money in ever-increasing amounts. The aura of past success was his principal asset: creditors willingly withheld their claims, and when he issued stock in the new company his fellow-townsmen bought half a million dollars' worth in a single day. But the resources of Flint were inadequate to Durant's needs, and he went far afield to sell his shares. Meanwhile, mounting demand for the Buick convinced him that his faith was justified. If he could secure enough capital to expand his enterprise, he knew that he would be rewarded with wealth, power and prestige as an industrial innovator.

As a result of his efforts, the new company was making money within two years. Raising capital by heroic efforts, Durant built the world's largest automobile plant, added five models to the Buick line, and launched into quantity production. In 1908, four years after taking control, Durant was building and selling more than eight thousand cars. One of the social effects of the automobile—to be demonstrated even more impressively by Detroit—was quickly made evident in the little city of Flint. It had been threatened by financial disaster; now, it became a boom-town. His expanding market, facing Durant with a need for constantly greater and more rapid production, soon brought about a labor shortage. To meet it, Durant instituted wage scales higher than those prevailing in other industries, and men flowed into Flint from all over the United States. The population doubled in five years. It continued to grow at a rate which overtaxed the supply of living quarters. For a time, it was common practice to rent the same bed to a day-worker at night, and a night-worker by day. Durant projected a large housing development for his workers, and the city began to sprawl over outlying farms. To the business men of Flint, this spectacular municipal expansion forecasted uninterrupted prosperity and pyramiding profits. In the golden glow of this prospect, nobody detected the emergence of an ominous social problem. But the welfare of the city would soon depend exclusively on the profitable operation of a single industry. This industry was in no respect socially accountable to the community which it dominated. It was responsible only to the stockholders who financed it. The fortunes of Flint, inseparably bound to those of its major product, would be determined by the fluctuations of the market, the efficiency of management, and the will of absentee proprietors largely indifferent to its social well-being.

Meanwhile, Durant was striving to cope with the problems

BOVE: "Why Won't It Go?"   RIGHT: A Prospective Purchaser Takes a Steering Test

Watching a Vanderbilt Cup Contest

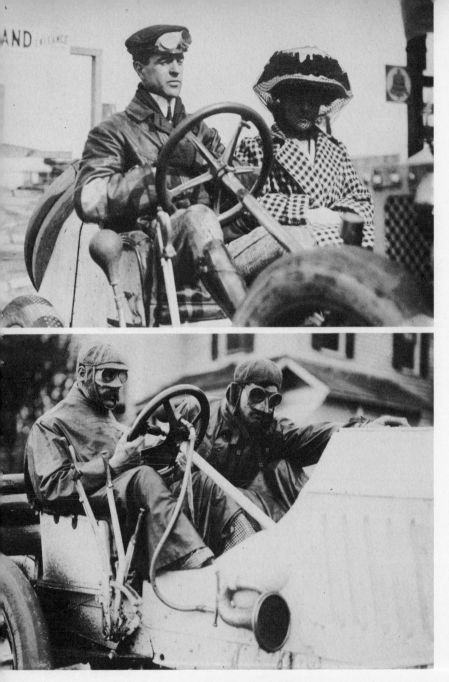

ABOVE: Mr. and Mrs. W. K. Vanderbilt, Jr.

BELOW: The Well-Dressed Racer

ABOVE: Returning from a Visit to the Milliner. Newport, 1904

BELOW: Harry Lehr and Mrs. John Jacob Astor in a Floral Parade

ABOVE: Governor Dix, His Wife and His Dog

BELOW: Boss Nixon Arrives at Tammany Hall

arising from his astonishing success. His appetite for adventure and incurable audacity were reflected by the character of his decisions. To meet the steadily enlarging demand for cars, he had increased and accelerated production; in his view, this made further expansion imperative. For he did not control the vital supplies upon which the output of his plant depended; delay in the delivery of some essential material, or fabricated part, could suddenly halt its operations. Any interruption of the production schedule was costly, but to Durant a prolonged one might bring financial ruin. In identical circumstances, other manufacturers built up financial reserves out of profits, and were protected against reduced production, unfavorable markets, or the abrupt drying up of sources of new capital. This was not Durant's way. One of the most adroit and successful promoters in American industrial history, he brought to the intricacies of finance only a genius for daring improvisation. Because his imagination forever outran his resources, no matter how large, he was always heavily mortgaged to the future.

Durant's optimism and self-confidence were extreme. He relied on his ability to sell stock, if other means of raising capital failed him. To keep his enterprise afloat, he was fully prepared to race production against the maturing of his rapidly mounting commitments. Expansion thus became a stern necessity. He saw that to insure continuous and steadily increasing production, he would have to achieve absolute productive independence. In some fashion, he would have to gain effective control of the chain of supplies and processes that contributed to a finished automobile. Having conceived this objective, Durant determined to reach it, so to speak, overnight. Four decades later, no manufacturer of automobiles—not even the colossus born of his decision—had yet succeeded in attaining the goal so confidently proposed by Durant.

But, as if this single goal was not sufficient to absorb all his energies, Durant simultaneously set himself another. Despite its prodigious and rapid development, the automobile industry, broadly viewed, remained violently unstable: an affair of boom-and-bust; a plunger's paradise in which new companies arose and collapsed with alarming frequency. No shares of any automotive company were either listed or traded in on the New York Stock Exchange. The great fountain of risk-capital in Wall Street could not be tapped, for leading bankers—not yet convinced that the automobile was anything more than a transient toy—refused to give the industry their support, and conservative investors, aware of its high mortality rate, had no faith in it.

As Durant realized, these circumstances also tended to depress the market for automobiles; prospective purchasers of cars wished to be certain that the manufacturers would remain in business during the active lifetime of the vehicles. His own extreme difficulties in financing Buick expansion had convinced him that stability could be assured only by control of a large fixed capital invested for long-range operations. But this kind of investment, he knew, could be attracted solely by conditions of economic security. Would not diversification of product yield these conditions? Why not bring together a number of companies making various types of cars at different prices? Such an arrangement would act as a precaution against unforeseen changes in public taste, and the operations of those divisions which were successful in any one year would carry the losses of those which were not. Absolute productive independence could be achieved by forming a vertical trust. Approximate stability, equally essential, might be gained by making the trust not only vertical, but horizontal also. Already launched on the course of combination—he had, by now, added three subsidiary companies to the Buick plant in Flint—Durant projected a giant holding corporation like those which had successfully invaded the field of public utilities.

Incorporation of the General Motors Company, in the early autumn of 1908, attracted no immediate attention. Its stated function was to purchase the securities of automobile and accessory companies, and it began life with a nominal capital of two thousand dollars. A fortnight later, this was increased to twelve and one-half millions, and thereafter Durant moved with a swiftness never before equalled in the history of industrial mergers. His policy was to pay for his acquisitions in stock of the new company, using as little cash as possible. This kept Ford, and several other leading producers, out of the combine. But, in little more than a year, Durant gained control of some twenty companies that built cars or produced parts and accessories. Among these, in addition to Buick, were three other major concerns: Henry Martyn Leland's Cadillac; the Oldsmobile, and the Oakland. Durant's operations, during the new company's first year, showed net sales of more than twenty-nine million dollars, and net profits of more than nine millions. He controlled twenty percent of the nation's total output of cars, and employed more than fourteen thousand people. When General Motors declared a stock dividend of one hundred and fifty percent, and increased its capitalization to sixty millions of dollars, the American people suddenly realized that a new industrial giant had been born, and that it was likely to gain a monopoly of the most promising, and hitherto least developed, field of enterprise.

Such, indeed, might have been the case, had engineering experience in the industry been more extensive than it was, and had Durant himself been of less impetuous temperament. Among his acquisitions there were many of unproved value; he had taken them over because they were believed to own basic patents, or rights to some mechanical improvement which might become important at a future date, or because they were thought to be promising sources of essential supplies. But Durant had to work with whirlwind speed, and often took vital decisions in an offhand way. Long afterwards, one of his early associates recalled that when Durant inspected a plant, it was like the visitation of a cyclone. He would lead his staff in, take off his coat, begin issuing orders, dictate at breakneck speed, call distant points on the telephone, close a series of deals, and abruptly take off for another place. On one occasion, he authorized the vast physical expansion of a plant after briefly inspecting a model; set men and machines at work within twenty-four hours; and began installing machinery in the new structures three weeks later. Deliberation, like caution, was alien to him; only a phenomenal memory enabled him to keep his deals straight—he worked so fast that the records were always behind.

It was not long before Durant's baby giant began to show

symptoms of acute indigestion: he had forced it to swallow more than it was able to assimilate. Its second year of operations told the story. Net sales, amounting to nearly fifty millions, exceeded those of the first year by some two-thirds; net profits, at slightly more than ten million dollars, showed an increase of little more than one million. Though volume of business had risen beyond expectations, the rate of profit had dwindled alarmingly, and the company's outstanding commitments had swollen to a huge figure. Undaunted, perhaps even ignorant of this situation, Durant had meanwhile undertaken further expansion. In doing so, he had closed one of the most misguided deals of all time.

This involved the purchase of what purported to be patent rights to an important innovation. The electric automobile lamp had just appeared and, as Durant correctly foresaw, it was destined to replace the acetylene and kerosene lamps then in use. Patent rights to a tungsten filament electric lamp were claimed by John Albert Heany, who had organized the Heany Lamp Company to exploit it. It was into this company that Durant bought heavily, paying, as usual, with General Motors stock. But Heany's right to a patent was being contested by so formidable a claimant as the General Electric Company, and the Patent Office presently dismissed his application. This made his lamp worthless, and Durant's purchase a complete fiasco. It had involved a loss of between five and twelve millions of dollars. Ultimately, the worthless lamp proved to be almost as miraculous as Aladdin's, but not for Durant. Between 1910 and 1927, fifty millions of dollars in dividends were paid by General Motors on the stock issued to the Heany Company, and its market value rose to three hundred and twenty millions of dollars.

On a smaller scale, some of Durant's other acquisitions proved to be almost as disastrous, and by the spring of 1910, less than two years after its birth, his enterprise was in grave jeopardy. The city of Flint, dependent on the Buick car, and the city of Pontiac, similarly dependent on the Oakland, suffered from the first repercussions. Building construction already under way suddenly stopped; layoffs, occurring with startling frequency, brought hardship to an increasing proportion of their new populations, and thus to local business men. To meet payrolls at the Buick plant, the company had its Boston distributor express suitcases containing cash; the funds could not be remitted through banks because the company's accounts were overdrawn. In Detroit, the Cadillac organization—which, during the year, had poured two million dollars into the General Motors treasury—was able to meet its payroll only because a joint emergency meeting of the directors of two banks furnished a loan of five hundred thousand dollars just before pay-off time. Durant, with characteristic intrepidity, took to the road in a desperate effort to raise enough money to save his tottering giant.

6 Wall Street Moves In

Bankers in New York and Boston, in Chicago, St. Louis and Kansas City refused Durant their aid. In a very few years, they would, as a matter of course, base the credit of a holding company on the earnings of its subsidiaries; in Durant's case, they rejected this policy with expressions of horror. To them, there was something deeply shocking in Durant's vision of the future, in his daringly adventurous methods and imperturbable optimism. They could feel only hostility to a man who had over-reached himself so spectacularly, who stood on the brink of ruin, but who nevertheless prophesied that, if permitted to continue in his courses, he would soon be building and selling one hundred thousand cars a year. For they distrusted the automobile industry as profoundly as they distrusted Durant. Clearly, the automobile "craze" would peter out in precisely the same fashion as had the earlier bicycle "craze"—in a sulphurous odor of widespread bankruptcy; and the fact that there were already nearly half a million cars registered in the land did not change this melancholy, but inevitable, certainty.

Nor could the bankers be persuaded that they were charged with a social responsibility, in the public interest, to come to the rescue of an industrial unit that dominated the economy of two American cities, and was also one of the largest employers of labor in the nation. Yet, by the autumn of 1910, certain social consequences of the situation were evident. In the cities of Flint and

Pontiac, the prospect of a complete shut-down of plant operations had produced financial uncertainty bordering on panic, and unemployment was giving rise to distress reflected in political unrest. The economic future of the state of Michigan was obviously involved, and it seemed likely that if Durant's weakened empire crashed, a nation-wide depression might follow.

During a last desperate trip to Eastern cities, Durant was informed that his empire could be saved, but only at the humiliating cost of his own abdication. At the outset of his feverish quest for money, eight million dollars would have met the emergency. Now, after six months, only a loan of twelve millions could avert bankruptcy. The banking houses of J. and W. Seligman, in New York, and Lee, Higginson, in Boston, were ready to rescue General Motors. Their terms were as harsh as if they had been military conquerors, not bankers. As a preliminary condition, they required Durant to give up his control of the company, and eliminate himself from its future management. This demand he had not foreseen, even allowing for the universal hostility of the banking fraternity. It meant unconditional surrender, and he could do nothing but assent.

The bankers thereupon loaned General Motors the sum of fifteen million dollars. For this, the company gave notes bearing interest at six percent, secured by a blanket mortgage on all its property. But although indebted, as to principal and interest, for the full amount, the company did not receive it. Two and one-quarter millions were retained by the bankers. This was their modest commission for making the loan. In addition, they exacted, and were given, more than six million dollars worth of the company's stock. Thus, before funds were made available, the bankers had assured themselves of a profit on the transaction amounting to very nearly fifty percent. Nor were they, even temporarily, out of pocket as respects the money they advanced. By disposing of the company's notes to private investors, the bankers retrieved their principal, and shifted the burden of their loan to others. Moreover, they insisted on the execution of a legal trusteeship. This gave the bankers complete control over the company's affairs and future operations. It likewise enabled them to issue securities for which they created a market on the New York Stock Exchange, thus for the first time making automotive shares financially respectable. In this fashion, the bankers transferred to the general public the speculative risks arising from their future conduct of an enterprise which—for their own immediate profit— they had already saddled with an enormous debt. As an historian of the industry remarked long afterwards, in a masterly under-statement, this whole loan transaction revealed, on a large scale, the high cost of financing automobile enterprises.

Few Americans, at the time, thought this situation irregular, or detected its irony. Having taken their tribute, conservative bankers were now masters of the largest productive unit of an industry in whose future they had no confidence whatever; and although they had themselves reduced it to bondage, what could be more logical than the assumption that, by doing so, they had miraculously restored its vigor and improved its opportunities? A vast increase in the demand for automobiles was soon evident. In five years, registrations of cars leaped from less than half a million to more than two million. For this, one engineering in-novation was largely responsible. Almost overnight, it doubled the market for automobiles by making them as available to women as to men. The bankers, believers in progress unsullied by risk, took a dim view of it.

One of the most discouraging hazards of driving a car was the initial task of starting it. For engines had to be cranked by hand. Wrestling with an obdurate crank, leaping from crank to spark-control to advance the spark and regulate the flow of gasoline before the temperamental engine went dead, was a gymnastic feat that daunted even the most enthusiastic motorist. The job of cranking, alone, was exhausting as well as back-breaking. It drove strong men to bad temper and profanity; it was hopelessly beyond the strength of nearly all women. And it was a fertile source of accidents. The most common mishap was a broken wrist produced by the backfiring of the engine; with the growing popularity of the Model-T, physicians began to describe this as a "Ford frac-ture." Gashed hands and broken arms were also prevalent among motorists. Even more serious injuries occurred when—as happened frequently—the engine had been left in gear, and the car charged forward on its careless cranker.

7 The Ladies' Aid

Inventors had long been tinkering with various types of self-starter, but none had yet succeeded in producing a practicable device. All this was familiar to Henry Martyn Leland when, in 1910, he agreed to examine a model built by a young man from Dayton, Ohio. Whatever his skepticism, Leland had a special interest in the matter. For an elderly friend of his had lately sustained fatal injuries while cranking a Cadillac car that had stalled on Belle Isle bridge in Detroit. Deeply shocked by this incident, for which he felt a personal responsibility, Leland determined that a way must be found to overcome the mechanical defect which more than any other, was certain to permanently limit the use of automobiles.

The young inventor from Dayton, Charles Franklin Kettering, had reached this conclusion even earlier than Leland. While other experimenters were trying to perfect self-starters using compressed air, or springs, or acetylene gas, he had been working with electricity. Why should not the same power that ignited a car's gasoline likewise start its engine, provide its lights and turn them on automatically? Kettering was thirty-four years old when he came to see Leland, and already had behind him considerable achievement. Born on an Ohio farm, he had graduated from normal school, taught school, taken his degree at Ohio State University, and worked for a telephone company before joining the National Cash Register Company, a leading pioneer in the new technology. Its general manager, Colonel Edward A. Deeds, had quickly recognized Kettering's talent and appointed him head of the inventions department. In this capacity, he had perfected several improved cash registers, among them one that was electrically operated and came into use only some years later.

Meanwhile, foreseeing the expanding part which science was to play in the future of big industry, Kettering persuaded Deeds to help him launch an independent organization to undertake industrial research in the fields of electrical and mechanical engineering. The Dayton Engineering Laboratories Company—its name was presently abbreviated to the initial letters—was set up in a disused barn and, while awaiting clients, Kettering devoted himself to developing his electrical self-starter. Manufacturers of batteries ridiculed his idea; no battery had ever been built with sufficient capacity to turn over a motor; obviously, therefore, none could be. When Kettering finally bullied one of them into making a battery according to his specifications, he met with an equally closed mind among the manufacturers of automobiles to whom he showed his model. None of them would have anything to do with it, and Kettering had little hope of success in demonstrating it to Leland.

To his astonishment, Leland's technical judgment approved his invention, and Kettering received an order to furnish four thousand starters for the Cadillac car. He had a laboratory, almost no machinery, and very little money. It was only with enormous difficulty that he was able to begin actual production of the device. Meanwhile, Leland was meeting savage criticism from the banker-appointed directors of General Motors, who predicted ruin for the company as a result of his extravagant commitment of funds to an allegedly impractical experiment. The directors brought in three eminent electrical engineers, all of whom insisted that Kettering's device could not possibly work. Everyone but Leland and Kettering gloomily awaited failure on the February day in 1911 when the first Cadillac equipped with a Delco starter was to be demonstrated. While the directors and their experts watched, Leland, white-bearded, benign and imperturbable, turned the switch, adjusted the spark and pressed the button. At once, the engine roared. Leland advanced the spark and reduced the gas supply, and the engine settled down to a steady drone of power. The forebodings of cautious bankers and their skeptical technical experts had been disproved.

The electrical starter was soon acclaimed as a major invention, for it made the automobile, at least potentially, a universal vehicle. During the years that followed, Kettering added a long and varied series of contributions to automotive development. He also perfected other devices, among them a lighting and power plant for farms, which materially changed the lives of many Americans. Invention brought him wealth and world-wide fame. Yet it was not his greatest achievement. This, ironically, implied the obsolescence of the individual inventor, struggling along by himself, working at random, often without adequate laboratory facilities, financial resources or contact with other minds absorbed by related problems. Kettering's most significant accomplishment was the support and authority that he gave to a new concept of science which, by the middle of the twentieth century, had exercised a profound, far-reaching effect on American society.

When he founded his embryonic research organization in Dayton, in 1909, Kettering realized that the main source of future industrial progress was the scientist's laboratory. "Unless we progress from year to year we lose ground," he said long afterwards. He never doubted, as a scientist, that "today's dream is tomorrow's actuality"—that discoveries in the realm of pure science, supposedly promising no practical benefit, can be made socially useful by means of technology and their results widely diffused by industry in the form of new or improved products. "Changes are born in men's minds," he said, "and worked out in laboratories." But as early as 1909 he understood that a new, large-scale industry based on science could not rely upon haphazard discoveries to secure the continuous improvements which it would find economically essential. Forty years later, the vast research laboratories of the General Motors Corporation in Detroit stood as the concrete expression of Kettering's major achievement. They realized his concept of science as a socialized enterprise, and exemplified his principle of organizing research as a group activity. By many Americans, Kettering might be honored less for his inventions than for having developed industrial research as a technique that insured both the continuous making of scientific discoveries, and their application to socially fruitful ends.

8   Return from Elba

It was William C. Durant who laid the groundwork for Kettering's achievement by commissioning him to organize and direct research for General Motors during the First World War, when technical

and scientific problems suddenly became of paramount importance to industry. For Durant, excluded from the management of
General Motors when the bankers took control of it, dramatically
regained possession of his giant five years later. The operation by
which he recaptured it was characteristically audacious and spectacular, and was to leave permanent effects on the structure of
the nation's economy. But it likewise had a comic aspect which
reflected his jaunty contempt for conventional mentality and
traditional methods. Durant determined to kidnap his giant from
its watchful banker guardians. It was genuinely like him to carry
out this exploit by forcing a pigmy to swallow the giant.

Though the bankers had ousted him from participation in the
affairs of General Motors, Durant retained his holdings of the
corporation's stock and a seat in its directorate. But, after abdicat-
ing, he had promptly turned to another automotive venture and,
within four years, drove it to triumphant success. The venture was
a new, light, low-priced car designed by the Frenchman Louis
Chevrolet, a daring racing driver whom Durant, some years
earlier, had employed to handle the Buick car in track contests.
The car met with immediate favor; Durant set up a system of
quantity production and nation-wide assembly; and when the
nation entered a business boom with the outbreak of war in
Europe, the new company enjoyed a meteoric ascent. At this
point, through the mediation of John J. Raskob, a wealthy industrialist who later rose to power in the councils of the Democratic party, Durant succeeded in forming a working alliance with
one of the nation's most powerful industrial and financial dynasties, the du Ponts of Delaware.

Of aristocratic French descent, this family had for many
generations been the largest producers of powder and other explosives in the United States, and in every armed conflict from the
War of 1812 their plants had been the chief suppliers of these
commodities to the nation's military forces. Each succeeding war
had forced the expansion of their plants, but the outbreak of the
First World War had caused an unprecedented increase in their
facilities and operations. The peacetime use of explosives in
mining, engineering, agriculture and other occupations had not

been sufficient, even before war broke out, to absorb the productive capacity of their plants, and they had already extended their operations to the field of general industrial chemistry. Now, anticipating the eventual termination of war in Europe, they were considering future markets for chemical products. Commanding immense financial resources, they were prepared to invest heavily in an industry likely to expand both as to its production and its use of their products. Their principle, in this matter, was the reverse of Durant's. He had been bent upon controlling all the sources of his essential supplies. The du Ponts cherished ambitions to control an assured, rapidly growing market for their products.

By 1915, more than two and one-quarter million automobiles were registered in the United States, and the annual production of cars was approaching one million. Clearly, the automobile was becoming an integral part of the American way of life. Demand for cars and trucks was continuously increasing, thus confounding those economic experts who asserted that the market must reach a "saturation point." The industry was permanently established; its new productive techniques were in use; its future prosperity appeared to be assured. And the automobile—itself a chemical device from the primary processing of its raw materials to the final explosion of its gasoline as it reached the junk-yard—promised to be a formidable consumer of paint, varnish, artificial leather, plastics and fabrics, and such other chemical products as the du Ponts were already manufacturing, or might conceivably introduce in the immediate future. In these circumstances, they were receptive to Durant's project for regaining control of General Motors. As finally worked out, the strategy of recapture was extraordinarily brilliant. Backed by the du Ponts, and relying on his personal influence with many General Motors stockholders, Durant incorporated the Chevrolet Motor Company of Delaware. Like the original General Motors, this was a holding company with very broad powers, among them the right to acquire the securities of other automotive companies, and a representative of the du Ponts was among its directors. It was the intention of Durant and his backers to have this company acquire, through negotiation and purchase in the open market, enough General Motors stock to insure a controlling interest.

The prize was a rich one, industrially as well as financially. Under banker management, General Motors had very nearly paid off its onerous mortgage debt. Its earnings were doubling every year. Plant capacity had been enlarged and manufacturing methods had been improved. For its industrial advance, the adoption of the self-starter and the introduction of the closed car were largely responsible, but the opportunities which these created were exploited by two remarkable, self-made, masterful men, both of whom were to play major roles in automotive development. These were Charles W. Nash and Walter Percy Chrysler.

Nash was born on an Illinois farm and when, at the age of six, his parents separated, he was bound out to a Michigan farmer for whom he was to work for board and lodging until he reached his majority. After six years he ran away; after six more years, having made money by buying a flock of sheep, he was profitably operating a portable steam hay-presser. Soon after marrying the daughter of a farmer for whom he worked, he became a grocery clerk in the city of Flint, and left this position for one in Durant's road-cart company, stuffing cushions at one dollar a day. It was later said that Durant, noticing the thoroughness and speed of his work, advanced Nash rapidly; within a very short time he became plant superintendent of the Durant-Dort carriage works. Here, he was responsible for a straight-line system of assembly that immensely increased production. When Durant took over the Buick car in 1904, Nash remained at the carriage works, rising to the position of vice-president and general manager. When the bankers eliminated Durant from General Motors, he persuaded them to engage Nash to take charge of the production of Buick cars.

Nash was then forty-six years old, without experience in the automotive field, but an expert in factory organization. Such was his driving force in lifting production that, two years later, he was made president of General Motors. In his old age, as a multi-millionaire living in California, he could look back on a career almost as spectacular as Durant's but more fortunate, and part of his success he attributed to being "the most common cuss that ever lived." "I belong," he once said, "to the common people,

and I'm proud I do. I'm proud that some of my workmen call
me by my first name." The common touch on which Nash prided
himself was also characteristic of Walter Chrysler, whom Nash
brought into the Buick organization soon after taking it over.

Chrysler, when he entered the Buick plant, was thirty-five years
old and almost as lacking in automotive experience as Nash. The
son of a locomotive engineer on the Union Pacific Railroad, his
first job had been as an apprentice, working for five cents an
hour, in the road's shops at Ellis, Kansas. Later, he took a correspondence course in engineering; this furnished his sole equipment
in scientific theory, but the practical side of the profession he
mastered on the job. He was superintendent of motive power on
the Chicago and Great Western when, in 1905, he attended the
Chicago automobile show and there conceived an irresistible desire
for a white, red-upholstered Locomobile priced at five thousand
dollars. He knew little or nothing about automobiles, but he had
developed an obsessive interest in any form of self-powered vehicle.
He had seven hundred dollars in the bank and, borrowing the
rest, bought the costly white-and-red monster. He didn't want
to drive it, and probably never did. He wanted to take it apart
and put it together again. Having done so, he was convinced
that he could build a better car for less money. Offered a job
building locomotives for the American Locomotive Company
in Pittsburgh, he accepted it, and two years later was general
manager of the works, at a salary of twelve thousand dollars a
year. Nash offered him precisely half this salary to join Buick,
and with scarcely a second thought he did so. Like Nash, Chrysler
proved to be a genius in plant economy and production, and
when Nash was promoted to the General Motors presidency,
Chrysler succeeded him at Buick.

The industrial achievements of Nash and Chrysler were
accurately gauged on the New York Stock Exchange, where the
price of General Motors shares had steadily risen even before
Durant, in 1915, began buying for control, driving the quotations
up from eighty-two dollars a share to a high, for the year, of five
hundred and fifty-eight. Wall Street knew that this runaway
market was largely due to his operations. But that Durant had

the du Ponts behind him was not known, and the Street was skeptical about the extent of his personal resources. The bankers who controlled General Motors were perhaps even more skeptical, for they ignored the accumulating evidence of danger. When the directors of the company assembled for their annual meeting, Durant, still one of them, strode in with a smile. He was accompanied by men carrying baskets filled with securities and proxies. In a dead silence, he emptied these on the great board-table. "Gentlemen," he announced quietly, "I control this company."

In effect, the Chevrolet Motor Company had captured General Motors. The pigmy had swallowed the giant, and legal experts were to have a field day in extracting it, so that the process of consumption might decorously be reversed. But in point of literal fact, Durant and his backers had carried out an exploit which, many years later, the sober New York *Times* was to describe as "one of the historic bluffs of financial history." For the mass of papers which Durant jauntily dumped on the board-table represented only forty percent of the corporation's stock. Had the bankers mobilized for resistance, the amazing hoax might have failed. In perpetrating it, Durant took advantage of a condition that was soon to be recognized as one of the characteristic features of finance capitalism. That managerial control of a vast enterprise can be—and usually is—held by owners of a minority interest, was taken for granted by Americans in the middle years of the twentieth century. It was an inevitable result of the wide distribution of securities, to a great extent in small holdings, among investors unknown to one another, without facilities for collective consultation or participation in policy, and for the most part not sufficiently vigilant to attend company meetings. In carrying out his daring coup, Durant was, as usual, ahead of the times. He captured General Motors with forty percent of the stock. In the future, the du Ponts were to retain it with little more than half that amount.

With Durant once again determining policy, General Motors resumed its career of rapid expansion. Nash, who had brought order out of the chaos born of Durant's irrepressible optimism, soon resigned his post, and Chrysler presently followed him. Both

went on to further triumphs as independent producers. In the
rosy aura of a post-war boom, it appeared that every American
wished to own a car; since not all could afford to purchase one, the
corporation organized a subsidiary to finance installment-plan
buying—and sales shot upward. In 1919, the colossus showed earnings of sixty million dollars. It had become a billion-dollar concern. It had absorbed, or bought into, a formidable list of
companies producing a great variety of commodities. It gave
employment to some eighty-six thousand Americans. Under Durant's administration, an exhaustive social study was made of the
corporation's labor relations, plant conditions and the welfare of
its employees. Among the practical results of this study were the
founding of the General Motors Institute of Technology in Flint;
the undertaking of large-scale housing programs for employees in
six cities; the initiation of bonus and investment plans. The
giant was becoming aware of its social responsibility, and beginning to realize that measures of fulfillment would contribute to its
prosperity. In the opinion of Alfred P. Sloan, Jr., a future president of the corporation, it was "sailing along at full speed, the sun
was shining, and there was no cloud in the sky that would indicate
an approaching storm."

But in the spring of 1920, falling grain prices presaged a post-
war deflation. By midsummer, train-loads of automobiles were
standing unclaimed in freight terminals. By autumn, a severe
depression had set in. Almost overnight, the colossus was, once
again, in serious financial difficulties. Meanwhile, Durant—hopefully striving to support the price of General Motors shares as
earnings swiftly declined—had been buying stock in increasing
amounts while its value dwindled, day by day, until quotations
registered a loss of fifty percent. When the day of reckoning came,
his personal commitments in the stock market totalled some
thirty-five millions of dollars.

The prospect that Durant would be sold out by his brokers
became more imminent as the market continued to fall. It was
obvious that a forced sale of his pledged securities would damage
the credit of the corporation, perhaps irreparably, and might even
bring about a financial panic. To avert such a sale, the du Ponts,

with the banking house of J. P. Morgan and Company, financed a settlement with Durant's brokers, thus taking his shares out of the market. Although his losses were reckoned at some ninety millions of dollars, a portion of Durant's fortune was saved. At the same time, the corporation obtained a loan of eighty millions from the house of Morgan, which thus joined the du Ponts in presiding over its future. When these arrangements had been concluded, Durant resigned for a second and last time. It is said that, calm, smiling and cheerful as usual, he left his office with the casual remark, "Well, it's moving day."

Single-handed, Durant had brought into existence what was to become the most powerful of all industrial enterprises. But the colossus that he created outran his capacities, and ironically made him an anachronism. Perhaps the greatest of all American promoters, he failed to recognize that the day of the promoter had passed, that the methods of the promoter had become obsolete, and that he, as much as any man, had brought this about. Even more clearly than his contemporary, Henry Ford, he had foreseen the transforming effect on society of the automobile, and its industrial future. But he had not foreseen the economic implications of the future, or realized that the corporate collectivism which was his objective would inevitably bring with it domination by such groups as the du Ponts and Morgans, who alone and in concert commanded the enormous resources of credit it required.

Banished a second time from the scene of his triumphs, Durant, at the age of sixty, plunged into new automotive ventures. Sixteen years later, he filed a voluntary petition in bankruptcy, listing liabilities at close to one million dollars, and assets amounting to two hundred and fifty—the value of his personal wardrobe. In his eighty-fifth year, the city of Detroit celebrated the fiftieth anniversary of the founding of the automotive industry, and Durant returned to appear publicly with the other surviving pioneers before a generation which scarcely knew their names. But in the near-by automotive city of Flint—he had once rescued it from economic disaster—there stood the Hotel Durant, and elderly citizens remembered the occasion of its building. For with the dropping of the old pilot, the automotive cities of Michigan

had experienced a sharp panic. Might not the absentee ownership
of Eastern capitalists and bankers bring them to ruin by moving
the great plants from Michigan to the East? It was to allay this
fear that, shortly after passing their decree of exile, the new rulers
had subscribed three hundred thousand dollars to build a modern
hotel named for a pioneer who had outlived his economic
usefulness.

CHAPTER V

The New Messiah

1 Efficiency Expert

In 1908, when Durant first tried to buy the Ford Motor Company, Henry Ford was vexed by other worries than the Selden lawsuit. The Model-T, newly added to his line, had been an instantaneous success. Ford cars were becoming increasingly popular, as was obvious from the sharply rising demand. Under James Couzens' vigorous leadership, sales were mounting each month. Yet this was a source of anxiety, not satisfaction. For Ford, who was in charge of the shop, couldn't build enough cars to keep pace with Couzens' orders. In their new three-story factory on Piquette Street, men worked for a sixty-hour week in two shifts. But even this schedule did not suffice, though visitors were impressed by the large number of chassis always on the lower floor, standing up-ended and resting against the walls. Expanding business had not brought any significant improvement in production methods. Cars were still assembled in very much the same way that they had been in the old plant back of Albert Strelow's shop. The major structural units of a car, built in separate departments, were brought to a specified location. There, one or two highly skilled mechanics put them together, thus producing a complete auto-mobile.

Though this was the only technique known, it was clearly inadequate. Nothing less than a drastic change in the system of production would enable Ford to cope with a prospective mass market. Recognizing their own inability to solve the problem, Ford and Couzens decided to turn it over to a specialist in manu-facturing procedures. The expert they called in was Walter E. Flanders of Ohio, a massive, powerful, curly-headed giant who could roar as loudly as Couzens, and was equally independent, hard-driving and autocratic. Flanders had been an eager student of the doctrines of Frederick Winslow Taylor, already famous as the apostle of scientific management and the prophet of an industrial efficiency greater than any yet realized—to be achieved through planning, a functional organization of processes, and a standardizing of tasks. Within a few months, Taylor himself was to lecture in Detroit, to a group of automotive technicians, and somewhat later one of his associates was to be employed by General Motors. Meanwhile, Flanders saw, in the Ford factory, a challenging opportunity to test out some of Taylor's principles. He agreed to expedite Ford's production, but laid down two conditions: he was to name his own salary; and he was to have an absolutely free hand in reorganizing and equipping the plant. Somewhat remarkably, Ford and Couzens not only consented but offered him an additional incentive. If Flanders succeeded in producing ten thousand cars in twelve months, an output never before reached by any plant, he would be paid a bonus of twenty thousand dollars. Introduced as the new production manager, Flanders promptly took off his coat and went to work.

Within a few weeks, he had transformed the plant, installing new machinery, relocating old equipment, reorganizing the operations of the thousand workers then employed. He was trying to apply the theory of "line production" which Taylor, some years before, had developed for the steel industry. This theory proposed that the product should pass, continuously and with as few interruptions as possible, from its initial form to its final one. This "flow" demanded the laying out of machinery according to a plan radically different from the one then in general use. Instead of grouping all machines of a single kind together, as was the common practice, they must be arranged in an orderly sequence corresponding to the successive processes through which the product would pass. To produce the maximum efficiency, the theory also required the greatest possible elimination of waste motion; both in the actual work performed by each man, and in the movement of workers from job to job.

In applying the theory, Flanders introduced notable changes; for example, in the process of final assembly. He assigned this to groups of mechanics who worked on a car simultaneously, each one being responsible for a specified series of operations. He provided helpers for these men, and runners to bring them small tools and parts as these were needed. Undistracted and well served, the assemblers were able to complete their job with greatly increased speed. After three nerve-racking months, Flanders had his new system of production working smoothly, and he succeeded in meeting the year's quota of ten thousand cars with two days to spare. But this unprecedented achievement did not prevent a disagreement with Henry Ford, and Flanders left the organization to become a partner in another automotive enterprise.

Nevertheless, Flanders had proved the efficacy of Taylor's principle of line production. He had also established the fact that mass output of automobiles would require standardization of tasks no less than standardization of parts and materials. By mechanizing the plant more thoroughly, and by subdividing many operations, he had gained speed, as well as volume, of production. The effect of his innovations was obvious in the next year's output, which very nearly doubled the record figure established by Flanders

himself. Meanwhile, aware that his new system had already out-
dated their three-year-old factory, Ford and Couzens determined
to build another one. Sixty acres of cheap land were bought in
suburban Highland Park, north of the Detroit city line. On this
tract was erected what Ford proudly described as a bigger factory
than the world had ever seen, and in 1910 operations were transferred there. Within four years, it was to become world-famous
as the birthplace of two changes—technological and economic—
having immense social consequences. As an industrial unit, the
Ford plant at Highland Park was the wonder of its day. But, after
only one decade, it was to be made obsolete by the powerful forces
which it released, and later it was to be superseded by a mammoth
twelve-hundred-acre plant on the River Rouge, in Dearborn.

During the first years at Highland Park, Ford's production
experts devoted themselves chiefly to perfecting and extending the
innovations in practice made by Flanders. The company was now
manufacturing nearly all its parts, and the principle of line production was applied to each. Careful job analysis revealed that
further subdivision was possible in both the mechanical and
manual operations necessary for the making of each part, and the
work was split, again and again, into smaller and simpler tasks.
This gave greater continuity to the line, but impeded the flow of
its product, since the part had to be carried or passed from one
operation to the next. To eliminate this waste motion, gravity
chutes were installed; the moment a worker finished his particular
job on any part, he dropped it into the inclined trough at his
elbow, and it slid to the next processing place. This simple expedient speeded up the production of small, light parts, but
threatened to swamp the assemblers, who could not keep pace
with it. A new method of assembly was therefore tried out. The
skeleton chassis of cars were mounted on pairs of wooden horses,
and set up in two parallel lines of sixty each. The groups of
assemblers were enlarged, and each man was charged with a more
limited set of operations. As the groups moved down the two
lines, each assembler merely repeated his set of operations on every
successive chassis. Under this system—the best that Ford technicians had been able to devise—final assembly of a Model-T

could not be accomplished in less than twelve hours and twenty-eight minutes. This was the situation in 1913, and Henry Ford had already conceived his "life desire." It was to produce cars at the rate of one a minute.

2   The Conveyors Move

Meantime, conditions on the final assembly lines were rapidly becoming chaotic, largely because of certain radical improvements that were being effected in the sub-assembly of parts. Two imaginative technicians, C. W. Avery and William Klann, had been inspired, by the effectiveness of the gravity chutes, to a brilliant extension of the principle which they exemplified. Was there not some more efficient method of keeping the work in motion, or "taking the work to the men instead of the men to the work?" Why not, indeed, mechanize the process of work-delivery? Casting about for a means of effecting this mechanization, Avery and Klann came upon a suggestive precedent. For many years, the Chicago meat-packers had been using a moving overhead trolley to facilitate the dressing of beef. Carcasses, suspended from this trolley, moved past the dressers, each of whom removed a specified cut until, at the end of the line, the job was finished. The beef-dressers were engaged, so to speak, in dis-assembly; but could not a similar device be applied to the assembly of automotive parts? Avery and Klann decided to experiment with a moving chain, and a moving belt.

In the spring of 1913, they applied the new technique to the assembly of fly-wheel magnetos. Previously, each workman had produced a complete assembly, requiring about twenty minutes for the task, and turning out from thirty-five to forty pieces in a nine-hour day. Avery and Klann broke down the assembly into twenty-nine separate operations, assigned one man to each, and started the mechanical conveyor moving at a speed of sixty inches a minute. This speed was too fast for the workers. It was reduced to eighteen inches per minute—and this proved to be too slow. A time-study established the proper speed at forty-four inches per minute; this gave each worker "every second necessary but not a single unnecessary second." The assembly-time for magnetos was cut to thirteen minutes, ten seconds; and when, after further study, the height of the line was raised by eight inches, the assembly-time was further reduced to seven minutes, and subsequently to five. As Henry Ford later boasted, this experiment made it possible for one man to do in a day somewhat more work than four men had accomplished before. Gratified by the results, Avery and Klann went on to mechanize the assembly of axles and motors. Motors, like magnetos, had been individually assembled by single workers. Avery and Klann broke down the process. Ultimately, it was subdivided into eighty-four separate operations with a worker assigned to each, and this force was capable of maintaining a production-level that had formerly required three times their number. More importantly, within six months, the time needed to assemble a motor was reduced from nine hours and fifty-four minutes to five hours and fifty-six.

But these prodigious achievements in sub-assembly had the disastrous effect of producing a bottle-neck on the final assembly lines, where parts were being delivered in greater profusion and at greater speed than the lines were capable of matching. Could the new "moving assembly" technique, which had worked such miracles on feeder-lines, be applied to the final task of putting a car together? Late in the summer of 1913, after long and careful preparation, Avery and Klann undertook to demonstrate that a car could be assembled while in continuous motion.

This demonstration took the form of a crude experiment performed before Henry Ford, James Couzens and other leading executives of the company. Two hundred and fifty feet of floor space were cleared. At one end stood a bare chassis, roped to a windlass at the other end. Stockpiles of parts and necessary tools had been deposited at calculated points along the route. Six assemblers, specially trained for the experiment, awaited the signal to begin work. When the signal was given, the windlass commenced to revolve, slowly dragging the chassis toward it. Immediately, the assemblers went into action. Sometimes walking beside the moving chassis, sometimes actually riding it, they picked up their tools and parts as they traveled, and kept steadily at work. From the moment when the windlass began turning, the bare chassis was, quite literally, in production. Five hours and fifty minutes later, it reached the end of its course, and came to rest. During the interval, it had been transformed into a completed car. Moving at the scarcely perceptible speed of eight and one half inches every minute, it had nevertheless reduced by more than fifty percent the time required for final assembly of an automobile. So elated was Henry Ford by this performance, that he ordered the immediate setting up of two permanent lines to institute moving final assembly.

In the triumphant success of their demonstration, Avery and Klann had unwittingly fixed the pattern of all subsequent developments in automotive technology. They had, indeed, done far more than this. For their crude experiment on that late summer day of 1913 could be reckoned as the annunciation of mechanized mass industry—the material agency which, more profoundly than any other, was to change the American social order as the twentieth century advanced. Not many years were to pass before Henry Ford would proclaim machinery to be the new Messiah, "accomplishing in the world what man has failed to do by preaching, propaganda, or the written word." For a large proportion of American workers, the advent of the new deity produced two momentous results. From their working day, it all but eliminated the necessity for thought; and it reduced their movement to a minimum. Wherever the Messiah was properly served, in the vast humming temples erected by industry, the American workman could expect to spend most of his productive years doing "as nearly as possible only one thing with only one movement."

The coming of the Messiah was not long delayed. It was probably hastened by a relentless drive for speed which crippled one of the new mobile lines for final assembly, and resulted in a destructive accident. But, in any case, it was inevitable. For, obviously, automatic mobility could be further perfected, and extended to final assembly. The Ford technicians soon solved this problem with a masterly invention: an overhead conveyor, continuous and completely mechanized; the very first of its kind. It consisted of a so-called "endless belt," sufficiently strong to lift the whole final assembly line off the factory floor, and elevate it to the height of a man's waist. Two of these devices were installed, to fit squads of different average heights. They brought a ceaseless succession of chassis, for "man-high" assembly, at levels of twenty-six and three quarter inches, and twenty-four and one half inches, above the floor. On January 14, 1914, they were set in motion for the first time, and the new Messiah arrived. Three months later, their revolutionary effect on production was fully evident. Less than one year earlier, no Ford car could be put together in less than twelve hours and twenty-eight minutes. Now, final assembly took only ninety-three minutes.

All during the next decade, the implacable march of mechanization at Highland Park astonished the world. Soon, the great conveyors of the final assembly lines were surrounded, on every side, by tributary systems. There were some five thousand parts in a Model-T. With the incessant splitting and simplifying of tasks, the number of departments making or assembling parts grew from one hundred and fifty to five hundred. Each was a little factory in itself. So there were mobile sub-assembly lines, carrying every part through its necessary processes, from raw material to finished product. And there were mobile feeder lines, delivering the finished parts to the final assemblers. Perfect timing, and faultless integration of each of these tributary systems into the total operation, were obviously essential. But however closely approximated, a perilous weakness always remained. For final assembly, upon which all other operations converged, depended upon their continuous functioning. A breakdown, or a suspension, on any auxiliary line, could quickly bring the whole vast organism to a standstill. It still functioned at the mercy of the human element. The worker was its most vulnerable factor.

The worker could not be eliminated. But to what degree could his imperfection be offset? How far could his technologically wasteful humanity be nullified? Three members of the Ford hierarchy were to be concerned with this problem. Charles E. Sorensen, a Danish immigrant, began his career as a skilled mechanic. He rose to power as the major expediter of Ford's production lines; became notorious for a generation as the factory boss most universally detested by American labor; and, after forty years of devoted service, was ignominiously dismissed by Henry Ford himself. William S. Knudsen, likewise a Dane by birth and a master mechanic, became a brilliant organizer of mass production. He built and directed Ford's earliest outlying assembly plants in the United States and abroad, set up to put cars together from parts made in Michigan. Resigning from the Ford organization after a clash with Sorensen, Knudsen later became president of General Motors, and, in 1940, under the national defense program, was named director of industrial production by President Franklin D. Roosevelt. Though he never achieved the notoriety of Sorensen or the fame of Knudsen, it was Carl Emde, the third member of this notable trinity, who contributed most to a solution of the problem that engaged them. Emde, a German by birth, proved to be a genius in technological innovation. His creative fertility was so great that, for a time, two hundred designers were kept busy working out his ideas. Long after both men passed from the Ford scene, Knudsen asserted that Emde, more than any other individual, had revolutionized the automobile industry.

Emde dealt with human fallibility as a purely technological problem; its solution depended on perfecting machinery, not on improving workmanship. He realized that mobile assembly lines and their tributary systems could never function automatically, with absolute precision, while any process along their route involved the element of hand labor, subject to the skill and speed of individual workers. So long as any manual work was performed on an embryonic automobile—whether in the casting, shaping, drilling of metal, or in any other operation—the whole productive process would be imperiled. The problem, therefore, was to replace hand labor completely by automatic machine tools. Since the subdivision of work had already been carried to a degree of minuteness never before attempted, this meant the use of innumerable highly specialized machines. Nothing remotely like them existed. They would have to be created, quite literally, out of the void.

One of Emde's early productions, for example, was a multiple drill which, plunging simultaneously in four directions, bored forty-five holes at one time in a cylinder block. Working at furious speed for a decade, Emde created a long series of automatic, single-purpose machines, and adapted others, already invented, to new uses. Once, when furnishing a manufacturer of machine tools with the design for one which he had invented, Emde specified that it have an output of two hundred units per hour. The manufacturer protested that no machine could attain this output, and Emde calmly showed him one already in use; it had been built expressly to test his specification. As a result of Emde's inventive wizardry, Henry Ford was able to startle the world, in 1922, by announcing that, at Highland Park, there remained not even a single vestigial hand operation. The victory of technology was all but complete. So far as it could do so, it had succeeded in eliminating the necessity for skill in any job performed by anyone. In the fourteen years that had passed since Flanders' first experiments, it had transferred the versatile mechanic into a mere servant of the machine. It had made craftsmanship an anachronism, and thought a superfluity.

3 Five-Dollar Day

But before achieving this victory, the new Messiah had effected another change. It was equally startling and destined to be equally seminal; and in one week it carried the name of Henry Ford around the world. This change issued directly from the relentless advance of mechanization at Highland Park. Ford and his associates identified mechanization and progress. The workers saw it only as regression, inevitably and swiftly carrying them toward the status of sub-human automata. For production jobs were degenerating into the doing of one thing, over and over again, always in the same way, at a speed automatically fixed by the conveyor-belt.

Moreover, the "speed-up," a natural concomitant of mechanization, was already in evidence. Horace Lucien Arnold and Fay Leone Faurote, the earliest authoritative analysts of "Ford methods," reported that by 1914 the speed-up was being enforced from top to bottom of the plant. To his highest executives, they alleged, Henry Ford made clear that, unless they stepped up production every day, they could not expect to retain their jobs. At the bottom, Arnold and Faurote described as typical the case of an operative compelled to lift his daily output to seven thousand units, after a time-study revealed that he had been making seventy thousand waste motions every day. Every Ford worker, they asserted, was "perfectly aware that he is under constant observation, and that he will be admonished if he falls below the fast pace of the department." Moreover, he was expected to keep repeating his particular set of motions at this fast pace for four hours at a stretch, without variation or relief. Everywhere, in the vast plant at Highland Park, machines crowded one another so closely that, as Arnold and Faurote noted, "There seems to be no room for the operators." The crowding, Henry Ford afterwards explained, was intentional: every foot of floor-space carried the same overhead charge; and if a man and his machine occupied more space than absolutely essential, money was being wasted. Efficiency brought Ford machines, he asserted proudly, "closer together than in probably any other factory in the world." Every man and every machine was given every square inch that he required, but not a square inch and certainly not a square foot more. And there wasn't much personal contact between the operatives, Ford reflected complacently. "The men do their work and go home—a factory is not a drawing room."

To Ford's workers, the conditions implied by this statement were a source of growing dissatisfaction. They were being paid the standard wage rate: two dollars and thirty-four cents for a nine-hour day. Yet they were leaving their jobs in staggering numbers. By 1913 when the plant required a complement of fourteen thousand workers, it had become necessary to hire fifty-three thousand men annually to maintain a constant force at this figure. From forty to sixty percent of the force were quitting every month, and the new technology of mass production seemed destined to founder on mass desertions. Meanwhile, the militant International Workers of the World, fresh from their sanguinary but victorious strike in the textile mills of Lawrence, Massachusetts, during the previous year, had invaded Michigan. They poured into the Upper Peninsula, and struck the great copper mines. Then they came down to Detroit, and paralyzed the Studebaker automobile factory for a week. They were attempting to organize the entire industry; they were preaching the eight-hour day; and at the very gates of Highland Park they denounced Henry Ford as "the speed-up king" whose factory was a "sweat-shop." Unrest within the plant soon rose to the boiling point.

In this emergency, James Couzens invented the policy that was suddenly to make Henry Ford world-famous; that was to be acclaimed as the miracle of an inspired social savior, and to be condemned as the mischief of an irresponsible social quack. Long afterwards, Couzens acknowledged that he had never given a thought to the welfare of labor until, one wintry day, he looked out of his office window to see a group of workers, demonstrating against a layoff, being put to rout by the icy torrent streaming from a fire-hose. To his indignation at this sight, Couzens attributed his subsequent plan for a "Five-Dollar Day" and his vigorous insistence on its adoption as company policy.

On January 5, 1914—exactly nine days before the great conveyors of the Ford final assembly lines began to move—Couzens and Ford announced the new policy in a meeting with representatives of the press. Couzens read from a prepared statement, while Ford, tilted back in his chair with his head resting against the wall, waited impatiently. A week thereafter, Couzens read, the company would "initiate the greatest revolution in the matter of rewards for its workers ever known to the industrial world." Believing that "social justice begins at home," the company wanted to share profits and future prospects with those who made them possible, for "The movement toward a better society does not need to be started universally and simultaneously." To give concrete effect to its humanitarian motives, it was instituting a basic "Five-Dollar Day," thus doubling the prevailing wage-scale for common labor. Furthermore, it was reducing the working day from nine hours to eight. The whole plan was based upon the principle of sharing anticipated profits; those for 1914 were estimated as being sufficient to justify a distribution among the workers of some ten million dollars. From the benefits of the plan, no "qualified employee" was to be excluded, not even "the lowliest laborer and the man who merely sweeps the floors."

To qualify for participation, employees had to be in the service of the company for six months or more. They fell into one of three classes: married men, living with and taking good care of their families; single men older than twenty-two years, of proven thrifty habits; youths less than twenty-two, and women who were the sole support of some next-of-kin, whose way of life was above reproach.

When Couzens finished reading his statement, Ford rose to add his personal endorsement of the policy. He preferred having twenty thousand prosperous, contented workers in his plant, he said, to enriching a few "slave-drivers" and making multi-millionaires. The various reforms embodied in the plan might, he surmised, serve as a foundation for a "new industrial order."

In the American press, reaction to the sensational announcement was immediate, but by no means laudatory. The New York *Times*, in an editorial, declared that, "The theory of the management of the Ford company is distinctly Utopian and runs dead against all experience." It pointed out that the country's other manufacturing industries could not follow the Ford example, so serious disturbances in the labor market were bound to follow; there would be dissatisfaction, unrest and probably a wave of strikes. "We think the weight of opinion will decidedly incline to the side of doubt," remarked the *Times*, "or to prophecies of certain failure for the experiment so manifestly based upon a vision of universal human uplift through a single venture in the field of beneficence." The *Wall Street Journal*, organ of the financial community, denounced the new wage-scale as an "economic crime." Had Ford set aside reserves to insure the continuance of the current wage scale, "It would have been scientific and according to the highest ethics and true laws of giving." But to double the minimum wage was "to apply Biblical or spiritual principles where they do not belong." Gloomily, it predicted that Ford's blunders would "return to plague him and the industry he represents, as well as organized society."

To the American public—and soon to the whole world—Highland Park ceased to be merely a unit of big industry. It took on the dual status of a laboratory and a model, formulating the theory of an industrial philosophy rich in the promise of social progress, and demonstrating that its application was practical as well as profitable. Like Miss Jane Addams' Hull House, in Chicago, Highland Park became even more significant for what it represented than for what it produced; and, like Hull House, it attracted visitors from distant lands, eager to study so radical, yet so incontestably successful, an experiment in the extension of human welfare. For, astounding as were the productive achievements of Highland Park (and the world had never before seen their like), were they not to be attributed to an ideal, and an ethical attitude, far more astounding? Certainly, to the plain people everywhere, it seemed obvious that Henry Ford was proving the efficacy of the Golden Rule; proving that, by becoming socially responsible, great industry would materially increase and multiply; proving, too, that twentieth-century capitalism could be made to yield a better life for all.

It was the Europeans who named the new industrial philosophy: "Fordism." Did it not signify more than the mechanized conveyors and automatic machines that many Europeans took to be its primary element? Most Americans were certain that it did, though they failed to agree on the nature of its major implications. Liberals, sociologists and reformers had few doubts. Jubilant at Ford's enlightened action in sharing profits by doubling wages, they were the more impressed because his social conscience did not find this sufficient. He seemed, indeed, to be as inspired a reformer as Miss Addams herself, as deeply imbued with the principles expressed by Hull House and other social settlements. For he set up a "Sociological Department," the private equivalent of a public welfare agency, to minister to the needs of his workers, many of whom were foreign-born and recent immigrants. It was the function of this agency not only to rehabilitate the misguided employee who was "wasting his substance," or "living unworthily as a profit-sharer" (his life and habits often required "complete revamping")—but likewise to aid, educate and "Americanize" the morally worthy, especially in using their augmented incomes for approved purposes; mainly those which, by making them more efficient workers, would also make them better citizens.

Organized by John R. Lee, a talented pioneer in industrial

ABOVE:
The Well-Dressed Lady Motorist

TOP, RIGHT:
Mrs. Leslie Carter Rides in Style

RIGHT: They Took No Chances
        with Wind and Dust

ABOVE:
The Skeptical Horse

RIGHT: Country
Roads Were a Danger

LEFT: This Became
the Lincoln Highway

BELOW: Help Needed

BOTTOM: A Spin
in the Country

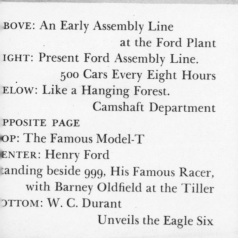

ABOVE: An Early Assembly Line
at the Ford Plant
RIGHT: Present Ford Assembly Line.
500 Cars Every Eight Hours
BELOW: Like a Hanging Forest.
Camshaft Department

OPPOSITE PAGE
TOP: The Famous Model-T
CENTER: Henry Ford
Standing beside 999, His Famous Racer,
with Barney Oldfield at the Tiller
BOTTOM: W. C. Durant
Unveils the Eagle Six

LEFT: Ford Family
in the First Ford Car

BOTTOM:
The Famous River Rouge Plant

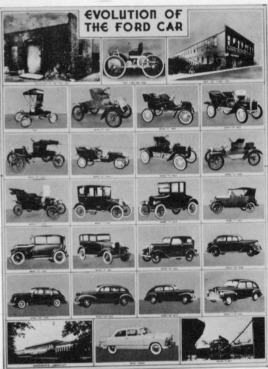

BELOW: The Handbill
           That Started the Riot

RIGHT: Frankensteen Is Slugged

BOTTOM Sit-Down Strikers
    Leave a General Motors Plant

Ford Workers

UNIONISM NOT FORDISM

Now is the time to Organize!
The Wagner Bill is behind you!
Now get behind yourselves!

General Motors Workers, Chrysler Workers, Briggs Workers
have won higher wages and better working conditions. 300,000
automobile workers are marching forward under the banner of
the United Automobile Workers Union.

JOIN NOW IN THE MARCH AND WIN:

**Higher Wages and Better Working Conditions
Stop Speed-up by Union Supervision
6 Hour Day, 8 Dollars Minimum Pay
Job Security thru Seniority Rights
End of Ford Service System
Union Recognition**

Organize and be Recognized - JOIN NOW!

| Union Headquarters for Ford Workers: | Michigan Avenue at Addison |
| | Vernor Highway West, and Lawndale |

*Sign up at Union Headquarters for Ford Workers or at any
office of the United Automobile Workers*

1324 Clay at Russell	8944 Jos. Campau at Playfair
2441 Milwaukee at Chene	11440 Charlevoix at Gladwin
11725 Oakland at Tuxedo	1343 East Ferry at Russell
4014 Leuschner at Dwyer	3811—35th Street at Michigan
11640 East Jefferson	2736 Maybury Grand at Michigan
10901 Mack at Lenay	4715 Hastings Street
77 Victor at John R.	Room 509 Hofmann Bldg.

Distributed by
United Automobile Workers of America

License No. 4   Printed by Goodwill Printing Co.

"The Pretzel." Grand Central Parkway and Queens Boulevard, New York

sociology, the department was soon taken over by Dr. Samuel S. Marquis, a longtime friend of Henry Ford, who had been his parishioner. In order to meet this opportunity for service, Dr. Marquis resigned the deanship of St. Paul's Cathedral in Detroit. "We want to make men in this factory, as well as automobiles," Henry Ford told him. "This company has outlived its usefulness as a money-making concern, unless we can do some good with the money. I do not believe in charity, but I do believe in the regenerating power of work in men's lives when the work they do is given a just return." But Dr. Marquis, who began his mission with practically unlimited means at his disposal, and certainly with boundless hope, resigned after five years, a deeply disillusioned man. And Henry Ford then explained to the world that paternalism had no place in industry, that welfare work was out of date. So the liberals, sociologists and reformers were deceived. Whatever else Fordism might imply, it did not connote the scientific application of social conscience to human welfare.

The discomfiture of financial magnates and industrial tycoons was even greater, and brought about more rapidly. These dispensers of economic omniscience, privately cursing Ford as a traitor to the interests of their class, sentenced him to the public pillory as an economic ignoramus. But a profound fear colored their verdict: twenty-three years later, in reporting on the industrial progress of Wayne County, seat of the city of Detroit, an official of the city's Board of Commerce asserted that the Five-Dollar Day had caused a greater flight of capital and migration of industry than the insurgent rise of industrial unions during the turbulent 1930s. In 1914, the masters of capital and industry freely predicted that Ford's follies would bring him quick ruin, as was only just. They also felt morally obliged to point out that he was undermining the nation's prosperity by his reckless assault on the established order.

Orthodox wisdom was founded on experience running back to the very beginnings of the Industrial Revolution, more than a century earlier: it showed that prosperity depended upon profit, and that profit resulted from keeping wages as low as labor would take, and pushing prices as high as the market would bear. When

Ford, six months after instituting the Five-Dollar Day, announced that, if the company succeeded in selling three hundred thousand cars during the ensuing twelve months, every purchaser would receive a rebate of fifty dollars—it seemed that economic heresy could go no further. Fifteen and one half million dollars were paid out in rebates during the summer of 1915. Meanwhile, although the Five-Dollar Day had cost Ford twelve million dollars in 1914, profits that year rose by five million dollars to thirty millions, and by 1916 had doubled, and stood at sixty millions.

4   A Doctrine Sanctified by Truth

However extreme their discomfiture, insight was not entirely lacking to the masters of finance and industry. Once the incredible figures began to come out, they arrived at a just estimate of the new philosophy. Their astuteness could be measured by the rapidity with which they imposed Fordism—though not under that name—as the official religion of the American economy. Like nearly every other official religion, it was to contain two bodies of doctrine. One, already composed, was suitable for communication to the people; in it, the overlords recognized a gospel admirably effective for the purpose of producing mass conversions; among its many merits was the remarkable one of having an element of demonstrable truth. The second body of doctrine was esoteric. Its fundamental theses, first worked out by Henry Ford himself, were gradually elaborated by the new industrial theocracy. They were intended to be kept secret; knowledge of them was to be restricted to the initiate, the great overlords who, in the exercise of their theocratic functions, further refined and perfected them. For this second body of doctrine provided the techniques which enabled the high-priesthood of industry to effect their awesome miracles, with complete assurance, in full view of a reverent world.

Among twentieth-century Americans, the public creed quickly became a cardinal article of faith. Its superior credibility was established by the immediate conversion of labor and its leaders; for years, workers fought to secure employment in the Ford plant, and their spokesmen extolled Henry Ford as the voluntary promulgator of labor's Magna Charta. Though the faith of labor and its leaders was to diminish, the middle of the twentieth century brought little evidence of any more extensive apostasy. By then the public creed had become so inseparable an element of the national culture that its restatement seemed superfluous. Its principal assumptions were extremely simple. Mechanized industry makes possible mass production, which in theory implies one great social gain: availability to the common man of goods which, under any other system, he could not hope to acquire. But mass production requires mass consumption of its products to operate at a profit. The unit price of its products must therefore be kept as low as possible. A low profit per unit, under large volume of distribution, will return immense aggregate profits.

Costs of production can be greatly reduced by economy and efficiency of operation. They can be further reduced by the payment of high wages, which not only furnish an incentive to increase volume of production, but create the maximum of buying power among the masses. Since, "by the application of engineering skill," high wages are transformed into low wages *per unit of production,* "the power of consumption will be steadily raised until poverty will become practically a voluntary matter having to do with the willingness to work." So ran the public creed, which in time became even more sacrosanct than the Declaration of Independence or the Constitution. But this, surely, was only fitting. For who could doubt the luminous truth first set forth by Henry Ford: "The Declaration of Independence is not a business charter, nor is the Constitution of the United States a business code"? And who could doubt that other truth which was its corollary: "There is something sacred about big business which provides a living for hundreds and thousands of families"? Under the benign rule of an industrial and financial theocracy, the ultimate sanctity of big business became, like faith itself, the substance of things hoped for. It was likewise the evidence of things unseen.

The things not seen—the esoteric doctrines and techniques that enabled Fordism to produce its ritual miracles—soon began taking shape in the practice of the master himself. By what magic, for example, were high wages converted into low? Clearly to the rank and file upon whose efforts the miracles of Fordism were based, the possession of skills was no asset. They learned their jobs within a few hours or a few days. To be employed, they had to satisfy only one criterion: that they should be potentially able to do enough work to pay the overhead charges on the floor space they occupied. For, as Ford himself remarked, he created the tradition "that pressing always to do work better and faster solves nearly every factory problem." It was this, in great measure, that he meant by the "application of engineering skill." These descriptive phrases merely disguised the speed-up and stretch-out, which industrial workers chose to define somewhat less enticingly as "cutting costs by taking it out of the men." In his effort to expand the mass market by reducing the price of his cars, Henry Ford came upon the item of cost, and deduced a novel economic theory. The way to discover what a cost ought to be, he surmised, was to set a price so low as to force all his workers to the highest point of efficiency; a minimum selling price would not only yield increased sales, but compel everyone in the organization to "dig for profits." As his production figures established again and again, this theory was entirely practicable. "If a man is paid six dollars a day in the Ford factory," Dr. Marquis wrote after quitting that temple to the new Messiah, "he is expected to earn it, and conveyors tuned up to a six-dollar speed leave little to the will of the operator."

Such cynicism was exceptional but, occasionally, disquieting questions were raised. In 1924, a challenging discussion of the effect of machinery on workers in the automotive industry was published in the *Annals of the American Academy of Political and Social Sciences*, an erudite journal probably not read by Henry Ford. Its author, Professor Charles Reitell of the School of Business Administration of the University of Pittsburgh, took issue with certain doctrinal affirmations of the new gospel. In particular, he pointed out that automatic machinery was depriving the workers of those satisfactions which confer a sense of human dignity and personal achievement. The success of the machine, this critic argued, must not be measured solely by the goods which it creates. "We must see to it that those who build and operate it," he urged, "share in a greater happiness because of this master giant now in our midst."

But the views of Henry Ford—many of which were adopted by other masters of mass industry—pointed to very different perspectives. A great business, he asserted, is really too big to be human. Sacred in itself, its continuance becomes a holy trust. Necessarily, therefore, its interests are more important than those of the individuals whose labors make it productive. Economically, it exists for the sole purpose of being prosperous. This purpose must take precedence over every other; because, as Ford declared, "We now know that anything which is economically right is also morally right." Large-scale mechanized industry could achieve its paramount purpose, Ford held, only by continuously expanding production. "To produce, produce," he exhorted; "to get a system that will reduce production to a fine art; to put production on such a basis as will provide means for expansion and the building of still more shops, the production of still more thousands of useful things—that is the real industrial idea." What matter that this ideal exacted the creation of an "impersonal system wherein the workman has become something less than a person—a mere part of the system"? The ideal was economically sound. It was therefore morally right.

Sympathy for the workman who became "something less than a person" was misguided, Ford held. It sprang from the absurd belief that all men are equal; to insist that they are is to do the maximum disservice to humanity. For, patently, men are not equal, and any democratic conception which strove to make them so was no more than an effort to block progress. The worker was endowed with a special kind of mentality, characteristic of the great majority of men. This type of mind found no terror in work which consisted only of performing one operation, over and over again, always in the same way. To the contrary; its ideal was a job in which a man did not have to think.

Indeed, Ford asserted, for most purposes and most people it was necessary to establish a routine and make motions purely repetitive—otherwise, the individual would not get enough work

done to be able to live by his own exertions. To such people—
the great majority, the workers—mechanized industry furnished
the best opportunity of gaining a livelihood. But industry retained the moral right to insist that its machines be utilized to
full capacity. In these circumstances, Ford argued, the cultivation
of "good feeling" in industry was nonsense, and morally debilitat-
ing nonsense, at that. Workers were in the factory for the sole
function of accomplishing the greatest possible amount of work,
in order to receive the highest possible pay. It was not necessary
for the employer to love the employee, or for the employee to love
the employer. "Business holds no place for democracy," he declared, "if by democracy is meant the shaping of policies by the
vote of a large number of people or their delegates." And democracy had nothing to do with the question, "Who ought to be
boss?"

Inevitably, this philosophy found acceptance among the masters of mass industry. But its social cost was not computed by the
American people until the fourth decade of the century. Then,
while the effects of the Great Depression still afflicted the nation,
it suffered a period of industrial warfare that was unprecedently
savage, widespread and prolonged. During its course, the practices to which the new industrial philosophy had given birth
received frequent and dramatic illustration. They were also expounded in publications issued by agencies of the Federal government. Americans who wished to reckon the cost, to their society,
of large-scale industry's adherence to the tenets of Fordism, no
longer lacked the materials required for appraisal.

Some were made available in exhaustive documentary records
published by the National Labor Relations Board. Others were
set forth in a sober, searing report issued by a sub-committee of
the United States Senate. This group, presided over by Senator
Robert M. La Follette, Jr., and responsible to the Committee
on Education and Labor headed by Senator Elbert D. Thomas,
investigated industry's violation of the right of free speech and
assembly, and its interference with the right of labor to organize
and bargain collectively. Their report, running to six closely
printed volumes, considered such practices as the maintenance

of private police systems, industrial espionage, and the recourse
of industry to professional, nation-wide strike-breaking services.
It, too, illuminated certain features of the American way of life
in the machine age—features previously ignored by many Americans not destitute of good will.

The practices thus exposed were not unfamiliar to workers in
Ford plants throughout the United States. Some had originated
during the early years at Highland Park. Others were instituted
at the vast new plant on the River Rouge. Both the old and the
new became standard in the outlying establishments of the Ford
empire. By the 1930s their systematic use had been developed to
an efficiency that, while not unique in American industry, was
not elsewhere excelled. Three factors contributed to the rapid
attainment of this efficiency. One was a crisis in the affairs of
the Ford company. A second was the rise to power, in the company, of a man whose mind was singularly attuned to that of
Henry Ford. A third was the swift upsurge of industrial union-
ism, and the spectacular victory achieved by the United Automobile Workers in their first collision with their employers.

5   The Fall of Lizzie and the Rise of Bennett

The crisis that broke upon the Ford company in 1926 had been
foreseen by almost everyone but Henry Ford himself. Fabulous
success had intensified his old obstinacy; had given him, likewise,
a conviction of personal infallibility. For a decade or more the
Model-T, child of his own mind, had accounted for one half the
automobile production of the United States. It had put a nation
on wheels, transformed the habits of a people, produced enormous changes in the American social order. But the mind that
had conceived this revolutionary product did not understand
many of its effects. In 1926, the Model-T was almost precisely
what it had been in 1909; it was uniquely unchanged in an
America that it had itself largely remade. And, abruptly, it was
made obsolete by the revolution which it had precipitated.

The approaching death of Model-T was presaged by ominously
falling sales, a condition from which it had been exempt since
the day of its birth. In the America of the post-war era, laced with

hard-surfaced roads, dotted with garish movie palaces and gaudy speakeasies, devoted to speed and jazz, incubating the greatest bull-market of all time, and yearning for the socially established proofs of personal success—in such an America, the gaunt, naked, slow-paced, unimproved Model-T was an anachronism; an historical relic of the age of impassable roads, isolated farms and garageless villages for which it had been designed. Ownership of a Model-T had become a public confession of personal failure.

For the mores of post-war America proposed a new criterion of social status: the possession of an up-to-the-minute car. The multiplying used-car lots of the nation were an outlet for the discarded models of yesteryear; in them, one could usually buy, for less than the two hundred and ninety dollars which the Model-T cost new, a more presentable vehicle. The American people had shifted the emphasis of their demand; it fell, now, on style rather than price. William S. Knudsen, at General Motors, had been quick to detect this; and in his redesigned Chevrolet he was offering them the kind of car they wanted. By 1926, Knudsen had displaced Ford from his position of preeminence in the industry—a position which Ford was never thereafter to regain. In the following spring, Henry Ford reluctantly acknowledged defeat. When the fifteen-millionth Model-T rolled off his conveyors, the great Ford plants shut down. For very nearly a year, while a new model was being designed and the plants were re-tooled to produce it, some one hundred thousand workers were forced to find other employment or go on relief. Many Ford agents skidded into bankruptcy. Wage-earners employed by firms supplying parts and materials to Ford found their livelihood threatened, or cut off. Uncounted merchants, small tradesmen, landlords, physicians and others were indirectly affected by an economic disturbance whose true source was the reactionary industrial thinking of America's most progressive industrialist.

When the Ford plants reopened for production of the new car, Ford's determination to win back his former market imposed a rigorous cutting of costs. This resulted, as usual, in a general reduction of wages, an accelerated speed-up, a more exhaustive stretch-out. These measures were made effective by Charles E.

Sorensen, whose single policy, according to Dean Marquis, was to "put the fear of God into labor." To aid him in carrying it out, Henry Ford created a new department, headed by a man who was to become one of the most sinister figures in American industrial history. It was Harry Herbert Bennett's function to build the Ford "Service Department" into a private militia, proficient in the arts of espionage, terrorism and labor-baiting. For these arts were apparently indispensable to the ultimate sanctity of big business, and had their warrant in the doctrine that whatever is economically right is morally right likewise.

To the discharge of this mission, Bennett brought modest qualifications. In youth he had served an enlistment in the United States Navy, earning some celebrity as a pugilist under the name "Sailor Reese." Subsequently, he had enjoyed a brief, but allegedly adventurous career in French West Africa, and after his return to the United States became a clerk in the Ford plant. While thus employed, Bennett attracted the attention of Henry Ford, who personally selected him for the post of chief watchman at the new plant under construction on the River Rouge. His success in this assignment led to his appointment as chief of Ford Service. Thereafter, his progress was meteoric. In less than a decade, "the little fellow"—as he was called, not always affectionately—emerged as Henry Ford's accredited spokesman, chief strategist, principal executive and political deputy. Jaunty, cocky, vain of his physical prowess and reputation for toughness, cynically indifferent to public opinion, contemptuously frank about his purposes and methods, Bennett used his power in ways that broadened the social education of the American people.

The private militia that he organized, reputedly the largest in existence, became a highly efficient instrument. In a statement at least half-true, Bennett once described them succinctly: "They're a lot of tough bastards, but every goddamn one of them's a gentleman." For a time, their membership included a sprinkling of college athletes. His acquaintance in pugilistic circles enabled Bennett to recruit boxers and wrestlers. Appointed to the Michigan Prison Commission, he did not forget Henry Ford's faith in the regenerative power of work in men's lives, but adopted it so wholeheartedly that Ford was able to boast that eight thousand former prison inmates were on his payroll. Still pursuing the elusive ideal of fused toughness and gentility, Bennett also dipped his net into the underworld of gangsters and racketeers. Two eminent representatives of this community—Joe Adonis, boss of gangs in Brooklyn, New York, and Chester La Mare, supreme overlord of Detroit's racketeers—in the guise of private enterprisers enjoyed profitable business connections with the Ford company. Bennett publicly acknowledged the closeness of his relations with Detroit's underworld, and openly cultivated some of its lesser leaders; obviously, they could furnish personnel for his army. He confided its training to an old friend, Norman Selby. Better known under his professional name of "Kid" McCoy, Selby was a discredited veteran of the prize-ring, recently paroled from a California prison where he had been serving a long sentence for an experiment in purely amateur killing.

But, although admirably taught by McCoy, an army did not serve to accomplish all of Bennett's purposes. He therefore contrived to have two of his henchmen appointed to public office in Dearborn, the site of the great River Rouge plant. One of them, Carl Brooks, remained for twelve years its chief of police; this, and other connections, assured Bennett's dominance over the city. Similarly, by exploiting his ability to provide Ford jobs at the request of politicians, and his reputed command of the votes of Ford employes, Bennett likewise gained considerable influence in Michigan state politics. At the peak of its development, Bennett's machine therefore constituted an outstanding achievement. It possessed a formidable private army; it was advantageously allied to the criminal underworld; it controlled major public functions in an American city; and its authority in the conduct of the public affairs of an American state was substantial. Even Henry Ford, dedicated to the concept of a universal machine, could not find fault with this one.

6 War and All Its Deeds of Carnage

Indeed, the efficiency of Bennett's machine, operating by remote control in every American city where a Ford plant was domiciled, made it possible for Henry Ford, an inveterate foe of labor unions, to prevent the organization of his workers, and to flagrantly defy the law of the land for more than half a decade. Even before he began this one-man counter-revolution, the nation was given a preliminary view of Bennett's militia in action. The celebrated "Ford Hunger March" of 1932 brought several hundred idle workers from Detroit to the Rouge plant in Dearborn, there to present a petition. It was not presented; instead, four people were shot dead, twenty seriously injured by gunfire, and many more otherwise hurt by the Ford militia and the Dearborn police. Five years later, on May 26, 1937, the nation learned of another engagement in which Bennett's troops staged an unprovoked attack and precipitated another sanguinary riot. In this episode, Walter P. Reuther and Richard T. Frankensteen, executives of the United Automobile Workers, having secured a city permit to distribute union leaflets to Ford workers leaving the Rouge plant, attempted to do so with the assistance of some fifty people, many of them women. All were roughly treated by Bennett's men—described by an eyewitness, Reverend Raymond P. Sanford of the Chicago Federation of Churches, as "thugs, hoodlums and brass-knuckle men"—and, in particular, Reuther, Frankensteen and others were slugged, kicked, gored, beaten and otherwise viciously injured. Once again, in April, 1941, when Ford workers finally struck the Rouge plant, the Bennett cohorts performed with their habitual virtuosity and finesse.

Meanwhile, in 1935, the Congress had passed a National Labor Relations Act sponsored by Senator Robert F. Wagner. This act guaranteed to labor the right of collective bargaining through representatives of its own choosing. Workers in the automotive industry had not been organized; the Chamber of Commerce of Detroit took pride in the fact that the city was "open shop," an exemplar of the "American Plan." But the young United Automobile Workers had the temerity, late in 1936, to propose the opening of collective bargaining negotiations with the giant General Motors Corporation. Rejection of this proposal touched off a spectacular "robot revolt"—a sit-down strike which for forty-four days paralyzed sixty General Motors plants and eventually won the union its first victory in the industry.

The major cause of this revolt was not widely understood; but it had already been defined by a committee of the National Recovery Administration, headed by Leon Henderson. Reporting on its investigation of conditions in the automotive industry, this body had sounded a clear warning: "The grievance . . . mentioned most frequently and . . . uppermost in the minds of those who testified is the stretch-out. Everywhere workers indicated that they are being forced to work harder and harder, to put out more and more products in the same amount of time and with less workers doing the job. There was a tendency to excuse the automobile manufacturer for the lack of steady work . . . but when it comes to increasing their work loads they are vigorous in denouncing the management as slave-drivers and worse. If there is any cause for conflagration in the Automobile Industry, it is this one."

After the Supreme Court had affirmed the constitutionality of the Wagner Act, in the spring of 1937, the United Automobile Workers set to work to organize the industry as a whole. Their prestige, immensely increased by the capitulation of General Motors, was further enhanced when their parent organization, the Committee for Industrial Organization, astonished the nation by securing the surrender of the United States Steel Corporation. By the end of 1938, every major producer of automobiles, with one exception, had signed collective-bargaining agreements with the United Automobile Workers, and these agreements recognized the manufacturer's rate of production as an issue for collective bargaining. The single exception was Henry Ford. Only in his plants were the workers unable, through their bargaining representatives, to exercise a degree of control over the speed of the great belt lines which moved past them inexorably, set in motion by a distant and invisible mechanism which also could imperceptibly accelerate that speed until the tempo of work became unendurable. As for Henry Ford, he merely declared to the world, "We'll never recognize the United Automobile Workers Union, or any other union."

With this declaration, Ford announced his rebellion against

the government of the United States and its laws; clearly, for him, the Constitution was not "a business code." He was to remain in rebellion for more than five years, during which time the National Labor Relations Board cited him more frequently than any other employer in the United States as a violator of the law which the Congress had passed to protect the rights of labor, and which the Supreme Court had ruled to be consistent with the nation's organic charter. From the outset it was obvious that, if Ford's defiance of the law succeeded, a pattern of nullification would be established, not only for the entire automotive industry, but probably for every other mass-production industry in the land. So the long, complex drama that unfolded was as significant for its ultimate implications as for its immediate import. Set in terms of a battle between Ford and the C.I.O., the real contest occurred between Ford and the National Labor Relations Board. It pitted the absolute master of a family-owned, billion-dollar corporation —the largest purely "private" enterprise in the United States— against a constitutional agency of the Federal government.

During the course of this contest, the Board passed on nine separate actions, relating to Ford plants in nine American cities. In all these actions, the Board's decisions adjudged the Ford Motor Company guilty of numerous, repeated, and varied violations of the Wagner Act. What the evidence disclosed was an organized program of violence, terrorism and intimidation that, emanating from the company's senior executives in Dearborn, extended to all its employees wherever situated. "No case within the history of the Board is known to the undersigned in which an employer has deliberately planned and carried into execution, a program of brutal beatings, whippings, and other manifestations of physical violence comparable to that shown by the uncontradicted and wholly credible evidence on which the findings herein are based. Blackjacks, loaded hose, cat-o'-nine-tails made of rubber stripping and electric-light wire were among the weapons used by the Ford Motor Company's strong-arm squad. There was no limit of brutality to which this squad and those who were directing it were unwilling to go if necessary, for at one stage, even murder was planned." So wrote Robert N. Denham, trial examiner for the

Board in the case involving the Ford Motor Company's plant at Dallas, Texas, in his official report. The case, he asserted, was neither local nor exceptional; it represented the working-out of "a comprehensive and overall plan for the prevention of the organization of Ford employees, and the discouragement of their entertaining any willingness or desire for such organization." But among Ford cases, it was perhaps exceptional in one respect: the bulk of its evidence took the form of sworn testimony offered by Bennett's own minions. It thus revealed, in classic perfection, and from within, the operations of Bennett's machine.

These operations, in Dallas and elsewhere, were made essential by Henry Ford's reiterated contention that his employees had no wish to be unionized; that, indeed, they actively resented any proposals to organize them. To give validity to this contention during the period of Ford's rebellion, Bennett discharged some four thousand workers who were either known to be, or were suspected of being, union members. He likewise secured, at one time, a "vote of confidence in the labor policies of Henry Ford" from more than ninety-eight percent of the Ford personnel. As one worker in the Dallas plant testified, "It didn't make any difference how we felt, we had to be against the C.I.O., and if we had not been, the strong-arm squad would have made us wish we had."

The Dallas plant employed some thousand or fifteen hundred workers, and preventive operations began there in the spring of 1937, shortly after the arrival from Dearborn of a deputy assigned by Bennett. A booklet entitled "Ford Gives Viewpoint on Labor" was distributed to every employee; its content was described, by the Board's trial examiner, as "inflammatory" and "scurrilous in its references to organized labor." Under the leadership of Bennett's deputy and a trusted employee of the Dallas plant, an "outside" or "strong-arm" squad of some twenty men was set up; it was their function "to use any method they saw fit to keep the plant from being organized." These men were detached from their regular production jobs, equipped with blackjacks, pistols, whips, and lengths of hose called "persuaders," and assigned to cruise the cafés, domino parlors, barber shops, bus terminals, and similar places in the city where union activity or sympathies might be detected. The effect of these two moves was not only to instill a distrust of unions among plant employees, but a fear of reprisals from their fellow-workers should they be accused of union sympathies. As a final step, "inside squads" were formed; it was their duty to persuade the entire personnel of the plant to search out and report union sympathizers wherever they might be found, and regardless of who they might be. The task of the "inside" squad was to compel every Ford worker to become an ardent anti-union agent and labor spy, if for no other reason than to protect his own skin from the delicate attentions of the strong-arm squad.

The strong-arm squad were instructed to run out of town all C.I.O. organizers, union advocates, or union sympathizers whose presence there might possibly lead to the organization of Ford employees. For this particular duty, the trial examiner found, the plant management chose "the most brutal, vicious and conscience-less thugs in its employ, who could be counted upon to accept an opportunity to indulge their sadistic desires in lieu of additional compensation." During the first six months of their activity, there were from thirty to fifty occasions when persons were assaulted and either beaten up on the streets of Dallas, or kidnapped and taken into the outskirts of the city, where they were beaten, flogged, blackjacked, tarred and feathered, or otherwise mistreated.

In 1941, a momentous decision of the Supreme Court warned Ford that his one-man rebellion was very nearly at an end. In spite of the operation of Bennett's machine, his plants were highly organized. A strike at his great Rouge plant ended in a victory for the United Automobile Workers. Ford's reputation with the press and the public had seriously diminished; the good will of his vast empire was being jeopardized. After an election in his plants showed the desire of his employes to be represented by the United Automobile Workers, Ford grudgingly announced his willingness to enter into negotiations with the C.I.O. for a contract. When the contract was finally drawn up, and its terms announced, the American people learned that Henry Ford had granted the union

far more than it had ever asked. Alone in the industry, Henry
Ford would operate every one of his plants as a "closed shop";
every employe would be required to join the union as a condition
of permanent employment; and the company itself would act as
the union's collecting agent by deducting its dues from the wages
of every Ford worker.

All that Henry Ford asked in return was the privilege of
stamping every car with the union label. Of such is the kingdom
of heaven.

7   Universal Evangelist

As an emergent public figure in 1914, Henry Ford himself was
one of the most significant social results of his revolutionary
technology. That he became a popular idol at once is not surprising. His career confirmed the old democratic faith of his countrymen. It proved that with ingenuity, perseverance and self-reliance,
a man might still rise, unaided, from the bottom to the top of
the heap. Other men of the day had also made a swift transit
from poverty to riches, but Ford was unlike any of them. For he
appeared to be in tune with the times: with the people's hope of
reform, the war being waged against abuses of economic privilege,
the crusade for social justice blessed by Woodrow Wilson in the
White House.

Latest of the tycoons, Ford behaved like a champion of the
plain people. In fighting the Selden patent case, he showed himself to be the foe of monopoly. In instituting the Five-Dollar Day,
he proved his valiant friendship for the common man. To countless troubled Americans, Ford's economic heresies implied a program for social progress. Did he not have a formula for equating
business prosperity with Christian principles; for preserving the
profit system and also procuring the benefits of a socialized
Utopia? The hostility of Wall Street merely confirmed their
belief in him. The shy, laconic, homespun inventor, having discovered God in the machine, might yet lead his fellow-citizens
into the Promised Land.

Shy though he was, Ford displayed no reluctance to collaborate
with circumstance. He did not refuse to put on the mantle of

leadership. Doubt about his evangelistic vocation never afflicted him. "I want to live a life, to make the world a little better for having lived in it," he told Dean Marquis. "The trouble with people is that they do not think. I want to do and say things that will make them think." After 1914, he seldom resisted this laudable desire. As it turned out, the wellsprings of his inspiration never ran dry. The flow of revelation proved to be almost continuous, and nearly all-inclusive in its range of reference. To communicate his provocations to thought, he enlisted a diaconate: copywriters, editors, journalistic ghosts, literary collaborators, biographers, a radio commentator, and the reporters stationed at Dearborn to await those happy occasions when Ford had something to say that would make news.

As a molder of public opinion, Henry Ford enjoyed an unrestricted franchise for more than thirty years. Anything he chose to do or say could, if he so wished, be brought to the attention of the American people. His wealth gave him access to the requisite facilities. His unique industrial eminence made his opinions, whatever their merits, and his activities, whatever their importance, newsworthy at any time. But for the far-reaching influence of the counsel that he sought to impose, Henry Ford himself could not be held responsible. Its influence resulted from two convictions deeply cherished by many of his countrymen. They correlated the value of his thinking with the size of his fortune; for surely a man astute enough to become so fabulously rich must also be very wise. And they believed that his preeminence in his own field implied a singular capacity in all others. Ford himself genuinely shared these convictions. That he did so, probably added to the effectiveness of his mission. But sometimes, to skeptical Americans, it gave that mission a grotesque and dangerous appearance; as of the blind leading the dumb. For, irrespective of their nature, the causes that he advocated, the doctrines that he preached, were invested with the magic of his millions and his myth. Along with them, into the scales of public judgment, went his incalculable prestige. Were they not, after all, the causes and doctrines of a man whose product had inaugurated a new era, whose methods prefigured a new kind of civilization?

Every one of Ford's many crusades sprang from a hunch; he had learned early in life, he said, to "grab the first hunch"; and it became his invariable rule to rely and act on his immediate impulse. To find people able to justify his hunches with abundant evidence was always easy for a man so rich. It was easier for Ford than for most wealthy men, since except in the field of mechanics he was incompetent to judge the value of any evidence produced, and he was predisposed by temperament to accept any that supported his own views. The Model-T was born of a hunch, and its history warranted his faith in the infallibility of his intuitions. Once his mind was made up, he could not be persuaded to change it. So he came, as Dean Marquis said, to have "an insulated mind in an isolated body." The good Dean's suggestion "that if he stuck to the things he knew, and let those alone about which his training had not qualified him to venture an opinion, he would avoid placing himself in a foolish position"—that this suggestion should go unheeded, should merely arouse all of Ford's native obstinacy, was inevitable.

When the First World War had raged over Europe for one year Ford embraced the cause of militant pacifism and began his career as an evangelist. The cause of war, he insisted, was "capitalism, greed, the dirty hunger for dollars." The villains of the piece were the international bankers and munitions profiteers. Presently, he chartered a "peace ship" to transport American delegates to a projected congress of neutrals in Scandinavia; its purpose was to work out peace terms acceptable to all the belligerents. Ford's announced intention to "get the boys out of the trenches by Christmas" evoked a storm of ridicule from the press, and abuse from many eminent Americans. The expedition was a foredoomed failure, in every respect, before it sailed. His continued pacifism, after his return, caused him to be denounced, by the Chicago *Tribune*, in terms which he considered libelous. He brought suit against the newspaper. When the case came to trial, in 1919, he gave the press a classic pronouncement. "History is more or less the bunk," he asserted. "We want to live in the present, and the only history that is worth a tinker's dam is the history we make now." Under a week's pitiless examination in the witness box, he revealed unsuspected depths of ignorance, and his

steadfast refusal to prove his literacy by reading aloud permitted
an impression to prevail that he found reading a difficult, if not
altogether impossible, task.

Meanwhile, Ford had unsuccessfully campaigned for election
to the Senate, at the purported request of President Wilson. He
had expressed his contempt for the parasitic principles of finance
capitalism in a sensational lawsuit brought by his minority stockholders, whom he afterwards bought out. And he had bought a
weekly newspaper, the Dearborn *Independent*, in which he presently embarked upon a long and virulent campaign against the
Jews. The defamatory material that he published proved useful
to the Ku Klux Klan, then powerful as a political force. Ten years
after Ford had made public recantation and apology, this material returned to the United States as Nazi propaganda, and Ford
received the highest decoration that could be bestowed by Adolf
Hitler as Chancellor of the German Reich.

In 1923, Ford allowed himself to be launched as an aspirant to
nomination for the Presidency by the Republican Party. At the
same time, he sought to acquire Muscle Shoals, the future nucleus
of the Tennessee Valley Authority, and the campaign of publicity
with which he buttressed his bid caused a migration to that
vicinity. For Ford let it be understood that he planned to create a
super-power network, eventually to become the property of the
American people, which not only would revolutionize their way
of life, but the nation's financial system also. But the terms of his
offer for Muscle Shoals evoked vigorous denunciation from
Senator George W. Norris, and despite the support which it received from various public bodies, Ford finally withdrew it. He
likewise renounced his presidential aspirations. But the popularity of his projected candidacy was unmistakable. A large segment of the American people was apparently eager not only to
have him take over Muscle Shoals on his own terms, but the
White House also. To them, he stood as a foe of political corrup-
tion; an enemy of Wall Street, finance capitalism, and economic
privilege; a champion of the common man; a proponent of fiat
money; and an industrial wizard who would somehow, if permitted to do so, invent a machine to produce Utopia.

At various times, Ford publicized his solution for the farm

problem, his views on the tariff, his philosophy of education, his opinions of current feminine fashions, his theory of medical ethics. He campaigned long and earnestly against the use of tobacco. He was so thoroughly committed to the cause of prohibition that he announced the permanent shut-down of all his plants should the inconceivable come to pass, and repeal of the Eighteenth Amendment be accomplished.

But perhaps the most engaging of all the crusades of the "sage of Dearborn"—as the American press fondly described him in his later years—was to make him the nation's leading patron and conservator of American folkways. This aspect of his career was first revealed, modestly enough, in an attempt to revive, at Dearborn, the traditional square dances which Henry Ford and his wife had enjoyed in their rural youth. The notion once firmly fixed in his mind, Ford imported from Massachusetts a full-time dance instructor, Benjamin B. Lovett; cleared space for a ballroom in his great engineering laboratory; engaged a group of musicians having a repertory of old-time melodies to remain in constant attendance; required his chief executives to acquire proficiency in the unfamiliar dance forms, and himself undertook to become a master of the art.

The sequel, because of Ford's temperament, was already implicit and predictable. It took him little time to inflate a personal hobby to the proportions of a national mission. The powerful publicity machine of the Ford company was hitched to his expanding purpose. In 1926, there issued from his private press a manual of the all but forgotten folk art: *Good Morning: After a Lapse of Twenty-five Years, Old-Fashioned Dancing Is Being Revived by Mr. and Mrs. Henry Ford.* This compilation of valuable research was, in addition, an essay on morals and a treatise on etiquette. Contests were held, often on radio broadcasts, for rural fiddlers all over the land, and the winners were brought on to Dearborn with appropriate fanfare. From Norway, Maine, a salty septuagenarian, "Mellie" Dunham, was transported to Dearborn in a special train, with a sudden rash of headlines in the press, to perform for the master and his guests. From Paris, another champion of the indeterminate future, Isadora Duncan, rebuked Henry

Ford for subverting American youth with "the servile courtesan movement of the minuet or the coquettish sex expression of the polka." Her protest was not heeded. Under Ford's patronage, Lovett set up courses in the early American dance for the physical-training departments of thirty-four universities, colleges and normal schools. Students at these institutions carried the renascence into the nation's school systems.

About ten years after taking up his hobby, Ford departed from his lifetime precedent of veiling in an honorable anonymity those who had contributed to his fame. To his dancing teacher, he paid a unique tribute in the erection of Lovett Hall, an immense and sumptuous ballroom floored in teak. There, at his invitation, the aristocracy of Detroit assembled on Friday nights, in formal evening attire, to move sedately through dances that had originated in the barns of lonely New England hamlets and the log cabins of the Western frontier. As the century reached its midpoint, American youth owed to the nostalgic whim of Henry Ford three elements of the culture that nourished them: a prosperous revival of the square dance; the broadcast ubiquity of hillbilly bands; and the preservation, on phonograph records, of a large musical literature associated with the diversions of the nation's adolescence.

But this nostalgic journey back into his own youth inspired Henry Ford with far more magnificent projects. The rebellious prophet who had asserted that history was "more or less the bunk"; who had declared that "a man can think better if he is not hampered by the knowledge of the past"; who had insisted that "all the world needs for the guidance of its life could be written on two pages of a child's copybook"—this disdainful condemner of yesterday and impatient spokesman of tomorrow underwent a curious transformation, probably more ostensible than real. For Henry Ford became an insatiable, determined conservator of the relics of a culture which he, more than any one other American, had successfully undermined. His first venture was born of the recollection of Longfellow's "Psalm of Life," associated with his schooldays and the McGuffey readers. Learning that the Red Horse Tavern at Sudbury, Massachusetts, was falling to decay, and told that this was the hostlery commemorated by the poet in *Tales of a Wayside Inn*, he promptly bought and restored it. The undertaking was not especially revealing, but a subsequent action, scarcely noticed by his fellow-citizens, illustrated the paradox of Henry Ford's personality. The Wayside Inn fronted on the Boston Post Road. Along this main artery of travel, there passed the interminable procession of vehicles he had popularized, clamorous witnesses to the new Messiah, destroyers of the carefully re-created tranquillity of bygone days. To keep *those things* away from his sanctuary—out of sight and earshot— he had the Boston Post Road re-laid for a distance of two miles, and gave to the Commonwealth of Massachusetts for one dollar a stretch of highway that had cost him a quarter of a million.

As a result of Ford's predilection for the American past, future generations were to have, within walking distance of one another, two mutually contradictory memorials to his bemused spirit, his incompatible ambitions and affections. The transit from his sprawling plant on the River Rouge to Greenfield Village required little time; but these monuments were separated by the abyss between two civilizations. At the Rouge, automobiles rolled off the assembly lines in an incessant stream. At Greenfield Village, they were forbidden entrance. Horsedrawn vehicles provided the only transportation on its winding, graveled roads. Along these roads, illuminated at night by gas lamps, there were quaint shops where handicraft workers plied their trades: a cooper, a cobbler, a miller, a blacksmith, a glass-blower, a watchmaker, an artisan in tintype photography. In the colossal near-by Rouge plant, some hundred thousand workers were so thoroughly disciplined to mechanized industry, so habituated to its routine of doing only one thing with one movement and no thought, that—as Ford himself foresaw— they would be unable to earn their keep without the aid of automatic machines. Those machines made the skilled craftsmen of Greenfield anachronisms, living museum-pieces. They followed their trades at the caprice of a billionaire industrialist whose revolutionary technology had forever removed, from their contemporary successors, all possibility of livelihood as independent enterprisers.

If the Rouge plant represented the fulfillment of Ford's ambitions, Greenfield expressed the pieties of a man who distrusted most of the results produced by his epochal life-work. For he was skeptical of the progress that he had so immeasurably advanced; he disliked, and largely failed to understand, the new age into which his simple contraption had trundled humanity; and his heart and mind, less flexible than his mechanical genius, lingered behind it, permanently enclosed in the narrow world of his youth. His friend John Burroughs, he thought, "had lived a wholesome life." Burroughs, the billionaire magnate noted with a touch of envy, "was fortunate to have as his home the farm on which he was born." In the outward aspect of Greenfield Village, Ford attempted to perpetuate, for future generations, a souvenir of that mid-nineteenth-century rural America which the Model-T had destroyed. There was a village green, or "common" and, clustered about it, were a church, a school, a court-house, a drover's inn, a town hall, a general store, a mill, and several farm houses. Here, empty of life, stood the shell of a society in which Ford had felt at home: one in which, "when a man is master of his own sphere, whatever it may be, he has won his degree—he has entered the realm of wisdom."

Here, too, were brought certain shrines that had kindled Ford's imagination. Edison's workshops at Menlo Park and at Fort Myers, Florida. The Michigan railroad depot where, in youth, he had been unceremoniously ejected from the train on which he sold newspapers, because he had set fire to the baggage car while making a chemical experiment. The birthplace of Stephen Foster; of doubtful authenticity. The bicycle shop of the Wright brothers, and the river-side cabin of Charles Proteus Steinmetz. Ford's primitive work shed, back of the Bagley Avenue house. John's Night Owl lunch wagon, a feature of Cadillac Square at the turn of the century. There were many others.

And there was a massive replica of Independence Hall. For Ford had personally commanded the erection of a counterfeit of the birthplace of that democracy which he feared and denigrated. Its function was to hold his vast collections of "Americana." There, on permanent display, was an overwhelming accumulation of miscellaneous relics, many of great historical value, many of little worth. The total fulfilled his intention to "have some of everything." There, among much else, were grandfathers' clocks, antique glassware, chandeliers, assorted old furniture and threshing engines; locomotives and railroad cars, music-boxes, churns, dolls and cigar-store Indians; spinning wheels, early automobiles, whatnots, baby-buggies and hearses. "When we are through," Ford had announced confidently, "we shall have reproduced American life as lived."

But even with the expenditure of twenty-five millions of dollars, life could not be reproduced as it had been lived in the America of Henry Ford's youth. He made other attempts to turn back the economic and social clock which he had so startlingly set ahead; to remake modern America in the image of the Dearborn of the eighteen-seventies. Nine country mills, set on the banks of various streams in Michigan, were carefully restored, then tooled to become feeder plants for the Rouge. In them, residents of the surrounding countryside fabricated certain light parts for his car, maintaining, in their off-hours and workless days, a limited cultivation of the soil. For America, Ford asserted, "it had been an evil day when the village flour mill disappeared."

Americans who came to maturity during the first half of the twentieth century habitually thought of Ford as the earliest, and perhaps greatest, pioneer in modern mechanized mass production, and this made him seem a prophet of the future. Yet, in all other respects, his career showed a retrospective, rather than prospective, cast. His reluctance to abandon the Model-T, though the roads of America passed from mud to macadam, to asphalt and to concrete, exemplified this; and he was similarly backward in recognizing the speedy obsolescence of Lizzie's two successors. The economic structure of his worldwide industrial empire was a defiant challenge of the old to the new; with William Randolph Hearst, whom in many ways he resembled, Ford remained an exponent of nineteenth-century industrial capitalism, as practiced by men like Andrew Carnegie, in an age of finance capitalism. His social ideas—which, during the second and third decades of the century, were taken with extreme seriousness—were those of a parochial mind formed in the penultimate years of the nineteenth century, nourished on the bitter revolts of Greenbackism and Populism. His prejudices, like his ideals, were those of a declining village culture in its last resistance to the overwhelming tide of industrialism. He had the villager's distrust of intelligence, of intellectual discipline, of book-learning, of the dangerous attraction of ideas; and he maintained, to the end, his conviction that ignorance was not only wisdom but virtue. To Charles Kinglsey's admonition to be good, and let who will be clever, he could add only the injunction to incessant work—in that, alone, lay the salvation of the world.

In April, 1946, the River Rouge was in flood, and at "Fairlawn," Henry Ford's great estate at Dearborn, the rising waters had cut off electric power, telephone and heat. The famed universal car—designed, forty years earlier, to give the farmer motive power for his machinery, as well as transportation—stood, silent and unfueled, in a museum. It could not provide its inventor's home with power for the conveniences that did not function. So the room in which Henry Ford lay dying, at the age of eighty-three, was very like the one in which he had been born: cold, illuminated only by oil lamp and candle, shut off from communication with a world he had helped to transform, but had scarcely understood. As life ebbed, a chauffeur was sent to the Rouge plant to telephone for a physician. But before medical aid arrived, Ford had died.

As the major architect of an industrial revolution, his place in history was secure. But what would posterity think of his social ideals, his evangelical missions, his attitude to the workers in his great plants? Perhaps future generations, trying to assess the worth of his inner light, might recall another rebellious spirit. For Lucifer, the light-bearer, the son of the morning, had once been an archangel. It was only later, in his pride, that he had fallen, and become Satan.

CHAPTER VI

A People on Wheels

1 Toy into Servant

The year of Henry Ford's death marked the golden anniversary
of the American automotive industry. Detroit, which it had lifted
from eleventh to fourth of the nation's cities in population,
honored the occasion with appropriate ceremonies.

Meanwhile, early in 1942, all the great assembly lines had
ceased moving. Production of cars for civilian use abruptly terminated. But there was scarcely an interruption before the industry's enormous plants began turning out the tools of war. Men
only middle-aged could recall a day when the infrequent appearance of a horseless carriage, spluttering and belching smoke, had

been an incentive to derision. Yet, when the last ones came off the lines, there were twenty-nine and one half million cars darting along the nation's highways—approximately one to every five adults and children living in the United States.

The absolute dependence of American society on the automobile was manifest during the wartime period of non-production. In order to achieve the highest productive level ever reached by the nation, it was necessary to keep as many of the existing cars as possible on the road. The Federal government therefore instituted such precautionary measures as gasoline rationing and the enforcement of a nation-wide speed limit, which prolonged their life, diverting to war production materials, men and machinery normally engaged by automotive requirements. Once a plaything for the rich, the automobile had become an indispensable servant of the masses. In this major transformation was summed up all the innumerable and pervasive changes which it had wrought in the American social order.

By the middle of the twentieth century, the results of this transformation were so familiar, so taken for granted as long-established features of the nation's life, that Americans were apt to forget the recency of its occurrence. The transformation actually began in 1919; for after the first World War a newly mature generation of Americans, adopting a radically novel attitude to the society which surrounded them, held a very different point of view on the automobile than that of their elders. They did not consider it mainly a luxury and an instrument of recreation. They regarded it as a year-round, day-and-night utility. For many of them, it seemed essential to livelihood, since possession of it obviously augmented their earning power. For all of them, it was a convenience capable of greatly increasing the comfort of personal existence. So the era of the linen duster, visored cap and goggles suddenly came to an end. The introduction of closed cars—usable at all seasons and in all kinds of weather—produced significant results. In ten years, the national registration of automobiles leaped from six to twenty-three millions.

Meanwhile, highway conditions throughout the country had improved little since the first national census of roads was taken, fifteen years earlier. But this, too, was to be changed with startling rapidity. By 1919, all the states had set up highway departments. Three years earlier, the Federal government had instituted a policy of granting financial assistance to the states for the development of rural post roads. In 1921, Congress passed the Federal Highways Act, which laid down a comprehensive program for road development, and pledged the Federal government, with respect to certain types of highway, to match state expenditures dollar for dollar. Thereafter, under the supervision of the state highway departments, localities within each state built and improved roads to create an integrated state-wide system. Under supervision of the Federal government, the states built roads which together formed regional systems. Collectively, all these projects combined into an integrated national system, covering the country with an immense fishnet of highways. By 1945, the nation had more than three million miles of road. Ninety-two percent of its primary state highways, and thirty-nine percent of its county and local roads were surfaced, thus being fit for year-round driving in all weathers. So successfully had the highway program been realized that some fifty-four thousand towns—or about half the communities in the United States—were without direct access to either railroad or river transport, yet were able to depend for their existence on automotive traffic exclusively.

2   Brightening up the Mores

Some of the drastic changes which the automobile was producing in the national mores quickly became manifest. A lifelong resident and shrewd observer of the Middle West, talking in 1925 with the sociologists Robert S. Lynd and Helen Merrell Lynd, asked: "Why on earth do you need to study what's changing in this country?" And he went on to remark, "I can tell you what's happening in just four letters: A-U-T-O!" In *Middletown*, the Lynds noted that ownership of an automobile had already reached the point of being an accepted essential of normal living. Houses were crowding closer to the front paving-line, and flowers, shrubbery and grassplots were giving way to the need for a garage, and a driveway to it. Families no longer spent summer evenings and Sunday afternoons on their porches, or in their yards; instead, they took to the road in their cars. As an evidence of social status, the make of a family's car had become as important as the physical appearance of its home. Indeed, the practice of mortgaging a home in order to buy an automobile was not uncommon.

Among the working-class families who furnished data to the Lynds, one-half owned cars; men who earned thirty-five dollars a week frequently used one week's income every month to pay for their cars. "We'd rather do without clothes than give up the car," a mother of nine children reported; and another remarked, "I'll go without food before I see us give up the car." A number of families who owned cars were satisfied to live in homes lacking bathroom facilities. This same condition was not uncommon in rural regions. An investigator for the Department of Agriculture asked one farm wife why the family owned a car when it didn't own a bathtub. She replied, with obvious surprise, "Why, you can't go to town in a bathtub."

Although ownership of a car was already recognized as a primary end in life, to which other traditionally approved purposes were to be subordinated, the automobile was upsetting various old-established social adjustments, and coming into conflict with emotionally charged sanctions and taboos. The Lynds remarked that it was making obsolete such time-honored dicta as "Rain or shine, I never miss a Sunday morning at church;" "A high-school boy does not need much spending money;" "Parents ought always to know where their children are." Because of the increasing custom of taking all-day motor trips on Sunday, the automobile was regarded, by conservative folk, as "a threat to the church," and clergymen, aware of the impatience of their congregations, were promising to dismiss them at an earlier hour.

Use of the family car was becoming a source of friction between children and their parents. Youngsters found it possible to join a crowd motoring to a dance in some neighboring town, without asking permission. Among high-school students, the family's ownership of a car was an important criterion of social eligibility. Boys seldom took girls to social functions without using a car, and some families were said to have bought more luxurious cars chiefly to buttress the social standing of their children. But the automobile was also producing disruptive effects on family life. Fathers, ruefully admitting the declining prestige of family meal-times, protested against the necessity for making dates with their children in order to see them. Mothers complained of the all but permanent invisibility of daughters constantly absent in other people's cars.

The automobile was displacing the parlor as the locus of pre-liminaries to courtship—was not this "endangering the home?" And motorized courtship was not always leading to honorable marriage. Houses of prostitution were few, but the judge of the juvenile court asserted that "the automobile has become a house of prostitution on wheels." Of the girls brought before him, during the previous year, on charges of "sex crimes," one-third had committed their offenses in automobiles. And, to "the desire of youth to step on the gas when it has no machine of its own" was attributed the theft of more than one hundred and fifty auto-mobiles during the same year. Thus, it was possible for some citizens of Muncie to consider the automobile "an 'enemy' of the home and society."

3 Urban Explosion

While upsetting long-established habits and customs, and chal-lenging traditional concepts of the proper conduct of life, the automobile was also precipitating an urban explosion throughout the country. Up to the turn of the century, most American cities grew compactly outward from the business center. Thereafter, suburban development cautiously followed the railroads and main turnpikes, but only to a limited distance. From 1920 onward, with increasing acceleration, American cities burst their bounds and sprawled indiscriminately over the surrounding countryside.

At first, the outward movement was largely confined to families in the higher income groups, for whom the lure of space, privacy, and rural scenery was indicated by an astonishing increase in the population of "developments" bearing names denoting such attractive physical features as heights, vistas, parks, and water-frontage. In the ten years between 1920 and 1930, this movement accounted for the rapid creation of what were virtually new, large communities. Thus, in the vicinity of Los Angeles, the population of Beverly Hills increased by nearly twenty-five hundred percent; that of Glendale by almost four hundred; those of Inglewood and Huntington Park by nearly five hundred percent. In the neighborhood of Cleveland, Ohio, the gain in population of Shaker Heights was one thousand percent, that of Garfield Heights five hundred, that of Cleveland Heights more than two hundred. Near Detroit, Grosse Point Park and Ferndale increased their residents by approximately seven hundred percent. Richmond Heights, a suburb of St. Louis, Missouri, showed an increase of more than three hundred percent; Webster Grove and Maplewood each more than seventy percent. The outward movement from Chicago swelled the population of Elmwood Park by a sevenfold increase, doubled that of Park Ridge, and added sixty percent to that of Oak Park.

But, because of the increasing diffusion of the automobile among the lower income groups, the exodus from the cities was by no means confined to the economically prosperous. Between 1930 and 1940, the decade of the Great Depression, the populations of one hundred and forty American cities increased by six percent, but those of the surrounding metropolitan areas showed an increase of nearly eighteen. The Lynds, reporting on Muncie, Indiana, once again in 1935, found that, under the impact of depression, "People give up everything in the world but their car." Relief authorities made no effort to discourage car-ownership among their clients, who were advised to use their cars in various ways to pick up small earnings. The automobile, the Lynds judged, was one of the most depression-proof elements of the city's life; far less vulnerable than marriages, divorces, new babies, clothing, and perhaps food. What was true of Muncie, was probably true of the country as a whole.

The drift toward outlying locations of low-income groups previously resident in metropolitan centers reflected, to some degree, a search for cheaper, if not more agreeable quarters. In part, it likewise reflected an increasing decentralization of industry. This was due, originally, to rising urban costs, traffic congestion in metropolitan centers, and growing reliance on automotive trucking for the delivery of supplies as well as the shipping of finished products. Working-class communities therefore sprang up around peripheral industrial plants. This movement was immensely accelerated, during the following decade, by the construction of huge war plants on the outskirts of major American cities. All these factors taken together resulted in a migration of low-income groups—but this would have been impossible without the automobile. The evidence recorded by a survey undertaken in the state of Michigan made this fact obvious: of eight hundred and fifty thousand workers employed in industry in Michigan, six hundred and fifty thousand depended exclusively on their cars to get to and from their work.

The phenomenon of urban explosion, produced by the automobile, created a new type of "supercommunity." Reporting on this, in 1933, for the President's Research Committee on Social Trends, H. D. McKenzie remarked that the automobile had "erased the boundaries which formerly separated urban from rural territory and has introduced a type of local community without precedent in history." This "supercommunity" differed from the old-fashioned metropolis, McKenzie asserted, in both the complexity of its institutional division of labor and the mobility of its population. Nor was it confined to the great cities; it had become "the communal unit of local relations throughout the entire nation." Every city in the United States, had, to some degree, become "the center of a constellation of smaller centers." This radically new social phenomenon, born of the automobile, generated problems which the automobile further aggravated—and for many of these the American people, toward the middle of the twentieth century, had found no effective solutions.

The optimistic hope of E. P. Ingersoll, expressed fifty years earlier, that the automobile would do away with traffic congestion, seemed almost ludicrous. The streets of American cities were so filled by automobiles that it had become almost impossible to drive one. "In some big cities," a writer in *Time* reported, "vast traffic jams never really got untangled from dawn to midnight; the bray of horns, the stink of exhaust fumes, and the crunch of crumpling metal eddied up from them as insistently as the vaporous roar of Niagara." In New York City's garment district, it often took fifteen minutes for a car to move one block. In Los Angeles—one of the most spaciously built of American cities— transit on certain streets at certain hours was slower than the horse-and-carriage traffic of the nineteenth century.

The effort to solve this single problem had given mid-twentieth-century America some of its most characteristic features. One was the multiple-laned concrete express highway, permitting non-stop traffic from the suburbs to the metropolitan center: Chicago's Outer Drive; New York's West Side Elevated Highway and East Side Roosevelt Drive; Detroit's sunken Davison Avenue were merely outstanding examples of a development to which nearly all large American cities were increasingly committed. Ironically, however, these developments, by facilitating access to the metropolitan center, merely intensified an already oppressive traffic congestion. Had the automobile's promise of immensely increased personal mobility been frustrated by its own enormous proliferation? There was evidence that it had. Traffic surveys conducted by the Federal government indicated that three trips of every four made by Americans in their cars were for necessity purposes; that trips less than five miles in length constituted the major portion of all trips made; that most family shopping was accomplished within a radius of three miles.

In 1922, the National Department Stores made a novel departure by erecting a branch establishment three miles out from the center of St. Louis, Missouri. Within the next twenty years, this innovation was followed, at greatly extended distances, by many department stores of the larger American cities, by the principal mail-order houses, and by leading operators of chain stores. Suburban shopping centers, with adequate parking space and gas stations, formed a new pattern of urban decentralization, encouraging those who had left the metropolitan center—presumably because the automobile made it accessible—to remain away from it as much as possible. In this respect the automobile, by precipitating urban explosion, had likewise promoted a new localism, and set up a counter-movement of decreasing circulation. In the suburbs populated by high-income groups that surrounded the country's very largest cities, only the man of the family regularly traveled to and from the city; often he had ceased to rely on his car for these trips and "commuted," as his father might have done in the nineteenth century, by train. Reflecting on one of the major ironies of the automotive age, he could ruefully quote the old hymn of Isaac Watts:

> *"And 't is a poor relief we gain,*
> *To change the place, but keep the pain."*

4 See America First

By 1937, fifty-two million people in fifteen million cars were spending an estimated five billion dollars on motor travel: one billion for gas, oil, garaging and repairs; another billion for lodging; approximately one and one-quarter billions for camping supplies and souvenirs; and some seven hundred millions of dollars on golf courses, soft drinks and hot dogs. Whereas in 1920, only one hundred and twenty-eight thousand cars entered the national parks of the United States, the number had risen, by 1940, to two million. In 1914, there were only two hundred golf courses in the country; in 1940, there were more than five thousand. In 1922, there were only some six hundred tourist camps or courts in the land; in 1940, there were approximately fourteen thousand, having an estimated annual business of thirty-seven millions of dollars. In addition to the accommodations which they furnished, some fifty thousand "tourist homes" offered their domestic amenities to the modern American centaur-on-wheels. The neon-lit plurals of "Eats," "Rooms" and "Cabins" supplied a working vocabulary for the American landscape.

The popularity of tourist courts and camps indicated their adaptation to the needs of that considerable segment of the American motoring public which did not enjoy an elastic income. The roadside camp always offered the privacy of an individual cabin, sometimes added the esthetic appeal of an attractive rural setting, and invariably spared its patrons the embarrassment which they might feel in entering an urban hotel in the clothes of the road. Yet, because of the regrettable imperfection of human nature, these specific advantages also recommended it to motorists not governed by "tourist psychology." In 1936, sociologists from Southern Methodist University, in Dallas, Texas, turned their inquiring minds to the social trends which might be manifest in neighboring tourist camps. Presumably, they were disconcerted by discovering that the principal clientele of these hospitable enterprises was composed, not of tourists, but of local couples whose use of their facilities rarely exceeded an hour's duration. They found that in one camp, a cabin was rented to sixteen different couples during the course of a single night. To non-academic observers this might have suggested a noteworthy deterioration of Southern gallantry during the automotive age. But the conclusion of the Dallas sociologists was that, "The growth of these institutions and their toleration by the community are evidences of a changed public attitude toward non-marital intimacies." As against the opinion of the judge of the juvenile court of Muncie, Indiana, expressed a short decade earlier, the report of the Dallas investigators established that progress had been accomplished, during the interval, if not in morality, at least in decorum.

But any disposition to regard abuse of the hospitality of tourist camps as peculiar to Dallas was rudely jolted by J. Edgar Hoover, chief of the Federal Bureau of Investigation. In a magazine article published in 1940, he described them as "camps of crime," imperiling the communities to which they were adjacent. Many tourist camps, he asserted, were "little more than camouflaged brothels." These were usually closed to the traveling public on Saturdays and Sundays, when anyone whom their proprietors suspected of being a bona-fide tourist would be turned away because there was "more money and a faster turnover in the 'couple' trade." In patronizing these camps at other times, Hoover warned, American tourists were exposing themselves to the attentions of prostitutes, the depredations of gangsters, and the profit-seeking scrutiny of "that lowest of parasites on law enforcement, the divorce detective." All in all, the American motoring public might have been expected to give tourist camps a wide berth. Yet they did nothing of the kind.

5   Lizzie's Double Life

But their disregard of Hoover's warning implied no special ad-
venturousness. It may merely have expressed a natural fatalism.
For, in the years after 1920, the automobile came to lead a kind
of double life. It was, on the one hand, an accepted essential of
normal existence, and in many families the most popular member.
It was, on the other hand, surrounded by an aura of violence,
danger and imminent death. A comparable position in society
could have been held only by a respectable matron devoted to her
household, who nevertheless consorted with criminals, slew people
indiscriminately, and inspired a wide variety of anti-social conduct.
On the American scene, the automobile functioned with precisely
this irresponsible dualism. Like many another gift of the age of
technological progress, it was by no means a pure blessing.

Before 1920, the hardy American tourist enjoyed a democratic
freedom resembling that of the wandering students who roamed
medieval Europe. Early tourists formed organizations for mutual
help and advice. One of these was called the Tin Can Tourists'
Association, and its members tied a tin can to the radiator caps of
their cars. Meeting one another on the road, they stopped, exchanged information about road conditions, detours, camp sites,
the best garage in the next town. In those days of comradeship and
innocence, to slow down when overtaking a pedestrian, and offer
a lift, was common practice; an extension to the whole nation of
the neighborly friendliness exercised at home. The kindly simplicity of the horse-and-buggy era survived into that of goggles and
duster.

Twenty years later, in 1940, the outlook and manners of the
American tourist had drastically changed. By then, he had learned
that his safety was dubious, whether in or out of his car. Neither
caution nor skill would fully protect him, and friendliness was a
luxury heavily charged with danger. He set off for his holiday
apprehensively. His attitude to his fellow-drivers was incurably
hostile. His view of all pedestrians was deeply colored by suspicion. He had become, when seated at the wheel, a dour misan-
thrope intent on self-preservation and the minding of his own

business. For this odd transformation, a number of factors were responsible.

The forty million drivers who infested American highways represented one out of every two inhabitants of the country old enough to drive. They included youngsters of fourteen, women, the very elderly, and many of the physically and mentally disabled. At the wheel of a complex mechanism requiring precise co-ordination, all persons were very probably not equal, yet the fit and the unfit, the trained and the untrained were alike permitted to pursue happiness in a car. Not surprisingly, this situation exacted a penalty: in an average year, automobiles caused approximately forty thousand deaths; brought about accidents which inflicted personal injuries on over one million people; and damaged one another to a cost of many millions of dollars. These statistics implied the normal hazards of the road, and the American motorist could scarcely be blamed for attributing them to the other fellow, whether pedestrian or driver. For even the experts could not agree on the appropriate endowment for a safe driver.

In 1948, James Stannard Baker, research director of the Northwestern University Traffic Institute, unqualifiedly stated that, "A high-grade moron makes the best auto driver." This mental type, he suggested, was an individual not too bright, but willing to learn, a plodding creature who kept his mind on the task at hand. Unlike the man of superior mind, the moron was not subject to daydreams and not easily bored with the mechanics of driving. Drivers with very high, or very low intelligence ratings, Baker asserted, were highway menaces; intellectuals found driving too easy, and simpletons were prone to witless wool-gathering. But to this reassuring diagnosis, J. R. Crossley, vice-president of the Automobile Club of New York, offered a horrified dissent. The safest driver, he claimed, was a person of normal intelligence. And he described the required qualifications as physical, mental and emotional soundness; adequate information about motor vehicle, highway and traffic laws; sound instruction in driving techniques; sufficient experience for the formation of protective habits, skill, and proper attitudes of responsibility, sportsmanship and courtesy. On the average, the American motorist conceived himself as exemplifying all the qualifications demanded by Crossley, and regarded his fellow drivers as not quite fulfilling those set by Baker. And the yearly toll in deaths, injuries and damages showed no substantial decrease.

Most of the forty thousand deaths annually caused by automobiles were avoidable; they were one of the unnecessary prices which Americans paid for equality of opportunity on the highway. A large majority of the accidents that injured one million Americans were likewise preventable. But not quite all. For in addition to the ordinary hazards of the road, motorists were subjected to others devised, for their disadvantage, by the criminal underworld. In the larger cities of the United States there flourished, from time to time, a prosperous racket based on the faking of automobile accidents to people on whose bodies the appropriate stigmata of physical injury had previously been produced. The racket was cultivated by astute criminals; they were leagued with physicians and lawyers of dubious repute; and careful preparations enabled their subordinates to present a convincing performance. The immediate, and often successful object was to swindle insurance companies as well as frightened motorists out of large sums of money. However skillfully and cautiously he drove, no motorist could consider himself absolutely safe at the wheel of his own car; in any large city, he might become the next victim of this racket.

Nor was he safe if a trusting nature inclined him to spontaneous hospitality while driving. The practice of hitchhiking, an amiable fad invented by youth in the 1920s, became prevalent as an economic necessity during the Great Depression. As a means of facilitating robbery and other crimes, it was quickly adopted by the underworld. By the 1940s, the wistful eye and frenzied thumb of the young, hopefully stationed along roads leading out of town, held a diminishing appeal for the solitary tourist, whose conscience often troubled him as he sped past, but whose car and wallet remained in his own possession when he arrived at his destination.

The new misanthropy of American motordom left few traces on other areas of the national life. It was, so to speak, an allergic disturbance, afflicting citizens otherwise kindly whenever they drove, and only then. It had become epidemic during the period of national prohibition, which brought about the rise to social power of gangsters and racketeers. The members of this new industrial aristocracy rapidly acquired control of the urban night-clubs and speakeasies, the outlying roadhouses, which distributed their products. The underworld elite was also quick in adapting the automobile to its business requirements. It used motor trucks for transport and hijacking. It bought custom-built cars like Al Capone's, with armor-plated bodies and bullet-proof glass, for personal use. It maintained fleets of arsenal-equipped cars for the punitive expeditions made necessary by competitive free enterprise. The practices of the time left a permanent fingerprint on the American language: to be "taken for a ride" no longer connoted a pleasure, but an unfortunate finality.

All these new phenomena suddenly increased the hazards of the road and—reported by the press, portrayed by the films, recorded by writers of fiction—produced, among motorists, a special form of jitters. The Dion O'Banion gang of Chicago, spraying the main streets of suburban Cicero with machine-gun bullets during a daylight raid on the headquarters of Al Capone; the later exploits of John Dillinger, a successful bankrobber and bandit who for several years terrorized Middle Western states—indicated, to innocent motorists, the perils of following the right road at the wrong moment. The guileless quest of a drink—illegal, but sanctioned by custom—might plunge them, inadvertently, into a shooting tangle between officers of the law and indignant enterprisers whose business was being interfered with. Mere nocturnal delay on lonely highways, sometimes made imperative by the conflicting purposes of the sexual instinct and the peculiar social vigilance of small communities, could involve unsuspecting motorists in hijacking episodes from which they were likely to emerge with wrecked cars, punctured bodies and damaged reputations. That these discouraging contingencies did not bring motoring for pleasure to an abrupt end was much more remarkable than that they contributed to souring the dispositions, and increasing the apprehensiveness, of American drivers.

6 The Transcontinental Bazaar

Nevertheless, tourism steadily increased, and within the lifetime
of a single generation turned winding dirt roads into broad concrete highways that resembled continuous, elongated bazaars. The
pleasant rural landscape, once the motorist reached it, had almost
disappeared under the encroachment of conveniences, commerical
solicitations, and ingeniously contrived services. Here and there,
state or local authorities managed to preserve a grove of trees,
relics of a bygone age, under which they set up picnic tables,
stoves and water fountains for the hasty use of tourists bent upon
getting from one place to another which looked almost precisely
like it. But, as he sped along, the motorist could enjoy the horta-
tory literature of the billboards. From the roadside stands operated
by farmers and their wives—the most up-to-date were furnished,
by city decorators, in old-fashioned ginghams and reproductions
of "early American" discomfort—he was able to buy vegetables,
fruits, eggs, chickens, jams and jellies. Other stands, in close
proximity to one another, offered him lawn furniture, "artistic"
weathervanes, sundials and garden sculpture, assorted antiques,
boxes of nuts assembled from the ends of the earth, golf hats and
clubs, fishworms and tackle, picture postcards of places he had
passed without seeing, domestic pets. To prove to himself that
he had actually been in the country, he could buy bunches of
wilted wildflowers from enterprising tots artfully arrayed in rags.

If trouble developed with his car, the great outdoor bazaar was
well equipped to attend to it. Service, by the middle of the
twentieth century, consisted chiefly in removing a worn unit and
replacing it by a new one, and the modern service-man had
electrical devices which helped him to analyze internal disorders,
as well as improved tools with which to straighten frames, bump
out bodies and fenders, and align wheels. Along American roads
there were nearly a quarter of a million filling stations; nearly
seventy thousand independent repair shops; more than thirty
thousand franchised dealers; and approximately twenty thousand
purveyors of accessories, tires and batteries. The filling station,
in particular, nearly always open for business, was a versatile
institution that offered replenishment to the car, and "rest rooms"

to its occupants; that sometimes sold toilet articles, canned goods, cigarettes, sandwiches and soft drinks; that often held a jukebox to furnish—while his car radio was turned off—the incessant music that was essential to the American motorist's happiness.

Nor did the motorist need to leave the great bazaar should he prefer not to snatch a bite at the nearest filling station. The quaint old village inns had largely disappeared. They had been replaced by the whimsies of "tea shoppes" and the costly elegance of restored, or merely counterfeited, historic "places" adapted to restaurant use. But, along the endless concrete emporium, there were other institutions that catered to the tourist's appetite. Windmills with parking lots served hamburgers subjected to rituals of glorification, glamorized hot dogs, polychromatic ice cream. Log cabins dispensed clams, lobsters, and chicken-in-the-rough divorced from knife and fork. In the far West, the tourist could turn into a "drive-in," give his order to a waitress garbed like a drum-majorette, contemplate the architecture of fantasy while waiting, and eat his repast from a tray hitched to his car-door, without ever leaving the wheel.

All along the Eastern seaboard, from Maine to Florida, there were belfry-capped buildings, vaguely "colonial," into which a far-sighted native of Massachusetts, Howard Johnson, had stretched his mother's recipe for homemade ice cream and his own masterly intuition that American motorists wanted meals that were good, familiar and quick. Johnson controlled nearly two hundred establishments that were standardized in architecture, cuisine and service, which his great fleet of trucks supplied with foodstuffs processed in his central kitchens. By sticking to Johnson all the way from Portland to Miami, the tourist could be sure of having almost identical meals every day, thus enjoying the advantages of travel while retaining digestively the illusion of comfortably remaining at home.

But the automobile, and the great bazaar through which it perpetually sped, might in time make home itself an obsolete superfluity in the lives of many Americans. The cult of selective transiency had proved very nearly fatal to old-fashioned resort hotels, formerly booking vacationers for a fortnight or an entire season, but now dedicated only to overnight guests and those too deplorably decrepit to sit upright in a car. It had made Americans reluctant to settle on a holiday place, buy a summer cottage, and return there year after year. The trailer, once a two-wheeled affair used to haul camping equipment, had been transformed into a mobile residence.

The Great Depression had popularized the trailer, the wartime housing shortage had made it a permanent feature, and by the middle of the century a family could pursue an ideally nomadic existence in an air-conditioned, centrally heated coach having sitting room, sleeping accommodations for four, and kitchen equipped with refrigerator, stove and sink. It seemed entirely probable that Americans born in the second half of the twentieth century would spend their infancy in ambulatory nurseries, be snatched off to education by school busses, carry on their courtship at the wheel, relax in drive-in movies, and go to their ultimate immobility in motor hearses. Even livelihood could be earned in transit: the president of a Texas ice-making concern had already acquired a super-trailer equipped with radio-telephone, to serve as executive office and retail sales establishment.

7   You Can't Keep Them Down on the Farm

The effect of the automobile on the lives of rural Americans was even more transfiguring than its effect on the lives of those who lived in cities. Almost overnight, it brought to an end the isolation and loneliness, the material meagerness of farm life; disrupted ancient patterns of existence; and changed the very look of the countryside. The crossroads general store, once the farmer's market and meeting place, was forced out of business by his new mobility; he could drive past it to the village, and—perhaps not finding there what he wanted—continue on to the nearest county seat, twenty or thirty miles away. Open-country churches were abandoned, and their congregations consolidated. Warren H. Wilson, a member of the Board of National Missions of the Presbyterian Church, discussed, in 1924, the case of a rural pastor who purchased a car, to the indulgent amusement of his flock, and used it to establish connections, on each Sabbath day, with eight services of worship. "I rode with him one Sunday over his circuit," Wilson noted. "He needed only two sermons, the same number as before, but he had quadrupled his professional efficiency." The one-room school succumbed to the same fate as the open-country church. Of the two hundred thousand existing in 1916, fewer than one hundred and fourteen thousand remained in 1940; the rest had been replaced by consolidated schools whose buildings and equipment compared favorably with those of any urban schools.

The change in rural medical practice impressively showed the effect of the automobile on American farm life. Kitchen operations and home nursing were still the rule in the century's first decade. In 1909, a young physician began practice in a Michigan town having a population of one thousand; five other doctors and fifteen practical nurses were also serving the town and surrounding countryside; the nearest hospital was more than twenty miles distant. After ten years of reliance on a pair of horses and a rig, the young doctor bought a Model-T. Though he could only use it in summer, he built up so large a practice that he required a stable of six horses to visit his patients in the winter. A few years later, he bought a closed car and dispensed entirely with his stable. Fifteen years later, in 1942, he was putting thirty-five thousand miles a year on his car, was on the staff of three hospitals all of which he could reach within a morning, and saw patients as far away as fifty miles. In his home town there were no longer any practical nurses, and there was only one other physician. Kitchen operations were unknown; the town maintained an ambulance, and patients could be speeded to any of several hospitals equipped with X-ray, blood bank, oxygen tent, and the latest operating facilities.

To the farm-wife, meanwhile, came the home demonstration agent, a missionary from the nearest agricultural college or state university, an expert in home economics. She chose the most intelligent farm women on her circuit, and trained them as local leaders. They, in turn, put on exhibits at grange meeting halls, schools and farm homes. They held cooking schools, health schools, canning demonstrations, home-furnishing and gardening programs. In 1920, there were fewer than one thousand home demonstration agents, and fewer than fifty thousand leaders. Twenty years later, the number of agents had nearly trebled, and the number of volunteer leaders had multiplied fivefold. By this time, farm wives were driving long distances in their cars to attend home demonstration meetings. In the Eastern states their round trips averaged seven miles; in the Middle West, thirteen; in the Far West, twenty-four, with trips as long as one-hundred and twenty-five miles to county-wide meetings a common occurrence.

Better farming also came to the farm in an automobile, with the county agent who brought the technical information of the state experiment station, and the Federal Department of Agriculture, to bear on local needs. In 1920, two thousand county agents drew to their meetings an attendance of twelve million farmers; in 1940, nearly four thousand agents reached forty-six million farmers. At the same time, an expanding network of new organizations were reaching into the sparsely settled regions of America, and enlarging their opportunities for a more satisfying life. Rotary luncheon clubs came in, along with junior agricultural clubs, the Boy Scouts and Camp Fire Girls. Co-operative marketing associations were formed, applying modern merchandising to the farmer's products; co-operative canneries and quick-freezing plants were established, to process them. The automobile, by breaking down the farmer's isolation, had socialized his occupation, furnished him with a pattern of community existence, and enlarged his horizon until it equalled that of the townsman.

8   The Madding Wheels of Brazen Chariots

All night and all day, toward the middle of the century, the main highways and feeder roads of America roared with the passage of the nation's six million trucks, its nearly two hundred thousand motor busses. The trucks alone required the services of four and one half million drivers, the largest occupational class in the American economy, except for farmers. They brought wider markets to farmers, increased services to city-dwellers and—with the busses—new life to the many thousand American communities that had no connection with the rest of the country except by highway. They were commonplace features of the American scene, integral elements of the national transport system; yet their origin dated back no more than thirty years.

Long-distance haulage by truck was born of the First World

War, which put a strain on railroads to which they were unequal. As chief of a Highway Transport Commission, President Wilson appointed Roy D. Chapin, who had driven the first Oldsmobile from Detroit to New York. Chapin, aware that the government had ordered some thirty thousand trucks for delivery to France, where they were essential to the distribution of ammunition, food and clothing to troops, determined to put them to immediate use. Ordinarily, these trucks would have been put on railroad flat-cars and freighted to Atlantic ports. Instead, Chapin had them loaded with war supplies, and driven to seaboard. These trucks, lurching over bad roads, detouring around unsafe bridges, pioneered the immense, swift highway fleets of the mid-century, transporting for at least a part of its journey everything that Americans ate, wore or used.

On the four-lane main highway between Los Angeles and San Francisco, California, the nocturnal tourist might pass no less than four hundred and fifty trucks with their trailers. These combinations measured fifty feet from bumper to bumper. The truck rode on ten immense tires, the trailer on twelve. The truck had pneumatic brakes, and fifteen separate gear shifts for various speeds and hill conditions. Each of these vast road-liners carried twenty tons of freight. Moving eastward over the Rockies, the tourist could pass the great Diesel-powered trucks of the Pacific Inter-mountain Express, bound on a five-day run to Chicago; the company, with its fleet, covered twelve thousand miles of route.

Out from Des Moines, Iowa, a newspaper dispersed its three hundred trucks to bring readers throughout the state their morning paper on the day of publication. Out from Grand Rapids, Michigan, there rolled the five hundred trucks and nearly seven hundred trailers of the Interstate Motor Freight System, to flow over a network of routes covering sixteen states; an intricate system with forty-one terminals and many more call stations, linked by teletype, and controlled from a dispatcher's office at headquarters. From the fifteen-acre market in Benton Harbor, Michigan—the largest growers' market in the world—the huge refrigerator trucks poured out to more than five hundred communities scattered over half the continent.

On a busy night Washington Market, in New York City, received sixteen hundred truckloads of produce drawn from a radius of more than two hundred miles, and five thousand truck trips were required to distribute the receipts to city stores. Over the nation's roads, at night, moved the great oval tank trucks, bringing milk to cities; the tank trucks of the oil corporations, delivering gasoline and oil to filling stations; the refrigerator trucks of the meat-packers; the bread trucks of vast bakery-plants, servicing the stores and restaurants of half a state; the vans of the chain-store corporations, replenishing stock in outlying branches; the giant padded vans of carriers who moved the household goods of itinerant Americans from one town to another; the trucks hauling livestock from farm to stockyard; the coal trucks bound from mine to city; the big semi-flat trailers carrying baled cotton to mills and warehouses; the frozen-food trucks speeding fish from New England and strawberries from Florida; the double truck-trailers moving new cars to dealers.

And with the trucks, by day and by night, rushed the busses that carried Americans into nearly every town on the map of their country. These were the lineal descendants of the "jitneys" that swarmed about American cities during the First World War; aged passenger cars that plied irregular routes, charging a nickel a ride. Some of the busses were swift and small, little larger than elongated sedans. Some were long-distance coaches, carrying thirty-six passengers in reclining armchairs. Some were "nite-coaches"—compact sleeping cars on rubber tires, with berths and tiled washrooms, radios and drinking fountains. Competing with the railroads, and often operating between points which the railroads did not serve, the nation's twenty-five hundred bus lines, covering more than three hundred thousand miles of route, were by the middle of the century carrying more than one-third of the country's total intercity passenger traffic.

9 Every Man Has Business and Desire

Less than sixty years after the first native horseless carriage rattled over a Massachusetts road, one million Americans were employed in the manufacture of motor vehicles and parts. Eight million more were employed in related automotive fields. Approximately one of every six business firms in the United States was in some way dependent, for its profits, on the automotive industry.

Practically all Americans with annual incomes of more than three thousand dollars were car-owners. Of approximately eight million, having incomes ranging from fifteen hundred to three thousand dollars, nearly six million owned cars. Of nine million, whose incomes were less than fifteen hundred, but more than seven hundred and fifty dollars, five million possessed automobiles. A survey, in 1936, of five and one half million families, not on government relief but having incomes of less than seven hundred and fifty dollars a year, showed that two million owned cars. And the same survey reported that there were Americans whose annual income, in cash, was as low as two hundred and fifty dollars—and who nevertheless were owners of cars.

The fact was that the automotive industry could not operate at normal capacity if it depended for its market on those who could actually afford to purchase its products and pay cash for them. Therefore—in what were euphemistically called normal times—it inveigled Americans into the habit of leaning the present against the future. It taught them that their first duty as citizens was to consume; and to hasten the process of consumption, it also persuaded them that prestige required their dissatisfaction with any model as soon as it had been superseded by a later one. For to develop a continuous mass market, the automotive industry had to sell to those who could not afford to buy; and it also had to make them—annually if possible—replace what they had bought but had not yet paid for.

This situation led to certain curious practices. You might suppose that automobile dealers were sellers of new cars. They were not. For every new car they sold, they had also to sell at least two old ones, sometimes more. When Joe Doakes wanted a new car, he didn't wish to put down much cash. He turned in his old car to the dealer. No matter what its value, he was usually given credit that approximated a down payment amounting to one-third the cost of the new car he proposed to buy. He then signed twelve or eighteen monthly notes covering the unpaid balance, with interest sometimes running as high as twenty-five percent. These notes were payable, not to the dealer, but to one of several great financing companies. Having completed this transaction, sometimes without any cash payment, Doakes drove off in his new car.

The dealer promptly discounted Doakes's notes; thus receiving, immediately, the cash that Doakes hadn't yet paid anyone for the car he drove off in. Then the dealer put Doakes's old car up for sale, at an established price fixed for its vintage. Usually, he had to accept a still older car from its purchaser. He repeated the note-and-discount routine, and tried to dispose of his newly acquired antique. This sale might involve the acceptance of a still more ancient relic. But at some point in the series of transactions that began with cashless Joe Doakes, a decrepit vehicle reached the junkyard.

About two-thirds of all American car buyers—whether they acquired new or used cars—did their purchasing, like Doakes, on the trade-in and "painless" installment system. This meant that the vast, complex mechanism of mass production and distribution was powered by a national alacrity in signing promissory notes. The economic, tangible reality which these notes represented was an endless procession of cars slowly making their way to the junkyard. But each car in that immense procession was so far removed from the note that it secured, that nobody cared where it happened to be, or who had possession of it. As Thurman W. Arnold pointed out, the procession supported installment paper (a credit instrument) in precisely the same fashion that the gold buried at Fort Knox supported the national currency and credit; everybody believed in its existence, and this universal confidence was sufficient. Faith in the junkyard-bound stream of antiques kept the assembly lines moving at a profitable rate of speed.

Somewhere along that dismal road, even very poor Americans were able to intercept cars that they could afford to buy—on the installment plan. They paid more for these cars than they were worth; so had the dealers who originally accepted them as trade-ins. For it was not to the industry's advantage to permit a cash—and competitive—market in used cars; such a market would inevitably depress prices to a point where Joe Doakes might find it more advantageous to buy a good used car than a new one.

The high cost of installment buying, the fact that the automotive industry was constantly taking mortgages on the future incomes of consumers, did not escape criticism. The social results were dubiously regarded by many authorities. Since installment purchase encouraged Americans to buy cars more costly than their means warranted, it also prompted them to reduce other expenditures; even for such presumably basic needs as food, clothing, shelter and medical service. In this way it operated to contract the economy; and this effect conceivably could reach a point where the market for cars itself would contract. But the major point made by critics was that installment purchase of cars deprived Americans of the satisfaction of important social needs.

To this, in ordinary times, the automotive industry had a ready answer. Without installment buying, it couldn't expand; it couldn't even stabilize production at a high rate. Unless it was able to do so, the jobs of nine million people would be imperilled; the business of one out of every six firms would be adversely affected; the whole national economy would be seriously impaired.

The dilemma appeared to be a real one.

Yet the average American looked at the whole situation from quite another point of view. A new car was a package containing about one hundred thousand miles of transportation. Well-to-do folk bought the whole package. Less advantaged Americans bought whatever portion of the package they felt they dared risk. It might be the last sixty thousand miles. It might be only the last six thousand. But whatever it was, it put wheels under them.

And to be on wheels was the desire of every American. The privilege of mobility was the criterion of happiness, the evidence of personal success. Was it not, therefore, more important than anything else? The conviction that it was had created the nation's most brutalizing industry, its most rebellious labor union, its largest corporate colossus, its second largest fortune.

And it had, besides, completely transformed the society and civilization in which Americans lived.

PART THREE

"Listen to voices

in the upper air"

CHAPTER I

Harsh Discords and
Unpleasing Sharps

1 Illustrious Pathfinder

It was Christmas Eve of 1906. Some of the vessels plying up
and down the Atlantic coast of the United States had been
equipped with the newfangled wireless apparatus. On these, in
wireless rooms behind the bridges, operators were sitting at their
instruments, wearing their headsets. Here and there, on land,
amateur tinkerers were tending their homemade receivers to
listen in, as usual, on any messages that might be traveling across
space in the familiar dot-dash of Morse code.

Most of them, picking up the reiterated "CQCQ" that prefaced
a message, eagerly awaited the buzzing of coded text that would

follow. All but a very few were unnerved by a sense of hallucination. Faintly, through their earphones, there came the sound of a man's voice, speaking. Presently, the music of a phonograph record. Then, someone playing a violin. The speaker's voice, unskillfully raised in song . . . On ships at sea, wireless operators shouted for officers to come and listen. Headsets were quickly passed from one man to another. The unnatural experience wasn't a hallucination, after all. To the mystified listeners, it took on the quality of a miracle. For nothing like it had ever been heard before. As far down the coast as Norfolk, Virginia, operators who had listened to the first of all radio broadcasts began reporting its reception to the new wireless station at Brant Rock, eleven miles from Plymouth, Massachusetts.

In the lonely little station, that Christmas Eve, a few scientists, invited to attend the demonstration of wireless telephony, had joined the staff. Everyone was eager and hopeful, but failure would have surprised nobody except the inventor himself. For Professor Reginald Aubrey Fessenden, as his wife remarked long afterwards, seemed to live by the theory advocated in *Through the Looking Glass*: "practise believing so many impossible things before breakfast." Tall, massive, rugged, his broad face fringed with whiskers, Fessenden was a commanding figure, and his air of quiet authority was amply justified, for at the age of forty he had long been recognized as one of the nation's foremost electrical wizards. "The program on Christmas Eve," he wrote later, "was as follows: first a short speech by me saying what we were going to do, then some phonograph music—the music on the phonograph being Handel's 'Largo.' Then came a violin solo by me, being a composition of Gounod called 'O, Holy Night' and ending up with the words, 'Adore and be still' of which I sang one verse, in addition to playing on the violin, though the singing of course was not very good. Then came the Bible text, 'Glory to God in the highest and on earth peace to men of good will,' and finally we wound up by wishing them a Merry Christmas and then saying that we proposed to broadcast again on New Year's Eve." In its form, the first broadcast was likewise the precursor of all radio variety programs.

So swift was the progress of science during the first half of the twentieth century that when Americans, forty years later, read about Fessenden's experiment, they found difficulty in understanding why it had been invested with the quality of magic. Yet in 1906 wireless telegraphy, only a decade old, was the latest of marvels. Wireless telephony, as a means of communication, was held to be a dubious possibility. But the notion of sending out into space, hour after hour and day after day, music and song to entertain listeners, had occurred to nobody. It had not even occurred to Fessenden, who regarded his demonstration, that Christmas Eve, partly as a scientific adventure and partly as a means of securing commercial publicity. For Fessenden, like other contemporary inventors obsessed by the problems of space-bridging, had a clear vision of the pot of gold that might lie at the other end of their elusive rainbow. The examples of Alexander Graham Bell and, more recently, Guglielmo Marconi, gave practical point to their dreams.

Unlike Bell, who was striving to perfect a "harmonic telegraph" when, almost by accident, he succeeded in inventing the telephone, Marconi had conceived his real objective at the very outset. Born in 1874 to an Italian father and an Irish mother, he was fascinated by the theory of electricity from childhood. Scarcely a decade before his birth, the great British physicist James Clerk Maxwell had advanced the theory that electrical impulses travel through space in the form of waves moving with the velocity of light. In 1887, the German physicist Heinrich Hertz confirmed Maxwell's theory by a successful experiment, proving that electrical waves could be sent out at will by an oscillating circuit. Thereafter, the so-called "Hertzian waves" became the subject of experiment in laboratories everywhere. In 1892 the British physicist, Sir William Crookes, writing in the *Fortnightly Review*, first pointed out the possibility of using these waves to achieve "telegraphy across space." All that remained to be discovered, so Crookes asserted, were a method of generating waves of any desired length; more delicate and selective detectors than had been devised; and some form of directional instrument. That same year, the French scientist Edouard Branly invented an improved

appliance for detecting electro-magnetic waves: the Branly coherer.

It was shortly after he read Crookes' essay that young Marconi
began his experiments. He introduced a Morse telegraph instrument into his circuit, perfected Branly's coherer, set up an aerial,
and by 1895 was able to transmit messages for a distance of more
than a mile. Rebuffed by Italian authorities whom he tried to
interest in his invention, Marconi went to England, where he took
out patents. In order to demonstrate his system of wireless telegraphy, he sent and received signals from stations set up in London
on opposite banks of the Thames. British capitalists were quickly
interested, and in 1897 a company was formed—Marconi's Wireless Telegraph Company, Ltd.—to which the youthful inventor
assigned worldwide patent rights for every country except Italy.
British interests had achieved an almost complete monopoly of
cable communication throughout the world, and they now hoped
to set up a worldwide wireless system. In 1899, Marconi came to
the United States, and under the auspices of the Navy Department
made a test of his system. The battleships *New York* and *Massachusetts* were equipped with his installations, and established
communication across thirty-six miles of ocean. Admiral Robley
D. Evans, commander of the fleet, convinced that the era of the
homing pigeon had passed, began pressing the Secretary of the
Navy to equip all naval vessels with Marconi's invention. An
American Marconi company was soon established, the dominant
controlling interest in which was retained by the British company.
But when the Navy sought to buy Marconi equipment for its
ships, the American company, although willing to lease it, refused
to make any outright sale. Incensed at this refusal, naval authorities negotiated for a wireless system produced by a German
inventor. The breach between Marconi and the United States
Navy was destined to have important consequences two decades
later, which would contribute, obliquely, to the American development of radio broadcasting. On Friday, December 13, 1901, the
first wireless signals spanned the Atlantic Ocean. The Morse
telegraphic letter "S," coded as three dots, transmitted by Marconi's station at Poldhu, in Cornwall, was received by the inventor
at St. John's, Newfoundland.

Marconi had liberated telegraphic communication by Morse code from its terrestrial bondage to wires and poles, its aquatic prison in a cable. He had, so to speak, flung it into the skies, made it free of the heavens. But he probably did not realize that he had likewise come within reasonable distance of an even more spectacular miracle. The discovery of a method of putting the human voice on the air, of filling it with music or speech instead of the impersonal clatter of telegraph keys, was made by Fessenden —a self-taught genius who, fundamentally, was a research scientist with an inclination to uncharted fields and a flair for achieving the improbable.

Fessenden, although born in Canada, was of American ancestry. Soon after graduating from college he secured a position at Edison's laboratories in Llewellyn Park and there, to make up for his lack of technical training, he spent his nights studying electrical theory and analytical mechanics. Released when financial difficulties overtook Edison, Fessenden taught electrical engineering at Purdue University and at Western University in Pittsburgh. By this time, he had made some important contributions to electrical theory, and also had perfected several revolutionary inventions. He had read the results of Hertz's experiments as soon as these were published, and his imagination was excited by the possibility of wireless communication. In 1889, even before the publication of Sir William Crookes' inspiring article, Fessenden had urged Edison to let him undertake research in the new field, but his project was not realized. At Purdue, however, and subsequently at Western University, he conducted extensive researches in the production and detection of the Hertzian waves. As a result, by the late 1890s, he became convinced that prevailing methods of transmission and reception were inadequate and that Marconi, who had incorporated these in his system, was launched on what might prove to be a wrong course. Fessenden's hope was to develop an entirely different system. In 1899, the United States Weather Bureau invited Fessenden to develop a system to be used in transmitting its weather forecasts by wireless, and for the next decade he was to be concerned exclusively with the development of the new medium of communication.

Late in 1900, at his Weather Bureau station at Cobb Island,

Maryland, sixty miles down the Potomac from Washington, Fessenden achieved his first notable triumph. He succeeded in transmitting intelligible human speech by wireless, between two masts fifty feet high and one mile apart. This was only five years after Marconi, in Italy, had first sent Morse signals over the same distance. Although the results of Fessenden's trial were far from perfect, they convinced him that he was on the right track. Some months earlier, with the same equipment, he had successfully transmitted telegraphic messages to the Navy wireless station at Arlington, Virginia, over a distance of more than fifty miles. Encouraged by these exploits, the Weather Bureau expanded the number of its experimental stations, and Fessenden concentrated on improving his receiving apparatus. By 1902, his results were sufficiently promising to enlist the interest of two Pittsburgh capitalists, Thomas H. Given and Hay Walker, Jr., who formed the National Electric Signaling Company to exploit Fessenden's patents and finance his subsequent experiments. The new company intended not only to compete, in the field of wireless telegraphy, with the Marconi system and others, but to develop a commercially practicable system of wireless telephony as well. By 1905, Fessenden had developed radical innovations in reception and transmission. Late that year, the company erected twin steel towers, four hundred feet high, at Brant Rock, Massachusetts and Machrihanish, in Scotland, and equipped them with his apparatus. On January 3, 1906, Fessenden established reciprocal message communication between these stations, and thus was the first to achieve two-way transoceanic wireless telegraphy.

It was to the field of wireless telephony however—the future medium of radio broadcasting—that Fessenden made contributions which were unique and destined to be of enduring importance. They were three in number. Two related to receiving equipment, and one to methods of transmission. His first invention was a detector, differing in principle from the crude coherer, and vastly superior to it in sensitivity. In appearance, the device resembled an electric bulb. It was a glass tube containing a filament of wire, one end of which was in contact with a solution of nitric acid. This solution had the peculiar property of so modifying the rapidly vibrating signals released into space that, when hooked up into a circuit with a telephone receiver, the device translated them into clear speech. Fessenden named this instrument the "liquid barretter"; it was equally efficient for purposes of wireless telegraphy, and soon displaced all previous receivers.

Meanwhile, he had attacked the far more difficult problem of inventing a new form of transmitter. For purposes of wireless telephony, the spark transmitter had two notable disadvantages. The alternating current that it created for a carrier was unsteady; as a result, over distance, the phenomena of "fading" and distortion were inevitable. Moreover, it emitted a continuous din which, also being transmitted, effectually drowned out the human voice. What Fessenden wanted was a device that would produce a strong, steady current oscillating above the range of audibility of the human ear. The fastest alternator then known would produce only some five thousand oscillations—or cycles—per second; but up to fifteen thousand were audible as noise. Fessenden, imaginatively exploring the then unknown domain of the higher frequencies, wanted a machine capable of one hundred thousand oscillations every second. No such machine had ever before been conceived.

His quest for a high-speed alternator was all but heartbreaking in its disappointments. He made his own designs, submitted them to various companies, then modified the designs which they produced. He built and rebuilt model after model. Finally, in 1903, Charles P. Steinmetz of the General Electric Company provided him with an alternator capable of ten thousand cycles per second. The following year, Fessenden renewed his request for a one-hundred-thousand-cycle alternator. This seemingly fantastic commission the company turned over, not to Steinmetz, but to a comparatively new member of its engineering staff, Dr. Ernst Frederik Werner Alexanderson, a native of Sweden. Alexanderson within a year furnished Fessenden with an alternator capable of fifty thousand cycles, and it was with this instrument that Fessenden succeeded in establishing two-way wireless communication across the Atlantic, and making the first of all radio broadcasts.

Fessenden's third invention, long afterwards to become of basic importance in radio broadcasting, was a receiver which he named the "heterodyne." This was a device capable of taking an inaudible high frequency, mixing it with a lower one, and obtaining as a workable product the difference between the two—an audible frequency. But there was no need, in 1905, for Fessenden's heterodyne, and it remained without practical use for a dozen years until, during the First World War, Major Edwin Howard Armstrong developed from it his "superheterodyne" system of reception which, still later, became the standard receiver circuit in all radios.

Shortly after making his epochal broadcast in 1906, Fessenden became convinced that wireless telephony was not likely to become commercially practicable, or financially profitable, for many years. He therefore devoted himself to wireless telegraphy, produced an invention which promised to revolutionize its technique, and appeared to be on the very threshold of great fortune when a quarrel with his backers, and subsequent litigation, wrecked his company. In the protracted legal struggle over the rights to his patents, Fessenden eventually sacrificed the use of his wireless inventions. As a result, he turned to other provinces of electrical science, continued making important discoveries, and enjoyed a long and distinguished career. But honors later came to him as the forefather of radio, a development which he had never anticipated, though he had been the first to pursue a course that led to it. For Fessenden was the earliest to conceive, and successfully undertake, the preliminary work that had to be done before the human voice, or music, could be broadcast. He had furnished a sensitive detector capable of snaring them, and reproducing their natural tones. He had taken the first steps in developing a reliable high-frequency current on which to transmit them. He had thus invoked the future.

2　Giver of Power

In 1901, a young Swedish electrical engineer landed for the first time in New York City. Although only twenty-three years old, Ernst F. W. Alexanderson was a graduate of the Royal Technical University of Stockholm, and had also taken a year of postgraduate work at the Technical University of Berlin, chiefly with Professor Slaby, co-inventor of the German Slaby-Arco system of wireless telegraphy. In Berlin he had read Charles P. Steinmetz's *Alternating Current Phenomena*, and this work so excited him that he determined to come to the United States to try to meet its author.

The day after his arrival in New York, Alexanderson went out to the Edison laboratories in New Jersey, hoping merely to catch a glimpse of the great inventor. That he might be able to talk with Edison never occurred to him; in Europe unknown young men were not granted such privileges. But Edison's gatekeeper showed no surprise when Alexanderson explained the purpose of his visit. He said that the inventor would be leaving his laboratory late in the afternoon, and if the young man wished to wait, he could probably have a word with Edison then. To Alexanderson's amazement, his patience was finally rewarded, for he succeeded in having a talk with Edison. This unexpected fortune encouraged him to go to Schenectady, New York, a few weeks later, and call at the home of his idol, the master-magician of the General Electric Company. Admitted and taken to Steinmetz, he was shocked by the physical appearance of the man whom he had expected to find almost godlike. Facing him was a misshapen little hunchback, clad in a black bathing suit, crouched over a table and smoking a long, thick cigar. Steinmetz barked questions at him—about his ambitions, abilities and experience. But, as the interview went on, Alexanderson forgot his inquisitor's gnomelike body, and when Steinmetz began finally to talk of his own work, the young man realized that he was listening to a genius.

In February, 1902, on Steinmetz's recommendation, Alexanderson was employed by the General Electric Company, and two years later became a member of its engineering staff, assigned to work on the designing of generators under Steinmetz's direction. His work was soon recognized as extraordinarily brilliant, but his first outstanding achievement was the production of Fessenden's fifty-thousand-cycle alternator. Later models of this invention, constantly improved, and with its potential continuously augmented, brought him worldwide fame. For the Alexanderson alternator, for many years fundamental in long-distance telephony over land lines as well as over wireless, proved to be an epoch-making invention. Because it was a technological instrument of primary importance, it became a central issue in the high policy of the United States Government. As a result, it led to a development which had immense significance for radio broadcasting—a still non-existent social agency.

In April, 1917, when the United States entered the First World War, the Federal government took over all high-powered wireless stations and placed them under the control of the Navy Department. The government likewise took over all patents in the field of wireless communication, creating a patent pool which made it possible to place orders for equipment with manufacturers irrespective of their individual patent rights. Two years earlier, in the spring of 1915, Guglielmo Marconi had come to the United States in order to persuade Owen D. Young, then head of the legal department of the General Electric Company, to sell the Marconi system exclusive rights to the use of the Alexanderson alternator. These negotiations had been interrupted by a summons from the Italian War Department recalling Marconi to Italy. However, an alternator capable of one hundred thousand cycles was installed in the station of the Marconi company at New Brunswick, New Jersey, which during the war was operated by the Navy. It was due to this alternator that, on January 8, 1918, President Woodrow Wilson was able to transmit to the entire world his momentous address to Congress on the Fourteen Points.

Shortly after the Armistice of November, 1918, the British-controlled Marconi company resumed its negotiations for exclusive rights to the Alexanderson alternator. This became known to the Navy Department. High officials of the Department recalled the Marconi company's refusal to sell its wireless equipment, two decades earlier. They concluded that exclusive possession of the alternator would give a British company absolute control over American wireless communication. They so reported to President Woodrow Wilson, then in Paris. The transmittal of his Fourteen Points to the world had already convinced Wilson that possession of a powerful wireless system was of the greatest strategic importance. He therefore sent Admiral Bullard as his personal emissary to Owen D. Young with a request that the General Electric

Company refuse to grant exclusive use of the Alexanderson alternator to any foreign-controlled wireless system.

Naval authorities nevertheless realized that the General Electric Company had every right to seek a commercial market for the alternator. So they developed a project which, with the approval of Franklin D. Roosevelt, Assistant Secretary of the Navy, was submitted to Owen D. Young. The Navy proposed to Young that the General Electric Company establish a subsidiary to furnish the United States an American-controlled wireless system; the company could then sell its alternators to this subsidiary. One difficulty stood in the way of this project. Neither General Electric, nor any other American company, individually owned all the patents required to create a complete wireless system. But this difficulty was finally solved in 1919 when, with official approval, Owen D. Young organized the Radio Corporation of America, and by negotiating a series of cross-licensing agreements secured for it an equivalent of the wartime patent pool created by the Federal government. This merging of all essential patent rights in a single organization became a major factor in the sensational development of radio broadcasting during the following decade.

Meanwhile, before and during the First World War, Alexanderson had made other inventions in wireless communication almost as valuable as his alternator. He produced a magnetic amplifier which made possible transatlantic wireless telephony. He invented a multiple-tuned antenna ten times more powerful than any previously used. Even more significantly, he brought to final perfection a device that was destined to displace both his alternator and magnetic amplifier. This was the audion, invented by Lee De Forest, which had been improved by Irving Langmuir of the General Electric Company—a celebrated chemist, and future winner of the Nobel Prize—and H. P. Arnold, of the American Telephone and Telegraph Company. To their work, Alexanderson added further technical improvements which eventually gave the world the vacuum tube that became the basic element in all radio broadcasting transmitters and receiving sets. After the First World War, Alexanderson developed the system of tuned radio frequency later incorporated in all selective receiving sets. He also invented the directional antenna; this was to find spectacular use when the

State Department began "beaming" radio programs to foreign lands. His many inventions in the field of radio brought Alexanderson a dramatic personal reward when, in 1923, broadcast descriptions of his six-year-old son, who had been kidnapped, led to the boy's recovery. One year after this episode, he demonstrated a new invention by transmitting the first facsimile message ever sent across the ocean by wireless—a greeting, in his own handwriting, to his father, in Sweden. Dr. Alexanderson was also one of the pioneer workers in the field of television, and in December, 1926, he gave the first demonstration of this new marvel to be offered in the United States.

Although honored by scientists throughout the world, Dr. Alexanderson was scarcely known by the millions of Americans whose lives were daily influenced by his inventions. In 1942, Herbert Asbury published a study of him in *Popular Science*. To Asbury, he seemed very unlike the popular conception of a scientist; he looked like a successful business executive. A graying, brown-eyed man with a close-cropped mustache, his expression was quizzical, his manner kindly. His favorite pastimes were sailing and reading; Asbury reported that his only idiosyncrasy was an apparent fondness for keys. On the end of a long chain attached to his belt, he carried "a bunch of keys and appliances, including can and bottle openers, as large as a grapefruit." Attached to the key-ring was an object which Alexanderson described as his most prized personal possession. It was the first purchase that he had made in the United States; a circular slide rule somewhat larger than a silver dollar. His interest was centered on contributing materially to the winning of the Second World War, then in progress. But he acknowledged another ambition. He had long wished to meet a native of Sweden who, like himself, had made a career in America—the motion-picture actress, Greta Garbo. "But I suppose," Dr. Alexanderson told Asbury, "she's very hard to meet."

3   Father of Radio

On the audion, subsequently perfected as a vacuum tube, was erected the whole structure of radio broadcasting and reception.

The Four Fathers of Radio

Fessenden:
    He Made the First Broadcast
Marconi: He First
        Telegraphed without Wires
Alexanderson: His
        Alternator Was Epoch-Making
De Forest: Radio Broadcasting
            Rests on His Audion

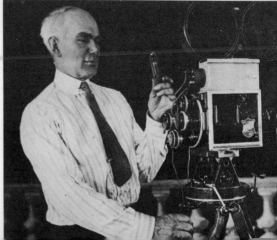

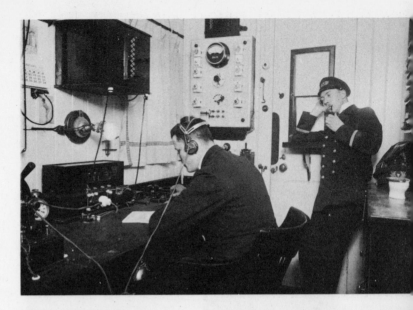

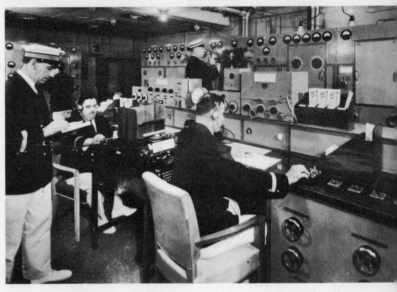

ABOVE: The First Wireless Room on an Ocean Liner

BELOW: Radio Room on the *Normandie*

OPPOSITE PAGE

ABOVE: An Early Crystal Set—An Early Microphone—A "Ham"
at His Hobby—BELOW: Antenna Sprouted in Back Yards

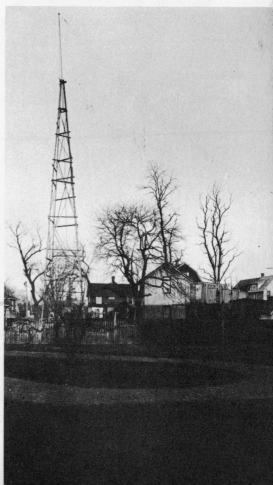

ABOVE: Dr. Frank Conrad's Station in His Pittsburgh Home

BELOW: Broadcasting the Harding-Cox Election Returns over KDKA

A little device made of glass and wire, it was invented in 1906 by Lee De Forest, who had determined to produce a detector more sensitive and efficient than any previously discovered. But by the middle of the twentieth century this electronic instrument was recognized to be man's most versatile servant. Its uses were apparently limitless. It resembled a universal, omnipotent genie. Without it, every radio station would be silent, and every receiver go dead. Television and facsimile broadcasting would cease; long-distance telephone circuits would fail; the movies and loud-speakers would become dumb. Airplanes, lacking radio beacons and instruments for blind landing, would fly under primitive conditions. The audion had given rise to industries said to represent an investment of six billion dollars. It had become uniquely valuable to the sciences of astro-physics, mineralogy and medicine. New purposes to which it could be applied were constantly being discovered. Yet to its inventor, this inexhaustibly useful instrument had brought relatively little happiness, though great fame.

For Lee De Forest had heard his invention derided in a courtroom. He had been severely reprimanded by an eminent jurist who had admonished him to "get a common, garden variety of job and stick to it." He had narrowly escaped criminal conviction on charges of fraud, only because twelve laymen were better able than officers of the law to determine that his audion was not a worthless hoax. He had won and lost four fortunes, and throughout his career had been involved in continuous patent litigation. But, as he neared his eightieth year, De Forest was still actively engaged in electronic research. He was a tall, thin, white-haired man whose emaciated face, with its high cheekbones, grim mouth, and deep-set, burning blue eyes few people ever forgot. And, even in old age, he seemed to be driven by a kind of nervous energy that allowed him no respite.

Born in Council Bluffs, Iowa, in 1873, De Forest was the son of a Congregational minister who shortly afterwards was appointed head of a school for Negroes in Talladega, Alabama. As a Northern child in a small Southern community during the bitter decade after the War between the States, his early years were lonely and unhappy. It was the era of miraculous new inventions: the gas engine, telephone, electric light and dynamo, among others. The poetry of science attracted him, even in boyhood. Reared in extreme poverty, he dreamed of great riches; shunned by other youths, he craved worldwide fame. He determined to become an inventor. By the time he was seventeen he had resolved to enter the Sheffield Scientific School at Yale, and after working his way through a preparatory school he did so. At Yale, he studied under a great scientist and great teacher, Josiah Willard Gibbs, the founder of physical chemistry. It was Gibbs who fired De Forest's ambition to explore the new domain opened by the experiments of Hertz; to take a postgraduate course in electrical engineering, and devote himself to research into the possibilities of wireless communication. Writing his thesis on the Hertzian waves, De Forest received, in 1898, his coveted doctorate, and found compensation for the higher learning in the form of a tedious, routine job in the Chicago plant of the Western Electric Company at the grandiose salary of eight dollars a week.

Like Fessenden, De Forest recognized the need for a detector superior to the Branly coherer, and it was to this problem that he returned every evening, after his day's work. "I study blue prints and apparatus during spare moments," he noted in his journal, "and at night come back to my bedroom to go deeper and deeper into the fascinating world of wireless. I feel that I am on the first rung of the ladder. It is very high and it grows wider and wider as I mount, but I can climb." Eventually, he received permission to conduct his experiments in the Western Electric Company's laboratory; later, in return for some hours of teaching every week, he was allowed to use a laboratory at the Armour Institute. The invention that finally emerged was a new type of detector, which he named the "responder," or electrolytic anti-coherer. By the summer of 1901, in two distance tests at Chicago, this device had proved its efficacy. To publicize it, De Forest hit upon the notion of taking his equipment to New York, and arranging to report, for a press syndicate, the international yacht races to be held off Sandy Hook. Arriving in New York, he learned that the Associated Press had contracted with the Marconi Company to furnish this service, but he persuaded the Publishers' Press Association to put him under contract, and talked a New York business man into financing him to the amount of one thousand dollars. Both news services widely advertised the new project of wireless reporting, but on the day of the race, the Marconi and De Forest signals jammed each other, and the rival press associations secured their reports by flag code. Both, however, announced their results as having been received by wireless, so De Forest achieved the wide publicity that had been his objective.

This publicity soon brought De Forest a visit from Abraham White, a gaudy, optimistic and highly persuasive promoter. The De Forest Wireless Telegraph Company was soon formed; a small factory was set up to manufacture equipment to be designed by De Forest; experimental stations were established in lower New York City, and on Staten Island. Meanwhile, with one of his assistants, he had developed an improved electrolytic detector which began to find a ready sale. But this device resembled Fessenden's liquid barretter, and the similarity provoked a lawsuit which was decided in Fessenden's favor. White, whose frenzied stock-selling campaign had already involved him in financial difficulties, forced De Forest to resign from the company. This decision was probably facilitated by the appearance of a new type of detector destined to play an important role in the eventual creation of an audience for radio.

It was this new device—the crystal detector—which, well into the nineteen-twenties, formed the basis of the homemade sets put together by thousands of amateurs who, spending their evenings wearing earphones, used it to translate into the faint tones of music or speech the equally faint signals in space that drifted down their aerials. In 1906, General Henry C. Dunwoody discovered that carborundum, when connected with an aerial, had the property of detecting signals and converting them into sound. At the same time, Greenleaf W. Pickard discovered that galena and silicon possessed the same property. The Dunwoody and Pickard receivers had the immediate effect of popularizing wireless telegraphy. By moving the point of a wire over the surface of a stone until maximum clarity of reception was attained, any amateur could enjoy the delight of eavesdropping on the world—a far more amusing pastime than listening in on the party-line telephone. The crystal receiver had one disadvantage: there was no feasible method of amplifying the sounds it picked up. But to American youth, it opened a new dimension of experience, a new field of exploration and experiment. All over the land, boys and young men, working in the isolation of their homes, began improvising apparatus with which to fish out of invisible space the clatter of Morse code. Many of them went on to build crude transmitters, and the air eventually was to become clogged with gossip in dot and dash.

To De Forest, out of a job because his company had adopted it, the crystal detector, in 1906, seemed both a nemesis and a challenge. He went to work once again, to devise, if he could, a receiver superior to the best that had been produced. The best in existence was the valve which had been patented in England two years earlier by J. Ambrose Fleming, technical adviser to the British Marconi company, and shortly afterward patented in the United States by the American subsidiary. Fleming's valve looked like an ordinary electric-light bulb. It contained a wire filament that glowed and became hot when the current was turned on, but it also contained a metal plate. It resembled a bulb which, thirty years earlier, Thomas Edison had designed and discarded. Edison's bulb had produced a peculiar effect for which he could not account; it had set up a current that leaped from the filament to the plate. Physicists later explained this "Edison effect" by the fact that the hot filament threw off a stream of electrons which passed to the plate. Fleming, constructing an improved model of the Edison bulb, connected its plate with an antenna, and its filament to the ground. This device reduced the frequency of signals to a point where they became audible when a telephone receiver had been introduced into the circuit.

It was this Fleming valve detector that De Forest set out to improve. For several months, he performed hundreds of experiments with no success. Finally, one day, he bent a piece of wire into the shape of a tiny gridiron. He inserted this "grid" into his glass tube, between the filament and the plate, and attached it to his antenna. The tiny grid acted as a sensitive control of the stream of electrons passing from filament to plate. The addition of this third element made the device a better detector than any which had ever been invented. De Forest named it the audion, and a patent application was drawn up late in December, 1906, but so poor was the inventor that it could not be filed until January 29, 1907, because he lacked the necessary fifteen-dollar fee required by the Patent Office. The miracles of which his audion was eventually to be capable were not foreseen by De Forest, and it was not until six years later that a student at Columbia, Edwin H. Armstrong, discovered that the audion could not only detect radio waves, but could also generate them.

De Forest determined to put his audion to use in experiments with wireless telephony, and during the summer of 1907, from a building on lower Fourth Avenue in New York City, carried on extensive test broadcasts in which he was assisted by Peter Cooper Hewitt, inventor of the mercury vapor lamp and an ardent wireless amateur, who had a laboratory in the tower of Madison Square Garden, three blocks away. Presently, the De Forest Radio Telephone Company was formed by a group of promoters, whose stock-selling activities within a few years would bring the company's officers and De Forest himself under prosecution for fraud. But, at first, the inventor's prospects appeared to be very promising. During one of his test broadcasts, he had invited a young soprano to sing two songs. The wireless officer on duty at the Brooklyn Navy Yard, astonished by hearing them, and unable to identify the source of this mysterious transmission, had promptly reported the matter to a New York newspaper, which printed the item. When De Forest read it, he cleared up the mystery. Meanwhile, the incident came to the attention of Admiral Robley D. Evans, who presumably listened to later broadcasts. One of the first naval officers to realize the importance of wireless, Evans now became a militant advocate of De Forest's system of wireless telephony. When an American fleet departed on a world cruise in the autumn of 1907, twenty of its vessels were equipped with wireless telephones.

De Forest's irrepressible flair for publicity led him, during the summer of 1908, to stage a spectacular feat. He made a broadcast from the Eiffel Tower in Paris, anticipating the future by playing a program of phonograph records. The program was heard as far away as Marseilles, a distance of five hundred miles, and the episode caused a brief sensation. Though his major purpose was to create a market for his telephone system, De Forest had already arrived at a concept of radio broadcasting as a social institution. "My ruling ambition, when I was entirely occupied with my work in radio," he wrote some years later in *Success Magazine*, "was to see the radio telephone, through the universal channels of broadcasting, become a medium for bringing into each home the very best in entertainment, education, information, which the leaders in all these fields have to offer. To see radio become an immeasurably potent medium for rapidly widening the mental horizons of people more isolated, less accessible to the better things in music, lectures and general culture than are the fortunate few who can have these things direct. . . . I saw in the radio telephone the ingredients of a new world cement, as penetrating and binding as it was invisible and intangible, to bind together the various peoples of the continent and finally of the globe in a quickened intelligence, a livelier sympathy, a deeper understanding." During the winter of 1910, De Forest demonstrated this concept in three remarkable broadcasts. For the first, he invited Mme. Marguerite Mazarin, a celebrated member of Oscar Hammerstein's Manhattan Opera Company, to give a brief recital on the air. For the second, he asked his mother-in-law, the eminent suffragist Mrs. Harriot Stanton Blatch, to give a talk on the extension of suffrage to women: this was probably the first lecture, as well as the first example of political propaganda, ever to be put on the air. But De Forest's third program was even more notable. On January 13, 1910, he succeeded in broadcasting, from the stage of the Metropolitan Opera House, a performance of *Cavalleria Rusticana* sung by Mme. Emmy Destinn and Enrico Caruso. This broadcast, the first ever made of an actual performance of opera, was heard by some fifty listeners in New York City and Newark, New Jersey; by wireless amateurs in Connecticut; and it was picked up by the wireless operator of the *S.S. Avon*, at sea.

Shortly afterward a series of misfortunes overtook De Forest in quick succession. The American Marconi company instituted a suit against him, claiming that his audion infringed their patent on the Fleming valve. Dissatisfied stockholders in his wireless telephone company—following a scandal in Great Britain caused by stock manipulation of Marconi shares—complained that they had been defrauded. The unfavorable publicity of a criminal trial, in which De Forest himself was exonerated but certain of his associates were convicted, ruined the fortunes of his company beyond repair. He had meanwhile succeeded in multiplying the capacity of his audion to amplify signals. He achieved this by connecting three audions in what he called a "cascade arrangement" whereby the output of the first was fed into the second, and the output of the second was fed into the third. The result of this arrangement was to increase amplification of sound twenty-seven times. While in the midst of his difficulties, De Forest had demonstrated this new improvement to officials of the American Telephone and Telegraph Company, for use as a telephone relay, and in 1913 the company purchased wire-telephone rights to the audion for fifty thousand dollars.

De Forest, however, retained the right to manufacture his tubes for sale to wireless amateurs, and in order to popularize the audions among the "hams," as they were coming to be known, he resumed his broadcasting activities. In 1916, he offered what was probably the first commercially sponsored broadcast in a program of lately issued records made by the Columbia Phonograph Company, and subsequently brought to his station in Highbridge various singers whom the company had engaged to make records. In the autumn of that year, he arranged the first "radio dance," the music for which was played at his station, and reproduced, through amplifiers, in a home at Elizabeth, New Jersey. And on the night of the presidential election, in conjunction with the *New York American,* he made the first continuous news broadcast ever put on the air, closing his program with the announcement that Charles Evans Hughes had been elected President of the United States—only to learn some days afterwards, with the rest of the nation, that Woodrow Wilson had been returned to office.

When the United States entered the First World War, in

April, 1917, the Federal government ordered all amateur wireless equipment to be disconnected and sealed. De Forest dismantled his station, and devoted himself to manufacturing wireless equipment for military use. During that year he sold his remaining rights in the audion to the American Telephone and Telegraph Company. Though he resumed broadcasting for a brief period after the war, leadership in this field passed into other hands, and De Forest presently retired from it. But he had not only provided the device which was to become the foundation of a major social agency. He had furnished the agency, even before its birth, with an ideal of social purpose and responsibility.

4   Great Inventor

"Had it not been for the radio amateur, there could have been no radio broadcast, and no radio industry as it exists today." So Lee De Forest, in the 1920s told Hiram Percy Maxim, president of the American Radio Relay League, the national organization of "hams." The man who most vividly illustrated the truth of this verdict was Edwin Howard Armstrong, professor of electrical engineering at Columbia University.

Like De Forest himself, Armstrong decided to become an inventor in boyhood. In 1904, at the age of fifteen, he read an account of Marconi's career, and surmised that the field of wireless telegraphy was still sufficiently new to yield important discoveries. Presently, in the attic room of his family's home in Yonkers, New York, he fitted up a wireless set, and thereafter spent most of his free time beside it, wearing a pair of earphones and listening eagerly for whatever signals might flow down his aerial. The weak detectors then available seldom picked up communications originating at any considerable distance, so that for the most part Armstrong overheard nothing more momentous than the coded chatter of other suburban hams. But this limitation, exasperating him as it did all enthuisastic amateurs, furnished a point of departure for his subsequent research.

Entering Columbia in 1909, he took courses for a degree in electrical engineering and carried on independent experiments in the laboratories after classes. He was still searching for a better detector when De Forest's audion tube came on the market, but although it was a vast improvement over any previous one, Armstrong was dissatisfied with its performance. He had an intuition that De Forest had not thoroughly understood the potentialities of his own invention, and that the tube, if handled in some different fashion, might prove to be a far more sensitive instrument than De Forest, or anyone else, surmised. There followed a long period of patient, careful investigation. One night in the autumn of 1912, he was thrilled by detecting signals from distances never previously spanned. Further experiments revealed that if he took the radio signal as it came from the audion, and fed back part of it to reinforce the signal coming into the tube, the reinforced signal would, in turn, be amplified further by the audion. Continuous reinforcement would increase the volume of the detected signal several thousand times. This was the principle of Armstrong's regenerative or "feed-back" circuit, which made possible the reception of transcontinental and transoceanic signals, and became fundamental to the development of commercial radio. But when Armstrong appealed to his father for money with which to patent his discovery, he was refused. An uncle, to whom he then applied, also refused him, but advised that he have the original drawing of his invention notarized, as a precaution, and Armstrong did this on January 31, 1913.

In his last year at Columbia, Armstrong took courses with Professor Michael I. Pupin, professor of electro-mechanics and himself a famous inventor. Continuing his experiments with the audion, Armstrong noticed that it was emitting a curious whistling noise. This led him to a second momentous discovery about regeneration. He found that when the amount of the signal fed back into the audion attained a certain level, the audion ceased merely to amplify high frequency waves, and began itself to generate them. This new principle, applicable to radio transmission rather than radio reception, revealed a second use for his regenerative circuit that was to become fully as important as the first. For by this discovery, Armstrong paved the way for the modern continuous wave system of broadcasting, and the vacuum tube transmitter.

After receiving his engineering degree in 1913, Armstrong accepted a position as assistant in the engineering school in order to continue using its laboratory. He applied for patents on his two inventions, and began working with Professor Pupin on the problem of eliminating static from radio reception. His regenerative circuit, for which a patent was issued in 1914, made a sensation among scientists concerned with wireless, and its significance was widely recognized. But Lee De Forest, as inventor of the audion tube, challenged Armstrong's claims, and filed an application for a patent, claiming prior invention of the circuit in both its amplifying and generating uses. Litigation over this issue continued for twenty years. In 1934, in a decision deplored by scientists and astounding to the radio world, the Supreme Court handed down a verdict in De Forest's favor. When, after this decision, Armstrong returned to the Institute of Radio Engineers the medal it had awarded him for his invention of the regenerative circuit, the Institute promptly re-awarded it. And subsequently, Armstrong received the medal of the Franklin Institute, and the Edison medal of the American Institute of Electrical Engineers, with specific inclusion of the regenerative circuit among the inventions for which these honors were bestowed.

It was while he was an officer of the Signal Corps in France, during the First World War, that Armstrong perfected the heterodyne principle, originally discovered by Fessenden, and developed his superheterodyne system of reception which, combined with the vacuum tube, was eventually to become the standard circuit in all radio receivers. In 1923, Armstrong undertook to demonstrate its merits before high officials of the Radio Corporation of America. He took a radio set, into which it had been built, to the apartment of Owen D. Young, and when he emerged from the elevator, carrying the set in his arms, the radio was in full operation, with an opera program in progress—an achievement unprecedented at a time when all sets required the use of an antenna. This demonstration so amazed the assembled company officials that they promptly decided to adopt the novelty. Within a very few years, it revolutionized the production of radio sets. The antenna disappeared, and receivers achieved a sensitiveness and selectivity previously unknown.

In 1935, Armstrong announced a development which, at the middle of the century, seemed likely to rank as his greatest contribution to the field of radio. This brought to a triumphant conclusion his long quest for a means of overcoming static, and it inaugurated an entirely new system of broadcasting. The standard system of broadcasting—known as amplitude modulation—imposed sound on a radio wave by varying the amplitude, or strength, of the wave. Armstrong's system—known as frequency modulation—imposed sound on a radio wave by varying its frequency, or pitch. Three major results were produced by this change in method. The new system virtually eliminated static whether man-made or the effect of such atmospheric disturbances as thunderstorms. It achieved a degree of fidelity in broadcasting incalculably superior to that of the standard system. And since FM transmission operated in the ultra-high frequencies, it opened an entirely new section of the radio spectrum to broadcasting. The success of the revolutionary new "high fidelity" system was made apparent by two facts. At the end of 1948, there were more than 700 commercial FM broadcasting stations operating in the United States. And annual production of FM receiving sets had reached a total of three million.

5 Industrial Prophet

On the last day of September, 1906, the chief engineer of the Marconi Wireless Telegraph Company of America refused to hire a telegraph operator, but offered the applicant a job as office boy at five dollars and a half a week. The applicant accepted the job. His name was David Sarnoff, and he was fifteen years old. Born in Russia, he had been brought to the United States by his parents six years earlier. As the eldest of five children, the death of his father had forced him to become a wage-earner at the age of ten. He had worked as a newsboy, then became a telegraph messenger. From his meager earnings he had bought an instrument, taught himself Morse code, and after six months had thought himself qualified for an operator's job. At the Marconi Company he studied persistently, and in 1908 was sent to the station at Nantucket to qualify as an operator. Two years later, he was made manager of the station at Sea Gate, New Jersey.

By this time, he had read every treatise on wireless telegraphy that he could procure, and was eager to take a course in electrical engineering at Pratt Institute in Brooklyn. When the John Wanamaker stores made arrangements with the Marconi system to establish experimental point-to-point stations in their New York and Philadelphia establishments, Sarnoff applied for assignment to the New York store, and was transferred there. In April, 1912, he picked up a terrifying message. "The *S.S. Titanic* ran into iceberg. Sinking fast." The great liner, new queen of the seas, was on her maiden voyage, westbound to New York. The *S.S. Carpathia*, receiving the same message at sea, steamed through the fog toward the doomed liner. Apprised of the tragedy, President William Howard Taft ordered off the air all wireless stations except those engaged in rescue work. Meanwhile Sarnoff sat at his instrument board for seventy-two hours without relief, picking up the heart-breaking details of the disaster, maintaining New York's only contact with the desperate search for survivors. Seven hundred and six of those who had been on board—largely women and children in lifeboats, or clinging to driftwood—were saved; fifteen hundred and seventeen perished in mid-ocean. That any lives were saved was due only to wireless, and the disaster profoundly impressed on the public the importance of radio service. A new law was passed by Congress, strengthening the existing requirements concerning equipment and operators on seagoing vessels. But out of the tragedy there had come a rumor that the work of rescue was impeded by the chit-chat communications of operators at sea. So Congress passed another law, requiring the licensing of operators and transmitting stations, including all amateurs.

By 1916, having risen through a series of promotions, Sarnoff was assistant traffic manager of the Marconi company. In that year he sent a memorandum to Edward J. Nally, the company's general manager, proposing an innovation which, at the time, must have seemed little short of fantastic. "I have in mind a plan of development which would make radio a household utility in the same sense as a piano or phonograph," he wrote. "The idea is to bring music into the house by wireless. . . . For example, a radio telephone transmitter, having a range of say twenty-five to fifty miles can be installed at a fixed point where instrumental or vocal music or both are produced. . . . The receiver can be designed in the form of a simple 'radio music box' and arranged for several different wave lengths, which could be changeable with the throwing of a single switch or pressing of a single button . . ." Painstakingly, and in detail, the twenty-five-year-old visionary went on to elaborate his project. The music box could be supplied with amplifying tubes and a loudspeaker, and a small loop antenna could be developed to go with it. Thus the music box could be placed on a table in the parlor or living room, the switch set, and the transmitted music be received. This device would do away with the headsets in current use. Within the radius specified, there would be hundreds of thousands of families, all capable of being served simultaneously by a single transmitter. In addition to music, lectures could be broadcast; events of national importance could be announced and instantly received; baseball scores could be transmitted through the air by the use of one set installed at the Polo Grounds. "This proposition," he argued, "would be especially interesting to farmers and others living in outlying districts removed from cities. By the purchase of a 'radio music box' they could enjoy concerts, lectures, music, recitals, etc., which may be going on in the nearest city within their radius."

By methods of mass production, Sarnoff suggested, his projected "radio music box" could be sold to the public for about seventy-five dollars; he thought one million sets might be sold within three years. "Aside from the profit to be derived from this proposition," he pointed out, "the possibilities for advertising for the company are tremendous; for its name would ultimately be brought into the household and wireless would receive national and universal attention." In making this suggestion, Sarnoff was not proposing that revenue could be earned by the sale of advertising time on the air—a project for which he would later offer a remarkable alternative. His memorandum was based on the assumption that the Marconi company would continue to do its major business in the field of wireless telegraphic service. But he felt that broadcasting could be made a secondary, and highly

profitable, activity. Lacking privacy of communication, radio telephony was unlikely to yield a large commercial traffic in the
immediate future. Fessenden and De Forest had already discovered
this, to their cost. But it was a fact that the chiefs of great communications services were not yet ready to acknowledge. Sarnoff,
in his memorandum, was the first to suggest a means of making
wireless telephony a profitable service.

But his project was actually a major prophecy. For it added,
to the experiments in broadcasting previously made, one vital new
element: the "radio music box." Sarnoff understood—as did
nobody else at the time—that, so long as listening was confined
to individuals each equipped with a headset, the radio audience
would inevitably be limited to youthful fans. Not until listening
could be made a group pastime, through an instrument like the
phonograph playable in the family living room, would radio
emerge from infancy. Only such an instrument would enable it
to become a medium of mass communication, a social agency of
incredible power, and a great independent industry.

This was the development prefigured by Sarnoff's memorandum. Foresight is not universally recognized and, like many
another visionary, Sarnoff had to wait.

CHAPTER II

Speak the Speech, I Pray You

1 Born in the Garret

When the United States entered the First World War, there were between three and five thousand amateur wireless operators in the United States. The Navy established two wartime radio schools, at Harvard University and Mare Island, San Francisco. Thus, by the time hostilities ceased, the number of "hams" had almost doubled. Because the war had brought about notable technical advances in radio telephony, most of them were keenly interested in this branch of communication. Their interest became a major factor in the development of broadcasting. For they constituted the first radio audience, and their home-built sets furnished the laboratory in which broadcasting received its earliest practical field tests. But broadcasting, as a commercial enterprise, was born of economic competition. It was an incidental result of a brief, spectacular warfare between a group of industrial titans. It was, so to speak, an accident, undesired and unforeseen; and its implications for the future were scarcely recognized by the magnates whose bitter rivalry produced it.

During the war, extensive research in radio telephony had been carried on by three great corporations. The General Electric Company of Schenectady and the Westinghouse Electric and Manufacturing Company of Pittsburgh dominated the manufacture of electrical equipment. As competitors, each wished to secure a preponderant share of the business that would result from any expansion of wireless communication. In this possible expansion the American Telephone and Telegraph Company was also vitally concerned. For, in addition to dominating the nation's telephone system, this company, through a subsidiary, the Western Electric Company, was likewise engaged in the manufacture of electrical equipment. To all of these great corporations, the future of radio implied only one possibility: the furnishing of facilities for commercial service by coded wireless telegraph or wireless telephone. In these circumstances, control of patent rights to fundamental inventions was of primary importance to all. General Electric owned rights to the Alexanderson alternator, the most efficient of all long-distance wireless apparatus. American Telephone and Telegraph had purchased rights to De Forest's audion tube. The Westinghouse Company, during the war, had assigned its assistant chief engineer, Dr. Frank Conrad, to the task of developing an improved radio-telephone transmitter.

This was the situation when, in 1919, officials of the Navy Department suggested to Owen D. Young of General Electric that he organize a subsidiary to create and operate an American-owned wireless system. The Radio Corporation of America was formed for this purpose. It promptly acquired the property and business of the American Marconi company, and negotiated exclusive agreements for the handling of its traffic with the British Marconi system, and the systems of the principal European countries. Shortly after the United States Navy relinquished its wartime control of high-powered commercial wireless stations, the Radio Corporation negotiated an alliance with the American Telephone and Telegraph Company. This covered a pooling of patent rights. In addition, the Radio Corporation became the selling agency for the amateur wireless equipment that was produced by General Electric and Western Electric.

These developments quite naturally perturbed the officials of the Westinghouse Company. They determined to enter the field of wireless service, and compete with their rival, General Electric. Their first step was to purchase control of a moribund corporation, the legal successor of the company originally organized to promote Fessenden's wireless system. Their second step was an attempt to gain a victory in the matter of patent rights. They purchased control of the regenerative circuit invented by Edwin H. Armstrong. By this time, the Westinghouse Company was committed to an expenditure of two and one half million dollars. Then its officials learned, to their dismay, that they had suffered an overwhelming defeat. By its exclusive arrangements with foreign wireless systems, the Radio Corporation had prevented them from entering the field of worldwide wireless service.

Meanwhile, the Federal government had rescinded its wartime prohibition of amateur wireless stations, and hams were once again free to operate. In April, 1920, Dr. Frank Conrad of the Westinghouse Company relicensed the station which, prior to the war, he had installed on the upper story of his garage in Pittsburgh. There, at night, he proposed to continue his experiments in radio telephony, particularly in the testing of transmitting equipment, and among the company's employees he had set up numerous listening posts to check the success of his broadcasts. He soon became bored by the necessity of talking on the air, and decided to use phonograph records as the material of his broadcasts. But this innovation had a disconcerting result. He presently began receiving letters and telephone calls from hams throughout the region, making such odd requests as that he broadcast particular records, or conduct a program at some specified hour. Finally, in the summer of 1920, Conrad announced that he would broadcast for two hours every Wednesday and Saturday night. This meant that he needed a fresh supply of records for each program; he arranged to borrow them from a local dealer, and by way of return mentioned the dealer's name as his source of supply. The dealer soon found that the records which Conrad used were out-selling all others. This was perhaps the first demonstration of the effectiveness of radio advertising.

As time passed, the philanthropic scientist grew weary of his self-imposed public service. His two young sons occasionally re-placed him, and introduced into the programs the novelty of local talent. The audience multiplied amazingly. Listeners de-manded more and more entertainment from this novel amateur studio; there were requests for baseball scores, and talks on radio. The Westinghouse plant experienced a small-scale boom in the sale of parts necessary to the home assembly of sets with which the growing audience was listening to Conrad's programs. Finally, in the Pittsburgh *Sun*, on September 20, 1920, an enterprising depart-ment store advertised radio receivers which would enable the public to pick up "Dr. Conrad's popular broadcasts."

In this advertisement H. P. Davis, vice-president of Westing-house, saw a means whereby the company might eventually retrieve its large and unprofitable investment in radio. Like Sarnoff, four years earlier, Davis suddenly realized that the efforts being made to develop radio telephony as a service for confidential communica-tion were misguided. But its radical defect of absolute publicity endowed it with a far different sphere of usefulness. Uniquely, it could be made the medium of instantaneous collective communi-cation. The success of Conrad's informal broadcasts proved that the appeal of its mystery fascinated a large segment of the public. Davis surmised that, properly exploited, the radio program might be made a service of universal application, which millions of Americans would be eager to receive. He was convinced that if Westinghouse put broadcasting on a permanent basis, it could develop an immense market for the sale of receiving sets. As yet, the company had manufactured no completely assembled sets, but nothing prevented them from doing so.

Davis gave orders for the immediate construction of a broad-

casting station on the roof of the tallest building of the Westinghouse plant in East Pittsburgh, which was licensed by the
Deparment of Commerce on October 27, 1920, and assigned the
call letters KDKA. The station was a primitive affair, a small
penthouse built of matched sheathing which, in addition to the
transmitter and microphone, contained two fifty-watt oscillators
and four fifty-watt modulators. Davis had determined to inaugurate broadcasting on the night of November 2nd, by announcing
returns of the presidential election in which Senator Warren
G. Harding and James M. Cox were the contestants. Bulletins
from all over the country were to be relayed to the station by
telephone from the newsroom of the Pittsburgh *Post*. The company had widely advertised its innovation. Special receiving sets
had been manufactured. These were distributed to officers of the
company and various other prominent individuals; some were set
up in stores and other public places throughout the city. On the
night of November 1st the transmitting equipment was tested and
found to be unsatisfactory. Adjustments were hastily made on the
following day. Dr. Frank Conrad became very nervous over the
prospect of the approaching broadcast, and before it began he
rushed to the amateur station in his garage, in order to take over
the program should anything go amiss at KDKA. Fortunately, the
broadcast proceeded without misadventure. About one thousand
listeners in the Pittsburgh region, and others elsewhere, heard
bulletins throughout the evening, and finally learned that Harding had been elected President of the United States.

As Davis had hoped, the inauguration of a permanent, professional broadcasting service was widely described by the press
throughout the country. The company was suddenly swamped by
orders for receiving sets, and presently negotiations were begun
by Owen D. Young to have Westinghouse enter the Radio Corporation of America. It joined that combination in June, 1921,
becoming a party to the collective patent pool and, like the other
members, appointing the Radio Corporation as sales agency for
its receiving sets. To create a nation-wide market for its sets,
Westinghouse realized that it must set up widely scattered broadcasting stations to bring entertainment to prospective purchasers.

By the autumn of 1921, it began operating WBZ at Springfield, Massachusetts, to serve New England; WJZ in Newark, to serve the metropolitan New York area; and KYW to serve Chicago and its vicinity.

Meanwhile, at the end of January, 1920, nine months before Station KDKA went on the air, David Sarnoff had revived his project for a "radio music box." As general manager of the Radio Corporation, he had sent to Owen D. Young, the chairman of its board of directors, the same memorandum that he had submitted to his superior at the Marconi company four years earlier. Though the project was apparently approved by Young, it met scant favor from the conservative directors. Sarnoff's prediction that sales of the device would produce a revenue of seventy-five million dollars within three years impressed them as being absurd. (The corporation's actual sales of home instruments between 1922 and 1924 were to total eighty-three and one half million dollars.) Besides, they had no desire to embark on the adventure of broadcasting; their interest was confined to the development of wireless communications service, and the machinery which it would require. So they took no action on Sarnoff's memorandum except—as a concession to Young's interest in it—to appropriate two thousand dollars for the experimental production of a model "music box" or "radiola."

Sarnoff, however, conceived a bold maneuver. For July 2, 1921, the boxing promoter Tex Rickard had arranged a great event. On that date Jack Dempsey and the French pugilist Georges Carpentier were to do battle for the heavyweight championship of the world. Sarnoff determined to broadcast this contest, and thus test the appeal of broadcasting for the metropolitan audience. The fight was to be staged in an open-air arena in Jersey City, Boyle's Thirty Acres. As yet, KDKA in Pittsburgh was the only broadcasting station operating in the country. To carry through his project, Sarnoff had to borrow a transmitter ordered by the Navy but not yet delivered. An antenna was strung between two towers of the Lackawanna Railroad in Hoboken, and a telephone circuit set up between the transmitter and the arena in Jersey City. Major J. Andrew White, then editor of *Wireless Age*, undertook to describe the fight, blow by blow, for the invisible audience. No sports event had ever been broadcast in New York, so White lacked any precedent to guide him. But his clear, enthusiastic, exciting word picture of the battle established a precedent for all future announcers. Later historians estimated that the broadcast was heard by some two hundred thousand sports fans in the metropolitan area. The response, by mail, telegram and telephone was phenomenal. It was apparently this daring experiment that finally persuaded officials of the Radio Corporation to participate in broadcasting. When station WJZ went on the air, it did so as the joint enterprise of Westinghouse and R.C.A.

Out in Pittsburgh, meanwhile, station KDKA, pioneering in the composition of programs, developed certain features that were later to become standard elements in broadcasting. A staff orchestra and a "little symphony," both composed of amateur musicians drawn from the company's employees, gave regularly scheduled performances. On January 2, 1921, the first church service to be put on the air was broadcast from the Calvary Episcopal Church. On January 15th, when Herbert Hoover was guest of honor at a banquet of the Duquesne Club, the radio audience heard his appeal for funds for European relief—and sent in contributions of more than twenty-five thousand dollars. One month later, Representative Alice M. Robertson, recently elected to Congress by the state of Oklahoma, made an address. Other innovations followed quickly: a boxing match in April; a performance at a local theater, in May; baseball games at Forbes Field during the summer; the market reports of the Department of Agriculture.

By such novelties as these, the future was being anticipated. But the economic foundation of broadcasting had not yet been discovered. Its commercial function was to promote the sale of receiving sets.

2 Charm the Air to Give a Sound

Eighteen months after the inauguration of broadcasting, two hundred and twenty stations were on the air in the United States, and a new craze was sweeping the country. "The rate of increase in the number of people who spend at least a part of their evening in listening in is almost incomprehensible," declared an editorial in the first issue of *Radio Broadcast*, in May, 1922. "To those who have recently tried to purchase receiving equipment, some idea of this increase has undoubtedly occurred, as they stood perhaps in the fourth or fifth row at the radio counter waiting their turn, only to be told when they finally reached the counter that they might place an order and it would be filled when possible. The movement is probably not even yet at its height. It is still growing in some kind of geometrical progression." Speculating about the future, *Radio Broadcast* surmised that "before the market for receiving apparatus becomes approximately saturated, there will be at least five million receiving sets in this country." In the next issue, the magazine's reporter on the Pacific coast described what had happened in that region. "The average man on the street had never more than vaguely heard of radio until two months ago. . . . All of a sudden it hit us. The first most of us saw of it . . . was in first-page, first-column headlines from New York . . . proclaiming that the East had gone mad over radio. Within twelve hours, the interest swept the coast."

During the autumn of 1922, listeners in the vicinity of New York gained a notion of the possible promise implicit in this new form of entertainment. Grantland Rice, leading sportswriter for the *Tribune*, gave a play-by-play account of the World Series baseball games. A similar report of the Princeton-Chicago football game was broadcast direct from the gridiron. A concert of the Philharmonic Orchestra was put on the air from Carnegie Hall. For the first time since De Forest's experiment, twelve years earlier, a performance at the Metropolitan Opera House reached the radio audience. Even earlier, station WJZ had made two prophetic broadcasts from its studio. A performance of Mozart's comic opera, *The Impresario*, with piano accompaniment, had been given by the members of William Wade Hinshaw's Little Opera Company, on their return from a long tour. And the popular comedian Ed Wynn—later to become a great star of radio—had brought to the microphone some numbers from *The Perfect Fool*, his current Broadway success. On this occasion, Wynn missed the response of an audience, and suffered from "mike-fright"—and, to save the show, the announcer hastily

assembled the entire personnel of the station: electricians in shirt
sleeves, scrub-women with their skirts tucked up, telephone operators and others whose applause restored Wynn's confidence.

Such events as these were, however, exceptional. For radio
stations were not yet spending money to bring talent to the microphone. Their managers were therefore under the necessity of
seeking to recruit, from the theater, vaudeville and the concert
stage, performers willing to contribute their services for the sole
reward of publicity. Surprisingly enough, they were often successful. The team of Billy Jones and Ernie Hare, whose phonograph
records had an immense sale, appeared regularly and, as a result,
became the earliest great stars of radio. The astute manager of
the Capitol Theater, a new movie palace on Broadway, quickly
perceived the audience-building potentialities of the new medium;
as "Roxy," presiding over the weekly antics of "Roxy's Gang,"
S. L. Rothafel soon achieved personal celebrity; so also did Major
Edward Bowes, who succeeded him after three years.

But, while talent was not being paid, the programs of even
major stations sometimes had an air of hasty improvisation.
Versatility and showmanship were requisite qualities for announcers, who identified themselves not by name but by assigned
initials. Despite their pseudo-anonymity, they rapidly acquired
loyal fans, like the unnamed favorites of early movies. At WEAF,
the station of the American Telephone and Telegraph Company,
there was Albert V. Llufrio, an announcer who was also an excellent pianist, and who was quite capable of putting on a one-man
program whenever need arose. There was also Graham McNamee,
a singer by profession, who had dropped into the station one day
to find out what radio was all about, and had promptly been hired
as staff-entertainer and announcer. A similarly casual entry into
the profession was made by Milton J. Cross, a student at the
Institute of Musical Art, who had visited station WJZ at the
instigation of a friend. Taken on as a singer, like McNamee,
Cross' remarkable speaking voice caused him to be pressed into
service as an announcer. Both Cross and McNamee were to
become among the foremost personalities of radio, known and
admired by millions of Americans.

Equally celebrated, over a long period, was the earliest "radio girl," Miss Vaughn de Leath, who had first appeared on the air for Lee De Forest. Miss de Leath for a time acted as manager of one of the smaller New York stations, serving also as its principal performer. She was a composer and singer, a talented pianist, and had likewise had a brief career as an actress. Her versatility and her wide professional acquaintance enabled her to put on programs which found immediate favor with a growing audience. On the occasion of one of her birthdays, a group of professional friends joined her at the station and improvised an all-star program in her honor. While it was in progress, allusion was made to the occasion which it celebrated, and something was said about Miss de Leath's fondness for angora cats. By the following day, there had arrived for her at the station two truckloads of birthday gifts, and five angora kittens. From the very outset, the radio public felt a deep sense of personal attachment to its chosen favorites.

This was to be demonstrated, rather spectacularly, by the later career of another early star, Miss Jessica Dragonette, a talented singer. In the late nineteen-thirties, after a financial disagreement with her sponsors, Miss Dragonette retired from radio. In some cities, fan-clubs announced that they would boycott radio until she returned. She set out on a concert tour. In Minneapolis, fifteen thousand people ignored a taxi strike and a blizzard to hear her sing; and later, an audience of one hundred and fifty thousand gathered in Grant Park, in Chicago, where she appeared as soloist at one of the city's free summer concerts. In the very early years of radio, singers and musicians of established fame ignored its existence. Their lack of interest continued until after New Year's Day of 1926, when Miss Lucrezia Bori, soprano of the Metropolitan Opera, and John McCormack, celebrated Irish tenor, gave a joint broadcast. By that time, transmission and reception had been greatly improved, and radio had found, in the commercial sponsor, a means of paying those who entertained its audience. Over the years, radio appearances were to become so highly profitable to opera singers that many of the more popular ones would give few performances at the Metropolitan, retaining their connection with the opera chiefly because of its prestige.

That musicians held radio in disesteem was not surprising. Even the early audience, once its novelty had worn off, found the conditions of reception discouraging. For the rapid multiplication of broadcasting stations, especially in metropolitan centers, produced chaos on the air waves. Interference and jamming were common phenomena, for only two channels were available to all stations; agreements between stations to "share time" were constantly broken. Listeners often found themselves receiving, not one but two or more broadcasts simultaneously. The Department of Commerce, charged with the supervision of commercial wireless communication under a Federal law enacted in 1912, before broadcasting existed, could do little to remedy this condition. Order was not imposed on the air waves until 1926, when Congress passed new legislation specifically dealing with broadcasting, and created the Federal Radio Commission to administer its provisions. In 1934, under more comprehensive legislation enacted by Congress, this body was superseded by the Federal Communications Commission, which thereafter exercised supervisory and regulatory powers over the radio industry.

3   Disinterested Good Is Not Our Trade

By the spring of 1922, it seemed certain that broadcasting was to become a permanent and expanding enterprise. In the opinion of David Sarnoff, it promised to be an activity of national, rather than merely local, scope. Broadcasting stations, he surmised, would "ultimately be required to entertain a nation." What kind of agency could best undertake so specialized and extensive a function? And how should this operation be financed? Sarnoff submitted a program for the future to the directors of the Radio Corporation. He proposed that they establish a separate, non-profit corporation to conduct broadcasting as a public service, free from any imputation of "money-making." Plans could be devised, he predicted, whereby such an agency "will receive public support and, in fact, there may even appear on the horizon a public benefactor who will be willing to contribute a large sum in the form of an endowment." For broadcasting stations, under this plan, would have the status of public libraries or museums. But, pending the arrival of a benevolent millionaire, Sarnoff proposed that public-service broadcasting be financed by the allocation of a fixed percentage of income derived from the sale of radio sets manufactured by the companies which owned the Radio Corporation.

This program was rejected. For bitter dissension had already broken out among the industrial titans who founded the Radio Corporation. This dissension was to be prolonged for a decade, until they voluntarily withdrew from the corporation in order to save it from prosecution—and possible dissolution—under the anti-trust law. But, just as the birth of broadcasting had resulted from their commercial rivalry, so its ultimate nature was to be determined by their subsequent conflict. In the radio industry, as earlier in the motion-picture and automobile industries, conflict was bred of the attempt to create a monopoly through control of basic patents.

The origin of dissension among the great companies was the phenomenon of broadcasting. The Radio Corporation had been set up to furnish transoceanic wireless service; its sale of wireless equipment to amateurs had been envisaged as merely a sideline. But in 1922, the corporation's income from wireless service was slightly less than three million dollars, while its income from the sale of radio sets exceeded eleven and one quarter millions. Broadcasting had produced a situation which none of the founders had foreseen—and for which their complex arrangements about patents had failed to make explicit provision. Under these arrangements, the Radio Corporation, the General Electric Company and the Westinghouse Company were prevented from using broadcasting as a source of direct revenue. All three companies operated radio stations, and the fact that they were prohibited from operating them for profit may have had some bearing on David Sarnoff's proposal to make broadcasting a public service. For, under existing arrangements, this disability did not apply to the American Telephone and Telegraph Company. If broadcasting could be technically defined as a form of one-way communication service furnished by wireless telephony, the Telephone Company was privileged to conduct it as a business for profit. Furthermore, the

Telephone Company occupied a position of strategic advantage. The use of telephone lines was essential in order to transmit programs (such as sports events) which originated at any point remote from broadcasting stations. The use of telephone lines would also prove to be essential for "chain" or "network" broadcasting, when a group of stations were linked to transmit a single program. Both these uses could be—and would be—denied to others.

This was the situation when, in the late summer of 1922, the American Telephone and Telegraph Company determined to invade the field of broadcasting. It opened station WEAF in New York City, having installed transmission apparatus far superior to that of any other station. Its station, the company announced, would furnish paid commercial service to "anyone desiring to use these facilities for radio broadcasting." No prospective clients responded, so the company sent out salesmen to bring in business. As a result, the first of all commercially sponsored radio programs went on the air at five-fifteen in the afternoon on August 28, 1922. Probably nobody connected with this broadcast realized that it presaged a day when Americans, tuning in their radio sets, would find that every passing hour, as it struck, was the private property of a manufacturer of watches; would listen to a half-hour program of excellent music interrupted four times by eulogies of a brand of tobacco; would acknowledge the sovereignty of hucksters over the dimensions of time and space. Yet all these things were prefigured by the first commercial radio program: a ten-minute advertising talk extolling "Hawthorne Hall," a recently completed co-operative apartment house in Jackson Heights, across the East River from Manhattan Island.

The injection of advertising into radio prorgams was resented by many listeners. It was severely condemned by *Radio Broadcast*. But the Telephone Company, disregarding all protests, continued to add to its paying clients. Four months later, sixteen sponsors were broadcasting commercial programs from its station. The roster included department stores, real-estate enterprises, automobile companies, manufacturers of rubber goods and radio appliances, oil dealers, an advertising agency, and the Y.M.C.A., which put an eminent clergyman, Dr. S. Parkes Cadman, on the air to drum up a desire for the spiritual life. Most of these advertisers offered no more stimulating entertainment than brief talks. The department stores favored bedtime stories for children. After some months, one of them resorted to the innovation of musical programs. Presently, dance music became the chief reliance of advertisers broadcasting during the evening hours. The practice of selling "time on the air" was quickly adopted by other broadcasting stations in the metropolitan area, and soon spread across the country. Stations operated by the Radio Corporation were, however, debarred from commercial activity. They therefore offered the privilege of free time on the air to advertisers who were willing to defray the cost of orchestras, or other performers, capable of providing suitable programs.

Meanwhile, this new development became a matter of public controversy. Secretary of Commerce Herbert Hoover called the first of a series of "radio conferences" for broadcasters, in Washington. "It is inconceivable," he told them, "that we should allow so great a possibility for service, for news, for entertainment, for education and for vital commercial purposes to be drowned in advertising chatter." The broadcasters agreed. They recommended that "direct advertising . . . be absolutely prohibited and that indirect advertising be limited to the announcement of the call letters of the station and the name of the concern responsible for the matter broadcasted." But the costs of broadcasting, the lure of profits, and the skill of copywriters, rapidly adapted to radio, conspired to defeat this program of abstinence. By 1925, the drum-fire of advertising on the air had become so insistent that Secretary Hoover considered the problem again. "The radio listener does not have the same option that the reader of publications has to ignore advertising in which he is not interested," he asserted, "and he may resent its intrusion in his set. It has been pointed out over and over again . . . that advertising in the intrusive sense will dull the interest of the listener and will thus defeat the industry. Furthermore, it can bring disaster to the very purpose of advertising if it creates resentment to the advertiser. If we can distinguish on the one hand between unobtrusive publicity that is accompanied by a direct service and engaging entertainment to the listener, and obtrusive advertising on the other, we may find a solution." To the American radio audience at the middle of the twentieth century, these words had a quaint, archaic ring, as if recovered from a civilization long extinct.

Yet Secretary Hoover, with remarkable prescience, analyzed a social problem the eventual solution of which was to be determined, not by the American people, but the masters of the air waves. "The ether is a public medium," he asserted, "and its use must be for public benefit. The use of a radio channel is justified only if there is public benefit. The dominant element for consideration in the radio field is, and always will be, the great body of the listening public, millions in number, countrywide in distribution." Freedom of the air, he argued, "cannot mean a license to every person or corporation who wishes to broadcast his name or his wares and thus monopolize the listener's set." And he declared that "no one can raise a cry of deprivation of free speech if he is compelled to prove that there is something more than naked commercial selfishness in his purpose." But it was precisely this cry that would be raised, two decades later, when the Federal Communications Commission, representing the American radio audience, challenged the right of broadcasters to use the air waves as they saw fit.

Almost immediately after Secretary Hoover made his statement, a development occurred which ultimately gave his words an effect of unintended irony. As a result of prolonged negotiations, the American Telephone and Telegraph Company determined to retire from the field of radio broadcasting. Two years earlier, in the presidential campaign of 1924, by using its own telephone lines to link twenty-two widely separated broadcasting stations, it had enabled President Calvin Coolidge to speak over a network that spanned the continent. The Radio Corporation had attempted to build a network by using telegraph lines, but these had given unsatisfactory service. When the Radio Corporation succeeded in purchasing the Telephone Company's broadcasting stations and network arrangements, it likewise acquired the long-denied privileges of using essential telephone lines in its future broadcasting operations, and of broadcasting for profit. The era of network broadcasting, with a national hook-up of stations simultaneously receiving a single program, had arrived.

With the opening of this era, domination of the air waves by advertisers became inevitable. For broadcasters could now offer them a larger circulation than any established medium afforded. There were already five million radio sets in use. By the middle of the century, there would be seventy-five million; the potential radio audience would include nearly every family in the nation. Quite naturally, advertisers hastened to exploit the new medium. They went on the air to gain good will for their products through entertainment, and so increase their sales. They associated their trademarks, as closely as possible, with the names of popular performers, orchestras, newscasters, commentators. Network broadcasting made radio the most powerful and pervasive of all advertising mediums. It transformed a plaything into the Fifth Estate.

The development of network broadcasting resulted from the pressure of two forces. One was the desire of early commercial sponsors to extend the range of their programs beyond the receiving area of local stations, and thus multiply the number of their potential customers. But equally influential was the demand that originated with broadcasters. Local stations, remote from such theatrical centers as New York and Chicago, faced a discouraging lack of talent capable of furnishing adequate programs. The public had "gone mad" over radio as a novelty. If it was to be held after the immediate novelty had worn off, better and better programs were requisite. Network broadcasting enabled the radio stations of Middletown and Main Street to bring to their audiences the talent of Broadway and, shortly afterwards, the talent of Hollywood.

To organize and develop its broadcasting activities on a nationwide scale, the Radio Corporation established a subsidiary, the National Broadcasting Company. The ambitious programs which it proposed to put on the air would be financed by revenue from advertising, but that the organization had a peculiar responsibility to the public was clearly recognized. Fourteen eminent Americans were therefore invited to serve as an advisory council on problems of program policy. They included two prominent educators; the general secretary of the Federal Council of Churches; William Green, president of the American Federation of Labor; Walter Damrosch, the famous conductor; the presidents of the Carnegie Foundation and the General Federation of Women's Clubs; and a number of well-known industrialists, bankers and lawyers, among them Charles Evans Hughes and Elihu Root. Soon afterwards, Walter Damrosch was retained as music counselor of the broadcasting company, and a decade later, Dr. James R. Angell, who had retired from the presidency of Yale University, became educational counselor of the broadcasting company. These arrangements expressed a characteristically American adaptation. They attempted to provide for public representation on issues of public policy. They acknowledged the people's vested interest in a social agency of incalculable power which, under the economic system of private capitalism, was being administered for profit by an industrial corporation.

Three years after the launching of the National Broadcasting Company, a rival organization appeared to challenge its supremacy on the air. This was the Columbia Broadcasting System, which was erected on the foundation of an abortive network by William S. Paley, the twenty-seven-year-old heir to a tobacco fortune. As advertising director of the family enterprise, Paley had experimented with a radio program broadcast over the failing network, and this had more than doubled cigar sales. Attracted by the medium which could produce such astonishing results, Paley bought the network and began building it toward its eventual position of equality with its competitor. Five years after Paley entered the field, the Mutual Broadcasting System was organized as the co-operative venture of a group of stations, each of which retained its independence in the field of program resources, and developed features that were tested locally before being given network time. Unlike the two older organizations, which supplied programs to their affiliated stations, the Mutual system originated no programs, but existed to provide network facilities for appropriate programs supplied by its affiliates. The fourth nation-wide network system in the United States, the American Broadcasting

Company, resulted from a ruling by the Federal Communications Commission, in 1941, which caused the National Broadcasting Company to divest itself of one of the two networks which it had previously operated. At the middle of the century, therefore, in addition to local and regional networks serving various listening-areas throughout the country, the nation was served by four competitive organizations operating on a nation-wide scale.

4   Politics, Panic and Persuasion

On Armistice Day in 1923, Woodrow Wilson made his only public address after retiring from the White House, broadcasting to the relatively small radio audience of the time. Four years earlier, the ill-fated President had broken down while seeking, in person, to carry his appeal for the League of Nations directly to the people of the United States. Long afterwards many Americans were to wonder whether, had radio on a nation-wide scale then been available, Wilson might not have won popular approval of his program; whether, as a result, the course of world history might not have been very different. The mere possibility of this specula-tion indicated that radio had produced vital social changes. Its influence was nowhere more evident than in the sphere of politics. William Jennings Bryan had not exaggerated when, at the Demo-cratic National Convention of 1924, he declared it to be "a gift of Providence."

In that year, for the first time, the national conventions of both major parties were broadcast. Thereafter, few political events of importance failed to reach the microphone. In constantly increas-ing numbers, citizens were able to listen to the controversies and debates, the statements of policy, the announcement of social and economic measures that were to shape the nation's course. On such occasions, radio restored the condition of the town meetings in which American political institutions had been born. It trans-formed the nation into a single, gigantic, cohesive community by shattering the last regional and cultural barriers that divided the people. Americans had never felt such intimate participation in their government as they were to know on the occasion of Presi-dent Franklin D. Roosevelt's first inaugural address, and on the

ABOVE: The Wide World Comes to the Farm

BELOW: Listening to the Radio in a Country Store About 1920

LEFT: A 1924 Broadcast by
Miss Olga Petrova

CENTER: Toscanini Leads
the NBC Symphony Orchestra

BELOW:
Sound Effects—Churning Water,
Anchor Chain and Ship's Bell

TOP: A Give-Away Program

CENTER: Broadcasting the 1948 Election

RIGHT: Walter Winchell—Gossip for the Millions

ABOVE: Election Returns by Television   BELOW: Televising Milton Berle

Sunday evening a week later when he explained in simple, reassuring terms the measures being taken to restore the country's collapsed financial system. The "fireside chats," in which President Roosevelt gave the people a periodic accounting of his stewardship, were an innovation that expanded the functioning of political democracy. These seemingly informal talks made it possible for him to discuss, with millions of his fellow-citizens, the activities of their government; to analyze the grave social and economic problems that confronted the nation, and describe the means that were being devised to solve them. In these fireside chats, the President took the attitude of putting problems squarely up to the people, and inviting their approval or censure of his proposed solutions. "It is your problem no less that it is mine," he emphasized in his first talk, and he repeatedly insisted that government required the co-operative effort of every citizen. The result was that he awakened many Americans to obligations and duties for which they had previously felt little responsibility. Gifted with a remarkable voice and an engaging manner, he also had the ability to make complex issues understandable, vivid and provocative. No President had ever addressed so vast an audience, yet none had ever spoken so intimately to the individual citizen. The confidence he inspired—largely as a result of his use of radio— was demonstrated by his triumphant election to a second term despite the aggressive opposition of three-fourths of the nation's press.

The social power of radio was made spectacularly obvious by a panic that swept the nation on the evening of Sunday, October 30, 1938. Shortly after eight o'clock that evening, several million families heard a series of news bulletins, commentaries and eye-witness accounts purporting to describe an invasion of the Atlantic seaboard by Martians armed with death-rays that enabled them to destroy all military forces sent to repel them. According to the broadcast, the Martians had landed near Princeton, New Jersey; martial law prevailed throughout New Jersey and eastern Pennsylvania; from Washington the Secretary of the Interior proclaimed a state of national emergency; the city of Newark was flooded with poison gas, then New York; other landings were being made at Buffalo, Chicago, and St. Louis. Ninety-two radio stations throughout the country carried this broadcast, which had been prefaced by the announcement that it was a dramatic performance of H. G. Wells' *War of the Worlds* by Orson Welles and the Mercury Theater.

Newspapers the next morning described the "tidal wave of terror" that spread over the whole country. In the state of New Jersey, hundreds of members of the National Guard telephoned to headquarters, asking where to report for duty; highways were blocked by the automobiles of families fleeing the danger zone; St. Michael's Hospital in Newark treated fifteen cases of shock, and dozens of listeners telephoned for inhalators, ambulances and police rescue squads. In Providence, Rhode Island, frightened residents demanded that the city be blacked out to save it from disaster. But at Concrete, Washington, where the electric power plant failed during the broadcast, people became hysterical and women fainted. A church service in Indianapolis, Indiana, was hastily dispersed when a woman dashed in crying that New York had been destroyed; she had heard it on the radio. In Memphis, Tennessee, the editorial staff of the *Press-Scimitar* was recalled to rush out an extra on the bombing of Chicago and St. Louis, and the threatened bombing of Memphis. In Pittsburgh, Pennsylvania, a woman snatched up a bottle of poison and was about to commit suicide when her husband entered the room and frustrated her intention. In New York City, eight hundred and seventy-five panic-stricken people telephoned to the *Times* alone, pleading for information about the reported cataclysm. Throughout the country, frantic telephone calls swamped the switchboards of newspapers, radio stations, police stations and army posts. As the extent of panic became apparent, radio stations put explanatory bulletins on the air, and the Associated Press issued a special bulletin over its wires. A fortnight after the event, an irate resident of Los Angeles brought suit against the Columbia Broadcasting System, which had transmitted the program, claiming damages of fifty thousand dollars for shock sustained by listening to it.

That this program, devised only to entertain, had terrorized many thousands of Americans, attested the immense social power of radio. A large proportion of listeners, especially in the lower-income and educational brackets, had come to rely on it, rather than on the press, for their news. As a source of news, a high degree of popular confidence attached to it. A few weeks before the broadcast, during the so-called Munich crisis when it seemed that Europe was about to be plunged into war, millions of Americans had kept their radios tuned to receive the latest news bulletins, and had learned to expect that any programs would be interrupted by the announcement of important developments. Since the dramatic form of the Martian broadcast exploited this situation, its credibility was notably increased. Subsequent investigations established that a large number of listeners who accepted it as a factual report, and were panic-stricken, tuned in too late to hear the prefatory announcement that it was a radio play, and either did not hear, or did not heed, three later statements to the same effect. More remarkably, many terrorized listeners failed to take the simple precaution of tuning their radios to other stations to ascertain whether or not the supposed emergency was being generally broadcast. All this suggested that a very large number of Americans had been conditioned to believe whatever they might hear on the radio, no matter how fantastic or improbable. The most significant conclusion to be drawn from this situation was phrased as a question in an editorial of the New York *World-Telegram*: "If so many people could be misled unintentionally when the purpose was merely to entertain, what could designing politicians not do through control of broadcasting stations?"

Five years after the Martian broadcast, another program contributed further evidence concerning the social influence of radio. On September 21, 1943, a popular radio star, Miss Kate Smith, undertook a marathon sale of United States war bonds. At the time, Miss Smith was regularly broadcasting one daytime program every day, and one evening program every week; her weekly audiences for these were estimated, respectively, at twenty-three million and twenty-one million people. On the day of her bond drive over the network of the Columbia Broadcasting System, Miss Smith announced that she would work uninterruptedly for eighteen hours; from eight o'clock in the morning until two o'clock the following morning. During this interval, she spoke for a minute or two approximately once every fifteen minutes. She pleaded with her audience and cajoled it. She demanded that her listeners buy war bonds. "She talked of neighbor boys from American towns and villages, now facing danger in other lands. And people listened. She told dramatic tales of generosity and sacrifice by soldier and civilian alike. People continued to listen. She invoked themes of love and hate, of large hopes and desperate fears, of honor and shame. Apparently there was nothing here of cut-and-dried radio script. This was presented as a personal message, iterated and reiterated in a voice often broken, it seemed, by deep emotion. And people did more than listen." By the end of her marathon broadcast Miss Smith had accumulated, from listeners throughout the country, pledges to purchase war bonds in the total amount of thirty-nine million dollars.

Miss Smith's broadcast furnished an extraordinary example of mass persuasion, and impressed social scientists as being a phenonemon of considerable significance. A group headed by Robert King Merton therefore subjected it to scientific analysis. Investigation disclosed that purchasers of bonds had been greatly influenced by their belief in Miss Smith's personal integrity. The scientists interpreted this as reflecting the conviction of purchasers that they were often the object of exploitation, manipulation and control by others actuated only by selfish interests; the conviction, partly based on experience, was magnified by anxiety. "The emphasis on this theme," the scientists concluded, "reflects a social disorder . . . in which common values have been submerged in the welter of private interests seeking satisfaction by virtually any means which are effective. It is a product of a society in which 'salesmanship'—in the sense of selling through deft pretence of concern with the other fellow—has run riot. Only against this background of skepticism and distrust stemming from a prevalently manipulative society were we able to interpret our subjects' magnified 'will to believe' in a public figure who is thought to incarnate the virtues of sincerity, integrity, good fellowship and altruism."

If salesmanship had gone berserk in American society, radio

appeared to be the origin and medium of its violent, destructive frenzy. Public reaction to both Miss Smith's and Orson Welles' broadcasts suggested that Americans might be developing a resistance to the clamor of advertising on the air. Many listeners who responded to Miss Smith's appeal for the purchase of bonds considered themselves victims of commercial exploitation and resented this. Many listeners to the Martian broadcast had tuned in late. They had thus missed the prefatory announcement of its nature. They had likewise apparently ignored similar announcements made midway during the broadcast, and at its end. This implied the possibility that radio listeners were training themselves to disregard the opening, middle and concluding moments of programs because they knew that these spots were normally consecrated to sales-promotion. Was any significant proportion of the vast radio audience indignant because the air was "drowned in advertising chatter?"

5 The Reign of the Hucksters

Radio celebrated its silver jubilee in 1945. In that year, the combined revenue of the four national networks from sales of time on the air amounted to more than one hundred and ninety millions of dollars. About three-fifths of this sum was paid by manufacturers of soaps, foods, drugs and toilet goods. The individual expenditures of radio's five most remunerative clients ranged from more than six to nearly fifteen million dollars. Was broadcasting being conducted, as the law optimistically required, "in the public convenience, interest and necessity?" Or was it being conducted, as certain critics alleged, not for the public, but for the benefit of advertisers? The four national networks included among their affiliates two-thirds of all the radio stations in the United States, a proportion large enough to make their use of the air waves a matter of general concern. It seemed scarcely probable that they would seriously oppose the policies of sponsors whose purchases of time ran to six, seven, eight, or nearly fifteen million dollars. There was little reason to doubt that, in defining the policy of his own company, George Washington Hill, president of the American Tobacco Company, had spoken for many other large-scale buyers of time on the air. "Taking one hundred percent as the total radio value," Hill declared, "we give ninety percent to commercials, to what's said for the product, and we give ten percent to the show . . . I don't have the right to spend the stockholders' money just to entertain the public."

The sensitive corporate consciences of men like Hill exercised a profound influence on what Americans were likely to hear whenever they tuned in their radios. In his satirical novel, *The Hucksters,* Frederic Wakeman gave radio listeners an adequate insight into the nature of that influence. Before writing his novel, Wakeman had been associated with the advertising agency which handled programs put on the air by the American Tobacco Company, and the tycoon who figured in *The Hucksters* was generally identified with Hill. "Remember, two things make good advertising," the tycoon declared. "One, a good simple idea. Two, repetition. And by repetition, by God, I mean until the public is so irritated with it, they'll buy your brand because they bloody well can't forget it. All you professional advertising men are scared to death of raping the public; I say the public likes it, if you got the know-how to make 'em relax and enjoy it."

To the profitable practice of making aural rape an enjoyable experience, three different professional groups devoted their collective talents. The broadcasters originated programs which were put on the air during periods for which no advertiser had contracted, and then attempted to sell them to prospective clients. But with a majority of the most popular programs on the air, broadcasters had nothing whatever to do. These were developed either by advertising agencies or package specialists. Until the Second World War, most commercial radio programs were built by advertising agencies which represented the sponsors. The agencies provided writers, actors, directors, musicians; created and produced the shows, charged the sponsors for all program costs, and collected a commission for their services. During the war, however, a new type of middleman entered the field. The maker of "package shows" was usually a talent agency, representing a radio star. Instead of selling the star's individual services, the talent agency, acting for the star, put together an entire program and sold it as a single "package" to an advertising agency acting for a sponsor. For various reasons, this arrangement was advantageous to stars, and presently many of the more famous radio performers adopted it. But whether radio shows were built by advertising agencies or package specialists, they were designed solely to fulfill the purposes of a commercial sponsor. Business, and not art or public service, dictated most of the entertainment with which broadcasters flooded the American home.

This fact had long been obvious to the Federal Communications Commission, official watchdog of the nation's air waves. In 1946, it issued a report on the public-service responsibilities of broadcasters which condemned many of their current practices. The Commission conceded that advertisers had a legitimate place in broadcasting, but denied that broadcasting "should be run solely in the interest of advertisers rather than that of listeners." It warned the radio industry to correct "advertising excesses." As an example, it cited the length, content and irritating qualities of many commercial plugs. It deplored the sponsor-imposed "piling up" of soap operas which filled the air during the morning hours, yet recruited only slightly more than twelve percent of the available audience. It called upon broadcasters to increase the time allotted to discussion of public issues, and the number of "sustaining programs," which were neither paid for by sponsors nor interrupted by commercial announcements. Admonishing broadcasters to mend their ways, the Commission warned them that renewal of licenses would be granted on the basis of their service to the public.

This was the severest castigation that the radio industry had yet suffered, and its pain was not assuaged by the fact that the Commission had called upon "forces outside the broadcasting industry" to demand better programs. As president of the National Association of Broadcasters, Justin Miller presently retorted. The term "public service," he asserted, had "no application to radio broadcasting." Furthermore, in the Commission's assertion of a right to review programs and practices, he saw a "subtle encroachment upon freedom of speech in radio." Any attempt by the Commission to pass judgment on the operations of broadcasters,

or on the character of their programs, so Miller declared, constituted an "encroachment upon the liberties of the American
people." But William S. Paley, head of the powerful Columbia
Broadcasting System, warned the Association of a growing volume
of criticism of American radio. "The most persistently repeated
charge against broadcasters is that we permit advertising excesses,"
he said. "Are we guilty? It is my opinion that we are, and I am
sure that most broadcasters would agree."

Under the financial sponsorship of the Association, surveys
were conducted by the National Opinion Research Center of the
University of Chicago, in 1946 and 1947, to ascertain the attitude
of the radio audience on a variety of issues. The results of these
surveys were analyzed and interpreted by Dr. Paul F. Lazarsfeld,
director of the Bureau of Applied Social Research of Columbia
University. Objection to advertising was the basis of the most
frequent criticism directed at radio, and came from slightly less
than one-third of the listeners who were polled. Complaint was
made of the interruption of programs by commercials, of over-
selling, of needless repetition. The most critical attitudes to radio
as a social force were expressed by college graduates, and those
in the higher income brackets. "The dissenting voices come from
very desirable groups in the community," Lazarsfeld reported to
the broadcasters. "They are solid citizens, the well-educated men
and women, able to express themselves clearly and likely to influence others. . . . The critics are a minority, but obviously a
very important one."

The redemption of radio from its mid-century bondage to the
hucksters might require aggressive action by the American people.
But they knew their power when aroused; and in the past they had
won many battles for reform.

CHAPTER III

Day and Night, Night and Day

1   In the People's Image?

"What have you done with my child?" asked the father of radio. It was the fortieth anniversary of his invention of the audion tube, and Lee De Forest addressed an open letter to the masters of the air waves. The ageing parent was appalled at the fate that had overtaken his child. It had been conceived, he declared, "as a potent instrumentality for culture, fine music, the uplifting of America's mass intelligence." He denounced the broadcasters for their selfish betrayal of this public trust. They and their sponsors, he charged, had debased radio, made it a laughing-stock. In their guardianship radio had become "a stench in the nostrils of the gods of the ionosphere."

De Forest's blistering indictment was widely publicized. For in the later 1940s controversy over radio ran high. This indicated that the American people were becoming increasingly aware of its power, as a social force, for good or for evil; of its profound, far-reaching influence on the nation's culture and civilization. When it first emerged as a mass medium, educators and social theorists predicted that radio would inaugurate an era of adult education. But early hopes for a true "university of the air" were never fulfilled. The broadcasting schedule came to be devoted principally to entertainment programs, and these proved to be the most popular form of fare with a mass audience. As radio became big, and ever bigger, business, the profits to be made by amusing the largest possible audience multiplied and soared. Though it could be assumed that hundreds of thousands of people would listen to serious programs, everyone knew that millions tuned in for comedy, popular music, drama, quizzes and audience participation programs, and the reports of certain columnists. Faced with a conflict between their alleged cultural responsibilities and their obvious commercial interests, the decision of broadcasters was almost inevitable. When, after three years, he retired from the radio editorship of the New York *Times,* the literary critic John K. Hutchens ruefully acknowledged that, "Radio is essentially a money-minded business, and . . . when the prospect of a dollar conflicts with the public interest, the dollar is an odds-on favorite to win." And the eminent news analyst Raymond Swing, deserting the air after thirteen years of broadcasting, stated the issue in another way. "When broadcasting first began, it seemed to offer a promise of democratic enlightenment such as surpassed the dreams of a Jefferson," Swing remarked, in his valedictory. "But what has been accomplished, good as it is, is miserably inadequate to the need and falls miserably short of the opportunity. . . ."

This, in essence, reflected the viewpoint of those Americans who charged radio with dereliction in its position of grave social responsibility. They did not take the extreme and intemperate attitude of Lee De Forest; they did not condemn radio for total failure. But, recognizing its undeniable achievements, they pointed out that these were exceptional, and contended that public response justified an extension which broadcasters were reluctant to undertake. In his interpretation of an audience survey conducted by the National Opinion Research Center, and devised by a panel of social scientists, Paul F. Lazarsfeld stated that one-fifth of the listening public expressed a desire for more serious programs, and showed that this segment of the audience was distributed very evenly among all educational strata. It constituted a minority—but this minority was composed of many millions. The conclusion was supported by other evidence. In the field of music alone, there was an immense audience for the superb orchestral concerts and performances of opera conducted by Arturo Toscanini, and put on the air by the National Broadcasting Company; for the weekly symphonic concerts of the New York Philharmonic Orchestra, offered by the Columbia Broadcasting System. When, in 1940, the Metropolitan Opera Company faced eviction from its domicile, one million dollars were required to assure its continued existence. Weekly performances of opera had been broadcast for nine years. Did a democracy consider opera a cultural institution worth preserving? An appeal for funds was made to the people—to the radio audience throughout the nation, most of whose members had never entered the old auditorium on Broadway. Approximately a half million dollars were received from one hundred and fifty thousand contributors in Middletowns and Main Streets all over the country. Radio effected a revolution by redeeming opera from its status as the fashionable diversion of a social elite, and making it the common property of the people.

Criticism of radio by no means ignored the remarkable social contributions that broadcasters were making. But it originated in a concept of radio's almost limitless potentialities for constructive social good. It emphasized the disparity that existed between radio's opportunities and its actual performance. Such criticism reflected a permanent premise in American life: an eternal dissatisfaction with things-as-they-are that was bred of the vision of what they might become; an abiding conviction that what ought to be, could be. Radio, to its critics, was an instrumental device endowed with unique power—for, on the average, Americans listened to it from three to four hours daily. Should it not, therefore, be made to serve the interests of a better life, a life more completely fulfilling to the spirit? To the critics of radio, its necessary bondage to the dollars of commerce did not preclude a far greater service to the liberation and enrichment of existence.

Yet even radio's most idealistic detractors acknowledged that it was an instrument responsive to democratic controls. Did not the possibility of its progress toward manifold opportunities for social achievement rest, in the end, with the public alone? A well-known star, the comedian Henry Morgan, candidly admitted radio's preponderance of "sponsored junk," and testified that "the most popular programs on the air today . . . are of poor quality . . . by the standards of the people who produce them." But he asserted that responsibility for this situation was chargeable to the audience, which not only failed to demand better fare, but refused to listen when superior programs were offered. And Victor Ratner, a prominent radio executive, carried this argument further. Criticism of radio, he asserted, pointed to the failure of the American educational system, which had neither raised the "cultural level" of the people, nor interested them in the "better things" during their formative years. Critics of radio professed to be shocked by its programs; actually, they were shocked by the tastes of the American people. Radio, this executive declared, was vulgar, fast, simple and fundamental. It was made in the image of the American people.

A mass medium, the defenders of radio contended, could gain and hold its great audience only by practicing what might be described as "cultural democracy"—by giving the majority of people what they wanted. Radio had to build its programs on the common denominators of mass interest.

2   Adam and Eve on a Raft

As the first half of the century rushed to its end, Americans were living in a high-powered world, and Dr. Oscar B. Anderson, an eminent psychologist, took a dim view of their way of life. The nation's businessmen were increasingly suffering from hypertension and cardiac ailments. In the main, he averred, these afflictions resulted from unnecessary stress and strain, and maladjusted home life. At the end of the day, all over the land, businessmen returned home carrying briefcases stuffed with extra work. They arrived on the domestic scene tense and upset, quarreled with their wives, had trouble with their children, and spent half the night working. Why did these unfortunates always have to be on the go and appear busy? Basically, Dr. Anderson asserted, because they were afraid to face themselves; afraid to see something they did not like. Reading his gloomy analysis of their domestic existence, Americans could find it confirmed by the ever-rising divorce rate. But science offered a crumb of comfort. Guinea pigs, it appeared, suffered from the same neuroses as humans; and although the statistics of voluntary celibacy among laboratory animals were not reported, it seemed likely that man was not alone in his domestic infelicity.

Had you tuned in your radio between the hours of eight and nine thirty on weekday mornings, you would have heard no echo of the acrimony in which, presumably, American families broke their fast. The air, at that cheerless time, vibrated to a multiple marital bliss. Over the tinkle of glassware, the rattle of dishes, the splash of liquid into invisible cups—whether real, or merely hallucinatory—there prevailed an insistent connubial cooing. This was the habitual utterance of radio's foremost mister-and-missus teams, supposedly enjoying their ritual breakfasts in an atmosphere of gratifying intimacy and fluent affection. As exemplars of conjugal etiquette, these eminent personages demonstrated the uses of reiterated endearment and reciprocal compliment. They also illustrated the high rewards with which Americans requited an impersonal and frugal hospitality. The morning repasts of two vocally sociable couples were reported to yield incomes in excess of seventy-five thousand dollars.

It became clear, during the course of their programs, that the elite of the ether had met, and valiantly conquered, an astonishing number of the anxieties that disturbed American households. They had accumulated spots on their clothes, and dust on their furniture; their good nature had been blighted by the lack of a truly superior coffee; their efficiency had been impaired by the want of a nourishing, yummy dessert requiring negligible preparation; and for years they had suffered from the absence of dentifrices, shaving lotions and other products having peculiar properties that changed the very look of life. But these overwhelming misfortunes were happily past. Delightedly, they reminded one another—and an eavesdropping congregation—of the discoveries that had brought them to their current state of carefree euphoria. In exchange for a modest sum of money, each of these was obtainable by anybody. Who, at such trivial cost, would consent to prolong a deprived existence?

They had, however, other experiences to share with their listeners. The audience of Pegeen and Ed Fitzgerald heard a folksy colloquy that reduced the life of metropolitan New York to village dimensions. Those who shared the breakfast of Dorothy and Dick entered a very different sphere. Dorothy Kilgallen was a columnist for the Hearst press; her husband, Richard Kollmar, was an actor and theatrical producer. From their table issued bulletins on café society, accounts of excursions into more exalted circles, and brief comment on the new plays. The specialty of Tex McCrary, a former journalist, and his wife Jinx Falkenburg, a former model and movie starlet, was interviews with guests. Occasionally, these were current celebrities, with whom the McCrarys became engaged in a contest of mutual admiration; more frequently they were people of undiscovered interest, and perhaps undeserved obscurity. From Hollywood, Athens of the West, where a cult of the intellectual life continued to flourish, the veteran movie-actor Adolphe Menjou and his wife, Verree Teasdale, addressed themselves to problems having philosophical implications. A quarter of an hour with the Menjous considerably thickened the mystery that enveloped such a topic as atomic energy, for example, but left listeners with an appreciation of its importance, and a gratifying sense that if what they had heard seemed obscure, it was the more likely, for that reason, to have been genuinely profound.

The most popular of all radio breakfasts was not a domestic meal, but a public repast. This was the tumultuous show con-

ducted, until his death, by Tom Breneman from his restaurant on
Vine Street in Hollywood. Broadcast over two hundred and twenty
stations—the largest network required by any program—it was
said to bring into use nearly one half of the nation's radio sets.
Though Hollywood was associated only with youth, glamor and
fame, Breneman's breakfast parties contradicted these popular
concepts. His guests were elderly; they were invested with no
glamor; none of them had achieved celebrity. Yet every weekday,
in the mists of dawn, more than four hundred women formed
in a patient line on Vine Street to await the opening of his
restaurant at six o'clock. After a substantial meal, they were
rewarded by participating in the hour of jovial banter, persistent
clowning and moist sentiment that Breneman put on the air. This
program brought him more than a thousand letters every day,
chiefly from ageing women who wrote in terms of unreserved
affection.

Breneman was a former vaudeville singer, middle-aged, portly,
gray-haired and sad-eyed. He moved his guests to shrieks of
laughter by making fun of their hats and their husbands; by telling
them innocent jokes and engaging them in bouts of repartee; by
commanding them to perform various ludicrous actions. But the
major features of his programs were interviews. As subjects, he
invariably selected very old women, and gently persuaded them
to talk about their own lives, their current interests, and what
philosophy they had managed to extract from their experiences.
At the end of these conversations, he kissed them, wished them
joy, and presented them with corsages of purple orchids. Whether
or not Breneman so intended it, his interviews furnished an
insight into the lives of the plain people of the United States. For
many of his subjects, existence had obviously not been easy. Their
unrehearsed answers to his questions indicated that they had
endured adversity and met with misfortunes. They had devoted
themselves to children of whom they were proud, and for whose
advancement they had willingly sacrificed personal desires. They
spoke gratefully of small, simple pleasures enjoyed in earlier
years. Conceivably, their autobiographies justified Thoreau's
assertion that most men led lives of quiet desperation. But the

elderly women whose quavering voices Breneman's microphone carried across a continent made no such melancholy admission. What they had to say implied that, like the American pioneers, they believed life to be a process which must inevitably go forward, whatever the obstacles or disappointments. They invited confidence in its worth, and faith in its ultimate good.

3   Ivory Apes, and Peacocks

Between the hours of ten-thirty in the morning and six in the afternoon, the air over America dripped a monotonous anguish. Approximately fifty dramatic serials, each fifteen minutes long and richly sauced in woe, were being broadcast to the nation's housewives. On this daily flood-tide of feminine tribulation and tears was borne the resonant advertising of several great corporations: manufacturers of soaps, food products, pharmaceutical preparations and toilet goods. In American civilization, the soap opera had become an established institution that touched the lives of twenty million women. Educators, social scientists and many psychiatrists deplored its influence. The daytime radio audience, composed almost exclusively of women, was itself sharply divided in its opinion of the merits of soap opera as entertainment. Surveys indicated that approximately one half of the housewives who were available and potential listeners habitually tuned in to one serial after another. The other half assiduously avoided tuning in to any. This division, it appeared, registered a difference in educational, but not economic, strata. In general, those women who had had the fewest educational opportunities derived the greatest pleasure from soap operas. Sponsors found the ventilation of washboard weepers highly profitable, and spent some thirty-five million dollars a year to broadcast them. At the middle of the century the oldest surviving radio epic had enjoyed eighteen years of uninterrupted, prosperous existence.

If radio could claim credit for the practice of "cultural democracy," the soap operas probably constituted one of its most significant achievements. The fact that they were designed as a vehicle for high-pressure, continuous merchandising made it imperative that they exemplify, without ever transgressing, the beliefs, standards and aspirations of their audience. Moreover, the audience exercised a censorious supervision of the activities of their favorite characters, and by reporting explicit approval or disapproval largely determined the content of soap operas. Millions of letters were annually received by the organizations which produced them, and an important proportion of these revealed that the writers were dominated by an illusion of reality: the characters of soap opera were, for them, not fictional personages, but living people. Thus, for example, a young actor played the roles of hero in several serials; in one, he figured as having been married for some time, but in another the exigencies of plot brought him to the altar. Accusations of bigamy, and indignant protests, followed promptly. Players in the serials were often favored with letters of advice and warning, addressed to the characters they impersonated and dealing with their fictional predicaments and problems. And the arrival of gifts for infants spawned in the ether, for characters stricken with illness or celebrating some joyous anniversary, was not unusual.

All this testified to the credibility achieved by the cliff-hangers, and the high degree of involvement into which they persuaded many of their devotees. An enterprising social scientist, Miss Herta Herzog, conducted an extensive research on the subject of their impact and appeal. Soap operas, she concluded, provided listeners with an adjustment to the kind of life they were leading, and gave meaning "to a world which seems nothing but a humdrum existence." Did so many million American women find their lives so intolerably dull? Existence in Soapland was certainly not humdrum, though its incessant turbulence might present, to non-addicts, a fairly desperate alternative. Just how desperate was shown by James Thurber, in a series of illuminating articles which he contributed to *The New Yorker* during 1948, after prolonged, courageous exposure to the current serials. Thurber's report on the world of soap opera did not make it seem a promising source of effective adjustment to reality.

But, appealing to millions of American women, and largely responsive to their will, the soap operas constituted a kind of social mirror, reflecting the values that they cherished and holding, as it were, their composite, transfigured image. What manner of society was this which, according to Miss Herzog, gave listeners "a sense that the world is not as threatening as it might seem by supplying formulas of behavior for various troublesome situations . . . ?" Its most arresting characteristic was unlikeness to twentieth-century America. It flourished, as Thurber pointed out, in "a peaceful world, a political and economic Utopia, free of international unrest, the menace of fission, the threat of inflation, depression, general unemployment, the infiltration of Communists and the problems of racism." This miraculously insulated region was dotted with small towns, all identically idyllic. The changing mores had scarcely touched their inhabitants, who continued to live under the stern moral code of the nineteenth century. True, automobiles sped along the highways; houses were equipped with telephones; and young women entered the professions and engaged in business. But the prevailing decorum might have been instituted by Mrs. Rutherford B. Hayes. By the towns of soap opera, the canons of Mrs. Emily Post would have been considered subversive.

Felicity should have been the lot of the virtuous women who presided over these communities. But rational happiness was a blessing perpetually denied them. Through no fault of their own, their lives resembled a spastic nightmare. They were beset by agonizing emotional problems that appeared to be unsolvable. Having eventually disposed of them, they were immediately confronted by others even more excruciating. Week after week, month after month, year after year they breasted seas of pain churned up by the follies, frailties and sins of men. Wicked men they confounded by exercising their infallible intuition, or redeemed by displaying their invincible righteousness. But good men had been created by God to lapse into folly and frailty. To the detergent Griseldas of soap operas, masculine frailty was as catnip to sedate hearthside felines; as the rumored unchastity of an appetizing blonde to middle-aged stockbrokers: an irresistible stimulus to action. Their mission was to sustain, ennoble and continuously strengthen the wayward children of Adam. To discharge it, they had to subjugate the errant creatures and thereafter direct them in all things. Since men displayed a distressingly protracted recalcitrance, the vocation of women required inexhaustible fortitude, nobility, self-sacrifice, resourcefulness, understanding, and universal capability. In soap opera, the whole intellectual life of man consisted in discovering, acknowledging, and ultimately rejoicing in his absolute dependence on women. The career of women was to foster, by any means possible, this pre-ordained but long-postponed consummation.

During his immersion in soap opera, James Thurber noted the peculiar susceptibility of its men to three forms of disease: temporary blindness, amnesia, and partial paralysis. All of these produced emergencies propitious to the mission of women, and were therefore productive of their happiness. But one curious fact might have enlightened American husbands. Among the most beautiful romances, and the most satisfying marriages celebrated by the serials were those which united a brave and soulful woman with a man totally paralyzed from the waist down. In this exquisitely symbolic prospect, soap opera appeared to fulfill its function of supplying a formula of behavior for a troublesome situation.

"We write successful stories about unsuccessful people," asserted Frank Hummert, the most prolific of all producers of radio's daily tear-jerkers. "This means that our characters are simply unsuccessful in the material things of life, but highly successful spiritually."

It depended, no doubt, on how you defined spiritual success.

4 Something for the Girls

During intervals between soap operas, radio provided the feminine audience with more stable fare. Programs devoted to the art of cooking had been one of the earliest experiments in broadcasting. Their success was immediate, and their subsequent elaboration became inevitable. By the middle of the century, homemaking programs had acquired an admirable comprehensiveness, and covered all phases of the domestic arts. Along with these, broadcasters developed a species of radio journalism directed to women. This took the form of programs conducted by feminine commentators who discussed topics in the news of interest to housewives, dealt with recent books and plays, and interviewed people whose current activities had won favorable attention in the press.

Of the many conductors of "women's hour" programs, Miss Mary Margaret McBride was probably both the best known and the most conspicuously successful. Broadcasting from New York City, and heard only along the Atlantic seaboard, she had nevertheless gained nation-wide celebrity and become one of the foremost personalities of the radio world. Over her devoted listeners she exercised an influence so remarkable that *Printers' Ink*, the advertising trade publication, described it as "perhaps the most outstanding reliance upon the word of a human being in the commercial field." The critic Philip Hamburger, in an article about her which he published in *Life*, recorded a characteristic example. At a time when carrots were glutting Eastern markets, her praise of a particular brand of the vegetable caused its daily sale to leap from two to ten carloads. To celebrate her tenth anniversary on the air, an afternoon reception was held at Madison Square Garden, and twenty thousand eager fans surged into the great arena. Even more significant, as evidence of her peculiar prestige, was the fact that several million people never referred to her by her full name. They knew her, thought of her and spoke of her only as Mary Margaret. This custom expressed their affection and esteem. But it likewise reflected a feeling of personal intimacy which radio alone, of all forms of mass communication, made possible and plausible. As friend, oracle and domestic arbiter of a vast public, Miss McBride was, so to speak, a social phenomenon produced by radio. She was also one of radio's most skillful broadcasters.

Her programs followed a simple pattern. She usually began by chatting informally with her audience. She then interviewed her daily guest-star. She devoted her concluding quarter hour to a whirlwind, breathless series of plugs for the products of her many sponsors, delivered like an urgent, unbroken cadenza. The extraordinary popularity of her program could not be attributed to its content, which was in no way exceptional. The source of its appeal was her personality. To listeners she conveyed an impression of spontaneity and naturalness. They were won by her obvious sincerity, her simplicity and her common sense. To many, she seemed a symbol of the average American: practical-minded, humorous, sentimental, full of good will, finding life a perpetual adventure and bringing to it a capacity for enjoyment and enthusiasm. Fundamentally, Miss McBride captivated her fans by thinking, feeling and talking precisely as they conceived that they did. She recounted experiences for which they could find parallels in their own lives. When she interviewed her guest stars, she asked them the kind of questions which most of her listeners might have proposed had they been in her place. For her fans, she discharged the duties of a public deputy. She moved in the exciting, glamorous, sophisticated world that they would never enter, but she saw it in terms that they recognized as their own.

5 The Great Achievements

Though radio was only thirty years old, it had become a familiar element of the natural environment in which Americans lived. A generation already middle-aged had never known its absence; their elders scarcely recalled what life had been like without it. It was largely taken for granted, and the spectacular changes which it had wrought were seldom noticed. Yet in the areas of its greatest achievement, these changes were little less than miraculous. Their sum amounted to an extension of opportunity without precedent in history. For radio had brought within reach of every American a range of intellectual experience and a repertory of art so massive as to daunt the imagination. These were made available, day by day. They could be incorporated in the existence of any individual, whether he lived in a city or a village, on a snowbound farm, in the lonely spaces of the Western ranch country. If, as a result, the general level of American culture had not been immensely elevated, the fault did not seem to lie with radio.

In the realm of art, radio opened a fund of great music incomparably more extensive and more various than that which, during any year, was offered in the concert halls of New York, the nation's most prolific musical center. Weekly performances of opera were broadcast from the Metropolitan Opera House, and a guild of radio listeners not only contributed to the maintenance of that institution, but were given a consultative participation in the yearly planning of its repertory. Symphony concerts by the Boston, Philadelphia, Detroit and New York Philharmonic orchestras were regularly put on the air. A series of concerts familiarized the nation with the orchestras maintained by other cities; and during the year that preceded his retirement, the radio audience could hear Dr. Serge Koussevitzky conduct actual rehearsals of the Boston Symphony. But radio, in addition to broadcasting public performances by the nation's major orchestras and opera company, likewise made an independent contribution. Both the National Broadcasting Company and the Columbia Broadcasting System maintained permanent symphony orchestras; the Mutual Broadcasting System organized a smaller permanent group of musicians. The orchestral concerts and operatic performances directed by Arturo Toscanini and other distinguished conductors were arranged for the benefit of the radio audience alone, and brought to every American who chose to listen to representative works from the vast body of classical music.

Furthermore, radio made available performances of works which, in its absence, might never have been heard by any considerable portion of the nation. Notable examples were furnished by the programs of the Bach Aria Group, the String Quartet, and the First Piano Quartet of the National Broadcasting Company; and the weekly half hour called *Invitation to Music*, put on the air by the Columbia Broadcasting System, featured eminent singers, instrumentalists and conductors in programs of important works by living composers, often produced with their active collaboration. One further development of potentially great significance for American culture could probably be awaited with confidence. There seemed little doubt that the four national networks would eventually bring to the public the works of young American composers whose talents still awaited wide recognition. By so doing, radio would notably advance the state of music as a creative art.

Meanwhile, in the opportunities which it afforded for an extension of intellectual experience, radio was performing an equally remarkable service. Undoubtedly its greatest single achievement in this sphere was a magnificent experiment in mass education undertaken as the Second World War was drawing to a close. That this experiment formed part of a commercially sponsored program was especially noteworthy because of its nature. It was conducted during intermissions of the Sunday afternoon concerts of the New York Philharmonic Orchestra, sponsored by the United States Rubber Company, and broadcast over the national network of the Columbia Broadcasting System. The experiment had as its object the awakening of the American people to the immense role which science played in their society, and it attempted to give them a broader and more authentic understanding of what science is and how it operates.

For three seasons, in talks of ten or eleven minutes' duration, and in terms so clear and universal that their ideas could be grasped by everyone, eighty of the nation's foremost creative leaders in science outlined the social implications of the advances being made in their respective fields. No university in the world had ever undertaken a program of comparable magnitude, difficulty, or social importance, and the results were as impressive as the experiment itself. Approximately a quarter of a million requests were received for printed copies of the individual talks, and the continuing demand ultimately brought about their publication in book form under the title *The Scientists Speak*. Popular response to the experiment, in the form of letters of inquiry and appreciation, was overwhelming. These letters—it was reported by the committee in charge of the programs—"were sent in by bank presidents and by filling station operators—by ministers and grocers and teachers and ambassadors and professors and inmates of penitentiaries—by ranchers and philosophers and housewives and business executives and school children. They came from New England and the back country of Arkansas and Tennessee; they came from the plains of Montana, from the cornfields of Iowa, from the hills of the Carolinas; they came from the city, the desert, the farm, the factory and the village." The results of this

unprecedented experiment in mass education made two points
abundantly clear. The average American radio listener was fully
capable of comprehending programs of substantial and difficult
intellectual content. He was also eager to have such programs
presented.

Radio was actually meeting this demand to a far greater extent
than many of its critics seemed aware. The National Broadcasting
Company maintained a "university of the air," the Columbia
Broadcasting System a "school of the air," both of which offered
organized and systematic courses of instruction, some of them in
co-operation with colleges and universities. Among the subjects
covered were world politics and economics, science, contemporary
literature, the evolution of orchestral music. The discussion,
largely by contemporary writers, of masterpieces of world literature
formed the basis of a weekly program broadcast under the title of
Invitation to Learning. Programs of discussion by panels of
authorities in various fields were frequently broadcast, and probably contributed to adult education by stimulating some listeners
to undertake independent study of the problems they presented.
But the subjects discussed were almost invariably too large in scope
to be susceptible of more than superficial treatment in the limited
time reserved for such programs. The most scholarly of these
programs was the University of Chicago *Round Table*, which
offered weekly discussions, by highly competent authorities, of
social, political and economic issues confronting the nation. Similar subjects were covered in the weekly broadcasts of *The People's
Platform*. Debate and controversy, rather than discussion, were the
objects served by the widely publicized *America's Town Meeting*
program, which often generated more heat than light. Throughout
the country, there were said to be some fifteen thousand organized
groups meeting together to hear radio discussion programs, and
continue consideration of the topics proposed after conclusion of
the broadcasts. But some of the best educational programs,
although available for broadcast over all stations of national
networks, were not carried by many affiliated local stations which
preferred, instead, to devote the time to local sponsored broadcasts
that yielded financial revenue.

One of the most promising developments in radio, from the standpoint of adult education, was the so-called "documentary" broadcast. Employing the technique of dramatic recreation of actual events originated by the *March of Time* motion pictures and radio broadcasts, the documentaries were first perfected by a special unit of researchers and writers in the Columbia Broadcasting System. They were devised as an effective method of presenting subjects of major public importance, and were most advantageously used to interest a large audience in problems requiring social action. Outstanding documentary programs, founded on extensive research and brilliantly dramatized, were devoted to such issues as juvenile delinquency, old age and unemployment, needs and resources for medical care, the constructive peacetime uses of atomic energy, the value of the motion picture as a cultural force. In general, these programs were given an hour of broadcast time, and it was noteworthy that most of them were presented in the evening and required the cancellation of regular sponsored programs. Their success with the public encouraged regional stations to produce documentary programs dealing with specifically local issues, with notable results. Thus, a station in Los Angeles exposed widespread medical malpractice resulting from the flourishing prevalence of "quacks" in California; a Chicago station dealt with slum conditions and the juvenile gangsters that they bred; a Minneapolis station forthrightly dealt with the problem of interracial relations in Minnesota, and with juvenile delinquency in that state. The social value of these documentary broadcasts was demonstrated by the fact that they aroused local public demand for remedial action, and brought about the enforcement of corrective measures.

To the city-dwelling American, one of radio's most conspicuous social achievements—its substantial and varied service to the nation's farmers—was scarcely known. That service began when, in the spring of 1923, Frank E. Mullen, an editor of *The National Stockman and Farmer*, inaugurated a broadcast of market and weather reports for Station KDKA in Pittsburgh. With the cooperation of the Department of Agriculture and the United States Weather Bureau, Mullen rapidly expanded his program, and eventually secured the collaboration of important authorities on agriculture, who contributed discussions of scientific methods that would enable the farmer to produce more efficiently and profitably. Four years later, Mullen produced for the National Broadcasting Company the *National Farm and Home Hour*, which eventually became a nation-wide program put on the air six days a week. This program brought the farmer information and advice from government agricultural scientists, practical farm experts, leaders of farmers' organizations; it brought to the farmer's wife the talks of home economists and leaders of national organizations serving rural youth. It furnished a model for other network programs designed to serve the rural population, and for programs originated by regional stations to deal with problems of a specifically local nature. How elaborately this form of rural public service could be developed was shown, in 1947, by a station in St. Louis, Missouri. To dramatize for farmers in the region the methods by which soil conservation principles could be applied to their own farms, an entire farm of nearly three hundred acres was remade in a single day, utilizing methods of conservation which normally would have required several years to apply.

By the middle of the century, radio had become an active force in the promotion of scientific agriculture. It was saving farmers millions of dollars annually by bringing them up-to-the-minute market reports, and hourly forecasts of the weather that determined their welfare. But its service to the rural population transcended these practical ministrations. As significantly as the automobile, and more extensively than the motion picture, radio had operated to integrate the American farm home in the broad currents of national life. It dispelled loneliness and helped to overcome rural isolation. It afforded farmers and their families the same opportunities for intellectual adventure, for the experience of hearing great music, for the enjoyment of a wide choice of entertainment as were available to residents of metropolitan centers. Above all, through its world-wide coverage of news, radio more than any other agency kept them abreast of the rapidly changing world in which they lived.

6   Oracles and Pundits

On the sponsored broadcasts with which national advertisers saturated the American air, the word of one man often had a decisive effect. C. E. Hooper maintained an organization which measured the radio audience, determined the relative popularity of programs, and published monthly ratings of their prestige. Over a long period, the Hooper ratings indicated that a particular quarter-hour program outstripped all others in popular appeal. On Sunday evenings at nine o'clock, a peculiar tension gripped the nation. Millions of citizens suddenly dropped whatever they happened to be doing, and turned on their radios. For this was the moment of revelation, of forecast and counsel. The voice of the oracle reached them in a rapid-fire succession of staccato barks, accompanied by the incessant clicking of a telegraph key. They learned who was blazing; who was blending with whom; who was becoming unstuck; what was actually in the bag or soon would be. They overheard momentous secrets being conveyed to high officials in Washington—the President, the Secretary of State, the Attorney General—with urgent suggestions for action. They were told what was cooking on the cosmic stove, and whether or not they ought to like the dish.

No journalist in history had ever commanded so massive or faithful an audience as Walter Winchell, who in one evening probably reached more people than James Gordon Bennett, Horace Greeley and Charles A. Dana had together reached in their entire careers. Winchell's ascendancy over the imaginations of Mr. and Mrs. America—as he called his public—was one of the most notable social phenomena of the second quarter of the twentieth century. But among social critics there was singularly little agreement about what this ascendancy implied, or even on what it was founded. As the extensive literature devoted to him proved, few public figures of the time had provoked greater curiosity and controversy or more violent feelings. The importance of his influence was generally recognized, yet its effect had not been determined and was perhaps indeterminable. In reporting his first broadcast under new sponsorship in 1949,

Variety, the trade paper of the entertainment world, described Winchell as "the man who, for better or for worse, has parlayed Sunday at nine . . . into America's number one spot for the molding of public opinion." It was as accurate a description as could be given.

Sunday evenings brought a second oracle to the air waves, as portentous in his manner as Winchell, though considerably less masterly a showman. Drew Pearson was the author of a widely syndicated column, *Washington Merry-Go-Round,* which purported to interpret, in the light of secret, exclusive information, the day-by-day political news of the nation's capital. In his weekly broadcasts, Pearson combined the elements of revelation and prophecy, exposing the allegedly true circumstances in which government officials and men in public life took important actions, and making explicit predictions concerning supposedly imminent developments. Much of this material was sensational, some of it hinted at scandal in high quarters, and to the radio audience most of it undoubtedly yielded overtones of drama. Pearson's reputation for infallibility as a keyhole journalist may have been enhanced, rather than diminished, by the severity with which his printed columns were denounced, at various times, by President Roosevelt, Secretary of State Cordell Hull, President Truman, and other less exalted personages. A poll of his professional colleagues, members of the Congressional Press Gallery, was taken in 1944; the result indicated that they considered him the Washington correspondent who exercised the greatest influence on the nation. But only two regarded Pearson as the correspondent who did the best reporting from a standpoint of fairness, reliability and analytical acumen. Whether or not Pearson's influence on public opinion was as profound as his colleagues surmised, it was clear that a large audience tuned in to his broadcasts for the enjoyment of a pleasure little more intellectual than that afforded by the divinations of a tea-shop gypsy.

Until September 12, 1938, radio's analysts and interpreters of general news received little attention from the American public. On that afternoon, Adolf Hitler delivered an address at Nuremberg which, for twenty days, promised to plunge the world into war. Five minutes after Hitler ceased speaking, a veteran commentator in the studios of the Columbia Broadcasting System in New York City went on the air to explain the import of the Chancellor's declaration. The Munich crisis made H. V. Kaltenborn's name familiar to every home in the land; remaining in the studios for the whole period of its duration, he went on the air eighty-five times to analyze the news that poured in from every European capital. Hitler's threat to peace swept away American apathy about world affairs. Thereafter, it was to radio that the nation turned for a report of events as they occurred, and for an interpretation of their significance.

By the middle of the century, the evaluation of news had become one of the most important services undertaken by radio "in the public interest, convenience or necessity." It was also, by its nature, one of the most delicate and difficult. For the meaning of the news is necessarily a matter of opinion. Specialists and experts, like all human beings, are subject to prejudice. And in certain fields—such as foreign policy, industrial relations, social legislation —the real implications of news may be a matter of controversy. On the whole, the evaluation of news furnished by the four national networks was singularly free from bias, partisanship and distortion.

A number of radio's news analysts were outstanding for their achievement in informing and educating public opinion rather than seeking to influence it. The Hoosier twang and quiet wit of Elmer Davis had become familiar to a nation-wide audience immediately before the outbreak of the Second World War. His career as a news analyst for radio was interrupted, after Pearl Harbor, when President Roosevelt drafted him to head the Office of War Information, which under his direction became one of the most conspicuously successful wartime agencies. Davis's wartime experience as a government official considerably enriched his broadcasts when, after the war, he returned to radio. His pictures of the Washington scene were clear, vivid and authoritative, and his analyses of Congressional debate and action were probably the most illuminating of any that radio brought to the public.

William L. Shirer, author of *Berlin Diary* and *End of a Berlin Diary*, specialized in the interpretation of foreign affairs and the analysis of foreign policy as it was being shaped in Washington. Shirer began making broadcasts from Berlin shortly after Hitler's rise to power, and his accounts of developments in Germany and Central Europe thereafter were as remarkable for their insight as for their factual detail. In the postwar years, when the future of Germany became a central issue in the relations between the United States and Russia, Shirer's critical evaluation of policies and events, founded on comprehensive knowledge of Central Europe, was a significant contribution to public enlightenment. The field of Far Eastern affairs was admirably interpreted by Cecil Brown, whose book, *Suez to Singapore,* had won a wide audience. American listeners first became familiar with his name in a dramatic broadcast which he made from Singapore in 1941, describing the sinking by the Japanese of the British warships *Prince of Wales* and *Repulse*; he had been aboard the *Repulse*, and his factual account covered the incident in every detail down to his own rescue from the sea. In later broadcasts, he reported with equal vividness the events leading up to the fall of Singapore. Brown's postwar interpretations of news were clear and precise, and revealed his gift for selecting salient material.

Two news analysts—Edward R. Murrow and Quincy Howe— were outstanding in the ability to interpret current events in terms of their general historical setting. Murrow had served as assistant director of the Institute of International Education before entering the field of radio; Howe came to broadcasting as an editor and author. Both had specialized in the field of international relations, and in that of social and political history. This background of scholarship enabled them to deal, more illuminatingly than any of their colleagues, with the social and political theories, the intellectual currents and the philosophical doctrines which frequently shaped the course of events. It was the signal merit of Murrow and Howe to extend the perspectives, and expand the frames of reference, of their listeners.

7 Laughter Shakes the Skies

The variety show, usually featuring a star, proved over the years to be the form of entertainment which had the most enduring appeal for the American radio audience. In its perfected form, the variety show exhibited a fairly rigid pattern, combining four elements. It opened with a period of patter by the star comedian, brought in the members of his supporting cast, proceeded to a musical interlude, and closed with a skit in which the star was joined by a guest. The variety show which dominated the night-time air waves was, in essence, a tabloid revival of the vanished vaudeville program.

It was an ironical fact that the project of bringing vaudeville to the microphone first occurred to a young man who knew very little about either vaudeville or radio. This was Rudy Vallee, radio's earliest crooner, first star bandleader, and pioneer producer. Born in Vermont, and brought up in a small town in Maine, Vallee as a boy was infatuated by the saxophone, collected the recordings of Rudy Wiedoeft, a celebrated player, and finally managed to buy an instrument. With the help of instructions which Wiedoeft gave him by mail, Vallee taught himself to play, and presently became an expert performer. He spent a year at the University of Maine— he was later to make its "Stein Song" a continental nuisance—and then transferred to Yale, where he formed his own dance band, the "Connecticut Yankees." The band achieved considerable local success, and eventually was booked to play a summer engagement at the Savoy Hotel in London. Vallee's popularity in England was spectacular, but he returned to the United States and Yale, took his degree, and finally secured an engagement in a New York night-club which had its dance music broadcast by a local station. Vallee had composed two songs, "Vagabond Lover" and "Deep Night," and his singing of these numbers on the air brought a flood of inquiries about the "soulful" music that was actually the first crooning ever heard. One year afterwards, on October 24, 1929, Vallee and his band began the weekly, hour-long broadcasts which were to continue, for ten years, under the same commercial sponsorship. It was thus appropriately to the strains of "Deep Night" that the Great Depression was ushered in.

Faced with an hour of broadcast time—too long to be filled by even the most popular bandleader in the country, though women swooned at his crooning—Vallee showed his creative talent as a producer by applying the formula of vaudeville. On his second program, he interviewed the Grand Duchess Marie of Russia, and subsequently followed this eminent guest with the pugilist Max Baer, the journalist Heywood Broun and other celebrities not connected with the theatrical profession. When this procedure was imitated by other programs, he began interviewing unknown members of the public who had performed some unusual feat, or had met with some extraordinary experience; this idea bore fruit, years afterwards, in a popular network show, *We, The People*. Later, Vallee brought to the microphone a number of stars of the stage— among them, Miss Ethel Barrymore, Miss Eva Le Gallienne and Walter Huston—in brief dramatic sketches that had been written, not for the theater, but for radio. He was one of the first producers to recognize that radio, like the motion picture, was a new and independent medium with resources and limitations peculiarly its own. But the promise of a radio drama which Vallee apparently detected was never fully satisfied.

The pattern which Vallee developed for the variety show was adopted, during the nineteen-thirties, by a constellation of comedians who remained, to the middle of the century, favorites of the radio audience. Eddie Cantor, Jack Benny, Bob Hope and Jimmy Durante, notwithstanding their individual differences, had certain qualities in common. Debarred from visual effects, radio had to make its appeal entirely in terms of the spoken word and the inferred personality of the speaker. These comedians were served by script writers whose effort was mainly directed to creating, in the listener's mind, an image of the star, a character or personality, that could be maintained from week to week. Thus, Benny was established as parsimonious, and the butt of derision by his stooges. Durante was made a perpetually rowdy clown. Hope was given a coating of bumptiousness and brashness. The penalty of this stereotyping was monotony. But apparently to a large portion of the radio audience monotony was unobjectionable.

More critical listeners found greater pleasure in the broadcasts of two other comedians. The performances of Fred Allen and Edgar Bergen were in the vein of comedy, not farce; both men achieved a degree of satire and social criticism seldom present in radio entertainment. Allen, a librarian in Boston, had taught himself juggling from books and undertook to perform on an amateur night program. He failed as a juggler, but scored an immediate success with a humorous retort, and ultimately entered vaudeville as a monologuist. For radio, Allen wrote most of his own scripts, and turned an acidulous, pungent wit on the follies of the day and the more characteristic features of the national scene. Bergen discovered his talent for ventriloquism while still at high school, earned his way through college by performing with the dummy that was later to enter American folklore. After taking his degree, Bergen went into vaudeville. Successful there, he was working as a night-club entertainer when Rudy Vallee invited him to be a guest on his variety hour. Bergen's success in radio was instantaneous, and over the years he made Charlie McCarthy, a wooden dummy, the most outspoken facetious character in American broadcasting. Aside from Allen and Bergen, only Marian and James Jordan used radio as a vehicle for the satire of American life and manners. Veterans of radio's very early years, the Jordans in their serial comedy, *Fibber McGee and Molly,* brought a dry humor to the domestic and civic predicaments of the average tough-minded, wisecracking, optimistic and somewhat overconfident American citizen.

8   Mrs. Hertz, Miss Hush and the Hush Puppies

Traditionally, Americans were convinced that to get on in the world you had to know all the answers. From this assumption developed the national passion for self-improvement which, for a century or more, bred antiseptic pastimes of a dubiously instructive nature. The spelling bee, the Chautauqua, charades, the game of "authors," the visiting British lecturer and, latterly, the crossword puzzle had all ministered to this predilection. A morbid appetite for miscellaneous information became endemic. It was inevitable that radio should both satisfy this appetite and turn it to profitable account. Quiz programs of one kind or another became popular in the 1930s. But the following decade brought their innocent excitement to an alarmingly sophisticated perfection. The result was a type of program which combined the attractions of a national lottery, a universal detective hunt, and a mental jag. It turned millions of citizens into cultural blood-hounds, undoubtedly decreased the life expectancy of librarians, and added a new frustration to the total depravity of existence.

The "give-away" program which became a national craze during the 1940s originated in the cupidity and frugality of sponsors. To keep the public's ears plastered to its radio receivers was their object, and to produce this aural hypnosis at moderate cost was their desire. In these circumstances an advertising agency was visited with inspiration. Why not run a quiz program, selecting members of the studio audience as contestants, under the sponsorship of a group of advertisers each of whom would contribute to a collective jackpot of prizes? The listening audience, however, must be kept amused. A succession of dull, stodgy and inarticulate contestants would cause their interest to wilt. Masters of ceremonies on these earliest programs quickly learned that the listening public enjoyed them more if the contestants were odd and bizarre specimens of humanity. This led to the incubation of a class of chronic quizzees, preponderantly feminine, who led a melancholy but hopeful existence perambulating from one program to the next in a state of continuous intellectual vivacity. One of these flowers of American culture, in 1946, attained the enviable distinction of becoming radio's number-one quiz program contestant. Mrs. Sadie Hertz, a voluble, whimsical sexagenarian housewife of Brooklyn, New York, had been able, without faltering, to define chicanery as "something you put in coffee to make it taste diff'runt;" a stalagmite as "a guy what believes in Stalin;" a caboose as "a girl papoose". As a reward for these and other feats of mental prowess, her four-room apartment bulged with electrical household equipment, table services of sterling silver and china, and an extensive personal wardrobe. The career of Mrs. Hertz appeared to offer substantial support to the instrumental theory of knowledge advanced by William James and John Dewey, but philosophers were disconcerted by the dim view which she took of epistemology. Through *The Saturday Evening Post*, Mrs. Hertz confided to the nation the secret of her success. "I'm a natural-born comedian," she declared proudly.

The rewards that accrued to Mrs. Hertz were soon eclipsed. For presently two remarkable refinements in quiz programs brought their pay-off to dizzying heights, and also induced a periodic, nation-wide hysteria. The quizzes were transferred from the studio audience to the listening public, by the simple expedient of making telephone calls during the program and asking the respondents to identify a song that was being played, a "secret voice" that had been broadcast, or solve some other puzzle. These contests often had to be continued from week to week, and the total jackpot snowballed from broadcast to broadcast, sometimes reaching a declared value of twenty-five thousand dollars. Endowed with such fabulous rewards, and invested with the tantalizing prospect that the ringing of a telephone might bring any citizen the opportunity of a lifetime, it was scarcely surprising that the "give-away" programs became a national craze.

Thus, for a long period, millions of Americans were probably more intensely preoccupied with the identification of successive mysterious Hushes of both sexes than they were with a presidential campaign or the progress of a cold war with Russia. The Hush contests began with obscure clues; as they ran their weekly course, the clues became broader, the prizes more dazzling, and the public more hysterical. No less than seven hundred thousand hopeful Americans were said to have stormed public libraries in an effort to identify a Miss Hush, originally described as a celebrity whose profession was somehow associated with Santa Claus (one of his reindeer was named Dancer), and whose name was later linked to a common cracker. Finally—after guesses had ranged from Miss Elsa Maxwell to Sister Kenny—Mrs. Ruth Annette Subbie, a housewife of Fort Worth, Texas, murmured into her telephone the name of Miss Martha Graham and promptly collapsed when informed of her victory. For her fortunate insight, Mrs. Subbie received, besides two thousand dollars in cash, an airplane, an automobile, a free foreign cruise, some expensive jewelry, and a bewildering assortment of incentives to a new life. Six hundred and ninety-nine thousand, nine hundred and ninety-nine frustrated citizens presumably compensated for their disappointment by entering other contests that rode the air waves.

Two quiz programs, however, became national favorites without exploiting the lottery principle. One of these, *Information, Please,* gave radio listeners the innocent pleasure of seeking to confound a panel of encyclopaedic experts. They were invited to devise questions which would tax the erudition of Franklin P. Adams, John Kieran and one or more celebrity guests, and their questions were presented by Clifton Fadiman, a witty, urbane master of ceremonies. The other program, *The Quiz Kids,* assembled a group of child prodigies ranging from the ages of six to fourteen, and tested their mental powers with questions which might have proved embarrassing to many fascinated adult listeners. On one historic occasion, the infantile geniuses competed against Senators Ball, Hatch, Burton and Hart. Mr. Justice Douglas, of the Supreme Court, presided over this contest. He declared it a tie. Whatever this indicated about the mentality of the nation's lawmakers, the result did not displease millions of Americans who—notwithstanding the philanthropic ministrations of broadcasters—remained insufficiently self-improved.

9   Radio Opens Its Eyes

As the century reached its midpoint, television promised to become the most important single new factor in the nation's economic, cultural and social future. In 1948, there were about two hundred thousand television sets in active use, and the audience was estimated at one million. In 1949, there were one and a half million sets in use; the audience was estimated at six million people; and sixty-four stations were making television service available to some forty percent of the country's population.

Already, television was bringing about changes in the homes and habits of its audience. Special rooms, looking remarkably like Pullman parlor cars, were being designed to accommodate it. Families rejecting the notion of architectural reconstruction learned that rearrangement of living-room furniture was necessary to make group viewing possible. This usually reduced conversational comfort, but conversation promised to become an art lost to television addicts. The home was enjoying a revival as a center of family life; father, mother and children saw more of one another than ever before, and exchanged fewer words. Sociologists and educators were asking how a generation of children would turn out, having been brought up with a continuous show going on in the home. Hospitality, to some degree reluctant, was being more extensively practiced; possession of a television set insured an incessant stream of visitors. As a result, the consumption of liquor increased, as did the consumption of cigarettes. Dinners, however, were sharply reduced; nobody wished to sit at the table while a show was on the air, and telefamilies packed snacks on trays, devoured them silently in the dark. Among addicts, movie-going declined, and the tuning in of radios practically ceased. Leisure had become identified with indolent gazing.

Television was the infant of radio, but broadcasters were wondering whether they had nourished a parricide. At the annual convention of the National Association of Broadcasters, Merlin Aylesworth, first president of the National Broadcasting Company, warned the industry that radio was doomed; it would be superseded by television, he predicted, within three years. The motion-picture industry regarded it anxiously. Would television, making every home a theater, empty the nation's movie-houses? From Hollywood, Samuel Goldwyn gloomily prophesied that Hollywood must perish unless a way could be found to adapt motion pictures to the new medium. Meanwhile, critics of television were asserting that it portended the "death of culture" in the United States, since the commercial excesses of sponsors would inevitably blight whatever arts television might annex.

In its lusty infancy, television had done little more than add sight to radio's sound. But its potentialities for social good appeared to be boundless. What America would make of its new and great medium only the American people could decide.

CONCLUSION

The Horn of Plenty

As the first half of the twentieth century ended, many Americans looked back wistfully to the past. The United States of their grandparents held, for them, a romantic charm. In that vanished, remote Arcadia existence was simpler, more leisurely, more gracious. For a period of fifty years the rhythm of life had continuously accelerated. Day by day, the hours seemed to have become more crowded, the activities that filled them more confusing. Had not the individual's available leisure, his margin of personal freedom, steadily diminished? Existence was felt to be an affair of speed, complexity and urgency, of coercive pressures and inexorable exactions. Homesickness for the past implied more than a pathetic need of refuge from the present. It revealed, however inarticulately, the old American desire for a better life.

Yet to project the image of that better life upon the past, and not the future, was almost certainly misguided. The lost Arcadia of 1900 was largely an illusion. As compared with his descendant of 1950, the American of that era had been time-bound and space-bound. He had worked harder, for longer hours, on more days of the week. His orbit was narrower, his material standard of living notably lower, his possible recreations far fewer and less diversified. If personal freedom could be reckoned in terms of the number of alternatives among which the individual was able to freely choose, the American of 1900 had never known such freedom as his descendant took for granted. For all his faith in the future, his boundless optimistic confidence in progress, he would have found incredible the miraculous transforming instruments which science and technology had placed at the disposal of a later generation, making them so universally accessible that they had become commonplace elements of the social landscape, the natural environment. Had he been granted a vision of the America of 1950, the American of 1900 might have been mystified by the dissatisfactions of his descendants, might have wondered at the inexplicable abeyance of their sense of values.

For if the nature of life, as a process, had not changed, its character as an experience had changed unrecognizably. Life as a process was animal in origin, but rational and spiritual in its possible fruits. Yet within the memory of living men their possibility had been incalculably enhanced. Life as an experience had acquired new dimensions of potentiality. The transforming instruments had brought within range a multiplication of opportunity apparently limited only by the insight, wisdom and good will of men. But however miraculous, they were only instruments; the values that might flow from them would be determined by the use to which they were put. The better, more abundant life for all that Americans had so passionately desired throughout their history seemed, at the middle of the century, closer to the nation's grasp than it had ever been before. This closeness intensified its challenge. In the circumstances Americans needed to understand a principle that one of their philosophers, George Santayana, had declared to be everywhere discoverable.

The principle was that human reason lives by turning the friction of material forces into the light of ideal goods.

Index

Date Due

MAY 6 '60			
DEC 2 '60			
JAN 20 '61			
FEB 3 '61			
FEB 1 6 '62			
MAR 2 '62			
OCT 19 '62			
APR 26 '63			
JAN 1 0 '64			
JAN 2 0 1969			
May 2			
DEC 10 1969			
JAN 1 7 1971			
	PRINTED	IN U. S. A.	